THE CLASSICS OF WESTERN SPIRITUALITY

HENRY SUSO

THE EXEMPLAR,
WITH TWO GERMAN SERMONS

TRANSLATED, EDITED, AND INTRODUCED BY
FRANK TOBIN

PREFACE BY
BERNARD McGINN

PAULIST PRESS
NEW YORK • MAHWAH

Cover art: MARION MILLER is a figurative painter with a background in philosophy. She is an Associate Professor in the Art Department of Mount Holyoke College in South Hadley, Massachusetts.

Library of Congress Cataloging-in-Publication Data

Seuse, Heinrich, 1295–1366.
   [Selections. English]
   Henry Suso : the Exemplar, with two German sermons / [edited and translated] by Frank Tobin.
      p.   cm.—(The Classics of Western spirituality)
   Bibliography: p.
   Includes index.
   ISBN 0-8091-0407-5 : $15.95 (est.).—ISBN 0-8091-2986-8 (pbk.) : $12.95 (est.)
   1. Mysticism—Early works to 1800.   2. Seuse, Heinrich, 1295–1366.   I. Tobin, Frank J.   II. Title.   III. Title: Exemplar, with two German sermons.   IV. Series.
   BV5080.S836213   1989
   248.2—dc20   89-8569
                                                                         CIP

Published by Paulist Press
997 Macarthur Boulevard
Mahwah, New Jersey 07430

Printed and bound in the United States of America

Contents

CONTENTS

CONTENTS

CONTENTS

CONTENTS

CONTENTS

NOTES

From the collection of the Bibliothèque nationale et universitaire of Strasbourg, Ms 2929. Used by permission.

Frontispiece:
The Mystical Way

← This is a reproduction of one of the eleven illustrations (in color) included in MS Strasbourg Bibliothèque Nationale et Universitaire 2929, a manuscript containing Henry Suso's *Life*. This earliest manuscript containing Suso's writings dates from about 1370. It is generally thought to resemble closely an archetype prepared under Suso's supervision in Ulm between 1360 and 1366. The pictures are the work, not of an illuminator, but of the copyist of the manu-script. Thus in conception and in execution the illustrations were most likely under the control of Suso himself. An introductory caption (not part of the picture) reads: "The following pictures show the presence of the naked Godhead in the Trinity of Persons and all creatures flowing out and flowing back within, and (they) show the first beginning of a person starting, his well-ordered breakthrough of progressing, and the most sublime spilling over of perfection beyond being."

The illustration is a diagram in which a (red) line running from one figure to the next indicates the life of the divinity and the mystical progress of the soul towards union with this divine life. The line begins at the top left and runs clockwise more or less in a spiral ending in one of the figures at top right. We begin top left with the dark round shape surrounding a light circle. The caption above it reads: "This is the limitless abyss of the eternal Godhead which has neither beginning nor end." (Notice that a smaller version of this divine abyss resides in the breast of all figures that are joined by the line and it is through this "divine abyss" that the connecting line passes!) From here the line progresses through a screen veiling the Godhead to three figures at top right. Caption: "This is the Trinity of Persons in substantial unity." The figure to the left with a child at his bosom is God the Father. The Son, with hands folded as the Man of Sorrows, stands to the right. The middle figure is the Holy Spirit. Below them is an angel. Caption: "This figure is the flowing out of angelic nature." Directly beneath the angel is a falling winged creature that has lost its "divine abyss"; no doubt a fallen angel. From the angelic nature the line proceeds down through a human figure. Caption: "This is created humanity, formed according to the Godhead." The three figures at bottom right do not share in the line of mystical progress. Above the figure with the scythe we read: "This is death." Below the scythe is a knight with sword, dancing with a lady attired in the fashion of the court. Caption: "This is the love of the world which ends in grief." The next three figures all seem to represent the human soul or, perhaps, Elsbeth Stagel. The first of these, at bottom center, is a figure in prayer with rosary. Caption: "I shall turn my path to God, for this life is short indeed." The large figure whose head is pierced with daggers and who is being assailed with arrows and by a snake and toad, symbols of evil, is encaptioned: "Behold how I must die and be crucified with Christ." This causes the soul to falter. The dejected figure seated at bottom right laments: "Abandonment is trying to despoil me. Alas, it was too much." However, after the line passes through Christ on the cross, the human figure above him says: "My senses no longer work. The superior powers (of the soul) have taken over." The divine-looking figure with halo just above this which has the human soul in its breast says: "Here the spirit rushes in and is found in the Trinity of Persons." The human soul to the right (now with halo!) says: "I have lost myself in God. No one can reach me here." From here the line returns to the bosom of the Father where the birth of the Son is taking place.

For more on the illustrations, see Bihlmeyer, pp. 45*–62*; and Colledge, Edmund and Marler, J.C., " 'Mystical' Pictures in the Suso 'Exemplar' MS Strasbourg 2929," *Archivum Fratrum Praedicatorum*, 54 (1984), 293–354.

Foreword

Certainly any attempt to survey the masters of Western spirituality would be incomplete without the inclusion of the fourteenth-century Dominican of the Upper Rhine, Henry Suso. Less speculative than Meister Eckhart and less renowned as a preacher than John Tauler, Suso's works complement those of his fellow Dominicans by describing the interior life as an intensely personal experience. Because its language was widely understood, his Latin work, the *Horologium sapientiae*, proved immensely popular. More manuscripts of it survive than of any work of its time except the *Imitation of Christ*. However, it is to the works he wrote in his native Middle High German that we must turn to experience both the breadth and intensity of what he wished to impart. Toward the end of his life Suso edited his vernacular works as he wished them to survive into a volume that he called *The Exemplar*. This work, which contains his *Life*, the *Little Book of Eternal Wisdom*, the *Little Book of Truth* and the *Little Book of Letters*, is translated here into English in its entirety from the original Middle High German for the first time. To this have been added the only two surviving sermons considered authentic. While Suso's way of experiencing God and the world remains undeniably medieval, his devotional practices point to future centuries and his literary talents give his writings universal appeal.

An expression of gratitude is due to Richard Kieckhefer for helpful suggestions regarding the Introduction, and to Bernard McGinn and Robert Reardon for thoughtful suggestions and for their careful inspection of the entire manuscript. I am also grateful to Professor McGinn for contributing a Preface which is both valuable and kind. No man is an island, and a student and translator of medieval spiritual texts certainly should not attempt to be one. It is hoped that the finished product measures up to the quality of their assistance.

1

Preface

Die deutsche Mystik has connotations in German that the English term *German mysticism* cannot really convey. Perhaps we can grasp something of the richness, the force, the distinctiveness of *die deutsche Mystik* by thinking of it as *the* German mysticism. Though there were mystics of importance in other eras of German history, the mysticism found in the German-speaking lands between about 1250 and 1470 was unique. The mystical texts that are our living witnesses to this outpouring of the Spirit must surely be reckoned as among the greatest contributions of German culture to the world. They form one of the supreme spiritual traditions of Western Christianity.

This German mysticism was a movement both extensive in time and varied in authors, themes and intentions. Although some of the most important figures, like Meister Eckhart and Nicholas of Cusa, also wrote in Latin, it was in the creative turn to the vernacular that the German mysticism found its distinctive voice. The German spiritual writers of the late Middle Ages were not alone in finding their mother tongue a more suitable instrument to express, or better suggest, the ultimately indescribable mysteries of the mystical life—the same was being done in the Netherlands, France, Italy, Spain and especially England—but they had no rivals in the depth and the richness of the spiritual literature they produced.

Like many other spiritual movements of the late Middle Ages, the German mysticism is also distinguished by the prominent role taken by women, not only in the religious orders and spiritual circles (such as the "Friends of God") that fostered the pursuit of Christian perfection, but also in the actual composition of many of the great masterpieces. (How much of Suso's *The Life of the Servant* is due to his disciple Elsbeth Stagel is a question that can probably never be

PREFACE

determined.) Though women writers had not been lacking in previous eras in the history of Christianity, it is in the late Middle Ages that we find the first large body of religious literature written by women, and German literature is second to none in this regard.

The thematic and theological variety of the German mysticism precludes any one description as adequate to cover the multitude of texts—authentic, pseudonymous and anonymous—that make up its corpus. Though direct influence is often provable, as in the case of Eckhart and Suso, and a community of themes can often be found, even where there is no proof of influence, the figures are too individual, the texts too varied, the disagreements all too real to homogenize the intensely varied world of the German mysticism of the last centuries of the Middle Ages. Where does Henry Suso fit into this world?

Suso's name is usually and quite correctly identified as one of the three great male mystics of the early stage of medieval German mysticism. Along with Meister Eckhart, his teacher, and John Tauler, his contemporary, these three Dominicans are seen as the founding fathers of this great spiritual tradition. Without denying this traditional status, Suso's special contributions to the German mysticism do not always come out clearly by linking his name to Eckhart and Tauler, however much they had in common.

In *Little Book of Divine Truth*, as well as in the final chapters of *The Life of the Servant*, Suso proved that he had a real gift for the kind of highly speculative dialectical mysticism found in Eckhart—and that he recognized the need to correct his beloved Master on some crucial issues. In the *Little Book of Eternal Wisdom* and in the *Little Book of Letters* his devotional and pastoral concerns have many affinities to those found in Tauler's sermons. But Suso is more than just a bit of Eckhart and a bit of Tauler, with some courtly literature thrown in!

Perhaps one way to suggest the distinctive nature of Suso's mysticism is to focus on the inner connection between the "exemplar," also the name he gave to the corrected edition of his works that he put together shortly before his death, and the title of "the servant" that he took for himself both in the *Life* and in his most popular treatise, the *Little Book of Eternal Wisdom*. As Frank Tobin notes in this volume, *The Exemplar* is not only the title of the collection but is also a description of the content of the four works. One can go further and say that Suso himself *is* the "exemplar," precisely insofar as he is the "servant." Like Augustine in the *Confessions*, Suso

4

presents himself as the model to be followed, but he is the model not for any of his own accomplishments but only in his status as servant, that is, as one who has cast himself totally upon the mercy of Jesus, the Divine Wisdom and Truth.

Suso's focus on his own interior spiritual growth is most evident in *The Life of the Servant*, the first autobiography, or to use Richard Kieckhefer's suggestive term, auto-hagiography in the German language. But the concentration on his own exemplary experience is also evident in the other three works. In the early *Little Book of Truth*, written about 1326–28 during the debates that led up to the condemnation of Meister Eckhart, he begins from an autobiographical observation that establishes his position as a worthy disciple of Divine Truth who will be able to convey the real meaning of detachment and discernment to counter false mystics. In the *Little Book of Eternal Wisdom* (probably 1328–30) he presents "common teaching in which both he and everyone else can find what applies to them," but he does so in the form of a dialogue between Eternal Wisdom and the servant that makes the devotional message both more particular and more personal. The *Little Book of Letters*, though carefully edited for final publication, is a series of intimate communications between the servant as spiritual guide and his beloved disciples and followers. Suso is always center stage in *The Exemplar* in a way that neither Eckhart nor John Tauler ever are in their writings.

The personal voice, of course, had not been lacking in Western Christian mysticism before Suso, as the mention of Augustine reminds us. In the *Confessions*, however, Augustine only described two mystical experiences, one at Milan (Book 7) and the other at Ostia (Book 9), and such personal accounts are rare before the thirteenth century. During the thirteenth and the fourteenth centuries first-person accounts of visionary and mystical experiences proliferated in a remarkable way, not least among the female mystics. One has only to look at the writings of Mechthild of Magdeburg among German authors to realize how powerful the personal voice had become.

Suso is the first important male mystic to incorporate autobiographical accounts of mystical experiences on such a large scale into his writings, but he does so, I believe, in a distinctive way. The Swabian Dominican, well-educated as he was in theology, presents himself, his pious practices, visions and mystical experiences as exemplary of profound theological truths. His literary artistry, with its great gifts for narrative presentation and its rhetorical richness, is always in the service of a theological agenda. As Frank Tobin puts it in his Introduction, "The expression of spiritual truths in literary form was Suso's ultimate goal."

This is certainly the case, though it may not be immediately evident, in *The Life of the Servant*, the most accessible of all Suso's writings to the modern reader. The *Life* can be read on many levels, though it would be a mistake to take it in a crudely literal sense, as the Introduction points out. In its deepest meaning, like the *Confessions*, it is a form of theological anthropology, an analysis of the meaning of human existence and the path to God presented through a life story of an individual who is also an everyman. A detailed literary and theological comparison of the *Confessions* and *The Life of the Servant* would have much to tell us about the differences between the spiritual world of late Antiquity and that of the late Middle Ages.

The theological program is patent in the *Little Book of Truth*, which might be described as a handbook to the proper understanding of the key speculative themes of the German mysticism: detachment, discernment, the divine ground, virtual existence, flowing-out, breakthrough, freedom, union, and the like. It is perhaps less evident, though no less real, in the *Little Book of Eternal Wisdom*. With its repetitions and richness of language, this work reminds us of the writings of the contemporary English hermit and mystic, Richard Rolle. Few works bring us as close to the imaginative intensity of late medieval piety—a form of piety not all will feel comfortable with, but which has played a large role in the history of Christianity and continues to exist in many parts of the world today. While primarily devotional in nature, the *Little Book of Eternal Wisdom* always bases its devotion on fundamental doctrinal themes, especially concerning the Passion, Divine Providence and the meaning of suffering. The *Little Book of Letters* can be analyzed in a similar way as displaying doctrinal truths in the form of practical advice for life and worship.

Suso was scarcely alone in endeavoring to fuse mystical devotion and sound doctrine. What makes him special is how he uses the intensity of his own devotional and mystical experiences as the exemplar for his theological message. Less adventurous and profound than Eckhart, he is more representative of the two currents that sought a perhaps impossible synthesis in the German mysti-

PREFACE

cism of the late Middle Ages—ecstatic visionary experience and lofty doctrinal and speculative thought.

This is the first time that the whole of Henry Suso's *Exemplar* has been translated into English directly from the Middle High German. The variations in Suso's style, from the lyricism and courtly subtleties of some passages to the Eckhartian complexities of others, make him a difficult author to translate well. The translator of such a work must not only possess considerable linguistic skills, but also needs to control an extensive knowledge of late medieval piety and especially of the speculative theology characteristic of the German mysticism. Fortunately, Frank Tobin possesses all the requisite skills in abundance. A noted scholar of Middle High German literature, Professor Tobin is also well-acquainted with the scholastic theology of the Middle Ages and with the history of Christian spirituality. Mystical literature is perhaps more prone than other forms of religious writing to invite fanciful, at times even bizarre interpretations. Frank Tobin always manages to be fair and level-headed, while still being original and insightful. This volume, with its helpful Introduction and excellent translations, will make Suso available to the English-speaking world as never before. It is a pleasure for me to be asked to take a small part in its presentation to the public by writing this modest Preface.

Bernard McGinn

I. The abbreviations used for the books of the Bible follow the practice of the New American Bible. However, for translations from the Bible, see Translator's Note.

II. Other frequently cited works are abbreviated as follows:

Suso's Works:

Hor.:	*Horologium sapientiae.*
LBEW:	*Little Book of Eternal Wisdom.*
LBL:	*Little Book of Letters.*
LBT:	*Little Book of Truth.*
Life:	Suso's *Vita* or *Life.*
Ser.:	Sermons

Other Works:

Bihlmeyer: Bihlmeyer, Karl. *Heinrich Seuse. Deutsche Schriften.* Stuttgart: Kohlhammer, 1907. All of the translations have been made from this edition of Suso's German works.

Essential Eckhart: Meister Eckhart: The Essential Sermons, Commentaries, Treatises, and Defense. Translation and Introduction by Edmund Colledge, O.S.A., and Bernard McGinn. New York: Paulist Press, 1981. Classics of Western Spirituality Series.

Künzle: Künzle, O.P., Pius. *Heinrich Seuses Horologium sapientiae.* Freiburg, Switzerland: Universitätsverlag, 1977. Spicilegium Friburgense, Vol. 23.

Seuse-Studien: Heinrich Seuse. Studien zum 600. Todestag, 1366–1966. E. M. Filthaut, O.P., ed. Cologne, 1966.

Teacher and Preacher: Meister Eckhart: Teacher and Preacher. Edited by Bernard McGinn with the collaboration of Frank Tobin and Elvira Borgstadt. New York: Paulist Press, 1986. Classics of Western Spirituality Series (companion volume to *Essential Eckhart*).

Introduction

I.   THE TIMES

When one examines northern Europe in the fourteenth century and seeks an explanation for the flowering of what is usually called mysticism within that environment, one finds several phenomena that can well be understood as contributing factors. And yet those of us who count ourselves among the followers of Euclid feel a certain distress that the whole to be explained seems so much greater than the parts with which we attempt to explain it. Since the facts of the matter are incontrovertible, let us recall some aspects of the age that provide, if not a satisfying explanation, at least a plausible setting for this blossoming forth of religious spirit.

The collapse of the Hohenstaufen dynasty and the ensuing Interregnum (1254–73) dealt a serious blow to the Holy Roman Empire both as a political reality and as an ideal. Confidence in an emperor's ability to achieve and maintain peace and political stability had been severely shaken. Chivalry was on the decline because of the deteriorating economic situation of the knightly class and the growth of the towns. Many knights had to give up their way of life, move into the towns and take up a trade to sustain themselves and their families. Others became outlaws living by robbery and plunder, as described in the German novella *Helmbrecht* (c. 1250). The ongoing struggle between the emperor and the papacy, which in earlier times had often worked for the good of society, now only contributed to social and moral decline. In the face of turmoil in Italy the popes took up their residence in Avignon (1309). Soon thereafter began the bitter power struggle between Emperor Louis IV (the Bavarian) and Pope John XXII. John, whose outlay for wars made up over half his budget,

13

excommunicated Louis in 1324, thus increasing scandal and confusion. One now had to choose between emperor and pope at a time when papal claims to moral leadership had been greatly compromised. The Franciscan Spirituals, including their most famous thinker, William of Ockham, fled the papal court at Avignon where they had been awaiting trial because of their allegedly heretical views on poverty and, taking up residence at the emperor's court in Munich, supported the imperial cause. Even aside from this major conflict the century had more than its share of wars, and social upheaval pervaded many areas not visited by outright military combat.

It was also a time of natural calamities. Frequent famines, floods and earthquakes unsettled men's minds. Plagues, culminating in the Black Death (1348), increased people's awareness of the futility of hoping for peace and stability on earth and contributed to an increase in apocalyptic thought. Small wonder that these calamities, especially the devastating plague which wiped out great numbers of inhabitants in many areas, were taken as signs of God's displeasure. Flagellants appeared, parading through town and country scourging themselves and each other in the pious hope that God would see fit to end his wrath. It was a restless age, unsure of itself and unsure of political realities and religious values that had seemed unquestionable in the centuries immediately preceding. The Black Death was not the cause of the general state of mind. It merely accented characteristics of the age already present, an age that has well been termed one of intensity and extremism.[1]

It is hardly surprising, then, that when faced with conditions so full of uncertainty and so lacking in promise many "turned inward." The internal workings of the soul became the focal point of attention. One strove to develop an interior life. There, within, was where one's riches lay. This turning inward is not unique to the fourteenth century. Faced with Napoleonic rule and the tyranny of the scientific spirit at the beginning of the nineteenth century, the German romanticists, too, turned inward to the rich world of their imagination. And poetic theories in our own century have posited that the poet creates a refined and very real world of his own in opposition to his crass physical surroundings. In the fourteenth century, however, turning inward was an experience clearly religious in character, and there was no danger of ending in solipsism, though it must be admitted that not all attempts to fulfill spiritual longings resulted in a sound religious life. Properly prepared for, however, turning inward resulted in an encounter with God. The goal of the interior life was the development of this relationship between Creator and creature in ways that allowed the creature to experience the heights and depths of love and all the nuances possible in this richest of personal relationships. Ultimately, the duality implied in "relationship" was in some very real but mysterious way overcome, and God and the human person became somehow one.

This emphasis on an intense personal relationship with God can hardly be considered an innovation of the fourteenth century. Within Western Christianity one can point to the writings of St. Augustine, especially the *Confessions*, and to those of St. Bernard of Clairvaux as clear evidence that an intense personal relationship with God was already established as a primary concern in the best traditions of Christian thought. And beginning around 1150 and continuing to Suso's time the secular lyric poetry in vernacular languages had been focusing almost exclusively on the intense personal relationship of a knight to his lady. The mendicant orders of Franciscans and Dominicans, who had made a vigorous impact on the previous century, had already contributed much to the thriving tradition of the spiritual life in times just prior to those of concern here. What differentiates fourteenth-century spirituality from that of other times is that this deep concern with the interior life gripped relatively large numbers of people, both clergy and laity, and that the pursuit of inwardness became such an intense and exclusive goal for so many. Meister Eckhart, perhaps the most famous mystic of the age, does not fit this mold of exclusivity because of his intellectual achievements as university professor and practical successes as an administrator. And yet his sermons center so exclusively on what is within and are so utterly devoid of any comments that might be used as references to time and place that they might just as well have been delivered on the moon as in turbulent fourteenth-century Strasbourg or Cologne.

Who were the practitioners of this spirituality? First of all, members of the mendicant orders as well as of other religious orders, but especially Dominican nuns. Second, men called beghards and women called beguines.[2] Third, large numbers of laypersons especially in the towns. The areas most deeply affected by this popular wave of religious fervor were those regions adjacent to the Rhine river, both along its upper reaches extending into Switzerland and in the Low Countries.

INTRODUCTION

The Dominican order's province of Teutonia, which included the Rhineland, had grown rapidly in the last half of the thirteenth and early part of the fourteenth century, with the establishment of convents for Dominican women making up most of the increase. Shortly after 1300 the province counted seventy such convents, seven in Strasbourg alone. Each convent numbered about fifty women, occasionally closer to eighty. These women frequently came from well-to-do families and were educated and cultured enough to be fitting recipients of more than just rudimentary instruction in the ways of the interior life. Some knew Latin. Probably the decisive event leading to the flowering of mysticism in the Rhineland occurred when the duty of supervising the spiritual instruction of Dominican convents was entrusted to the Dominican friars. Because of the tremendous burden this put on the order, Dominican superiors at first resisted. Only friars well-trained in theology would really be suitable for the task, and assigning them to these duties would mean taking them away from their studies and other important tasks. However, the command of Pope Clement IV in 1267, reiterated by the Dominican provincial of Teutonia, Herman of Minden, in 1286 and 1290, had to be taken seriously. Hereafter, the *cura monialium*, as the responsibility for the spiritual guidance of nuns was called, would be one of the main occupations of the Domincan friars. Later their responsibility was extended to women of other religious orders as well. This combination of enlightened spiritual advisors and recipients who were both eager and qualified provided the basis for much of the intense spiritual activity of the times.

Not all those seeking a rich spiritual life were able to gain acceptance into a religious order. Convents were required to be financially self-sustaining. Hence they existed through the beneficence of a wealthy founder or through the dowries that were required of those entering. Those unable to gain entry because of financial or other considerations were forced to pursue their goals in other ways. This gave rise to beguines and beghards. Beguines were religious women leading lives of chastity, generally grouped in convents, supporting themselves by manual work and engaging in prayer and other religious practices, but without any fixed rule, organization or permanent vows, and without ecclesiastical approbation. Since women seem to have outnumbered men at the time, many women who had little chance of marrying may have perceived this as a

16

viable way of life. Thus the attainment of lofty spiritual ideals may not have been, in all cases, a woman's exclusive motivation for joining a beguine community. Also, it is likely that some who could have entered religious orders simply preferred to become beguines. Beghard was the usual name for the male equivalent of the beguine. Beghards often led a less fixed existence and frequently lived by begging. How beguines and beghards were perceived by their contemporaries varied greatly. Some looked upon them as religious frauds and hypocrites, while others defended them as more religious than most monks and nuns. The majority seem to have been admirable, pursuing their spiritual goals seriously. Frequently the spiritual direction of such communities also fell to the friars, and it is probable that this task at times comprised part of Henry Suso's pastoral activity, although spiritual direction in Dominican houses of nuns appears to have taken up a larger portion of his time.[3] Occasionally in Suso's writings, as well as in the spiritual writings of his contemporaries, the phrase "friends of God" occurs. It seems unlikely, at least in the case of Suso, that he has any specific and formally constituted group in mind when employing the phrase. Nor does it appear that he restricts it to beguines and beghards. Rather, the term simply signifies anyone seriously pursuing a religious interior life.

One of the religious currents of the age was something often referred to as the brothers and sisters of the Free Spirit. These people were most likely not an organized group or sect but rather loose associations of like-minded individuals, much like the "hippies" of recent times.[4] However, they were perceived by church authorities as a unified group inimical to orthodoxy, and their supposed teachings were considered dangerous. Several of these teachings were condemned by the Council of Vienne (1311–12). Those of the Free Spirit were accused of maintaining that one can attain a state in this life in which it is impossible to sin; that in this state ascetical practices are unnecessary because reason is no longer affected by the sensuality of the body, and hence one is free to accord to the body all one wishes; and that in this state one is not subject to the laws of the church but has freedom in the spirit of the Lord. They were said to characterize this state of perfection as the soul's annihilation in the nothingness that is God. On the other hand, they were accused of teaching that God can be an obstacle to the attainment of perfection. The council described those propagating such views as beghards and beguines, but that all or even a majority of these groups or individuals were disseminating such heretical views seems unlikely. A few clerics were accused of holding these views as well. The learned Dominican theologian and mystic Meister Eckhart is alleged by some, both accused and accusers, to have been the source and authority for much of this heresy.[5] In any case, the brothers of the Free Spirit and the reaction they provoked were characteristic of the intellectual and religious climate of the times, and the controversy left its mark on the life and writings of Henry Suso.[6]

The case of the so-called brothers and sisters of the Free Spirit reveals the problems that arose when the serious pursuit of the interior life became popular among those without formal education in theology. The fate of Meister Eckhart, who was condemned by papal decree for presenting "many things as dogma that were designed to cloud the true faith in the hearts of many, things which he put forth especially before the uneducated crowd,"[7] demonstrates some of the dangers theologians might face if they strove to provide untrained minds with an understanding of the philosophical and theological underpinnings upon which rest the interior life and man's personal relationship with God. And yet it is misleading simply to dwell on the darker side. Anyone who believes that the life of the mind and the unquantifiable but intense experiences within the human person comprise what is best and most important in human existence will be forced to view the movement as a whole as an important enrichment of the human spirit.

The fact that it was a popular movement meant that most of the writing and preaching connected with this focusing on the God within oneself would have to be done in the vernacular. Learned thinkers and deeply sensitive spirits would strive to express in their native tongue things for which, until then, Latin had seemed the only proper medium. The impact on the vernacular language can be perceived even today. Religious art received strong impulses from the movement as well. And the achievements in language and art in turn became the means that fed this religious fervor, helping to insure that it would continue to thrive. We shall now turn our attention to one of the major contributors to this awakening of the religious spirit and, by furnishing information about his life and writings, attempt to give the reader more ready access to him and his works.

INTRODUCTION

II. SUSO'S LIFE

Chronology and Main Biographical Details

Because Henry Suso's autobiography or *Life* centers on the interior experiences of the protagonist and does not progress chronologically, it is not as helpful as one might wish in supplying factual knowledge about his life. Other documents of the times, especially those of the Dominican order, must be used to supplement what the *Life* offers.[8] One must be careful not to overestimate the reliability of the facts in the *Life*, nor to conclude too readily that information from other sources refers with certainty to Suso.[9]

The day of Suso's birth, March 21,[10] can be much more easily determined than the year. Nevertheless, 1295 is a very close approximation. He was of noble birth, and his original name was Heinrich von Berg. The von Berg family into which he was born was probably that von Berg family who were originally ministerials to the Archbishop of Constance but who, by Henry's time, had moved from the countryside into the town of Constance and, while retaining their nobility, had been forced by changing circumstances to take up some trade not considered demeaning. His mother's maiden name was Sus or Süs, and she came from the town of Überlingen which, like Constance, was situated on the shore of the Lake of Constance. Later, out of veneration for her, Henry assumed her family name.[11] What we learn of his parents from the *Life* should be viewed against the background of that work's genre.[12] The only other offspring of Henry's parents we hear about is a sister, who also entered religious life and at one point was a source of great concern to her brother.[13]

Of his life as a child we know little except that he was often ill.[14] This frailness may partially explain why Henry was not destined to pursue a career that would further the family fortunes but was instead, at the age of thirteen, brought by his parents to the Dominican house in Constance. In this friary, beautifully situated on an island where the Rhine flows out of Lake Constance, Suso would spend a larger part of his life as a Dominican than anywhere else. The fact that he entered religious life at thirteen, two years younger than normally allowed by church law, would trouble him severely. Since an exemption had obviously been made in his case, and since his parents had made a donation to the order upon his entrance into it, he was tortured for ten years by thoughts that he was doomed to hell and that nothing he did was of spiritual value because his acceptance into the order had been secured through simony, the sin of gaining spiritual profit in exchange for material goods. It was only by confiding his fears to Meister Eckhart, probably while studying in Cologne, and being reassured by him that he became convinced that his fears were unreasonable and was thus freed from these tormenting thoughts.[15] This incident bears witness to the force and authority of the revered master's personality even apart from his learned lectures and preaching, and it indicates that the impact he had on Suso went far beyond what the latter might have learned as a student of theology.

Suso's first years as a Dominican were, by his own admission, ordinary in every sense. We should hardly be surprised at this. What thoughts about religious life can we expect from a thirteen-year-old brought to the friary by provident parents? He went through the paces of living the life of an average friar, as did those around him, but apparently did so rather mechanically and without much reflection, satisfied, as he tells us, to lead the life of a religious just well enough not to compromise his reputation.[16] It took several years for the insight and feeling to grow to maturity within him that something was lacking. And then quite suddenly, after being a member of the order for five years, he underwent a conversion that marked the true beginning of his religious life.[17] Since this event stands at the beginning of his *Life*, we must give it the same prominence in his spiritual development that Suso himself did.

Since the *Life* tells us so little, we shall run through in some detail what kind of education and religious training the young Dominican was exposed to during his years of formation. Henry would spend his first year at the house in Constance as a novice, after which he would profess his religious vows of poverty, chastity and obedience and thereby be accepted into the order. Ordinarily, one could not pronounce these vows before the age of fifteen, but Henry was probably only fourteen at the end of his novitiate year. During his year as a novice and during the two or, in the case of one so young, possibly three years that followed, Henry would devote much of his time to studies and religious practices. To the extent that study before his coming to the friary had left him deficient, he would have to give time to perfecting his command of Latin.[18] Beyond this he would familiarize himself with the Bible, learn and engage in the recitation of the Divine Office, be instructed in the rules and constitution of the Order of Preachers, and read extensively in ascetical literature. These ascetical readings, such as the lives of St. Dominic, the founder of the order, and of other early Dominicans, the *Collations* of Cassian, and the lives of the desert fathers, would help introduce the young Dominican to the time-honored traditions of asceticism and monasticism, which he was expected to mirror in his own life, while, for the time being, sparing him the intellectuality required for the contemporary theology of the schools.

Following this he would spend several years studying philosophy. For the first two or three years he would devote himself to what was called *philosophia rationalis*, which was mainly a thorough grounding in basically Aristotelian logic in all its medieval breadth. This was what remained of the traditional trivium in higher studies. There followed two or three years of *philosophia realis*. Here the presence of such subjects as physics, geometry and astronomy bear witness to the old quadrivium, but one also studied Aristotelian metaphysics, ethics and politics with the aid of medieval commentaries. Suso would have been thus occupied for most of the time between 1313 and 1319. One of these branches of philosophy may have been offered at his home friary, but it is very likely that he also spent part of this time studying away from Constance.

Where he spent those two to three years allotted to theology for all Dominicans who were to engage in the ministry as priests is also uncertain, but Constance itself or Strasbourg are the most probable locations. Theological studies centered on an examination of the Bible and what teachings were drawn from it; however, Peter Lombard's *Sentences* and the many commentaries on this fundamental text were also studied. In Suso's time Dominicans relied heavily on the works of Thomas Aquinas in their approach to scriptural theology and the *Sentences*.

After concluding those studies that comprised the training given to all Dominican friars, Suso was chosen to continue and was sent to the Dominican house of advanced studies, the *studium generale* in Cologne. This was a tribute to his intelligence and previous success since only a few were chosen for this honor. Further study was usually restricted to those destined to teach, and most of those chosen would then be assigned to direct the philosophical and theological training of young Dominicans. The Dominican house in Cologne was already steeped in tradition in Suso's time since it had been founded in 1248 by Albert the Great, who had gone there taking with him his illustrious student, Thomas Aquinas. Thomas was canonized in 1323, either the very year of or the year previous to Suso's arrival there.

The thirty to forty students from the German provinces and eastern Europe studying at Cologne devoted themselves to expanding and deepening their knowledge of theology and of sacred scripture. They were expected not only to absorb what they heard in lectures but to engage regularly in disputations and to preach on learned theological matters, in Latin, to the Dominican community there. The course of studies generally lasted three years and was directed by a professor who was aided by an assistant holding the rank of lector. Suso's professor during at least part of this time was probably Meister Eckhart, who came to Cologne from Strasbourg in 1323 or shortly thereafter and is assumed to have taught theology in addition to what we are certain that he did: preached sermons in the vernacular to Dominican and Cistercian nuns and probably to laypersons as well. The impact that Eckhart's powerful personality had not only on the young Suso's mind but on his total person as well is borne out in the latter's writings.[19]

Suso must have had direct knowledge of at least the beginnings of Eckhart's difficulties with ecclesiastical authorities concerning the orthodoxy of many of his teachings while still a student in Cologne since he remained there at least until sometime in 1326 and perhaps until 1327. After appealing to the pope on January 24, 1327, and sometime after February 13 of that year, Eckhart left for the Avignon court of Pope John XXII to defend his orthodoxy. His dismal fortunes and posthumous papal condemnation must have affected his admiring student deeply. In the *Life* Suso describes how the deceased Eckhart appears to him to say that he "lived in overflowing glory" and that "his soul had been made utterly godlike." He further recommends to his former student "deep detachment" receiving "all things from God and not from creatures," and adopting "an attitude of calm patience toward all wolfish men."[20] That Eckhart had ultimately triumphed over his wolfish adversaries must have consoled Suso, who would need encouragement soon when he encountered wolfish adversaries of his own in a similar situation.

In 1326 or 1327, his studies complete, Suso returned to the friary in Constance, which would be his home for the next twenty years or so. His first years back there were spent in the post of lector, the logical consequence of his years of extra study.[21] With the help of an assistant he would direct the studies of the younger members of the community still in their years of formation. However, his magisterial duties extended to the rest of the community as well. Even the prior was expected to attend lectures and disputations when possible. One of the most painful experiences of Suso's life occurred when he was removed from this office in a manner causing him dishonor. He was summoned before a provincial chapter, or meeting, most likely in Maastricht in 1330, to answer to charges of heresy in his writings.[22] This seems to have caused his dismissal from the office of lector. At least this is the usual interpretation of his remarks in the *Horologium* that the grove he had nourished from youth (learning) was taken from him and given to another, and the chair of honor (lectorship) overturned.[23] Whether this interpretation of the facts is correct or not, the public humiliation did not last very long. Soon thereafter he was chosen as prior or superior of the house in Constance. He was released from this office in 1334 in a routine manner. Possibly he became prior a second time, but the evidence is not conclusive.

What was the condition of religious discipline in the Dominican houses at the time? The *Life* gives us several glimpses into the matter, but are there reasons to think that what Suso writes is an objective assessment, or are his critical comments those of someone overzealous and holier-than-thou?

The general impressions we gain from Suso's descriptions are corroborated from other sources. Both the diocese of Constance and the Dominican province of Teutonia, which included the Rhineland, were in a state of decline after the turn of the century. In Constance factions made the election of a bishop difficult, and the struggle between Pope John XXII and Emperor Louis the Bavarian undermined the religious observances of the laity. The bishop, who owed his post to the pope, held to the papal party while the town government took the side of the emperor. As a consequence, from 1326 to 1334, the bishop permitted no public religious services in the town. The Dominicans, with a few exceptions, remained loyal to the pope.

In the Dominican order during this same period there was also a noticeable departure from the life dedicated to evangelical perfection and the ideals of the order. The observance of poverty was relaxed. Many members of the order held on to private possessions, and an air of worldly elegance pervaded many of the houses for religious women. There was a general neglect of studies while many sought ecclesiastical honors and privileges. Many of the nuns filled their time with idle infatuations. There were those who seriously strove to fulfill their obligations, but the general tone in many houses made this difficult. The constant attempts to introduce reforms into the province of Teutonia by the pope and the order's general had only limited success. And at mid-century the consequences of the Black Death compounded the difficulty of reform.[24]

After his term as lector, and aside from the time spent as prior, what were Suso's activities during his years in Constance? We can well imagine him, in accordance with the special goals of his order, preaching in towns and throughout the countryside. Indeed, the *Life* describes several such journeys into parts of Switzerland, into neighboring Alsace, and down the Rhine. Only two sermons judged authentic have come down to us, and both are of good quality.[25] Certainly he preached, but when one reads the *Life* and takes into account what little we have from other sources, it appears that he was much more effective when in pastoral contact with smaller, more intimate groups or in counselling individuals.

It is his work advising women of which we hear most frequently. Some of these were daughters of the nobility whom he persuaded to enter a convent. Others would surely have been beguines, whose houses he visited as spiritual advisor. The preponderance of his time and effort, however, was doubtlessly devoted to the *cura monialium*, or spiritual direction, of Dominican nuns.[26] The order took this work very seriously and often assigned to it those who had gone on to advanced studies or even those who had received the *magister* or doctorate.[27]

Dominican friars did not normally serve as resident chaplains in convents. The daily mass and other regular duties were usually the responsibility of a secular priest. The friars acquitted their duties, rather, by regular visits to the convents. There they would preach, give instruction in theological matters, hear confessions and make themselves available for individual spiritual counselling. The friar was thought of as the spiritual father and the nuns as his children or spiritual daughters.[28] Often the relationships thereby established became quite intense and were spiritually profitable for both parties. Suso was probably a regular visitor at several Dominican convents, some close by and some as far away as Colmar and Freiburg. But we are best informed about his activities at the convent in Töss, near Winterthur, because it was there that his best-known spiritual daughter, Elsbeth Stagel, lived.

Töss was a thriving Dominican convent where at times the community numbered as many as one hundred sisters. Suso probably made the acquaintance of Stagel shortly after she entered the convent in the mid-1330s, and he remained in contact with her, at least through letters, until her death about 1360. She was from Zurich, of noble birth, and well-educated. The first chapters of the second part of the *Life* (chapters 33 and 34) are a delightful narration of the beginnings of Suso's friendship with this spirited young woman. She collected his letters to her and to others, and of her importance for the *Life* more will be said later. She also authored a collection of short biographies of some of the saintly departed sisters of her convent. One can well wonder whether all the extant works of the Dominican friar would have survived without her and how their content might have differed.

In 1338 the hand of Emperor Louis had been strengthened in his struggle with the pope, so that at the Imperial Diet at Frankfurt on August 6 he was in a position to counteract the continuing papal interdict and command that public worship be reinstated in the towns of the empire. Severe punishments would befall those not obeying by January 13 of the following year. Under pressure from the town fathers and against the wishes of the bishop, most of the clergy in Constance capitulated to the emperor's demands. The Dominicans, however, with the exception of four of their number, refused and were thus forced to leave their friary in Constance and go into exile. Their path did not lead far. Eight of their number found refuge in nearby Diessenhofen, while the rest were taken into the Schottenkloster, a monastery just outside the walls of Constance. Where Suso was stationed during this period is uncertain. Some of the friars returned to Constance briefly in 1346, and all had returned by 1349. Statements made in some sources that Suso was prior during part of this period are not based on convincing evidence.

Toward the end of the time of exile Suso was transferred to the Dominican house in Ulm, which became his home for the rest of his life. The move occurred about 1348, the year in which the Ulm Dominicans returned from a similar exile. During his years in Ulm

INTRODUCTION

he no doubt continued his pastoral journeys and spent time completing the *Life* and editing the other works to be included in the *Exemplar*. Otherwise, we know little of his life there. There is no evidence for the claim that he was again called before a chapter of his order to answer charges of heresy.[29] He died in Ulm on January 25, 1366, and was buried in the Dominican church there, already venerated by many in his order and by others in those areas where he had been engaged in preaching and other pastoral activities. In the following century one finds him often referred to as *beatus* (blessed). In 1831, after an investigation of Suso's life, Pope Gregory XVI confirmed the popular cult and set aside March 11 in the Dominican calendar for the celebration of the feast of Blessed Henry Suso.

III. SUSO'S WORKS

Toward the end of his life, most probably in the years 1362–63, Suso undertook to edit for posterity what he considered his most important vernacular works. One reason for doing so was that some of these writings were in circulation in versions either truncated or error-ridden. Hence he felt it necessary to assemble an authorized version "according to how God originally inspired it in him."[30] Another of his purposes in undertaking this volume was to publish for the first time his autobiography, which until then he had considered too private. Realizing, however, that reading it could be of benefit to many people and that it would either be lost after his death or appear in an unauthorized version, he decided to include it.[31] This volume bears the title *Exemplar* and, in sequence, contains the following works: the *Life*, the *Little Book of Eternal Wisdom*, the *Little Book of Truth* and the *Little Book of Letters*. In the present volume the *Exemplar* is translated into English in its entirety for the first time directly from the Middle High German original along with two extant sermons considered authentic.[32] Since Suso's works are so varied in their nature, and since he did not leave us with a unified system of mystical thought or spirituality that runs through the works as a whole, the best way to introduce him to the reader is to offer some analysis of and commentary on each of his vernacular works. In doing so we shall proceed not according to the order in which they appear in the *Exemplar*, but chronologically, as they were composed by their author.

26

INTRODUCTION

Little Book of Truth

Citing both internal and external evidence, authorities generally agree that this is the earliest of Suso's works. It has been suggested that its author may have revised it considerably as he prepared it for inclusion in the *Exemplar*,[33] but we must balance this possibility with the author's stated aim, namely, that he wished to capture the original divine inspiration of each work. In any case the influence and the thought of the schools is much more in evidence in the *LBT* than elsewhere in Suso's writings, as is the influence of Meister Eckhart.[34] It was written sometime during the period 1326–28. Since Eckhart's death is now known to have occurred before April 30, 1328, and probably not before the second half of 1327,[35] and since in chapter 6 (p. 327) of the *LBT* Suso speaks of him in the past tense, at least this part of the *LBT* seems to have been written after Eckhart's death. At any rate, the author's intellectual preoccupations while composing it were the concerns of the current scholastic philosophy and theology and, more particularly, the scholastic thought of Eckhart and Eckhart's troubles with ecclesiastical authorities. Such concerns coincide well with Suso's assignments during this period: concluding his studies in Cologne and assuming the role of lector in Constance. Certainly one of the author's major aims in writing the *LBT* was to defend his revered teacher from those interpreting him wrongly. However, although one finds nowhere a word critical of Eckhart, there are indications that Suso is also distancing himself from some aspects of his teacher's thought. This conclusion is not without its problems. It assumes that Suso thoroughly understood Eckhart's metaphysics, especially his concept of being, and also that we today, in making such a judgment, have grasped it—two great assumptions. Another difficulty in interpreting the *LBT* or determining its relationship to Eckhart's thought stems from the many obscure passages of the work that have thus far not been convincingly illuminated. In addition, certain passages appear to contradict the tenor of the work taken as a whole.

The form in which Suso chose to cast his thoughts is that of the dialogue, a form he returns to in his next work, the *LBEW*, and in the last chapters of the *Life* as well. In contrast to the *LBEW*, where the voices in the dialogue take on individual personalities and psychological depth, the speakers here, the disciple and eternal Truth or, in chapter 5, the disciple and the "wild one," are simply left at the level of a didactic device, albeit an effective one. Suso was in no way original in his choice of form. The dialogue was very familiar through the *Consolation of Philosophy* of Boethius, a basic text in medieval education. Also, allegorical dialogues were not uncommon in the vernacular literature of courtly love. More pertinent, however, in pointing to a literary awareness in our author is his comment in the introduction that the servant's prayer for enlightenment would be answered "in the manner of an explained allegory, as though the disciple were asking and Truth answering."[36] In other words, Suso was consciously choosing a literary form that would modify whatever "raw experience" was at the foundation of his writing. The result would be, in some sense, a figurative explanation. We must return to this idea later.

The author's aim in this dialogue is to achieve clarity concerning the nature of *detachment* and *discernment*. Although there is an ascetic component to detachment as here conceived, the way to its attainment betrays its Eckhartian origins. True detachment begins with an awareness of who God is and what creatures, especially the human creature, are. Since the result of such deliberations and any mystical consciousness based upon them will be that a person emphasizes the oneness of God and creature, a second awareness must come into play, one governed by discernment. Discernment is the ability to distinguish carefully and to avoid the pitfalls on the path of detachment. Besides the danger of assuming a metaphysically incorrect unity between self and God, one seeking detachment must not be led to embrace "unrestrained liberty." Despite the perils, however, we are urged not to lose heart, for the possibility of evil should not be allowed to stifle the worthy pursuit of detachment.

Chapters 1 and 2 elaborate on who or what God is. As Suso struggles to describe God, the influence of Eckhart is unmistakable. However, given Eckhart's present or past difficulties with church authorities, Suso prudently chooses to quote a supposedly unimpeachable source whose ideas are very similar to those of his mentor—pseudo-Dionysius, whom everyone at the time assumed to have been a disciple of St. Paul. For him, as for Eckhart, God, the origin and goal of all things, is nameless, infinite, beyond the grasp of logical concepts. He is a being beyond all limited modes of being. Since all names are incorrect when attributed to him, it is better to call him nonbeing or nothing. If name him one must, then one should call him an intellect whose being is simply and infinitely to know, to live and to be. In the Godhead or ground of this nothing where darkness beyond all light pervades, all multiplicity—even that of the trinity of divine Persons—is somehow lost. Any multiplicity we imply by attributing to God different concepts, such as good, just and the like, has no foundation in God but is due rather to our inadequate grasp of this infinite nothing beyond being who is really utterly simple or one.

What then are creatures? In chapter 3 Suso replies by describing their twofold existence. In a sense they have existed eternally in God who is their Exemplar. They existed as ideas in the divine mind. Truth then states the startling but inevitable conclusion that follows from the eternal existence of creatures: "All creatures in God *are* God."[37] This reference to man's eternal existence *in* God and *as* God, coupled with the terms "flowing out" and "breakthrough" at the beginning of the following chapter, make it very likely that he wishes to call to mind what is perhaps Eckhart's most well-known sermon, German Sermon 52 on poverty of spirit.[38] In this sermon the learned Dominican defines poverty of spirit as having no will, no intellect, not even a being of one's own. One is to become as free of oneself as one was before one "flowed out" from God. In other words, the mystical goal to be striven for is described in terms of a return to that way of existing one enjoyed when one was nothing else but an idea in God. This return to God, or breakthrough, is viewed as superior to one's flowing out into independent creaturely existence.

If, by employing key terms from Eckhart, Suso did wish to recall this sermon to the minds of his readers, it was not to show that he embraced this line of thought without qualification. Rather, he wanted to give it a more clearly orthodox ring. When asked to compare and evaluate the two existences of the creature, Truth responds that a creature does not have true existence in God and thus is in a sense nobler in its independent existence.

This same care to distance himself from questionable formulations is again evident at the beginning of chapter 4 when the author takes up the term *breakthrough*, but in actuality uses it merely as a synonym for another favorite Eckhartian theme he wishes to touch upon: becoming the Son. While Eckhart had stressed the unity of Christ and creature that occurs through the process of man's becoming the Son, Suso is careful to point out the differences that continue to separate God and creature. Eckhart had stated on occasion that in becoming

29

the Son the human creature undergoes a change in substance, just as bread is changed in substance into the body of the Lord in the mass.[39] Truth, on the other hand, states to the disciple very clearly that in a person's becoming The Son through detachment no transubstantiation occurs. The creature remains essentially creature. In order to clarify Truth introduces five ways of understanding *self*: as being, as vegetative existence, as sentient existence, as possessing human nature, and as an individual; and it is only this last self that one leaves through detachment, not the other four, which determine one as a creature. It is only this last self that one can develop and modify as to accidents, but not as to substance, through the exercise of one's will. True detachment consists in freely divesting oneself of possessiveness and losing this self by withdrawing into Christ's self. However, this involves no metaphysical change in the human creature. This leads Suso to qualify another Eckhartian doctrine: that creatures are a pure nothing.[40] Truth feels obliged to point out that one cannot leave one's creaturely self in such a way that it becomes absolutely nothing. It is one's attitude that must change through detachment, not one's nature.

Finally this chapter poses the question whether complete happiness is attainable on earth or is only possessed in heaven. Again, the author's ulterior motive for having the disciple pose the question would seem to be to clarify Suso's position and distance it from heretical views. This time, however, it is less likely that it is Eckhart whom Suso has in mind since this was not one of Eckhart's central concerns. The possibility of achieving ultimate happiness while on earth was a teaching of the brothers of the Free Spirit, at least as perceived by church authorities at the Council of Vienne as well as in other contexts.[41] Truth denies that such happiness is possible in our earthly condition but speaks of a mystical state attainable on earth that affords one happiness beyond what the senses or intellect can achieve.

Chapter 5 is long and in many ways confusing, and readers must generally be left to their own devices. However, three points do emerge clearly. First, borrowing from Eckhart yet another manner of describing the union of the detached person with Christ—that of one's being the image of Christ—Suso has eternal Truth refine the disciple's powers of discernment concerning Christ's preeminence by instructing him that Christ alone is taken up in his humanity into the subsistence of the second Person of the Trinity.

INTRODUCTION

The creature can only take on the form of Christ's image (a staple of Augustinian thought). At best, one can become an image more or less similar to the image of Christ, which is united with his divinity. Second, the reader is informed that there are two aspects of detachment: *interior*, in which one sees Christ with the intellect through contemplation, and *exterior*, through which, by means of ascetic practices, one carries interior detachment over into one's physical existence. Both are necessary and those who possess only external detachment lack the gentle and generous spirit of Christ, whom they should be imitating. They are as harsh and severe as their ascetic practices.

Finally and repeatedly, Truth clarifies an important point concerning ecstatic union. The disciple began this chapter by expressing a desire to converse with someone who had been taken up into God. Such a one seems to lose himself so completely in the divinity during such experiences that nothing is left of him as creature in any way still distinct from God. What is the role of discernment here? Truth insists that one keep clearly in mind the distinction between what such a person experiences and what the metaphysical facts of the matter are. While experiencing such a transport the person is completely unaware of anything but union. However, this does not change physical or metaphysical reality. No matter what a person experiences or thinks he knows, the fact is that throughout the experience he retains his essence and being as creature. And yet, any attempt to conceptualize anything concerning the One who is nameless must remain essentially inadequate. One must get beyond what can be presented in words: "To say that this nothing is intellect or being or fulfillment is certainly true according to what anyone can tell us about it. However, in true point of fact, it is as far and farther from these things than if one were to call a fine pearl a chopping block."[42] In this fanciful comparison we cannot help but detect an echo of Eckhart's condemned claim that "whoever would say that God is good would be treating him as unjustly as though he were calling the sun black."[43]

In order to recapitulate many of the points made thus far, to elucidate additional Eckhartian themes and to clarify who is in need of such elucidation, the author constructs in chapter 6 an imagined dialogue between the disciple, who has achieved a state of enlightenment, and a person named the "wild one." This wild one describes himself in terms of divine nothingness and says that he is moved by

31

"unrestrained liberty," which he defines as living according to one's impulses. This understanding of liberty was frequently attributed to those whom the Council of Vienne, in the decree *Ad nostrum*, had rebuked for their spirit of liberty.[44] The disciple counters with the idea of true or "ordered" freedom, which is learned through discernment. When the wild one implies that his own ideas are derived from a "learned teacher" (Eckhart) who denied all distinctions, the disciple responds by giving an explanation both of the unity in the Godhead, which allows for the Trinity, and of the unity between a person lost in God and God, which allows for the distinct being of each. The wild one then refers to two other incriminating teachings centering on Eckhart's conception of the just man's oneness with God as Justice. Suso's spokesman, the disciple, demonstrates he is well-versed in one of the most important features of Eckhart's thought, namely, his application of the *inquantum* principle. Christ is perfectly one with Justice because he is totally born from Justice and from nothing else. The just human creature, however, imperfect and limited in the possession of justice as he is, is one with Justice only *insofar as* he is born from Justice. In concluding, the disciple again criticizes the wild one's lack of discernment and the latter shows himself contrite and submissive to further instruction.

In the short final chapter the disciple wants to know how from externals one can discern a truly detached person. In other words, how does the person act who has utterly abandoned self? After paradoxically stating that the detached person's freedom consists in free submission to God and then enumerating a few characteristics of one so living, Truth cuts off further discussion with the observation that questions do not bring one to the goal. Only exercising oneself in detachment does. The disciple has received enough theoretical instruction. It is now time to practice detachment, for only by so doing can one make one's own the hidden truth awaiting one beyond the ordinary grasp of human understanding.

Little Book of Eternal Wisdom

Except in the concluding chapters of the *Life*, never again would Suso write so under the influence of his theological schooling. Nor would he ever again feel the need either to defend his teacher,

INTRODUCTION

Meister Eckhart, or to clarify his own theological positions. Indeed, the abrupt change in the author's style and approach between the *Little Book of Truth* and the next of his writings, the *Little Book of Eternal Wisdom*, has puzzled many. The goal of the *LBT* is the exploration of the ascetical-mystical term *gelassehheit* (detachment), but in spite of its dialogue form, it is perhaps most aptly characterized as a theological tract. The *LBEW*, on the other hand, makes no attempt at intellectual sophistication and can best be termed a manual of devotion whose purpose is edification rather than instruction.

Several reasons have been brought forward to account for this change in direction. First, there is the unpleasant matter of Suso's being called before a chapter of his order to answer, among other things, the charge "that he wrote books containing false teachings that were soiling the whole country with their heretical garbage."[45] The chapter in question was most likely the already mentioned provinical chapter held in Maastricht in 1330.[46] Certainly such an uncomfortable experience would be enough to turn one away from matters where one's orthodoxy might easily come under attack. However, since Suso employs the plural, *books*, and since no other of his writings that we know of could be meant but the *LBT* and the *LBEW*, the latter might well have already been finished or known at least in some version at the time of the chapter. Thus, if one is inclined to take the plural, *books*, seriously, Suso's sobering experiences in Maastricht would not account for the sudden shift in direction.

Second, in the *Horologium sapientiae*, the Latin version of the *LBEW*, Suso expresses his dissatisfaction with the theology of the schools and the motivation of those pursuing it.[47] He finds that such school learning is dry and that it nurtures the vanity and egotistical pedantry of those engaged in it, while there is little about it that promotes the spiritual life. This, combined with his own natural tendencies and talents, was certainly a factor contributing to the change. When one examines his works as a whole, one is forced to conclude that speculative thought was neither his main interest nor his strong suit. Undoubtedly his intellectual capabilities were considerable, as the decision of his superiors to send him on for further studies in Cologne and the *LBT* both attest. Yet his talents as a narrator and devotional writer are greater. The *LBEW* was the product of his natural inclinations and abilities, whereas the *LBT* had been the result of complex and abstract acquired knowledge. It should not be surprising that readers have difficulty with some sections of the *LBT*, as well as with the speculative chapters concluding the *Life*. The fault is not entirely theirs. Finally, the purpose of the *LBEW* and the intended audience surely were determining factors motivating the change. The book was composed to foster the spiritual progress of those, both members of religious communities and others, who had little formal training in theology. That Suso could so easily drop the language of the schools and adapt his writing to suit his new goal so quickly and so successfully confirms his abilities as a writer and also indicates that narrative and devotional discourse are where his natural talents lay.

We do not know exactly when the *LBEW* was written, but the *Horologium sapientiae*, which builds upon the *LBEW* and definitely follows it, was finished in the first half of 1334. If, as seems likely, the *LBEW* was objected to at the Maastricht chapter, it would have been completed by 1330. Suso probably began work on it sometime in 1328.

Because of its importance in its own right and because of its relationship to the *LBEW*, a brief explanation of the *Horologium sapientiae* is in order. Suso does not tell us why he decided to prepare a Latin version of the *LBEW*. Several possibilities come to mind. Because of the difficulties his earlier vernacular writings had caused him, he would have been well-advised to put his ideas in a form making them accessible to higher superiors in his order who could not read German. Since Latin was a more refined medium, he could express himself more clearly and thus avoid formulations whose orthodoxy might be impugned. Then there was the question of how Suso himself, in typically medieval fashion, perceived his mother tongue. He speaks of how cold and lifeless it seems in written form.[48] He might also have had in mind reaching a wider audience. In any case the Latin version did achieve great popularity outside of Germany: in the Netherlands, France, England and Italy. If one can judge a book's impact by the number of its extant manuscripts, the *Horologium sapientiae* was surpassed in popularity in the later Middle Ages only by the *Imitation of Christ*.[49]

Horologium sapientiae means "clock of wisdom." The author explains the title as the result of a vision in which a clock adorned with roses and from which heavenly music is issuing forth serves as a symbol for the book as it proclaims the mercy of the Savior and

34

INTRODUCTION

uplifts hearts.[50] The work is divided into twenty-four chapters, representing the hours of the day and night. Since books of this type, called *horologia* (clocks), antedate the *Horologium sapientiae*, the aforementioned vision does not appear to be the exclusive or crucial reason for the book's title.

The *Horologium sapientiae* is not simply a translation of the *LBEW;* it has even been referred to as almost a different book.[51] Much of the material of the *LBEW* is expanded or reorganized. Additions have also been made. These include several autobiographical remarks, references of interest to trained theologians, material more directly affecting members of religious orders—especially remarks criticizing the lack of religious observance—and some allusions to contemporary political events. Finally, the idea of betrothal to Wisdom is given more prominence.[52] Clearly a different audience is intended, and the prologue addresses the general of the order as one of the book's intended readers. Occasionally the tone is more learned, but the dialogue flows less smoothly than in the *LBEW*, and it lacks the structural unity of the vernacular version.

In contrast to the *LBT*, the *LBEW* demands little in the way of schooling in theology or even of intellectual acuity from the reader and thus requires little explanation or analysis. Again, Suso has chosen the dialogue form. This time, however, his role is not that of disciple but rather of servant of eternal Wisdom. Why Suso chooses this name for himself is best understood by reading chapter 3 of the *Life*. That Truth is replaced by Wisdom as chief partner for the dialogue seems to be a natural progression. Truth's function is to enlighten. Wisdom's function is to order one's life, as one of the pictures included in the *Exemplar* informs us through a quotation from Aristotle.[53] Besides eternal Wisdom, the servant also has Mary, the sorrowful Mother, and a person dying unprepared as partners in dialogue. As in the previous work, the author warns us not to consider what is portrayed as the description of things that actually occurred. They are literary constructions or allegory.

The author's purpose in the *LBEW* is to renew the interior life of his readers by providing them with a means to meditate on Christ's passion. The book is divided into three parts of unequal length. The first and longest section takes as its principal subject, with several digressions, the passion of Christ both as he and as his mother

35

experienced it. The events are narrated by the Savior and his mother. The servant responds appropriately and receives instruction. The chief digressions are a vivid allegorical depiction of the sorry state of monasticism and graphic descriptions of the pains of hell and the joys of heaven. The second section deals with four topics of basic asceticism: how to die well (portrayed in an emotionally charged conversation between the servant and a man about to die who has previously given no serious thought to death and now finds that it is too late to prepare properly); how to live interiorly; how to receive the eucharist properly; and how to praise God. The third part contains, by way of an appendix, the short hundred meditations which, as the author tells us, were the point of origin for the *LBEW*.

The *LBEW* was the most widely distributed and frequently read German manual of devotion during the one hundred and fifty years following its completion.[54] What accounts for its popularity then and its being considered a classic of its kind even today? Certainly it is not the originality of its subject matter. The reader is presented with the staples of instruction on the interior life as these had been understood and written about since the beginnings of Western monasticism. In turning away from the scholasticism of the *LBT*, the author has embraced instead the rich ascetic traditions of an older Christianity. Nor is it the format as such that holds the reader, although the author has chosen it judiciously. Rather it is the literary quality of the piece and the immediacy with which time-honored teachings are presented that justify its reputation. For example, the Hound of Heaven motif with which the *LBEW* begins goes back to the beginning of Augustine's *Confessions*. Suso was aware of this fact, as were most of his thoughtful readers. But the fact that the motif is borrowed is incidental, because God's pursuit of the errant soul has been so assimilated by the author that he has made it truly his own, expressing it with a freshness and intensity that reflect and bear witness to his rich interior life. The author wishes his readers to experience with this same intensity and, to accomplish this, makes use of his vivid imagination to recreate the story of the passion and the feelings of the two chief participants. By allowing his readers to imagine and feel so immediately the events of the passion, Suso enables them to unite with Christ as he brings about their redemption. The appropriate response is not to understand but to commit oneself completely.

INTRODUCTION

Little Book of Letters

Of the works included in the *Exemplar*, the *Little Book of Letters* is the least known and perhaps most underrated. This collection of "letters" had its origin in Suso's editorial activity as he was preparing the *Exemplar* for dissemination. Elsbeth Stagel originally collected many letters that Suso had sent to her and to others of his spiritual children. That collection, or one deriving from it, has been preserved and is included in Bihlmeyer's edition of Suso's German works under the title *Great Book of Letters* (*Das große Briefbuch*). It would appear that the *LBL* was compiled late since, in his short prologue to the work, Suso characterizes this epistolary activity as being over with.[55]

That he refers to the contents of the book as *instruction* shows that even the author was aware of the changed nature of what he had compiled. The letters are not such in the modern sense of personal communications. They have clearly been edited with an eye to making them both public and exemplary. All strictly personal aspects have been removed, although the psychological condition of the type of person addressed in each letter helps determine the tack taken. Some of the original letters have been combined with parts of others, the spiritual topic to be elaborated on serving as the principle of unity.[56] In their tone and form the resulting eleven letters remind one of Seneca's *Moral Epistles*, with which Suso was familiar. In their ability to impart concise practical wisdom they are models of religious instruction and exhortation.

Their author has ordered the letters to follow a line of progression from the first steps in religious life to its ultimate goal. The first is directed to a woman who has just left the world to take the veil and become the bride of Christ. The transitory and deceptive nature of what the world offers is contrasted with true freedom, which is serving God. The author's description of the dangers inherent in religious life is striking, particularly his depiction of the sorry condition of those who have committed themselves totally in a formal way by becoming members of religious orders, but who idle away their days preoccupied with utter trivialities. Ensuing letters take up such topics as humility and subordination, suffering as the mark of God's special friends, and steadfastness and independence in pursuing the goal in the face of self-serving advice from those less idealistic. One letter was written to strengthen and console someone who was dying and taking it badly. We are told that the letter had the desired effect. Another is addressed to someone who has just become a religious superior; it suggests in what spirit the assignment should be undertaken and what problems can be expected. In formulating his advice, the author could no doubt look back to some of his own experiences as prior. The final three letters touch upon such sublime subjects as peace of heart, the way of light and truth once one has become truly detached, and praise of the name of Jesus.

More than any other of his writings, the *LBL* displays Suso's rhetorical talents. His epigrammatic formulations show high linguistic virtuosity. And his ability to strike a tone suited to the needs of the intended audience and their situation reveals his gift for empathy. Occasionally wit and humor show through, as in Letter 8 when he describes the disproportion existing between someone experiencing spiritual bliss and someone in a drab and sober mood. The exuberance of the former is as difficult for the latter to re-create as it is for one on an errand of mercy thirsting in the wilds to comprehend and empathize with someone in a wine cellar whose high spirits are fueled by the alcohol he is imbibing. In urging a spiritual daughter not to give up her lofty resolve, he concludes by saying that one who has been invited to become the bride of Christ should not become a (spiritual) barmaid.[57] The letters are well-suited for the use Suso suggests for them in the Prologue: to provide a kind of spiritual recreation for the reader.[58]

Life

In many respects the *Life* is the most interesting of Suso's works and has found the most resonance in modern scholarship. It certainly poses the most puzzles. It has been called the first autobiography in the German language.[59] And yet one can justly question whether the term *autobiography* really applies and whether Suso can rightfully be declared its author. With regard to the second question, let us begin with what the introduction to Part One tells us. Without his knowing it, Elsbeth Stagel wrote down what Suso told her in conversations about his life. When he learned about her "theft," he demanded she turn everything over to him, and he burned what he could. As he was about to destroy the rest, a "message from God" prevented him. Thus, what remains is largely what she wrote down, except what he added by way of good instruction after her death.[60] Is the *Life* basically her writing? Since the narrative parts surviving have a sense of completeness about them, what was lost through the burning? Besides the "good instruction" at the end (chapters 46–53), there seem to be other parts that Stagel did not write. And concerning the matter of the unsuccessful attempt to destroy the work and the message from God, modern observers, try as they might to rid themselves of their Voltairean cynicism regarding things supernatural, may well find it difficult to suppress the uncomfortable feeling that perhaps they are dealing less with fact than with a well-worn literary device. Even if we ignore for the moment this last problem, the best we can offer concerning the other difficulties of authorship is to delineate the sensible but vulnerable *sententia communior* or generally accepted opinion.[61] Part One (chapters 1–32) is taken to be basically what Stagel wrote down from her conversations with Suso. The narrative sections of Part Two (chapters 34–44) were left largely in their original form: the form of letters. Exceptions to this are chapters 33 and 45, which are considered to be the direct work of Suso. In addition, within the narrative sections there may be material that was subsequently added. Most of the stories concerning the woman Anna might well be such. Chapters 46–53 in Part Two, which are not narrative and, in part, present difficult mystical teachings, were added by Suso after Stagel's death, as he himself tells us.[62] These are most likely the sections he sent for approval to Master Bartholomew.[63] Another matter about which one cannot but be terribly curious is how much Suso changed those parts written down by Stagel, both as to content and as to style, as he was editing the *Life* for inclusion in the *Exemplar*. Because other extant writings of Stagel do not measure up to the *Life* in style, aesthetic sense and theological sophistication, Bihlmeyer was convinced that Suso undertook extensive changes while editing.[64] However, no one has devised a convincing method for confirming this view or getting beyond such generalizations. Besides Bihlmeyer, Gröber undertook to distinguish "genuine" sections of the *Life* from later additions.[65] However, his results have been criticized for excessive dependence on psychological probability and modern judgments in matters of literary taste.[66] And there the matter uneasily rests. Both as to content and literary quality, the *Life* seems to have Suso as its principal source; but the inclusion of material not authored by him cannot be ruled out. However, it appears unlikely that such material would constitute enough of the total work to alter in an essential way the *Life*'s content, intent or tone.[67]

Perhaps more important still for the modern reader is the question: To what extent is one justified in calling it an autobiography? If the reader fails to grasp the kind of work it is, misunderstandings about its content will abound. Put simply, how should the *Life* be read? Certainly the *Life*'s concern with incidents in the protagonist's life and with his interior reaction to them persuades us that the *Life* has characteristics of autobiography. However, the reader is well-advised not to assume that the only, or even principal, concern of the author is to re-create the incidents as they really happened.[68] If the *Life* takes some of its characteristics from the tradition of autobiography, it is clearly to the "confessional" autobiography, as exemplified by St. Augustine's *Confessions*, that it owes the most. Like the *Confessions*, it is the story of a spiritual journey: First the soul of the progatonist feels within itself the stirrings of restlessness and longing for an unrecognized goal, then progresses along an arduous path, and finally finds rest in the attainment of the goal. And, like the *Confessions*, it wishes to confess or proclaim how the protagonist's life bears witness to God's love for humanity. In its openness with the reader the *Life* also bears incidental resemblance to Abelard's *History of My Calamities*, another autobiography Suso might have read.

In spite of these similarities to autobiography, it has been well-argued that Suso's *Life* more properly belongs to another genre: hagiography. The legends or lives of the saints had been in existence since the early centuries of Christianity, and the lives of the desert fathers deeply influenced Suso's perception of how the spiritual life should be led. However, even more interesting for our purposes is the nature of the hagiographies written in the fourteenth century. Richard Kieckhefer has investigated these lives of the saints not in order to determine what these people were really like, but rather to determine what ingredients people of that age considered essential to sanctity.[69] Because the protagonists in these hagiographies were so stereotyped, so hidden behind conventions, and because the content of such hagiographies was greatly determined by what people expected to find when reading about the life of a person of extraordinary holiness, one is likely to learn from them more about what people thought a saint was than about the actual lives of the people depicted. Kieckhefer determined that the chief ingredients of sanctity expected in the narration of a holy person's life at this time were the following: remarkable patience in suffering, devotion to the passion, penitence, and raptures and revelations. The *Life* dwells on these facets of Suso's spiritual journey to such a degree that it can well be considered a classic fourteenth-century hagiography. Kieckhefer suggests we call it and similar works auto-hagiography.[70] Overshadowing any claim they might make to the portrayal of actual people and events, such documents were written to edify readers by presenting them with spiritual heroes they could admire for their larger-than-life struggles and deeds and could imitate in the basic spiritual orientation of their lives.

This "exemplary" character of Suso's *Life* forces us to consider it at least as much hagiography as autobiography. While we are given intimate glimpses of the man, large portions of the book are so obviously intended to make the protagonist serve as a spiritual model for the reader that strictly autobiographical traits are deeply colored by pastoral concerns. When, for example, we are told how the servant conducted himself at meals (chapter 8), how he observed silence (chapter 14), or of the three circles that enclosed him in the priory (chapter 35), we are being presented with models for imitation and, more particularly, models eminently suited to cloistered nuns. Especially effective in this regard are delineations of how he creatively turns secular holidays, such as New Year (chapter 8), pre-lenten Carnival (chapter 11), or May Day (chapter 12), into festivals of the spiritual life.

Not only is Suso portrayed according to the stereotyped norms of sanctity, at times he takes on the posture of Christ himself. He goes up onto a mountain to pray in order to gather strength for impending spiritual combat with the forces of evil.[71] And as he spends an evening discoursing to some beguines after supper, much as Christ had done with his apostles on the night before he died, the miraculous increase of wine in the little bottle he has blessed must be viewed in the light of Christ's multiplication of the loaves and fishes, especially since the spiritual daughter bringing the bottle echoes Andrew's remark to Jesus (Jn 6:9), saying, "What help would that be among so many?"[72]

Seeing the *Life* mainly in terms of fourteenth-century hagiography also provides a more plausible context for judging those sections that describe the severe penitential practices the servant imposed

INTRODUCTION

upon himself. Although he later rejects them as not being what God
ultimately expects of him and cautions his spiritual children against
them, they are an essential element in the life of a saint. If not
something offered the reader for imitation, they are nonetheless
practices designed to stir his admiration for the superhuman side of
the hero. And their presence, whether fact or fiction, in the lives of
the desert fathers and other saints would have led Suso to consider
them necessary for one pursuing sanctity on a heroic level, as clearly
he did.

If the demands of hagiography and the obvious pastoral intent of
the author affect the content of the *Life* in ways that make it illegitimate for us to consider it as a naive portrayal of raw bits of reality,
the evident aspirations of the author to artistic or literary achievement also left their imprint on his striving for form, which again
affects content. Suso has long been recognized as an author of great
literary talent and subtlety, and writing in compliance with the
demands of literature influences and alters in many ways the raw
experience portrayed. Literature has its own laws and its own truth.
In other works Suso stated his awareness that the higher truths he
was seeking to present were not always best served by or limited to
factually accurate descriptions.[73] And in the prologue to the *Exemplar* there occur veiled comments in a similar vein concerning the
Life.[74] The expression of spiritual truths in literary form was Suso's
ultimate goal. Historical accuracy was but one means of expressing
them.

Literary intent reveals itself in the way the *Life* is structured.
Although it is clearly not of a piece artistically, the *Life* is also not
bound by the order of chronology. Rather, chapters or groups of
chapters are often structured thematically. In chapter 23, for example, independent episodes are grouped together because they all
refer to humiliations the servant suffered. Chapters 2 and 3 are
juxtaposed not because of any chronological proximity but because
they are alternate and complementary descriptions of mystical
union, each chapter employing one of the two chief ways of describing such union found in Christian tradition. Chapter 2 concentrates
on the tradition of ecstasy and light, while chapter 3 employs the
tradition of bride mysticism. Chapters 15–18 include all materials
relating to the self-imposed corporal penances characteristic of
Suso's life as a beginner. His rejection of these penances at the close
of chapter 18 signals the end of his neophyte existence. Chapter 19

42

marks the beginning of a clearly new level in his interior life, introducing the reader to the servant's "advanced schooling" in the practice of detachment; and chapters 31 and 32 conclude this section on advanced spirituality by focusing on suffering, not as self-imposed, but as something to be accepted as God's will and as a sign of his special love.

In implementing intent the author employs literary motifs and techniques. Thus in chapter 20, when the servant has just progressed to a higher level where he expects to encounter less struggle and more leisure, he meditates one morning on Job's words that life is a battle (*militia est*). He then describes a vision that draws on the fading world of knighthood as it had been idealized in courtly romance. Told that he is now expected to ascend from the level of squire to that of true spiritual knight, and that he can expect an increase in the number of battles he must engage in, Suso receives enlightenment about the real nature of the transition from neophyte to spiritual manhood.

The role of knighthood and Suso's adaptation of the ideals of chivalry to his spiritual quest have been greatly emphasized in secondary literature, especially by Germanists,[75] perhaps more so than the topic deserves. Viewing his work as a whole, one would do better to see chivalric thought as one of several factors influencing the way he expresses himself rather than to give it special preeminence.[76] However, there are several passages where the influence of courtly literature is evident. And Suso devotes all of chapter 44 of the *Life* to a comparison of knighthood and the spiritual life. This chapter well illustrates not only how he employs the ideas of chivalry for spiritual purposes but also how literary and pastoral concerns shape what was probably in some sense an actual occurrence. While crossing Lake Constance by boat to preach, the servant meets a knight and strikes up a conversation with him. The knight informs him that his task is to arrange chivalric tournaments. The servant inquires about the nature of such contests and the prize and learns that the prize is a golden ring presented by a lady of great beauty, and that the knight who wins the ring must be the best, unyielding in combat and enduring every blow. The servant reflects on the difficulty of the struggle and the paltry reward, insignificant when compared to the eternal reward promised to one who, like him, aspires to spiritual knighthood. Soon thereafter such difficulties overtake the servant that he forgets his noble resolve and gives himself over to depression and womanish weeping, until an inner voice recalls to him the promises he had made, and he is able at last to laugh through his tears.

If we reflect on this episode, it becomes obvious that the incident inspiring the chapter has been fashioned to suit the spiritual lesson Suso wished to impart. Whatever the nature of the actual conversation, Suso was most certainly already aware of the nature of knightly contests and prizes. Hence his seeking such information is a pose to provide a vehicle for the spiritual message to be conveyed. And the servant in the episode is not simply the real Suso. He functions as a mask, a speaker in a dialogue that, though skillfully executed, has as its goal not the portrayal of an actual event but the communication of a spiritual message. Even in his weakness the servant is a model playing a role, bringing comfort and encouragement to those who feel overwhelmed. When one examines the role of chivalry in the anecdote, one sees that it fares poorly as an ideal or system of values in comparison with the servant's spiritual quest and its reward. It has been reduced simply to a literary means serving a spiritual end.

Suso demonstrates great talent as a narrator; the most memorable parts of the *Life* are doubtlessly the anecdotes told on himself. His experiences in pursuit of his wayward sister, the tribulations encountered as he is accused of well poisoning, his walk through the forest with the murderer are all vividly portrayed and fix themselves firmly in the mind of the reader.[77] That his wish to tell a good story often modified the original experience is almost a certainty. Thus, when he is elected prior in a time of financial crisis, he tells us of the chapter meeting he called, and he describes it not only from his point of view, but also from a point of view to which he could not have been privy. We hear two of the more cynical members of the community whispering that not only is their superior incompetent and able to respond to the crisis only by gaping up to heaven, but they themselves are stupid for having elected him.[78] We also learn from this incident something we should at least suspect from other parts of the *Life:* Suso had a sense of humor and by means of it actually achieved distance from the role he assigned himself in the *Life*.[79]

To observe Suso functioning as a literary artist, we can examine at some length one of his most effective and detailed narrative episodes: his sufferings at the hands of the recidivist woman who accuses him of fathering her child (chapter 38). Before the actual narrative begins we are presented with a vision that foreshadows the impending misfortune. In the vision the servant is forced to sing the mass of the martyrs and is given ominous replies when he seeks to understand why only this mass may be sung. Certainly an effective lead-in to the story. Upon awakening he tries to explain the agony about to overtake him to a companion but is met only with incomprehesion, just as Jesus was misunderstood by his disciples when he tried to inform them of his imminent passion.[80] Following this indirect allusion to Christ's suffering the narrator adds to the mood of gloom by mentioning the dark and dreary winter season—a standard symbol for sadness in medieval poetry—and heightens the effect of all this by stating bluntly the tormented condition of the servant's mind and soul. We are then told of the nature of his affliction. As the story of his kindess to the fallen woman and her evil cunning unfolds, we see Suso forced into the torturous predicament of having to choose between his virtue and his reputation. A true model for us all, he chooses to preserve his virtue and, in so doing, he travels the same path that Susanna had trodden before him.[81] Echoes of the story of Suso's biblical counterpart abound, which leads one to believe that he consciously tailored the story to fit this already existing pattern.

Enter a second woman who consoles the hero and suggests a simple solution to his problem: She will kidnap the child and either bury it alive or stick a needle through its brain, assuming with her conventional wisdom that once the cause of the scandal is removed people will forget the whole incident. In exemplary fashion Suso rejects this morbid solution, calling the woman a murderess and pointing out to her and his audience that the child, after all, had been formed in God's image and redeemed by the blood of Christ.[82] Unmoved, the woman continues to find his anger at her proposal excessive, and she suggests the friar have the child brought secretly to the church as an orphan in order that he avoid any financial responsibility for it. The servant rejects this idea also and commands the woman to bring the child to him in secret. If we assume that everything really happened just as we find it written down, we are faced with accounting for the numerous improbabilities in these events. For example, how could Suso be so unthinking as to bid a woman who is wielding a knife and has just proposed that she murder the child most foully to bring that same child safely to him?

And how does the woman accomplish this without the mother's knowing or reacting? If we acknowledge the didactic purpose and the literary nature of the story, we feel less troubled in concluding that some liberties have been taken to move the story along and to subordinate actuality to pastoral intent.

Suso's meeting with the child is best taken in the same vein, formed as it is, at least to a degree, by a concern for artistic and pastoral effect. His concern for the child is so moving that even the heart of the woman who brought the child is touched, and she weeps. Considering how she has been portrayed until now, one could question the psychological probability of this conversion—unless one views it in the light of the genre of hagiography, where the exemplary actions of a saint often move otherwise incorrigible sinners to tears. The blows of fate continue to rain down upon the servant. Friends desert him. The future influence of his books for good is sneeringly called into question. But a voice from within provides momentary consolation as he is about to lose heart. In anguish over the insight that it is God's supposed friends, namely Christians, who are treating him like a skinned animal, like insects treat a skinned carcass, he nevertheless humbly realizes that ultimately it is actually God acting through them. Christ had his Judas; the servant complains that nowadays, in his own case, there is not just one Judas—there are several. Added to this burden is his fear of the damage this scandal will do to his order and of what his fate will be at the hands of his superiors. Deep in despair he goes off alone to ponder why God has forsaken him, but, as the Christ-figure he is, he struggles ably to the perfect Christ-like response: "Thy will be done." A departed spiritual daughter appears to him and promises all will be well.[83] Finally he is vindicated and his enemies die off. As with Job, all is restored to him and the experience has enriched him greatly.

The foregoing comments are not intended to keep the reader from taking this episode and others like it seriously. Their purpose is, rather, to show the reader *how* to take them seriously. The conscious use of prototypes (Susanna, Job and Christ), the posturing of the hero so that he is consistently exemplary, the intent to edify the reader, and the deft use of literary narrative techniques are so clearly in evidence that one must consider these elements as co-determinants of the content of the episode. Just as it is unwarranted to consider the story a complete fabrication, so also is it ill-advised to believe that the chief purpose of its narration is factual accuracy or that such accuracy is even approximately achieved. Exactly how much the events have been changed in the telling is impossible to say.

This same attitude of circumspection well becomes the reader regarding other features of the *Life*. So, for example, the servant's visions gain in plausibility if we try to rid ourselves of modern preconceptions about such phenomena and approach them in a spirit resembling that of Suso himself. Visions were an essential characteristic of the life of a holy person, and a lack of them reflected badly on an author's understanding of what a hagiography was supposed to contain. Besides this impetus for the supernatural emanating from the genre, there are several other factors that the modern reader should be aware of when considering Suso's descriptions of visions and mystical states.

First, one should keep in mind that the terms used to describe mystical conditions are frequently just as applicable to ascetic states and goals as they are to clearly mystical states. Second, in the *Life* most of these terms occur in those sections that offer a theoretical treatment of mysticism,[84] not in the sections that relate events in the life of the servant. Third, within these narrative sections the servant's descriptions of most of his visions are relativized by the language used to introduce them. Three relativizing elements frequently occurring are these: first, what he is experiencing through the senses begins to fade away; second, the use of a phrase such as "it seemed to him";[85] and third, the use of the subjunctive to describe the action of the person appearing, for example, it seemed to him "that Christ *were* coming to him."[86] At times, even when all these elements are not present to introduce a vision, the author seems to presuppose that the reader is acquainted with his standard introduction and will therefore properly understand an abbreviated one.

Fourth, the reader cannot help but notice similarities many of these visions have to dreams. Most of the visions are said to happen in the early morning after the servant has returned from prayer or matins.[87] He is usually sitting in a relaxed position. In fact, in the *LBEW* he describes himself as "lightly napping" or "asleep" when visions occur.[88] And the visions themselves usually reveal the weakened causality and the gaps in the sequence of events normally experienced in dreams. This connection between dreams and visions is made explicit in chapter 51 when, in discussing the means of distinguishing true from dubious visions, the servant refers to this problem as it affects visions one has when asleep. He then cites a passage from the *Confessions* in which Augustine's mother tells her son that God had given her the ability to distinguish between a vision using images and an ordinary dream of no significance. When Suso adds that one who has this gift cannot explain it to one who has not experienced it, the only apparent justification for this remark is that he felt he, too, had this gift.[89]

Fifth, we should consider these visions both in the light of Suso's own comments on visions and according to their role or roles in the *Life*. In his discussion of visions just mentioned, he assigns value to them according to how intellectual and free of images they are.[90] Thus a vision of the pure Godhead ranks highest because it is a purely intellectual seeing—without images. Their value also seems to be determined by how detached they are from the normal activity of the senses and how separated the visionary is from external activity.[91] Although most of the visions described in the *Life* can be viewed as occurring apart from normal use of the senses and external activity, few appear to achieve the intellectuality of that pure seeing that Suso valued most. And when we consider the roles of visions in the *Life*, we find that, supernatural though they may be, they tend to be more decorative than essential to the spiritual life the servant attempts to lead and that he advocates for others.

Sixth, even the most spiritual or intellectual raptures experienced by the servant must be seen as undergoing modification as he attempts to formulate them. In chapter 2 we are presented with his most well-known supernatural experience, his rapture when alone in the chapel on the feast of St. Agnes.[92] Whatever the nature of the experience, Suso expressed it in part by alluding to an experience described by Paul,[93] by using the most frequent symbol for such experiences, light, and by repeating two common literary cliches of the time: that if this was not heaven, he did not know what heaven was, and the fact that no amount of suffering was equal to this joy. Suso's descriptions of what he experienced points up the fact that no experience, mystical or otherwise, occurs in a vacuum. All previous experience—education, culture and all other aspects of one's background—modifies, if not the rapture itself, at least the telling of it. An absolutely pure mystical experience is by definition inexpressible.

Finally, we should ask ourselves whether some of our modern

assumptions about visions and similar phenomena were shared by the person who here describes them. More specifically, did Suso assume, as many moderns do, an essential difference and unbridgeable gap between what is natural and what is supernatural? Despite his training in scholasticism and his obvious ability to make fine distinctions, does one not read the *Life* more in the spirit in which it was written if one sees its world as one where such boundaries are fluid, where the so-called supernatural is immediately present to the natural order even though it is generally not perceived? And if we judge the author to be naive in this, we must also call to mind the sophistication of his most explicit statement concerning the visions described in his works. In the prologue to the *Horologium sapientiae* he says concerning the visions contained in that work that "they are not to be taken literally (*ad litteram*), although many literally happened." They are to be understood, rather, as "a figurative way of speaking" (*figurata locutio*).[94] Perhaps we can do no better than to leave the matter hovering, as Suso does, between actual event and symbolic function.

Besides visions, another main stumbling block for the modern reader of the *Life* must certainly be the excruciating corporal penances Suso inflicted upon himself—his hairshirt replete with nails, the barbed cross worn next to his bare back, his prodigious fasting, the self-imposed suffering from thirst, and all the rest. Regarding these, too, as we have said, one can mention that they were a staple of the hagiographies of the time and served the readers' need for superhuman heroes, if not their need for sensible ascetic practices. There is no doubt that in his early years Suso himself considered such ascetic athleticism essential to his pursuit of heroic sanctity. Fortunately for him, he came to realize that such practices, taken to the extreme, do not necessarily result in sanctity, but rather in broken health and ultimately death.[95] His reorientation regarding them was not limited just to his discovery that God no longer expected such practices of him.[96] More important, he came to realize that they were at best preliminary to attaining a higher level of the spiritual life where something more difficult would be expected: accepting all the afflictions imposed from without as being God's will. That he consistently cautioned his spiritual children to moderation in such penances may well have been the result of wisdom gained through sad experience.

In the final chapters (46–53) of the *Life* the author gives up all pretense of narrative. What is found there can be considered autobiographical only in the sense that it contains mature wisdom gleaned from the author's long and intense practice of the interior life. Although he continues to maintain that following Christ's example is the most secure path, he returns again to the concerns of his early work, the *Little Book of Truth*, and imparts to his spiritual daughter some knowledge of the "lofty path of intellect"[97] which so occupied her when the servant first made her acquaintance.[98] Here, as earlier, he is concerned to distance himself from any taint of heresy, and he carefully differentiates between the characteristics of true detachment and mysticism and doctrines attributed to the brothers and sisters of the Free Spirit and similar suspect groups. However, his principal purpose is to set forth sublime teachings of mystical theology about God's being and our experience of it as it is reflected in the universe. In expressing his thoughts about God and in explaining how our most intense and spiritual experiences of God on earth are but a foretaste of blessedness to come, he draws on a wealth of sources. His originality consists largely in his ability to bring all the material together into an eloquent and artistic whole.

If we try to characterize Suso's particular contribution to Western spirituality, we cannot point to unusual powers of intellect, as we can in the case of his revered teacher, Meister Eckhart, although it is easy to underestimate the subtlety of his mind. Nor can we imagine him swaying large audiences by the force of his preaching, as a Bernard of Clairvaux was wont to do, though the two sermons we do possess show him to be very capable in the pulpit. If any direction can be noted in the progress of his thought, it is away from the scholasticism of his contemporaries and toward the older traditions of Christian asceticism and monasticism. One aspect of his spirituality, however, does reveal him to be a precursor of things to come. The "devotional" facet of his works—for example, his devotion to the "divine name of Jesus,"[99] or his devotional approach to Christ's passion, which bears a great resemblance to the subsequently popular stations of the cross[100]—points to his interest in religious practices and points of view that later centuries will cultivate. Evidence that Suso actually influenced the development of such devotional practices is lacking, but his own interest is apparent. That he did through his writings influence others was in great measure due to

INTRODUCTION

his unusual ability to put things well. His literary talents were considerable. He reveals an awareness of the complexities of literary form and its relation to meaning that one otherwise finds only in the most celebrated medieval authors. Yet, though he was literary, and though he exploited his familiarity with the courtly literature of the time, literature remained a means rather than an end for him. His genius lay rather in the intensity with which he lived within himself, the intimacy with which he was able to share his interior life with others, and his ability to transform his own experience into a source of inspiration and guidance for others.

HENRY SUSO
THE EXEMPLAR,
WITH TWO GERMAN SERMONS

A NOTE ON THE TRANSLATION

While translation, like politics, is an art of compromise, I have tried to compromise the original as little as possible in rendering both meaning and style, as long as excessive violence was not done to English. I have not striven to make Suso more readable or clearer in English than he is in Middle High German, although occasionally a sentence of the original has been broken into two sentences and a pronoun rendered as a noun when its clarity in the original could not be duplicated in the translation. Parentheses are used to add words or phrases not actually in the original, but which seemed necessary or helpful for clarification. Occasionally such additions may be felt to cross the border between translation and interpretation. Translations from the Vulgate, the Latin edition of the Bible used by Suso, are generally my own and are usually rendered with an eye to accommodating whatever use Suso wished to make of them. Occasionally the Vulgate differs from recent English translations of the Bible so markedly that the latter are of little use in clarifying Suso's thought.

Prologue[1]

(This is the *prologus*, that is, the preface to this book.)

In this *Exemplar* four good books are contained. The first book in its entirety describes by concrete example[2] the life of a beginner and demonstrates in a veiled manner how a beginner should order his inner and outer self according to God's dear will. And, since good actions are, without a doubt, more instructive and uplift one's heart somehow more than words alone, it describes by many examples many holy deeds that really happened as depicted. It describes a person making progress: how through renunciation, suffering, and (ascetic) exercises one should break through one's unmortified animal nature to acquire great and praiseworthy sanctity. There are people whose mind and heart are struggling to achieve what is best and most perfect, but they are lacking in powers of discernment and as a consequence are confused and misguided. Hence this book provides many good criteria for distinguishing true from false reasoning, and it teaches how one shall attain the pure truth of a blessed and perfect life.

The second book treats a common theme, dealing with the contemplation of our Lord's passion and how one should learn to live inwardly, die in blessedness, and similar topics. Because, however, in distant and neighboring lands this and some others of his books have long been copied in excerpt fashion by all kinds of unqualified copyists of both sexes, in such a way that one would add whatever he thought good while another would in like manner leave things out, the servant of eternal Wisdom[3] has collected them all together here and put them in order so that one can find a correct exemplar[4] according to how God originally inspired it in him.

The third book, which is called the *Little Book of Truth*, has this as its purpose: Because in our times some uneducated but intelligent people have falsely understood their teachers with respect to the lofty meanings of sacred scripture, twisting it according to their own undisciplined natures and even writing things down, but not according to the true sense of sacred scripture, this book instructs people in these same lofty meanings, but with discernment, pointing out the right path and simple truth that is intended by God according to Christian interpretation.

The fourth book is called the *Little Book of Letters*. His spiritual daughter[5] collected all the letters which he had sent her and his other spiritual children and turned them into a book. From this he took parts of the letters and shortened it, as one finds it here below. The purpose of this short book is to afford refreshment and relief for a detached spirit. The pictures of heavenly scenes,[6] which precede or follow, serve the purpose of allowing a religiously minded person, when he leaves the world of the senses and enters into himself, always to have something to draw him away from this false world, which pulls him down, and upward toward our beloved God.

One should also know that the manuscript of the first book, rich in insight as it is, lay for many years secretly locked away, awaiting the servant's death, because he was quite unwilling during his lifetime to reveal himself to anyone. Finally, his good sense made him realize that, given the downward path mankind is presently following,[7] it would be better and safer with God's good grace to present the book to his religious superiors while he was still alive and able to vouch for the genuineness of all the parts. After his death it could happen that some foolish people whose words should not be regarded seriously might judge the book falsely, not wanting to recognize his good intentions in it or not being able to understand something better themselves because of their lack of sophistication. It could easily have turned out that after his death the book might become the property of the lukewarm and those fallen from grace who would devote no effort to having it circulated to God's praise among eager people. Thus it would disappear without being of use. It could also happen that it might immediately fall into the hands of those blind in knowledge or those full of spite who would suppress it out of their vice of malice, as has also frequently happened.[8]

PROLOGUE

And so with God's help, plucking up his courage, he picked out from this book the most abstruse ideas and exuberant sections contained in it and gave them himself to a learned professor to look over. This man had been richly endowed by God with virtue and was experienced in theological matters. In addition, he was an important superior over German territory in the Order of Preachers. His name was Master Bartholomew.[9] The servant humbly turned it over to him, and he read through it with deep pleasure and thought that, all in all, it would be like a secret sweet kernel from sacred scripture for all well-intentioned people. Afterward, when the more ordinary teachings had been added—so that everyone might find something for himself—and the servant wanted to show him the ordinary part too, dear God plucked the respected teacher from this life. When the servant heard that he was dead, he became very depressed because he did not know what should be done with the book. He came before eternal Wisdom with great earnestness and begged to be shown what was best in the matter. At some later date his request was answered, and the aforementioned teacher appeared to him in a brilliant vision and told him that it was God's will that he circulate it among all benevolent people who desired it with the right intentions and intense longing.

Anyone who would like to become a good and blessed person and share special intimacy with God, or whom God has singled out by severe suffering—which he is accustomed to do with his special friends—such a person would find this book to be a comforting help. Also, for well-disposed persons it lights the way to divine truth and for thoughtful people it points out the right path to supreme happiness.

The Life
of the
Servant

Part One

There was a Friar Preacher in Germany, a Swabian by birth.² May
his name be written in the book of life.³ He had a longing to become
and be called a servant of eternal Wisdom. He became acquainted
with a holy enlightened person who was beset with hardship and
suffering in this world.⁴ This person asked of him that he tell her
from his own experience something about his sufferings so that her
own stricken heart might take strength from it, and she kept after
him for a long time. When he would visit her, she would draw him
out with personal questions about his beginning and progress, about
some of his practices and the sufferings he had experienced. He told
her about these things in spiritual confidence. Because she found
comfort and guidance in these things, she wrote it all down as a help
for herself and for others as well; but she did this surreptitiously so
that he would know nothing about it. Sometime later, when he
became aware of this spiritual theft, he reproached her for it and she
had to hand it over to him. He took and burned everything he got
hold of at that time. When he got the rest of it and was about to do
the same with it, this was hindered by a celestial message from God
which prevented it. Thus what follows remained unburned, as she
wrote most of it with her own hand. A bit of good instruction was
added by him in her person⁵ after her death.

The first beginnings of his life as the servant occurred when he

63

was eighteen years old. Although by that time he had already worn the habit of his order for five years, his spirit was full of distraction. If God would keep him from those many failings, which might compromise his reputation, then, it seemed to him, things would in general not be so bad. But God somehow protected him from (persisting in) this (attitude) by his noticing an emptiness within himself whenever he gave his attention to things he desired. It seemed to him that there must be somehow something else that would calm his undisciplined heart, and his restlessness caused him torment. He continually felt something nagging at him, but he did not know how to help himself until God in his kindness freed him from this by causing a sudden conversion. Those around him were surprised at this sudden change. How had it happened? This person gave one explanation, that one gave another. But no one hit upon what had really happened. For God had drawn him in a hidden but illuminating manner, and this is what caused the sudden change.[6]

CHAPTER 1

The First Struggles of a Beginner

After God's influence had touched him, he began to experience struggles in himself through which the enemy of his well-being wanted to confuse him. And this happened as follows: The interior urgings, which arose in him from God, demanded of him a painful rejection of everything that could be an obstacle for him. Temptation stood in his way by suddenly posing this consideration: "Better think it over! It's easy at the beginning, but sheer drudgery to finish." An inner voice reminded him of God's strength and help. An opposing voice countered that there could be no doubt about God's power, but that what was open to question was whether he wanted to help. But on this point the servant was reassured because God had graciously confirmed with kind promises from his own divine mouth that he truly wanted to help all those who begin in his name.

As grace was gaining the upper hand in this dispute, a treacherous thought came in the guise of a friend advising him thus: "It may be well for you to strive to become better, but don't try to attain this with exaggerated efforts. Begin in moderation so that you can finish it. You should eat and drink with zest and should treat yourself well, but in so doing you should be on your guard against sin. Be as good as you want inwardly, but still with such moderation that people do not find you repulsive outwardly. As people say, 'If the heart is good, all is good.' You can be quite friendly with people and still be a good person. Other people want to get to heaven, but they do not lead such an austere life." With these and similar ideas he was very severely assailed, but eternal Wisdom refuted such perfidious talk, speaking with him as follows: "The person who wants to catch a slippery eel by the tail and enters upon a holy life with a lukewarm spirit is doubly deceived. Just when he thinks he has it, it gets away from him. Whoever expects to overcome a pampered and contrary body by being lenient is in need of common sense. Whoever wants to possess the world yet serve God perfectly is attempting the impossible and is perverting God's own teaching. And so, if you are going to back off (from living spiritually), then back off completely." How long this clash lasted he did not know. Finally, he boldly pulled himself together and, with great determination, turned his back on (worldly) things.

His undisciplined disposition died to a great extent when he broke away from frivolous people. Nature sometimes overcame him so that he would go to them to cheer himself up, but it usually happened that he went there in good spirits and left them unhappy because he found no pleasure in the conversation and entertainment that they engaged in, and they found his company unbearable. Sometimes, when he would come to them, they would tempt him verbally like this. One would say, "What a strange way of behaving you have taken on!" Another would say, "An ordinary life would be the safest." A third would say, "This is not going to end well." Thus would one hand him over to the next. He remained silent as a mute and thought, "Help, dear God! The best thing to do is flee. If you had not listened to this talk, it could not hurt you." One fact caused him sore distress. He had no one to whom he could express his troubles, no one who was searching the same way for the same thing he was called to. And so he went about, an unloved stranger, and with great self-discipline he stayed away; but doing so caused him much joy later on.

THE EXEMPLAR

CHAPTER 2

The Supernatural Rapture He Experienced

One time on the feast of St. Agnes,[7] when he was still a beginner, it happened that he went into the choir after the community had eaten their midday meal. He was alone there and was standing in the lower row on the right side of the choir. At this particular time he was being especially oppressed by severe sufferings assailing him. And as he was standing there sadly with no one around him, his soul was caught up, in the body or out of the body.[8] There he saw and heard what all tongues cannot express. It was without form or definite manner of being, yet it contained within itself the joyous, delightful wealth of all forms and manners. His heart was full of desire, yet sated. His mind was cheerful and pleased. He had no further wishes and his desires had faded away. He did nothing but stare into the bright refulgence, which made him forget himself and all else. Was it day or night? He did not know. It was a bursting forth of the delight of eternal life, present to his awareness, motionless, calm. Then he said, "If this is not heaven, I do not know what heaven is. Enduring all the suffering that one can put into words is not rightly enough to justify one's possessing this eternally." This overpowering transport lasted perhaps an hour, perhaps only a half hour. Whether the soul remained in the body or had been separated from the body, he did not know.[9] When he had come to himself again, he felt in every respect like a person who has come from a different world. His body experienced such pain from this short moment that he did not believe anyone could experience such pain in so brief a time and not die. He somehow revived with a deep sigh, and his body sank to the ground against his will as in a faint. He cried out interiorly and sighed in his depths saying, "O dear God, where was I? Where am I now?" And he continued, "Joy of my heart, this hour can never be lost to my heart." He walked along in body and no one saw or noticed by his exterior anything unusual, but his soul and mind were full of heavenly marvels within. Flashes from heaven came time and again deep within him and it seemed to him somehow that he was floating in the air. The powers of his soul were filled with the sweet taste of heaven, just as when one pours fragrant balsam from a container and the container keeps the pleas-

66

ant aroma. This heavenly fragrance stayed with him long afterward and gave him a heavenly longing for God.

CHAPTER 3

*How He Entered Into a Spiritual Marriage
With Eternal Wisdom*

The course that his life took for a long time after this in its interior activity was a constant effort to achieve intense awareness of loving union with eternal Wisdom. How a start was made in this can be learned from his *Little Book of Wisdom*, both in German and in Latin, which God made through him.[10]

From his youth he had a heart filled with love. Now eternal Wisdom presented itself in sacred scripture as lovable as an agreeable beloved who gets herself up in finery to please male inclinations, speaking softly, as a woman does, so that she might attract all hearts to her. Sometimes she would say how deceiving other lovers are but how loving and constant she is. His youthful spirit was drawn by this and he was affected like the wild animals of the forest when a panther giving off its sweet fragrance draws them to itself.[11] She displayed this charming manner often and attracted him lovingly to her spiritual love, especially through the books called the Books of Wisdom.[12] When these were read at community meals and he heard such expressions of love read from them, he felt great exhilaration. He would then begin to feel torment and would frame the thought in his love-crazed spirit: "You should really try your luck. Maybe you can win the love of this exalted lady beloved. I hear great marvels told of her. Your young untamed heart certainly cannot long remain without its own object to love." Often in looking at things he would become aware of her; he thought lovingly of her, and both his heart and his mind found her attractive.

It happened one morning when he was sitting as usual at table that she called to him in the tones of Solomon and said, "*Audi, fili mi!* Listen, my son, to the worthy advice of your father. If you wish to devote yourself to sublime love, you should take gentle Wisdom as your dearly beloved, because she bestows on her lover youth and vitality, nobility and abundance, honor and advantage, great power and an everlasting name. She makes him handsome and teaches him courteous behavior, and how to win people's praise and fame in battle. She makes him dear to and esteemed by God and man. Through her the earth was fashioned; through her the heavens were put in place and the abyss hollowed out. Whoever possesses her walks with confidence, sleeps untroubled, and lives free from care."[13] As he listened to these beautiful sayings being read to him, his longing heart thought immediately: "Ah, what a beloved this would be! If you could become mine, I would certainly have all I need!" But strange images intruded and he thought: "Am I to love what I have never glimpsed, whose nature I do not know? Better to have a handful of something real than a houseful of expectation. The person who builds grandiosely or loves passionately often sits at the table hungry. This noble beloved would be a good object of one's affections if she saw to it that her servant's material needs were well taken care of. But she says, 'Good food, strong wine, and long sleep—whoever is interested in these things should not attempt to win Wisdom's love.' "[14] When was a servant ever faced with such a hard contest? A divine thought countered: "It is an ancient law that suffering is part of love. No one can be a suitor unless he is a sufferer, nor can anyone be a lover unless he is a martyr. Hence it is to be expected that a person encounter occasional hardships if he chooses such a lofty object to love. Just imagine all the unhappiness and unpleasantness worldly lovers have to endure whether they want to or not." Because of this and other urgings he was again strengthened to the point of wanting to go through with it. This same thing happened to him time and again. Sometimes he kept his firm resolve, and then again he would let his heart pursue transitory love. As he was searching here and there, he would always discover something that would speak against his turning away from creatures entirely. And this would fling him back again.

Once as a passage from Wisdom was being read in the refectory, his heart was deeply moved. She said: "Just as the fair rosebush blossoms, just as precious incense gives off a fragrance while yet uncut, and just as pure balsam smells, so am I a blossoming, fragrant and pure beloved who causes neither discontent nor bitterness but only immeasurable loving sweetness. All other lovers offer sweet words but a bitter reward. Their hearts are death traps, their hands manacles, their words sweetened poison, their pastimes the loss of honor."[15] He thought: "This is certainly true!" And he said to himself without hesitation, "Certainly it has to be the right thing. She must be my beloved, and I shall be her servant. O God, if I might just catch a glimpse of my dear one! If I could just once talk with her! What must my beloved look like if she has so many delightful things hidden within her! Is she divine or human, man or woman, art or knowledge or what?" And to the extent he was able to imagine her through the explanatory examples of scripture with his inner eyes, she presented herself to him thus: She was suspended high above him on a throne of clouds. She shone as the morning star and dazzled as the glittering sun. Her crown was eternity, her attire blessedness, her words sweetness, and her embrace the surcease of all desire. She was distant yet near, far above yet low, present yet hidden. She engaged in activities with others, but no one could claim her. She towered above the summit of heaven[16] and touched the bottom of the abyss. She spread herself out sovereign from one end of the earth to the other and ordered all things sweetly.[17] The minute he thought her to be a beautiful young lady, he immediately found a proud young man before him. Sometimes she acted like a wise teacher, sometimes like a pert young thing. She presented herself to him endearingly, and greeted him smiling, saying kindly, "*Prebe, fili, cor tuum mihi!* Give me your heart, my child."[18] He bowed down at her feet and thanked her profusely from his humble innermost being. This is what he experienced at that time. More was then impossible for him.

After this, whenever he was going along lost in thought about his dearest beloved, he usually posed the question inwardly, inquiring of his love-seeking heart, "Alas, dear heart, tell me, where is the source of all love and charm? Whence arises gentleness, beauty, heartfelt joy, and all endearing qualities? Does not all this gush forth from the spring of the naked Godhead? Onward, then, dear heart, mind and spirit, into the endless abyss of all charming things! Who can stop me now? Today, as my burning heart desires, I shall embrace you!" And then the original abundance of everything good forced its way—I know not how—into his soul, and he found in it spiritually all that was beautiful, dear and attractive; but it was there in an inexpressible manner.

After this, whenever he heard songs of praise being recited or sung, it happened regularly that his heart and mind were suddenly transported by a detached gazing at his most dearly beloved from whom all good flows. How often he embraced his dearly beloved, with eyes filled with tears of love and with a heart endlessly wide, and pressed her tenderly to his loving heart it would be impossible to tell. He often felt just like a baby whose mother is holding it up under the arms while it stands on her lap. Just as it stretches upward with its head and the movement of its body toward its caressing mother and shows the joy in its heart by displays of laughter, so too did the heart in his body often go out toward the delightful presence of eternal Wisdom, with feeling charging through him. Then he would think, "O Lord, if I were married to a queen, my soul would boast of it. But, alas, you are now empress of my heart and the bestower of all graces. In you I have riches enough, and power as much as I want. I no longer want anything that the earth offers." Thinking such thoughts, his face would become cheerful, his eyes friendly. His heart would rejoice and his whole interior would sing: "*Super salutem*, etc. Above all happiness, above all beauty, you are my heart's happiness and beauty; for happiness has followed me with you. All that is good I have received in you and with you."[19]

CHAPTER 4

How He Inscribed the Beloved Name of Jesus on His Heart

At this same time an immense fire was sent into his soul that inflamed his heart utterly with love of God. One day, as it came over him and divine love surged up in him, he went into his cell, his hiding place, and he entered into loving comtemplation and said, "Gentle God, if only I could think up a sign of love that would give testimony as an eternal symbol of the love between you and me, one that no forgetting could ever erase." In this state of fervent earnestness he threw aside his scapular,[20] bared his breast, and took a stylus in hand. Looking at his heart, he said, "God of power, give me today strength and power to carry out my desire, for today you shall be engraved in the ground of my heart." And he began to jab into the flesh above the heart with the stylus in a straight line. He jabbed back and forth, up and down, until he had drawn the name IHS right over his heart.[21] Because of the sharp stabs blood poured profusely from his flesh and ran over his body down his chest. Because of his burning love he enjoyed seeing this and hardly noticed the pain. After he had done this, he went exhausted and bleeding from his cell to the pulpit under the crucifix. Kneeling down he said, "My Lord and only Love of my heart, look at the intense desire of my heart. My Lord, I do not know how to press you into me further, nor can I. Alas, Lord, I beg you to finish this by pressing yourself further into the ground of my heart and so draw your holy name onto me that you never again leave my heart."

He went about thus wounded by love for a long time until he recovered. I do not know how long this took. The name IHS remained over his heart, as he had wished. The letters were about as thick as a flattened out blade of grass and as long as a section of the little finger. He carried this name over his heart until his death. And as often as his heart beat, the name moved. At first the letters were quite visible. He bore the name in secret, so that no one ever saw it except for one friend to whom he showed it in divine confidence.[22] Afterward, whenever adversity struck him, he would look at this dear sign of love and the trial was easier to bear. His soul once said in an intimate conversation, "Look, Lord, the lovers in the world inscribe the name of their beloved on their clothes. O dear Love, I have inscribed you in the fresh blood of my heart."

Once after matins, when he had come from prayer, he went into his cell and sat down on his chair and put the *Book of the Ancient Fathers* under his head as a pillow.[23] He then drifted away and it seemed to him that some kind of light flooded out of his heart, and he looked toward it. There on his heart appeared a golden cross into which many precious jewels had been skillfully inlaid. These sparkled beautifully. Then the servant took his cowl and threw it over his heart thinking that he would like to cover the bright light bursting forth so that no one could see it. But no matter how much he hid it, the light flooding forth glowed so delightfully that nothing could diminish its powerful beauty.

CHAPTER 5

*The First Manifestations of Divine Consolation
With Which God Attracts Many Beginners*

When he went into the chapel, as was his custom after matins, and sat down in his chair to rest—he sat there only a short time, just until the watchman announced the coming of the day—he then opened his eyes, fell to his knees, and greeted the bright morning star as it rose, the gentle Queen of heaven, and he thought: Just as little birds greet the day in summer and receive it with good cheer, so he in joyous expectation greets the Lightbringer of eternal day. And he did not just speak the words; he spoke them in his soul as a sweet, soft melody.

Once at the same hour he was sitting there resting when he heard somehow within him such captivating music that his heart was deeply moved, and a voice sang with pure, sweet clarity as the morning star rose. It sang these words: "*Stella Maria maris hodie processit ad ortum*. Mary, the star of the sea, has risen today . . ."[24] This singing resounded with such a supernatural surge within him that it carried him along with it, and he sang along joyously. When they had finished their spirited singing, he experienced an indescribable embrace during which he heard the words: "The more lovingly you embrace me and kiss me in a spiritual manner, the more lovingly and affectionately shall you be embraced in my eternal splendor." Then he opened his eyes and tears flowed down over his face, and he greeted the rising morning star in his usual way.

Following this morning greeting came the second greeting, also accompanied by a *venia*,[25] to gentle eternal Wisdom, a short prayer of praise, which he wrote in the *Little Book of Letters*. It begins: "*Anima mea desideravit*, etc."[26] Then followed the third greeting with a *venia* to the supreme loving spirit of the Seraphim whose blazing love flames up toward eternal Wisdom, so that his fervent spirit might make his own heart burn with divine love, that he in turn might be on fire himself and might through his endearing words and instruction inflame all men. This was then his daily morning greeting.

One time just before Lent he had continued his prayers until the watchman sounded the break of day. The thought came to him: "Sit for a minute before you receive the bright morning star." And when his senses were calmed a bit, the heavenly youths intoned in a loud voice the beautiful response: "Shine forth, shine forth, Jerusalem."[27] And this sounded sweet beyond measure in his soul. The singing had hardly begun and his soul was so full of the heavenly song that his frail body could no longer endure it. His eyes opened, his heart overflowed, and tears of fervor flowed forth.

Once when he was sitting there at this same hour it happened, as in a vision, as if he were somehow led into a different land. It seemed to him that his angel was standing very kindly in front of him to his right. The servant got up quickly and embraced the beloved angel, hugging him and pressing him to his soul as lovingly as he could. There seemed to be nothing at all separating them. From a full heart he began to speak with a lamenting voice and weeping eyes, "Alas, my angel, whom dear God has given me for consolation and protection, I beg you by the love you have for God not to abandon me." The angel answered and said, "Do you dare to mistrust God? Look, God has embraced you so lovingly in his eternity that he shall never leave you."

And once in the morning after a period of suffering it happened that he was surrounded by the heavenly hosts in a vision. He asked one of their shining heavenly princes to show him what the hidden dwelling place of God in his soul looked like. The angel said to him, "Look with joy into yourself and see how dear God plays his games of love with your affectionate soul." He quickly looked inside and saw that over his heart his body was as clear as crystal, and he saw in the middle of his heart eternal Wisdom sitting quietly with a pleasing appearance. Nearby the soul of the servant was sitting and longing for heaven. It was inclined in love at God's side, embraced by his arms, and pressed to his divine heart. There outside itself and immersed in love it lay in the arms of its beloved God.

On the eve of the feast of the Angels[28] he put on a new penitential chain. And it happened as in a vision that he heard angelic song and the sweet melodies of heaven. This made him feel so good that he forgot all his suffering. And one of the angels said to him, "Just as you enjoy hearing the music of eternity from us, so do we like to hear the song of eternal Wisdom from you." Then he said, "This is part of the song that the chosen saints will be singing in joy on the day of judgment when they see that they are secure in the everlasting joy of eternity."

Once after that on their feast day he spent several hours contemplating their joys. When it was nearly day, a young man came who acted as though he were a minstrel from heaven whom God had sent him. Along with him came I know not how many other fine young men with the same manner and bearing as the first, except that the first one had a certain preeminence, as though he were an angel prince. This same young man came up to him in a very pleasant manner and told him that they had been sent down to him from God to give him heavenly joys in his suffering. He should, he said, cast his sufferings out of his mind, join their company, and take part in their heavenly dancing. They took the servant by the hand for the dance and the young man began a cheerful little tune about the baby Jesus, which goes *In dulci jubilo*, etc.[29] When the servant heard the beloved name of Jesus so sweetly sung, he was so happy in heart and mind that all the sufferings he had ever endured disappeared. Now he looked on with joy as they leaped about gracefully and boldly. The lead singer knew how to make things go well. He sang first and they followed, singing and dancing with rejoicing hearts. The lead singer sang the refrain three times: *Ergo merito*, etc. The dancing bore little resemblance to dancing on earth. It was somehow a heavenly flooding out from and an ebbing back into the untamed abyss of divine mystery. He experienced these and countless other kinds of heavenly consolation in these same years, especially at times when he was overwhelmed by great suffering, and these then became lighter to bear.

Once when he went to the altar to celebrate mass, he appeared to a holy woman in a vision; and he shone with the finery of a bright love. She saw the dew of divine grace descending into his soul and that he became one with God. Behind him there came up to the altar very many charming children with burning candles, one after the other. They stretched out their arms and embraced him, each separately, as tenderly as they could, and pressed him to their hearts. Puzzled, the woman asked who these children were and what this all meant. They said, "We are your sisters in religious life now enjoying eternal blessedness in praise and joy. We are with you and are guarding you always." She said, "O dear angels, what does it mean that you embraced this man so very warmly?" They said, "He is so very dear to us that we have much to do with him. Know that God performs many marvels in his soul, and whatever he seriously asks of God, God will never deny it to him."

CHAPTER 6

Visions

During this time he had very many visions of future and hidden things, and God gave him somehow a sense, to the extent that this is possible, of what heaven, hell and purgatory are like. It was quite usual that souls would appear to him when they had departed this world, telling him how things had gone for them, how they had earned their punishment, and how one might help them, or what their reward from God was like. Among others were the blessed Meister Eckhart[30] and the holy Brother John der Fuoterer of Strasbourg.[31] Meister Eckhart informed him that he (Eckhart) lived in overflowing glory in which his soul had been made utterly god-like in God. The servant desired to find out two things from him. The first was how those people were in God who were satisfied with seeking the eternal truth in true detachment without duplicity. He was shown that it could not be captured in words how these people were taken within the limitless abyss. He then asked what the most profitable exercise was for someone wishing to achieve this state. He (Eckhart) answered, "Such a person should, with respect to his 'selfhood,' withdraw from himself in deep detachment and should receive all things from God and not from creatures, and should adopt an attitude of calm patience toward all wolfish men."

The second person, Brother John, showed him in a vision the delightful beauty by which his soul had been transfigured. From him also the servant begged for the answer to a question. This was: Which of all the exercises was the one that caused a person the most hardship and was the most useful. He received the answer that nothing was more painful and profitable for a person than for him, with an attitude of detachment, to go out from God with patience toward himself and thus leave God for the sake of God.[32]

His own father, who in his time had been a child of this world, appeared to him after his death and showed him the sorry sight of his horrifying suffering in purgatory and what had contributed most to his deserving it, telling him especially how he should help him. And he did do this. The father afterward appeared again and told him that he had been freed because of it. His holy mother, through whose heart and person God had done marvelous things during her lifetime, also appeared to him in a vision and showed him the great reward she had received from God. This same thing happened to him with respect to countless souls. He drew pleasure from this, and it often gave him a graphic example and support for the life he was living.

CHAPTER 7

His Conduct at Meals

Whenever he was about to go to a meal, he knelt down and directed his heart to the inward contemplation of eternal Wisdom, begging it affectionately to go along with him to table and eat with him. He would say, "Dearest Jesus Christ, it is the great desire of my heart to invite you and I ask you, just as you provide food generously for me, that you also grant me today the honor of your presence." When he was sitting at table, he would have the beloved guest of a pure soul sit opposite him as his table companion and look at him with great affection, sometimes leaning toward his heart side.[33] With every dish set before him he would take the serving plate and offer it to his heavenly Host, asking him to give it his holy blessing. Often he said with loving intimacy, "Gentle Guest, now eat with me. My Lord, help yourself and eat with your servant." And he would use such expressions of affection toward him as these.

When he was about to drink, he raised his cup and offered it first to him to drink. At meals he usually drank five times and did so because of the five wounds of his beloved Lord; but because water and blood flowed from God's side, he drank this (fifth) time twice: the first mouthful and the last he consumed in the love of the most loving heart the earth is capable of harboring and in the most fervent love of the highest spirit of the Seraphim that such love might be completely granted to his heart. Food that caused him upset he would ask to be dipped in the heart wounded for love in the belief that it would then do him no harm.

He had a taste for fruit, but God did not want to allow this. In a vision it seemed that someone offered him an apple, saying, "Take it. This is what you have been craving." Then he said, "No, all my desire is for dear eternal Wisdom." Then he realized that that was not true and that his yen for fruit was much too strong. Within himself he became ashamed because of this and for two years he did not eat a single piece of fruit. The two years went by, not without some craving; and in the following year the crop failed, so that the friary had no fruit. With many a struggle he selflessly resolved not to want something special in the way of fruit for himself at meals. So he asked God, if it were his will that he should eat fruit, to supply fruit for the whole house. And this happened. In the morning a stranger came and brought to the friary quite a sum in new coin. He only wanted to contribute this if they would buy apples with it. So it happened that they had plenty for some time; and so, gratefully, he began to eat fruit again.

Large pieces of fruit he divided into four parts. Three parts he ate in the name of the Holy Trinity, the fourth part in the love with which the heavenly Mother gave her tender child Jesus an apple to eat. This part he would eat unpeeled because children usually eat it unpeeled. From Christmas day until some time thereafter he would not eat this fourth part. He offered it in his contemplation to the gentle Mother to give to her dear young Son. For this purpose he was willing to give it up. When he sometimes began to eat or drink too quickly, he would grow ashamed of himself because of his esteemed Guest. And when he failed to observe any of these table practices, he would impose a penance on himself for it.

Once a good person came to him from a different place and said to him that God had said the following in a vision: "If you want to have proper table manners, go to my servant and ask him to tell you all his practices."

CHAPTER 8

How He Celebrated the New Year

In his native Swabia it is the custom in some places on New Year's Eve for young men to go around frivolously asking for presents. That is, they sing songs, recite nice poems, and by exercising courtly behavior bring it about that their sweethearts give them flower wreaths. This impressed his youthful affectionate heart so strongly, as he heard of it, that he, too, on that same night went to his eternal Sweetheart and asked for a present. Before dawn he went up to the statue of the pure Mother pressing to her heart the gentle Child, beautiful eternal Wisdom on her lap. Kneeling down he began to sing in the soft sweet tones of his soul a sequence to the Mother, that she allow him to obtain a wreath from her Child. And when he did not know how to have her help him, he became very serious and felt the need to weep, and hot tears flowed forth. When he had finished the song, he turned to darling Wisdom and bowed at her feet. He greeted her from the deepest recesses of his heart and in praise proclaimed her beauty, gentility, virtues, gentleness, freedom and constant dignity to be above that of all the beautiful young ladies of this world. He expressed this in words and song, in thought and desire, as best he could. And he wished to be in a spiritual manner a herald of all lovers and loving hearts and a source of all loving thoughts, words and feelings so that he could praise his esteemed Lady lovingly enough, unworthy servant though he be.

Concluding he said, "You are certainly, Beloved, my happy Easter, the summer joy of my heart, my pleasant hour. You are the Beloved that alone my youthful heart loves and thinks about. It has scorned all earthly love for your sake. O intimate Companion of my heart, let me enjoy the benefit of this and let me today obtain a wreath from you. Alas, dear heart, do this for the sake of your godlike qualities, for the sake of your natural goodness. And don't let me today, as the new year begins, go away from you empty-handed. O dear Sweetness itself, would that be fitting for you? Remember that one of your dear servants tells us of you that in you there is not 'yes and no,' but only 'yes and yes.'[34] Therefore, Love of my heart, offer me today the sweet 'yes' of your heavenly gift and, just as the rowdies are given a charming wreath, so may my soul be offered some special grace or new light from your fair hand today as a New Year's gift, gentle dear Wisdom." These and similar things he said there and he never went away unanswered.

CHAPTER 9

Concerning the Words "sursum corda"[35]

He was asked what his reaction was when he sang mass and before the canon of the mass introduced the preface with *sursum corda*. In the vernacular these words are commonly interpreted thus: *sursum*—aloft, into the heights all hearts to God![36] The words left his mouth so full of longing that those who heard it could have received a special spirit of devotion. He answered the question with a deep sigh and said, "When I sang these venerable words *sursum corda* at mass, it usually happened that my heart and soul dissolved in tearful longing for God, a longing that immediately caused my heart to flee out of itself. Three uplifting fantasies usually arose in me then. Sometimes one would come, sometimes two, sometimes all three, in which I was lifted aloft into God and through me all creatures.[37]

"The first illuminating fantasy was: Before my inner eyes I placed myself along with all that I am, with my body, soul and all my powers; and around myself I placed all the creatures that God ever created in heaven, on earth, and in the four elements, each with its own name, be it the bird of the air, the beast of the forest, the fish of the sea, the foliage and grass of the earth, the countless grains of sand of the sea, and, in addition, the tiny particles of dust reflected in the sunlight and all the drops of water, which as dew, snow or rain have ever fallen or will fall; and I wished that each of them was sending aloft a pleasant stringed melody torn from the essence of my heart and was thus playing a new exhilarating song of praise for the beloved gentle God from eternity to eternity. And then in joy the loving arms of his soul stretched out and reached toward the countless numbers of all these creatures. And his intention was to make them thereby happy, just as when a lusty, hearty lead singer urges his singing companions to sing cheerfully and to raise up their hearts to God: *sursum corda!*

"The second fantasy was this," he said. "In thought I placed before me my heart and the hearts of all men and imagined what pleasures and joys, what love and peace those enjoy who give their hearts to God alone, and, on the other hand, what loss and suffering, what pain and unrest transitory love brings to her subjects. And with great emotion I proclaimed to the ends of the earth, telling my heart and all the other hearts what they are: 'Arise, captive hearts, from the fetters of transitory love! Arise, slumbering hearts, from the death of sin! Arise, vain hearts, from the lukewarmness of your lazy neglectful life! Raise yourselves aloft by turning fully and freely to your loving God: *sursum corda!*'

"The third fantasy was a friendly appeal to all persons of good will who are not detached and who live inwardly confused. They hold neither to God nor to creatures because their heart is pulled this way and that. These and myself I call upon to dare the complete risking of self by turning away utterly from self and from all creatures."

This was his response to the words *sursum corda.*

THE EXEMPLAR

CHAPTER 10

How He Celebrated the Feast of the Purification[38]

For Candlemas Day, the feast of our Lady, he prepared beforehand, with three days of prayer, a candle for the heavenly Mother in childbed. The candle was wound out of three strands thus: the first with a thought to her chaste virginal purity, the second for her endless humility, and the third for her maternal dignity. These three qualities she alone possessed among all mankind. He prepared this spiritual candle every day before the feast by reciting the *Magnificat* three times. When the day of the blessing of the candles arrived, very early before anyone had gone into the church, he went up before the main altar and waited there in contemplation of the Mother in childbed until she might come with her divine treasure. When she approached the outer town gate, in the longing of his heart he would outrun all the others and would run to meet her with the procession of all God-loving hearts. In the street he fell down before her and begged her to halt for a while with her retinue until he had sung her a hymn. Then in such spiritual soft tones that his mouth moved but no one heard him he began to sing the text "*Inviolata*,"[39] as lovingly as he could, and then bowed to the ground singing "*O benigna*,"[40] begging her to show her generous kindness to a poor sinner. Then he got up and followed her with his spiritual candle in the desire that she never let the burning flames of the divine light go out in him. Afterward, when he came to the crowd of devoted hearts, he began the song "*Adorna*,"[41] and urged them to receive the Savior with love and to embrace his Mother longingly. Thus he led them with songs of praise to the temple.

After this he went eagerly beforehand to where the Mother would enter and present her Son to Simeon. He knelt down in front of her and, raising his hands and eyes, asked her to show him the Child and also to let him kiss it. And when she kindly offered it to him, he spread out his arms to the ends of the earth, took the beloved Child, and embraced it countless times. He looked at its pretty little eyes, gazed at its tiny hands, and kissed its tender little mouth. All the tiny limbs of the heavenly treasure he looked at carefully and, raising his eyes, he cried out in amazement in his heart that the bearer of the heavens is so great and so small, so beautiful in heaven and just a Child on earth. He busied himself with him as the occasion

80

allowed, with singing, with weeping, and with spiritual exercises. Then he quickly gave him back to his Mother and accompanied her, staying inside until everything was accomplished.

CHAPTER 11

How He Celebrated Carnival[42]

When lent was drawing near, on the evening when one begins omitting the *alleluia*,[43] and the fools of this world begin their unrestrained frolicking, then he would begin to organize in his heart a heavenly pre-lenten carnival. This is how he did it. First of all, he called to mind the fleeting harmful pleasures of the earthly carnival and how for many long suffering follows upon a brief pleasure, and he would recite a *miserere*[44] to God on high for all the sin and dishonor committed against him during this same wild celebration. This carnival he called the carnival of the peasants because they do not know any better. His second carnival was a consideration of the prelude to eternity—how God entertains his chosen friends even in this mortal body with heavenly consolation. He considered with grateful praise what had been his share and felt content that his share was God.

When he was still beginning, God once granted him a spiritual carnival that was as follows. During carnival time he had entered a warm room before compline[45] to warm up because he was cold and hungry. However, nothing was quite as bad as the thirst he suffered. He saw people eating meat and drinking good wine. Because he was hungry and thirsty, this disturbed him inwardly. He then went outside and began to feel sorry for himiself, sighing deeply from the bottom of his heart. That same night it seemed to him in a vision that he was in a sickroom. Outside the room he heard someone singing heavenly music, and the melody sounded more pleasant than any earthly harp had ever produced. It was as though some twelve-year-old schoolboy were singing alone. The servant forgot all about any earthly food as he listened to the dulcet tones and said longingly, "Ah, what is this music? I have never heard any melody so delightful on earth." A fine young man standing there answered him and said, "Know that this boy who sings so pleasantly sings for you. You are the reason for his song." The servant said, "Oh, dear

THE EXEMPLAR

God! Ah, young man from heaven, ask him to keep on singing!" He sang again and it echoed high in the air. He sang three heavenly songs from beginning to end. When the singing was finished, it seemed that this same boy with the beautiful voice came in the air to the small window of the room and offered the young man a pretty basket full of red fruit that were like ripe, red strawberries, large and well-formed. The young man took the basket from the boy and offered it to the friar, saying, "Look, friend and brother, this red fruit was sent by your dear friend and divine Lord. This was the charming boy and Son of the heavenly Father who sang for you. He really cares for you very much." The friar was set afire and his face became flushed for joy. He took the basket eagerly, saying, "Alas, dear heart, this is a dear present from the lovely Boy from heaven. This shall always fill my heart and my soul with joy." And he said to the young man and the rest of the heavenly court that was present, "Dear friends, is it not right that I love this Boy from heaven so rich in grace? Truly, it is right for me to love him, and whatever I would know to be his most gracious will I would always carry out." He turned to the previously mentioned young man and said, "Tell me, dear young man, am I not right?" The young man smiled kindly and said, "Certainly you are right. It is right for you to love him because he has favored and honored you more than many others. And so you should love him very much. I shall tell you this as well. You will have to suffer, and suffer more than many other men. And so prepare for this." The servant said, "This I shall gladly do with all my heart, and I ask you to help me to visit him and thank him for his beautiful gift." The young man said, "Now come here to the window and look outside." He opened the window. There, standing outside the window, he saw the most gentle and charming schoolboy that eyes had ever seen. And when he tried to go to him through the window, the boy turned toward him endearingly, bowed kindly to him, and with a friendly blessing disappeared before his very eyes. Thus did the vision disappear. When he came to himself again, he thanked God for the fine carnival he had been granted.

CHAPTER 12

How He Celebrated May Day

On the eve of the first of May he usually began by planting his spiritual Maypole and would show it honor once every day for a considerable length of time. Of all beautiful branches that ever grew he would find nothing more like the beautiful Maypole than the fine cross beam of the holy cross, which is richer in blossoms of grace, virtue, and all beautiful adornments than any Maypole ever was.

At the foot of this Maypole he made six *veniae*,[46] and with each *venia* he contemplated and wished to decorate this spiritual Maypole with the most beautiful things summer could bring forth. In front of the Maypole he spoke and sang inwardly the hymn "*Salve, crux sancta*"[47] thus: "Hail, heavenly Maypole of eternal Wisdom on which has grown the fruit of eternal happiness. First, instead of red roses I offer you today for your eternal adornment my heartfelt love. Second, in place of tiny violets I bow down in humility. Third, instead of delicate lilies I offer a pure embrace. Fourth, instead of all kinds of bright and colorful flowers that any heath or field, woods or pasture, tree or meadow has ever produced, or ever would or will, my heart offers you a spiritual kiss. Fifth, instead of all the cheerful songs of the birds spiritedly sung as they perch on a burgeoning branch, my soul offers you boundless praise. Sixth, instead of all the decorations that adorned any Maypole on earth, my heart raises you aloft today with a spiritual song, and I bid you, blessed May, to help me so praise you in this brief existence that I shall be able to enjoy you, living fruit, forever."

This is how May Day was celebrated.

CHAPTER 13

How He Accompanied Christ on His Wretched Way of the Cross When He Was Led Out to Die

At first God spoiled him for a long time with divine consolation, and he craved it passionately. Whatever belonged to the Godhead was a joy for him. But when he was supposed to contemplate the sufferings of our Lord and to devote himself to imitating him in them, this he found hard and bitter. Because of this he was then severely scolded by God, and he heard it being said inside him: "Don't you know that I am the gate through which all true friends of God must force their way if they are to achieve true blessedness? You must fight your way through by means of my suffering humanity if you are really to come to my pure Godhead."

The servant became frightened. This was for him a difficult saying. Nevertheless, he began to focus his attention on it, however distasteful it was, and he began to learn what he was unable to before, and he surrendered himself to it with great detachment. The first step was that every night after matins[48] in his customary place—the chapter room[49]—conforming himself to Christ, he would devote himself to feeling sympathy for everything his Lord and God, Christ, had suffered before him. He arose and went from corner to corner to shake off all laziness and to remain wide awake in feeling the suffering. He began by joining with Christ at the Last Supper and suffering together with him from place to place until he accompanied him to Pilate. Finally, he took his condemned Lord to his trial and went with him then the lonely way of the cross from the place of judgment all the way to under the cross.

His way of the cross was as follows: When he came to the doorstep of the chapter room, he knelt down and kissed the first footsteps Christ made when, already condemned, he turned and was about to go to his death. He began to recite the psalm of our Lord's suffering: "*Deus, deus meus, respice me.*"[50] And then he went through the door and into the cloisters. There were four paths on which he accompanied him to his death.[51]

He accompanied him on the first path to death through a desire to abandon both friends and transitory goods, and to suffer hopeless abandonment and voluntary poverty in praise of him.

On the second path he resolved to reject transitory honor and dignity, to be despised willingly by this whole world, realizing that Christ had become a worm and was scorned by all men.[52]

At the beginning of the third path he knelt down again and kissed the ground to symbolize a voluntary surrender of all unnecessary comfort and pampering of the body, to the great pain of his soft body, and he imagined, as it is written there, how Christ's strength dried up and his nature died away.[53] And as they drove Christ forward so woefully, he called to mind how right it was for all eyes to grow damp and for all hearts to sigh.

When he came to the fourth path, he knelt down in the middle as though he were kneeling in front of the gate through which Christ would have to go out. Falling down in front of him, he kissed the ground, calling upon him and asking him not to go to his death without him, and that he let him go along because he had a right to go along. He imagined all this to himself as vividly as he could, and he spoke the prayer "*Ave rex noster, fili David,*" etc.[54] and let Christ lead the way.

After this he knelt down a second time facing the gate and received the cross with the verse: "*O crux ave, spes unica,*"[55] and let it pass by. Then he knelt down facing the gentle Mother, who in her immeasurable grief was led past him. He noticed how distressed she was—the hot tears, the plaintive sighs, the sorrowful demeanor. He remembered her with a "*Salve Regina*" and kissed her footsteps.

Then he got up quickly and strode after his Lord to catch up to him. His imagining was sometimes very vivid, just as if he were really walking at his side. He recalled how, when King David was banished from his kindgom, his most gallant knights rallied around him and loyally came to his aid.[56] Then he surrendered his will. Whatever God did with him, for the sake of Christ let it always be. Finally he took up the epistle from the prophet Isaiah that is read during holy week, which reads, "*Domine, quis credidit auditu nostro,*"[57] which clearly portrays his being led out to his death. Then he went to the door of the choir and climbed up the stairs to the pulpit. When he came beneath the cross, where he had once experienced the hundred thoughts on the passion,[58] he knelt to watch his Lord being stripped of his clothing and nailed to the cross. Then he took the discipline[59] and with heartfelt agony nailed himself on the cross with his Lord, begging him that neither life nor death, joy nor sorrow be able to separate his servant from him.

He had another interior way of making the way of the cross, as follows: When the "*Salve Regina*" was being sung at compline, he imagined in his heart in contemplation that the chaste Mother was at that very moment at the grave of her dear Child, sorrowing as a mother for her buried Child, that it was time to take her back home, and that he should take her there. And so, in his heart he made three *veniae*,[60] by which in contemplation he brought her back home.

The first *venia* was on the grave when one began the "Hail, Holy Queen." His soul would bow to her and in a spiritual manner take her into his arms. He commiserated with her tender heart, which was then so full of bitterness, dejection and deathlike sorrow; and he consoled her with the thought that because of this she was now an esteemed queen, our hope and our sweetness, as the hymn proclaims.

When he brought her to the city gate of Jerusalem, he walked on in front and looked back at her, seeing how sorrowful she looked as she entered, spotted with the warm blood that had dripped down upon her, flowing from the open wounds of her beloved Child. How abandoned she was and bereft of any consolation! Then he took her again in his arms with a second *venia* of the heart at the words, *"Eya ergo advocata nostra,"*[61] and told her she should take heart because she was now the honored advocate for us all. Out of love for her sorrowful appearance he asked her to turn her merciful eyes to him, and after this vale of tears to allow him to look with love upon her revered Son, as the hymn begs.

The third interior *venia* was made in front of the door of the house of St. Anne, her mother, where she was led in her sorrow. He thanked her and recommended himself to her kindness and her maternal sweetness with the devout words *"O clemens, O pia, O dulcis Maria."*[62] And he asked her to receive his poor soul on his last journey and to be its companion and protectress against the evil enemies until it passed through the gate of heaven to eternal happiness.

CHAPTER 14

The Practical Virtue Called Silence

The servant had an urge in his interior life to attain real peace of heart, and it seemed to him that silence might be useful to him. And so he kept such guard over his mouth that in thirty years he never broke silence at meals except once when he was coming back from a chapter[63] with many fellow Dominicans and they ate on the boat. That one time he departed from his practice.

In order to master his tongue better in all situations and not talk carelessly or to excess, he introduced three spiritual masters into his contemplation without whose special permission he would not speak. They were three dear saints: our father St. Dominic, St. Arsenius and St. Bernard.[64] Whenever he wished to speak, in his imagination he would go from one to the other and ask for their permission, saying, *"Jube, domine, benedicere."*[65] And if it was a proper time and place for talking, the first master would give permission. If the conversation involved no external attachments, the second master would allow it. And if speaking was not going to cause him to be disturbed inwardly, it seemed to him that he had the permission of all three. Then he would speak. If these conditions were not met, he thought he should remain silent.

When he was called to the door,[66] he tried to carry out these four things. First, to welcome each and every person kindly. Second, to keep such matters short. Third, to have people leave comforted. Fourth, to go back into the cloister without having formed an attachment.

CHAPTER 15

The Chastisement of the Body

In his youth he was very lively by nature. When this became evident to him and he noticed that he was being overwhelmed by it, he found this bitter and difficult. He sought all kinds of remedies and practiced rigorous penances to make the flesh subject to the spirit. For a long time he wore a hairshirt and an iron chain[67] until he bled like a fountain and had to give it up. For his lower body he had an undergarment of hair made secretly with thongs worked in to which a hundred and fifty pointed nails had been attached. They were of brass and had been filed sharp. The points of these nails were always turned toward his body. He would tighten the garment around him, binding it together in the front so that it would fit more tightly against his body and the pointed nails would press into his flesh. The garment was made long enough to reach up to the navel. He would sleep in it at night. In summer, when it was hot and he was tired from having to travel on foot and had become weak, or when he had gone for bloodletting[68] and was lying a captive of his misery and tortured by vermin, he would sometimes lie there, groaning to himself and gnashing his teeth, and he would turn this way and that, as a worm does when it is being pricked with a sharp needle. It often seemed to him that he were lying on an anthill because of the vermin creeping over him. When he tried to go to sleep or had fallen asleep, they would bite and suck at him in keen rivalry. With heart full, he sometimes said to God, "Alas, gentle

87

God, what a way to die! Those that murderers or large animals kill quickly have it over and done with. But I lie here dying in the midst of these nasty creatures and cannot even get it over with!" Never were the nights so long in winter or so hot in summer that he would refrain from this practice.

In order that he not get any relief from this suffering, he thought up something else. He bound part of a belt around his neck and cleverly attached to it two rings of leather. Into these he slipped his hands and locked his arms inside it with two curtain fasteners. The keys he put on a board near the bed until he got up for matins and unlocked them himself. His arms were each drawn upward in their bonds to his throat, and he made the locks so secure that, if his cell had been burning, he could not have helped himself. He kept this up until his hands and arms began trembling badly from being so stretched. Then he thought up something else. He had someone make him two leather gloves, like the ones laborers usually wear when they are pulling out thorny growth. Then he had a tinsmith fasten pointed brass tacks to them all over. These he would put on at night. He did this so that, if in his sleep he tried to take off his undergarment of hair or to get some relief from the biting vermin, the tacks would prick him. And it worked, too. When, while asleep, he tried to use his hands to help himself, he would run the pointed tacks into his chest and scratch himself. This caused ugly gashes, as though a bear had clawed him with its sharp nails. This all began to fester on the skin of his arms and around his heart; but when after many weeks he had recovered, he would continue all the more and cause fresh wounds. He kept up this torturous practice for about sixteen years. Afterward, when his blood had been cooled and his nature crushed, there appeared to him in a vision one Pentecost a heavenly gathering that announced to him that God no longer wanted this of him. He put an end to it and threw everything into a river.

CHAPTER 16

The Barbed Cross He Wore on His Back

More important than all his other practices was his idea and desire to bear on his body some sign of his heartfelt sympathy for the intense sufferings of his crucified Lord. And so he made for himself a wooden cross as long as the breadth of a man's outstretched hand and proportionately wide. He hammered thirty iron nails in special remembrance of all his wounds and of the five signs of his love.[69] He fastened the cross to his bare back on the skin between his shoulders and carried it day and night for eight years to praise his crucified Lord. Then, in the final year, he hammered seven needles into it in such a way that the points extended out quite a bit but the needles themselves remained fixed in the wood. The back parts of the needles he broke off. The wounds caused by these sharp needles he bore in praise of the deep sorrow of the pure Mother of God that so utterly pierced through her heart and soul at the time of his wretched death.

When he fastened this cross to his bare back for the first time, his human nature recoiled from it and he thought he would not be able to endure it. He took it off and bent the sharp nails a little on a stone. Soon he regretted his unmanly cowardice, and so he sharpened them all again with a file and put it back upon himself. It rubbed his back open where his bones were, making him bloody and torn. Wherever he sat or stood, it seemed to him as though the hide of a hedgehog were covering him. When anyone touched him unintentionally or bumped against his clothing, this injured him. To make this painful cross all the more agonizing for himself, he carved on the back of it the dear name IHS. For a long time, besides wearing this cross, he took the discipline twice daily in the following manner.[70] He struck the cross with his fist driving the nails into his flesh where they remained stuck, so that he had to pluck them back out again with his clothing. He struck these blows onto the cross so unobtrusively that no one was able to notice it. He took this first discipline when he had come in his contemplation to the pillar where his handsome Lord was so cruelly scourged. He begged him to heal his wounds together with his own. He took the second discipline when Christ had come to the place of the crucifixion and was being nailed to the cross. He would nail himself to Christ, never to leave him. The third discipline he would not take every day but only when he had allowed himself too much comfort or enjoyment in eating, drinking, or the like.

Once he had shown carelessness by taking the hands of two girls—with nothing evil intended—into his hands while they were sitting next to him publicly in the congregation. He soon regretted this thoughtless conduct and decided such inordinate behavior required penance. When he left the girls and entered the chapel he went to his private place, and to atone for his misdeed he threw himself onto his back where the cross was fastened. The pointed nails stuck in his back. Also, because of this misdeed he would not allow himself to go after matins to his usual place of prayer in the chapter room, to the pure court of heaven which had there been present to him in contemplation. Sometime later, when he wanted to atone for this misconduct completely, he hesitantly ventured in and fell at the feet of his Judge and in his presence took a discipline with his cross. Then he went round and round to the images of the saints on each side of the room and took the discipline thirty times, so that blood ran down his back. Thus did he bitterly make amends for his inordinate pleasure.

When matins had been sung, he went into the chapter room to his secret place and prostrated himself a hundred times and then genuflected a hundred times, each time contemplating a particular object. These movements were very painful because of the cross since he had bound the cross to himself as tightly and was wearing it as snug against his body as when a cooper fits a hoop around a barrel. When he fell to the ground, as was his custom, and made his hundred prostrations, the movements caused the nails to stick in him. When he then stood up, he pulled them back out. At the next prostration they would make new wounds, which caused him great pain. If they remained sticking in one place, it was bearable.

Before this exercise he performed another one. He made himself a scourge out of a leather strap into which he had pointed brass tacks driven. They were as sharp as a stylus and protruded through each side of the strap in the form of a triangle. Whichever end struck his body caused wounds. He made a scourge out of this and would get up before matins, go into the choir, and in front of the main altar where Christ was bodily present take the discipline vigorously. He did this for an undetermined length of time until his fellow religious became aware of it. Then he stopped.

On the feast of St. Clement[71] at the beginning of winter he once made a confession of his whole life. And when he was alone, he closed himself up in his cell, took off his clothes except for the undergarment of hair. He took out the scourge with the sharp thorns and struck himself over his whole body, arms and legs so that blood ran down, as happens in bloodletting. There was one special tack on the scourge that was in the form of a hook. Wherever it caught the flesh, it would rip it out. He struck himself so hard with it that the scourge broke into three pieces. One piece stayed in his hand and the ends flew against the walls. He stood there bleeding and looking at himself. It was a very sorry sight and reminded him again and again in many ways of the scene where dear Christ is being cruelly scourged. Out of pity for himself he began to weep from his heart. He knelt down in the cold, naked and bloody as he was, and begged God to wipe away his sins from his loving sight.

Afterward, on the Sunday before lent,[72] he again went into his cell during the community meal, as he had done before. He stripped himself and struck himself so severely that blood flowed from his body. As he was about to beat himself more intensely, a fellow friar, who had heard the noise, came by and he had to stop. Taking vinegar and salt, he rubbed them into the wounds to increase his pain.

On the feast of St. Benedict,[73] the day on which he had been born into this wretched world, he went into his chapel during the period of light refreshment, closed the door, and took off his clothes as before. He took out the scourge and began beating himself. Somehow a blow hit him on the left arm striking the median vein or some other one. Since it had been struck squarely, blood spilled forth, running down to his feet and between his toes onto the floor where it formed a puddle. His arm quickly swelled up severely and turned blue. This frightened him and he did not dare continue striking himself.

At this same time, at the very hour when he was thus scourging himself, a holy woman named Anna was at her prayers in a castle in another place. She had a vision in which she was brought to the place where he was taking the discipline. When she saw the hard blows, she was moved to such pity that she went up to him. And when he had raised his arm to strike himself again, she got in the way of the blow and, as it seemed to her in the vision, was struck on the arm. When she came to herself again, she found the blow traced in dark dried blood on her arm, as though the scourge had hit her. These marks were noticeable and were very painful for her for a long time.

THE EXEMPLAR

CHAPTER 17

His Bed

In this same period of his life he somehow came into the possession of an old door that had been thrown away. He put it in his cell on his bed frame under himself and he lay on it without any kind of covering. To provide some ease, he had fashioned a very thin mat from reeds. This he laid on top of the door. The mat reached down to his knees. Beneath his head, instead of a pillow, he placed a little sack filled with pea straw and on top of that a very small pillow. Nowhere did he have any bedclothes, and he went to bed at night clothed as he was during the day, except that he took off his shoes and wrapped himself in a thick cloak. Thus did he acquire a wretched place to sleep. The pea straw lay in a lump under his head. The cross with the sharp nails stuck him in the back. He had tight bonds on his arms and the undergarment of hair around his hips. The cloak was very heavy and the door hard. He lay there so miserably that he could not move any more than a block of wood. When he wanted to turn over, it was very painful because when still in his sleep he turned firmly onto his back with the cross under him, the nails would dig into the bone. And then he would very often let out a groan to God. In winter the cold caused him much pain because when in his sleep he would from habit stretch his legs out they would be bare on the door and would freeze. When he then tried to pull them up under him, the blood would throb wildly in them and cause him much pain. His feet became diseased, his legs swelled up as though he were getting dropsy. His knees were bloody and open, his hips full of scratches from the undergarment of hair, his back covered with wounds from the cross. His body was wasted because of immoderate fasting, his mouth parched from not drinking, and his hands shook from weakness. In such torment he spent day and night.

Later he changed his practice of sleeping on the door. He moved into a small cell and used the chair one sat in for his bed. The chair was narrow and so short that he could not stretch out. He remained for eight years in these confining quarters or lying with his accustomed bonds on the door. In winter after compline, when living at the friary, his custom for twenty-five years was never to enter a heated room or come near the friary stove to warm himself, no matter how cold it was, unless there were other reasons for going there. In these same years, in order to cause his pleasure-seeking body discomfort, he refrained from all bathing, water baths and sweat baths. For a long time he ate only once a day, summer and winter. And not only did he abstain from meat, but from fish and eggs as well. For a long time he practiced such poverty that he would neither accept nor even touch a penny, either with or without permission. He was so intent on purity that for some length of time he would not scratch or touch his body anywhere except his hands and feet.

CHAPTER 18

How He Restricted His Drinking

He once took up the painful practice of allowing himself only a very small amount to drink. And so that he might not measure the amount wrong, both at home and away, he got a small cup of the right size. This he carried with him whenever he went out. When he was very thirsty, it was only enough to cool his parched mouth, as one does for a sick person with a high fever. For a long time he drank no wine except on Easter Sunday. He did this to show honor to this important day. Sometimes when he was thirsty but, because of his own strict practice, did not want to satisfy his thirst either with water or wine, he gazed upward to God very pitiably, and he once received inwardly the following answer: "Look how I was thirsty as I was dying with only a little vinegar and gall. And yet all the cold springs of the world belonged to me."

It happened once before Christmas that he had renounced completely all bodily comfort, and he adopted three practices aside from the usual ones that he had done for a long time. The first one was that after matins he would stand in front of the main altar on the bare stone until daybreak. This was at the time of year when the nights are longest and the bell for matins rang very early. The second one was that he did not go to any warm place, either day or night; nor did he warm his hands over the coals burning at the altar. His hands swelled up terribly because this was the coldest time of year. After compline he would go to his chair to sleep chilled to the bone. After matins he stood in front of the altar on bare stone until daybreak. The third practice was that he refrained completely from drinking throughout the day, except for something in the morning while at table, no matter how thirsty he was. And when it would get on toward evening he would be so terribly thirsty that his whole being yearned for something to drink, but he repressed it all with much bitter suffering. His mouth was as dry inside and out as that of a person suffering from fever. His tongue became cracked and would not heal for more than a year. When at compline he was standing there so dry and holy water was sprinkled about, as is customary, his dry mouth would start to open expectantly and would then open wide in the direction of the sprinkler in the hope of having a tiny drop of water fall on his tongue and thus cool it a little. At collation[74] or dinner when, thirsty as he was, he would push the wine away from him, he would sometimes raise his eyes and say, "O heavenly Father, accept as a sacrifice this blood of my heart, this cool beverage, and satisfy with it the thirst which your Son felt as he was dying on the cross." Sometimes he would pass the well very thirsty, look at the water splashing in the tin basin, and look toward heaven with a sigh from his heart. Sometimes when he was completely done in, he would say from his inner depths, "Alas, eternal Goodness, for your hidden judgments! The broad Lake of Constance is so near and the clear Rhine flows all around me. Yet a single drink of water is so precious for me. What a sad state of affairs that is!"

This continued until the Sunday when one reads in the gospel how the Lord turned water into wine.[75] There he sat that same Sunday at supper, depressed since he was not enjoying the food because of his thirst. After the thanksgiving after meals had been recited, he hurried quickly to his chapel. Because he was done in by his great suffering, he could no longer contain himself and he broke out in freely flowing, bitter tears. He said, "O God, you alone see the sufferings and distress of our hearts. Why was I ever born into this world that I have to suffer such want in the midst of abundance!" As he was thus lamenting, it seemed to him that within him somehow a voice spoke into his soul thus: "Cheer up! God will soon make you joyful and console you. Don't weep, valiant knight. Get hold of yourself!" Somehow these words made his heart happy so that he quit weeping. He was not given over completely to grief, but because of his pain he was not able to be completely happy either. Though the tears were still falling, something within him forced him to laugh about a divine future event that he would soon experience through God. Thus did he go to compline. His mouth sang with a trembling heart and it seemed as though all his suffering would soon be turned to joy. And this actually happened a short time later. That very night it began in part thus: It seemed to him as in a vision that our Lady came with her dear Child Jesus as he was on earth as a seven-year-old. He held in his hand a little jug of fresh water. The jug was sparkling and was a little larger than the cups used in the friary. Our Lady took the jug in her hand and offered it to him to drink from. He took it and drank with great eagerness, satisfying his thirst to his heart's desire.

Once he was walking across a field. On a narrow path coming the other way was a poor, respectable woman. When the woman came closer, he stepped aside from the dry path onto wet ground to let her go by. The woman turned around and said, "Dear sir, why did you, an honorable lord and priest, yield so humbly to me, a poor woman. I should much more fittingly have yielded to you." He said, "Dear woman, it is my custom to show freely politeness and honor to all women for the sake of the gentle Mother of God in heaven." She raised her eyes and hands to heaven and said, "I shall ask this same esteemed Lady that you not depart from this world without her granting you some special grace, since you show her honor through all of us women." He said, "May the pure Lady of heaven help me achieve this!"

Soon thereafter it happened that he went away from a meal thirstily as usual, although there had been an abundance of various things to drink. When he went to bed that night, there came and stood before him in a vision the figure of a woman from heaven. The figure spoke thus: "It is I, the Mother who brought you something to drink in the jug last night; and whenever you are so terribly thirsty, I intend out of pity to give you something to drink." He then spoke very timidly to her: "Ah, wonderful Lady, you have nothing at hand that you can give me to drink." She answered saying, "I shall satisfy you with the healing drink that flows from my heart." He then became so frightened that he did not know how to respond because he realized how unworthy of this he was. Then she said to him with much kindness, "Because the divine treasure, Jesus, has so lovingly penetrated your heart and because your parched mouth has earned it in so much agony, you shall receive from me a special consolation." She continued, "It is not a drink for the body, it is a beneficial spiritual drink of true purity." And so he let it be done and thought to himself, "Be sure to drink enough so that you can really quench your great thirst." When he had drunk of the heavenly liquid, something like a small, soft lump remained in his mouth. It was white, like the bread of heaven. He kept it in his mouth for a long time as proof that this really happened. Afterward he began to weep intensely, and he thanked God and his dear Mother for the generous graces he had received from them.

That same night our Lady appeared to a very holy person who was living somewhere else and told her how she had given the servant to drink. And she said to her, "Go there and tell my Child's servant what one finds in the writings of the exalted teacher called John Chrysostom of the golden mouth: When he was a student, he was kneeling in front of the altar where there was a wooden statue of the heavenly Mother with her Child on her lap letting him drink, as a mother does. The figure of the mother then asked her child to stop drinking for a while and allowed the aforementioned student to drink from her heart, too. This same favor has now been granted by me to him (the servant) in a vision. As proof of the truth of this, be informed that the teaching that comes from his mouth from now on will be heard with more longing and joy than before." When the servant was told this, he lifted up his hands, eyes and heart, and said, "Praised be the outpouring richness of the Godhead and great praise to you, sweet Mother of all graces, from me, a poor unworthy man, for this celestial gift." This same story is found in the first part of the book called *The Mirror of Vincent*.[76]

This saintly woman began again saying, "I am supposed to tell you something else. Know that our Lady came to me last night with her Child in a vision. Our Lady held in her hand a beautiful pitcher of water. The Child and the Lady said very nice things of you. She held up the pitcher of water toward the Child and asked him to bless it. He performed his holy blessing over the water and the water immediately turned to wine. Then he said, 'It is enough. I do not want this friar to continue any longer the practice of being without wine. From now on he should drink wine because of his weakened condition.' " And since it was thus allowed him by God, he began to drink wine again, as he had earlier.

At this time he had become very weak because of the excessive burden of these exercises, which he had practiced for so long a time. Our Lord appeared to a saintly friend of God with a box in his hand. She asked him, "Lord, why do you have this box?" He said, "I am going to attend to my servant who is sick." Then our Lord visited the servant with the box and opened it. Inside was fresh blood. He took some of the blood and spread it onto the servant's heart so that it was completely covered with blood. Then he spread it over his hands and feet, and all over him. She said to him, "My Lord and my God, why are you marking him so? Are you trying to press your five wounds onto him?" He said, "Yes, I want to mark his heart and whole being lovingly with suffering, and then I shall treat him and make him healthy. I want to make out of him a man after my own heart."

After the servant had led a life filled with the exterior penitential exercises that have been in part described here from his eighteenth to his fortieth year, his whole physical being had been so devastated that the only choice open to him was to die or to give up such exercises. And so he gave them up. And God made it clear to him that such severity and all these different practices together were nothing more than a good beginning and a breaking of the undisciplined man within him. He instructed him that he must make further progress, but in a different manner, if he were to reach his goal.

CHAPTER 19

How He Was Directed to the School of the Spirit and Instructed in the Art of True Detachment

Once after matins the servant was sitting there in his chair deep in thought and unaware of things around him, and it seemed to him in an inner vision that a fine young man came down from above, stood in front of him and said, "You have spent enough time in the lower school. You have practiced enough at that level and have graduated. Come with me. I shall now lead you to the highest school that exists on earth.[77] There you shall diligently learn a most lofty art that shall place you in divine peace and bring your holy beginning to a blessed completion."

This made him happy and he stood up. The young man took him by the hand and led him, as it seemed, into a spiritual land where there was a very beautiful house that seemed to be the dwelling of religious people. In it lived those who were practicing this same art (of detachment). When he entered, he was received kindly, and all greeted him pleasantly. They hurried to the chief teacher and told him that someone had come who also wanted to be his disciple and learn this art. He replied, "First I want to see him for myself, whether I like him." When he saw him, he smiled very kindly at him and said, "Let me tell you that this guest can very well become a capable religious teacher of our exalted art, if he is willing with patience to betake himself into the confining living quarters where he must prove himself."

The servant did not yet understand these mysterious words. He turned to the young man who had brought him there and asked him, "Tell me, my dear companion, what is this most advanced school and its teaching of which you have told me?" The young man said, "The advanced school and the teaching that is lectured on is nothing other than complete and perfect detachment from oneself, so that a person becomes so utterly nothing, no matter how God treats him, either through himself or through other creatures, in joy or sorrow, that he strives continually to be in the state of going away from his 'self,' to the extent that human frailty allows, and he aims alone at God's praise and honor, just as dear Christ did with regard to his heavenly Father." When the servant heard this, he was pleased and thought he would live according to this art. Nothing could be so difficult that it could draw him away from it. He intended to live there and engage in much serious activity. But the young man kept him from doing so and said, "This art requires that one be free for inactivity. The less one does, the more one has really accomplished." The activity he had in mind was that which in doing a person becomes an obstacle to his own progress and does not carry out purely in praise of God.

After these words the servant soon came to himself and sat there very quietly. He thought very seriously about them and realized that they were utterly true, as Christ himself taught. He began to talk to himself inwardly and said, "If you look inward seriously enough, you discover that your 'self' is actually still there and you become aware that, in spite of all your external penitential exercises, which you performed out of your own ground against your 'self,' you are still not detached enough to accept adversity coming from outside you. You are still like a scared rabbit that lies hidden in a bush and is startled by every leaf that falls. In your case you are startled the whole day by some suffering falling your way. You blanch at the sight of your adversary. When you should stand firm, you run away. When you should boldly show yourself, you hide. When someone praises you, you are all smiles. When someone finds fault with you, you are depressed. It can well be that you are in need of this advanced schooling." And so with an inward sigh he looked upward to God and said, "O God, I have really been told the unadorned truth. When shall I ever be a truly detached person?"

CHAPTER 20

A Painful Transition

After God had forbidden the servant to engage in such outward exercises that endangered his life, his exhausted nature was so elated that he wept for joy. When he thought back on his severe bonds and all that he had thus suffered and attained in the struggle, he said to himself inwardly, "From now on, dear Lord, I will lead an unperturbed and free life and be good to myself. I will completely satisfy my thirst with wine and with water. I will sleep on my sack of straw without being in bonds, something I frequently in deep sorrow begged God for—that he grant me this comfort before I should die. I have been spoiling things for myself long enough. From now on it is time for me to relax." Such were the presumptuous thoughts and notions running through his mind and, alas, he had no idea what God had in store for him!

After he had gone around for several weeks entertaining these enjoyable thoughts and being very pleased with himself, he happened to be sitting in the chair that he used for a bed, and he began meditating on the words of truth that Job in his suffering had spoken: *"Militia est:* Man's life on earth is nothing else but a knightly contest."[78] Deep in such meditation the world around him faded, and it seemed that a fine young man looking very virile entered carrying two elegant knightly boots and other clothing usually worn by knights. He came up to the servant, clothed him with knightly garb, and said to him, "Be a knight! Until now you were just a squire. Now God wants you to be a knight." He looked at himself in his knightly boots, and with his heart filled with amazement said, "Help, God! What has happened? What has become of me? Am I supposed to be a knight now? From now on I was going to devote myself to quiet repose." He said to the young man, "If God expects me to be a knight, I would much prefer to become one in a praiseworthy manner through a contest." The young man turned away a little and smiled. Then he said to him, "Don't worry. You shall have enough combat. He who endeavors to lead the life of a spiritual knight of God with valor will encounter many more dangerous battles than happened of old to the famous heroes in the bold knightly contests the world proclaims in song and tale.[79] You seem to think that God has removed your yoke from you and cast off your fetters, and that you should live a life of ease. This is not how it is going to be. God is not taking your bonds off you. He just wants to change them and make them heavier than ever they were." At this the servant became deeply frightened and said, "O God, what are you going to do to me? I thought I was near the goal, but now it seems to me it turns out that the real struggle is just beginning. Dear Lord in heaven, what do you want from me? Am I the only sinner around and is everybody else just, that you use the rod only on poor me but spare it with regard to so many others? You have been treating me like this since I was a child when you tormented my tender nature with long, hard periods of sickness. I thought by now it was enough!" The youth replied, "No, it is still not enough. You have to be tried in all things to your very ground if things are to turn out right for you." The servant said, "Lord, show me how much suffering I still have before me." He answered and said, "Look up to heaven. If you can count the limitless numbers of the stars, you can also count the sufferings still in your future. And just as the stars seem small but are really large, so too will your sufferings seem small to the undiscerning eyes of men; but as you experience them, they will be difficult to bear." The servant said, "Lord, show me the sufferings beforehand so that I recognize them." He said, "No, it is better for you not to know so that you will not lose heart. However, among the countless sufferings awaiting you, I shall name only three.

"First, until now you have been punishing yourself with your own hand and, if you felt pity for yourself, you stopped whenever you wanted. Now I will take you away from yourself and hand you over defenseless to be dealt with at the hands of others. Then you will have to accept the public destruction of your reputation in the estimation of some blind men. This blow will strike you harder than the suffering you endured from the pointed cross on the wounds of your back. Your earlier exercises caused you to be highly esteemed by people, but now you shall be beaten low and must be utterly ruined.

"The second suffering is this. However often you have inflicted bitter and deathly agony upon yourself, by a determination of God you have kept your tender, loving nature. It is going to happen that in those places where you especially look for love and loyalty you shall experience deceit, much suffering, and hardship. The suffering will be so manifold that those people who have a special loyalty toward you will have to suffer along with you out of pity.

"The third suffering is this. Until now you have been a baby and a pampered sissy, and have moved about in divine sweetness like a fish in the sea. This I shall now take from you and will let you wither and go to ruin. You shall be abandoned both by God and the whole world, and shall be persecuted publicly by friends and enemies. In short, everything that you undertake out of joy or to be consoled will go awry, and whatever is suffering or repulsive to you will prosper."

The servant grew so frightened at this that his whole being trembled. Wildly he sprang up and then fell to the ground in the form of a cross. His heart crying out and his voice wailing, he called out to God and begged him, if it could be, that in his gentle fatherly kindness he might spare him this terrible woe; but if this could not be, that the will of heaven and his eternal plan should be fulfilled through him. When he had been lying there in distress a good while, it spoke within him thus: "Pull yourself together! I shall be with you myself and shall graciously help you to conquer these prodigious visitations." He got up and surrendered himself into God's hands.

When it became light after mass and he was sitting in his cell disconsolate, pondering these things and freezing because it was winter, something spoke in him: "Throw open the window of your cell. Look and learn!" He opened and looked out. There he saw a dog running around in the cloisters, dragging a tattered doormat in his mouth. He had a strange way of playing with the mat. He would throw it into the air and then to the ground, tearing holes in it. Then the servant looked upward and sighed within himself, and it was said to him: "Exactly this shall happen to you in the mouths of your fellow friars!" He thought to himself, "Since it cannot be otherwise, surrender yourself to it. See how without a word the mat lets itself be ill-treated. Do the same yourself!" He went down and kept the doormat for many years as his exquisite jewel. And whenever he was about to give vent to his impatience, he took it out so that he might recognize himself in it and remain silent before others.

When he sometimes rudely turned his face a little away from people who irritated him, he would be inwardly punished for it and a voice would say, "Remember that I, your Lord, did not turn my fair face away from those who spit at me." He would then be very sorry and would turn toward them again in a friendly manner.

In the beginning, when some suffering would befall him, he would think, "O God, when is this suffering going to end? If only I had escaped it!" Then the Child Jesus came to him in a vision on the feast of the Purification of our Lady and scolded him saying, "You have not yet learned to suffer well. I shall teach it to you. Look, when you are suffering you should not be looking to find out when the present suffering will end on the assumption that you shall then have peace. While one bit of suffering is going on, you should be preparing yourself in patience to receive another. This is part of it all. You should do as a young girl does who is picking roses. When she breaks off one rose from the bush, she is not satisfied, but takes it into her head to pick more of them. You should do the same. Prepare yourself beforehand. When the present suffering comes to an end, you will soon encounter another one."

Among the various friends of God who foretold to him his future sufferings there came to him a respected and holy woman who told him that after mass on the feast of the Angels[80] she had prayed to God very earnestly about him. Then it seemed to her in a vision that she was led to a place where the servant was. And she saw that above him a beautiful rosebush had begun to bloom. It was full on all sides; it was beautifully formed and covered with fair red roses. She looked toward heaven and it seemed to her that the sun was rising in splendor against a cloudless sky. In the brightness of the sun stood a beautiful child in the form of a cross. And she saw radiance coming out of the sun toward the heart of the servant, so brilliant that all his veins and limbs glowed. But the rosebush bent down in between and was trying with its thick branches to block the rays of the sun from reaching his heart, but it was unable to do this because the rays bursting forth were so powerful that they shot right through the branches and shone into his heart. Then she saw the Child coming forth out of the sun and she said to it, "Dear Child, where are you going?" It said, "I want to go to my beloved servant." She said, "Gentle Child, what is the significance of the sun's radiance in the heart of your beloved?" It said, "I have illuminated his loving heart so brightly that the reflection of this radiance shall emanate from his heart and shall draw the hearts of men to me in love. The thriving rosebush signifies the numerous sufferings that are yet to come for him. It cannot hinder this from being nobly accomplished in him."

Because it is very profitable for a beginner to be closed off from everything, he resolved to remain shut off from the whole world in his friary for more than ten years. When he left the refectory, he would shut himself up in his chapel and stay there. He did not wish to engage in long conversations or even see either men or women at the door of the friary or anywhere else. He put a tight rein on his eyes and would not look at anything more than five feet away. He always remained at home not wanting to go into town or into the country, and wanting only to preserve his solitude. All this watchfulness was of no help because during these same years sufferings befell him in full view of all around him, and he was so hard pressed by them that he was the object of his own and other people's pity.

To make his prison easier for himself to bear during the ten years he kept himself shut up in the chapel—staying there of his own accord without fetters—he got a painter to sketch for him the holy ancient fathers and their sayings, as well as much other devotional material that motivates a person in suffering to be patient in adversity.[81] But God did not want him to become too enamored of this. After the painter had sketched the ancient fathers in the chapel in charcoal, his eyes became diseased, so that he did not see well enough to do the actual painting. He took a temporary leave and said the work would have to remain as it was until he got better. The servant turned to the painter and asked him how long it would take him to recover. He said, "Twelve weeks." The servant asked that the ladder, that had been taken down, be put up again where the sketches of the ancient fathers were. He climbed the ladder, rubbed his hands on the pictures, and stroked the aching eyes of the painter saying, "By the power of God and the sanctity of these ancient fathers I command you, master, to come back here tomorrow with your eyes completely well again." When it was morning, he came happy and hardy, and thanked God and the servant that he had recovered. But the servant attributed this to the ancient fathers on whose images he had rubbed his hands.

During this period God treated him as though he had allowed the evil spirits and all mankind to torment him. He suffered immeasurably from the evil spirits who inflicted terrible pain and sorrow on him, taking on horrible forms in wild excesses. This happened both day and night, whether he was awake or asleep, and it caused him much distress.

Once he was beset by a temptation: the strong desire to eat meat, which he had done without for many years. After he had eaten the meat and satisfied his appetite, in a vision there came and stood before him a monstrous creature from hell who spoke the verse: "*Adhuc escae eorum erant.*"[82] With a bellowing voice he said to those standing about, "This monk deserves to die and I am going to oblige him." When they would not let him do this, he pulled out a hideous-looking auger and said to him, "Since I cannot do anything else to you now, I am going to torture you with this auger, driving it into your mouth. This will cause you pain equal to your pleasure in eating the meat." And he went at his mouth with the auger. Immediately his chin and gums swelled up, and his mouth swelled shut so that he could not open it or eat meat or anything else for three days except what he could suck in through his teeth.

CHAPTER 21

Interior Sufferings

Among his other sufferings then there were three interior sufferings that caused him much torment. The first of them was unorthodox ideas against faith. Something like this would occur to him: How could God become a man? He had many such thoughts. The more he resisted them, the more confused he became. God left him in this sorry condition for a good nine years, with his eyes weeping and with his heart crying out to God and to all the saints for help. Finally, at some point, it seemed to God that it was time, and God freed him completely from this, and he received from God great firmness and enlightenment in faith.

The second interior suffering was immoderate sadness. He was constantly so depressed in heart and mind as though a mountain were weighing down his heart. Part of the reason for this was that his sudden conversion was so uncompromising that his lively nature suffered very serious depressions because of it. This wretched condition lasted about eight years.

The third interior suffering was that he fell into the state of thinking that there was no hope for his soul and that he would be damned forever, no matter how good his actions or how much penance he performed. All this would not help him in the least to become one of the saved; all was already lost. These thoughts tormented him day and night. Whenever he was supposed to go to choir or perform some other good action, thoughts of despair would rise up in him and say accusingly, "What good does it do you to serve God? You are cursed; there is no hope for you. Give it up now. You are lost no matter what you do." Then he would think, "Wretched man that I am, where shall I turn? If I leave the order, hell will be my fate. If I remain, it is hopeless anyway. Dear God, was ever anyone worse off than I am?" He would sometimes stand lost in thought emitting many a deep sigh with tears streaming down. He would strike his breast and say, "Dear God, is there no help for me? What a wretched situation this is! Must I be here and hereafter miserable? Oh, why did my mother ever bear me!"

This trial had its origin in excessive fear. He had been told that his reception into the order had been the result of temporal goods changing hands. This is where the sin called simony comes from—when one buys something spiritual with something material.[83] He buried this in his heart until he finally worked through his suffering. When this horrible suffering had been going on for about ten years, during which he considered himself simply as a damned person, he went to the saintly Meister Eckhart and lamented to him his suffering. He helped him get free of it, and thus he was released from the hell in which he had existed for so long a time.

CHAPTER 22

How He Undertook to Bring Spiritual Help to His Fellowmen

After he had spent many years fostering his own interior life, he was impelled by God through many kinds of revelations to work for the salvation of his fellowmen, that he also might fulfill this (task). The sufferings that befell him because of these good works were numerous and severe, even though many souls were really helped by him. God revealed this once to a chosen friend of God named Anna, who was one of his spiritual daughters. Once she was deep in her devotions and saw the servant celebrating mass high on a mountain. In him and on him she saw a countless number of persons suspended, and each was different from the others. The more each one possessed God, the more room each one had in him; and the more space was within him, the more God turned to each one. She saw how earnestly he prayed for them all to God whom he held in his priestly hands, and she begged God to tell her what this vision meant. God answered her thus: "The countless number of children suspended from him are all those people who go to him to confession, who are taught by him, or, aside from this, who are particularly devoted to him. These people he has brought to me in such a way that I shall direct their lives to a good conclusion, and they shall never part from my happy countenance. Whatever suffering he may endure because of this, I shall generously repay him for it."

Before this same noble person mentioned above had become acquainted with the servant of eternal Wisdom, she received from God an inner impulse to see him. And it happened once when she was in a rapture that she was told in the vision that she was going to come to where the servant was and see him. She said, "I shall not recognize him in the midst of all the friars." She was told, "He is easy to recognize in the midst of others. He wears a green crown on his head, which is adorned all over with red and white roses mixed together like a garland of roses. The white roses signify his purity and the red roses his patience in the various kinds of suffering he must endure. And just as the golden halo that one usually paints around the head of saints signifies the eternal happiness which they possess in God, so this bright crown of roses signifies the various sufferings the dear friends have to bear as long as they are still serving God on earth with knightly endeavor." Then the angel in the vision led her to where he was, and she quickly recognized him by the bright crown of roses which he wore round his head.

During this same period of his suffering, his greatest inner support was the eager help he received from the heavenly angels. Once, when he had entered a state of withdrawal from his external senses, it seemed to him in a vision that he was led to a place where there were many of the angelic community and one of them who was closest to him said to him, "Hold out your hand and look!" He held out his hand, and looking, he saw in the middle of his hand a beautiful red rose spring up with tiny green leaves. The rose was so big that it covered his hand to the fingers. It was fair and bright, a feast for his eyes. He turned his hand this way and that. Front and back it was a delight to see. With great amazement in his heart he said, "Dear friend, what is the meaning of this sight?" The young man said, "It means suffering and more suffering, and then some more suffering and still more suffering that God wishes to give you. These are the four red roses on both hands and feet."[84] The servant sighed and said, "Gentle Lord, that suffering causes men so much distress and yet at the same time should make them so beautiful spiritually, this is certainly a strange dispensation of God."

CHAPTER 23

Sufferings of Many Kinds

He once came on foot to a small town, and close to the town there was a wooden figure of Christ crucified covered over by a miniature house, as is the custom in various places. And people believed that many miracles occurred there. For this reason they brought images made of wax, many of them, and hung them up there in praise of God.[85] Since he was passing by, he went up to the crucifix and knelt before it. After he had prayed for a while, he got up and went with his companion to the inn.[86] A child, a seven-year-old girl, had seen him kneeling and praying in front of the crucifix. That night thieves went to the shrine, broke open the door, and stole all the wax they found there. When it was daylight, the news of this was brought to the town and to the townsman who took care of the shrine. He started an investigation into who had committed this terrible crime. The previously mentioned child said that she knew very well who had done it. And when they began to press her to come out with it and identify this evil person, she said, "The person guilty of this crime is none other than this friar here." She was referring to the servant. She continued, "I saw him late last night kneeling near the crucifix and then go into town." The townsman accepted the girl's statement as the truth and spread the news all around so that the slander concerning the friar was being spread throughout the town and this base action was being imputed to him. Many evil opinions were bandied about concerning how they should bring him to ruin and because of his low character quickly remove him from the world. When he heard all this, he was terribly afraid, though he knew himself to be completely innocent, and sighing within himself he said to God, "O Lord, since I am about to suffer and there is no avoiding it—if you were to give me ordinary suffering that would not cause me dishonor, I would bear it cheerfully. But now you are cutting me to the quick with the ruin of my reputation in this affair. It is the worst thing that could happen to me." Thus he remained in the town until all the talking died down.

In another town it happened that a public outcry was raised against him, so much so that the town and the whole area was filled with it. There was a monastery in the town in which there was a stone figure of Christ crucified that was said to have the same dimensions as Christ had. Once during lent fresh blood was discovered on this figure under the mark of the wound in its side. The servant came running along with the rest to see the miracle. When he saw the blood, he pushed forward and got a drop on his finger. Everyone standing around saw this. The gathering crowd from the town was becoming very large. They forced him to stand up publicly in front of everyone and say what he had seen and touched. This he did but with such circumspection that he did not offer his opinion as to whether it had been caused by God or by men. Such a judgment he left to others.

These stories spread far through the countryside, and people added something to it as it suited them. It was alleged that he had stuck himself in the finger and spread the blood onto the crucified figure so that people would think that the figure was bleeding by itself, that he had contrived to have the crowd gather out of greed—that he might relieve the people of their valuables. Similar defamatory statements about him were being bandied about in other places. When the townspeople of this town became aware of these accusations of fraud, he had to escape from the town at night. The townsfolk hurried after him and would have killed him if he had not escaped. They offered a large reward to anyone bringing him in dead or alive. Such defamations and ones like them were frequent. Wherever these stories were aired, they were accepted as truth and his name was the object of much abuse and curses. Many a rash judgment was made about him. Some there were with keener powers of discernment who knew him and said he was innocent. These were so savagely contradicted that they had to be silent and leave him to his fate. A respected woman of that same town, when she heard all these strange and terrible things the poor man was going through despite his innocence, came to him, moved by pity at his distress and gave him the advice that he should obtain a notarized declaration of his innocence from the town for use elsewhere, since many in the town knew quite well that he was innocent. He said, "Dear lady, if it were this suffering alone and nothing besides which God has ordained that I endure, then I would seek such a credential. But this suffering and others like it that befall me every day are so numerous that I just have to entrust the matter to God and do nothing else about it."

Once he traveled to the Netherlands to a chapter.[87] Suffering was being prepared for him in advance. Two important members of the order attacked him there and were very diligent in their efforts to try him sorely. With a trembling heart he was called before a tribunal where many different things were imputed to him. One of them was that he wrote books containing false teachings that were soiling the whole country with their heretical garbage.[88] Because of this he was very badly treated with verbal attacks and threats of great suffering, though God and the world recognized his innocence in the matter. This severe affliction did not satisfy God; he increased the number yet more. On the return trip God sent him sickness resulting in a high fever. In addition, a worrisome sore developed near his heart. And so, because of both inner distress and burdens from without, he came so close to dying that no one thought he would live. His companion would often look at him as though expecting his soul to depart.

As he lay there in a strange Dominican house feeling wretched and unable to sleep at night because of his terrible sickness, he began to call God to account and said, "God of justice, you have utterly overburdened my weak nature with bitter suffering and have deeply wounded my heart with the great dishonor and scorn I have received. I am surrounded by severe trials both within and without. When will you hear and answer me, gentle Father? Or when will it seem to you to be enough?" The fear of death that Christ experienced on the mountain[89] took hold of his mind. Deep in such thoughts he crawled out of bed and onto the chair in front of the bed and sat there, since he could not lie down because of the sore. As he was sitting there sorrowfully, it seemed to him in a vision that a great crowd of the heavenly court came to him in the room to console him. The celestial host began to sing a heavenly dance melody. This sounded so delightful to his ears that his whole nature was transformed. As they sang so cheerfully and the sick servant sat there so sad, a young man came to him and said very kindly, "Why do you remain silent? Why don't you sing along with us? You certainly know well heavenly music." The servant answered him in the deep sadness of his heart and said, "Don't you see in how much pain I am? Was there ever a dying man who was happy? I am supposed to sing? Now I am singing a woeful lamentation. If I ever sang happily, that is now over with. Now I am waiting for the hour of my death." The young man said quite cheerfully, "*Viriliter agite:* Get hold of yourself. Be happy. Nothing is going to happen to you. You shall yet in your lifetime sing a hymn that shall praise God in eternity and console many a suffering person." At this his eyes filled and he burst out weeping. And suddenly at the same time the sore broke open and drained, and he was immediately well.

Afterward, when he arrived home, a pious friend of God visited him and said, "Dear sir, although you were more than a hundred leagues from me while on this journey, nevertheless I was intensely aware of your suffering. One day I saw with my inward eyes the divine Judge sitting on his throne, and with his permission two evil spirits were released to inflict suffering on you through the two important (Dominicans). I called upon God, saying, 'Gentle God, how can you endure this great and bitter suffering of your intimate friend?' He answered and said, 'I have chosen him for myself, that through such suffering he be formed according to my only-begotten Son. Still, because of my justice, the great injustice being done to him will have to be avenged by the untimely deaths of the two who tormented him.' " Soon afterward this actually happened and in such a way that it was known to many people.

CHAPTER 24

The Great Suffering That His Own Sister Caused Him

The servant had a sister who belonged to a religious order. It turned out that, while her brother was living elsewhere, she started going out of the cloister and joining up with bad company. Once, when she had gone out with such company, she strayed and fell into sin. And because of the suffering and agitation that befell her she left her religious community and ran off, he knew not where. When he arrived home, the wretched business was being whispered about. Someone came and told him what had happened. He was petrified with sadness and his heart died within him. He wandered about like a man out of his senses. He asked where she was, where she had gone. No one could tell him. He pondered, "I was ready for new suffering. But this! Well, buck up and see whether you can at all help this poor lost soul. Offer up all worldly reputation to our merciful God. Cast aside any merely human sense of shame. Jump down into the deep mire and lift her up!"

As the community was assembled for the Divine Office, he walked through the assembly and turned utterly pale. It seemed as though his hair was standing on end. He did not dare approach anyone because everyone felt ashamed of him. Those who had been his companions before now shunned him. When he sought help from close friends, they turned away from him in disdain. Then he called to mind poor Job and said, "Now it is up to God to comfort me since the whole world has deserted me."

He asked all around, wherever he could, that he might hurry after the lost soul. Finally he was directed to a place, and he went there. This was on the feast of dear St. Agnes,[90] and it was cold. It had poured during the night and the streams were full. When he tried to jump over a stream, he fell into it because of his weak condition. He got up when he could. His inner distress was so great that he hardly noticed his external problems. When he got there, a small hut was pointed out to him. He directed his sad steps in that direction, went in, and found her there. Looking at her he collapsed onto the bench where she sat. Twice he fell into a faint. When he came to, he began to cry out hoarsely and to weep, clapping his hands together over his head, and he said, "O my God, why have you forsaken me!" And his sight failed him, his mouth remained motionless and his arms raised. Thus he lay for a time dead to the world in his weakness. When he had again come to himself, he took his sister in his arms and said, "Alas, my child, my sister, what I have had to go through because of you! St. Agnes, kind virgin, how bitter has your feast day become for me!" Then he sank down again and lost consciousness.

Then his weak sister got up, fell at his feet with many bitter tears, and pitifully spoke to him thus: "O, reverend father,[91] what a

wretched day that was that brought me to this earth, since I have
lost God and caused you such great suffering. Because of it my
unhappy heart will forever and ever sigh in pain and shame. O loyal
rescuer of my wayward soul, even though I am not worthy that you
speak to me or look at me, take this thought into your faithful heart
and ponder it: that you can never show God more true devotion, nor
act more as he does, than in your relations with an outcast sinner
and an overburdened heart. God has made you kind toward all who
need pity. How could you then deny your pity to me, a poor
rejected sinner, especially since I have now become an object for
God and the world to pity, and my serious guilt has so quickly and
without my realizing it made me worthless in men's eyes? What
everyone else disdains and finds repulsive you have searched out.
While everyone is ashamed of me, as they should be, your eyes
pursue what is a painful object of loathing for them and seek me out.
Sir, I beg you with a heart filled with everlasting sorrow, prostrate
and bowed down at your feet, that you do God the honor of completely forgiving me, a poor fallen sinner, for this base and evil deed,
which I have committed against you and against my own miserable
soul. And remember, if I have compromised your honor in this
world and damaged your life, you shall receive special honor and
eternal consolation because of it. And be moved to pity. I am the
one who is miserable and who has fallen into the net, who in time
and in eternity with heart and with soul must bear the consequences
and be a burden to myself and everyone else. Here as well as there
let me be your poor one in need. Since I no longer have the right to
be called or to be your sister, my heart no longer desires anything
more than in your mercy to be your lost sister and, according to
what is right, to be your beggar in need that has been found and
rescued. This way of thinking is so firm in my heart that if someone
calls me your sister or if someone wanted to present me as such, I
would find it very bitter. I feel very sorry for you, being here,
seeing me face to face and suffering because of it, because you
cannot protect yourself, as I well know about you, from all this that
a heart naturally finds shameful. From now on I shall not and
cannot have any other relationship with you except that you feel
shame and fright at the sight or sound of me. These lasting effects I
shall bear and will offer them to God for my shameful sin, that you
might obtain generous pity and true resolve from God for me, a

poor sinner, and that you might help my poor soul to enjoy again God's favor."

When he had regained his composure, her brother responded to her pitiable words in this fashion: "Oh, hot tears! Burst forth from a full heart that can no longer contain its grief! Alas, my child, only joy of my heart and soul from the days of my childhood, from whom I expected to experience joy and comfort. Come here and let me press you to the lifeless heart of your unhappy brother. Let me flood the face of my sister with my eyes' bitter tears. Let me weep and mourn over my dead child. Alas, a thousand deaths of the body are small pain! Alas, the death of the soul and honor are immense pain! Alas, the pain and sorrow of my unhappy heart. Dear God, merciful God. What I have gone through! Alas, my child, come to me. Now that I have found you, I shall quit my mourning and weeping and shall receive you today in grace and mercy, just as I want our merciful God to receive me, a sinner, at my final departure. I shall freely and completely forgive you the immeasurable suffering and grief that you caused me and that I must suffer to the end, and I shall vigorously help you atone for your sin and make amends before God and the world." This touched the hearts of all who saw it and heard the lamenting of them both, so much so that no one could keep from weeping. Thus behaving so sorrowfully and kindly giving comfort, he so touched her heart that she resolved to devote herself again immediately to the religious life.

After he had returned the lost sheep in his arms to our benevolent God with indescribable shame, great cost and effort, God brought it about most mercifully that she was received into a much more trustworthy house than where she was before. And her zeal toward God and her well-tempered and holy way of life remained so strong in virtue until her death that in the eyes of God and the world he was richly compensated for all the suffering and grief he had ever experienced because of her. When this devoted brother saw that his suffering had had such positive results, it caused him pleasure and joy. And he recalled God's mysterious ways—how for a good person all things come to good. And then he looked up to God with great gratitude and his heart dissolved in praising God.

THE EXEMPLAR

The Great Suffering That One of His Companions Once Caused Him

Once, when he was going to set out on a journey, he was given a companion, a lay brother, who was a dimwitted person. He did not like taking him along because he thought back on all the unpleasantness due to companions he had already endured. Nevertheless, he gave in and took him along.

Now it happened that they arrived in a village before breakfast on the day of a fair, and all kinds of people were coming there. His companion had gotten wet in the rain and went into a (public) house to warm himself by the fire. He told the servant that he could go no farther, that he could take care of the business without him, and that he intended to wait for him there. As soon as the friar left the house, the companion stood up and went over to join a group of strangers and hucksters who had come to the fair. When they saw that the wine was going to his head, they grabbed him, after he had gotten up and was standing in the doorway looking about emptily, and they said he had stolen some cheese. As these low characters were treating him so impudently, four or five notorious men of arms came up and, joining in the attack, said the evil monk was carrying poison. This was the time when there were widespread rumors about the poisoning of wells.[92] They took hold of him and raised such a din that all kinds of people came running. When he saw how things were going and that he was a captive, he very much wanted to help himself. Turning around he said to them, "Wait just a minute. Stop for a moment and let me explain things. I shall confess and tell you how it all happened. For evil things have unfortunately been done." They quieted down and many listened. He began to speak thus: "Look, you can plainly see that I am a fool and a stupid person. No one pays any attention to me. My companion, however, is a shrewd and clever man. The order has entrusted little sacks of poison to him, and these he is supposed to drop into wells all over the country all the way to Alsace. That is where he is now headed, intending to ruin everything with evil poison wherever he goes. See that you get him quick or he will commit crimes that can never be made good. Here, too, he took out a little sack and threw it in the village well so that everyone who has come to the fair and drinks the water must die. This is why I stayed here and

114

was unwilling to go on with him. The whole business is repugnant to me. As proof that what I am saying is true, know that he is carrying a large book sack that is full of these sacks of poison and gold pieces, which he and the order have received from the Jews to commit these crimes." When this wild bunch and all those who had crowded around heard this, they raged and shouted at the top of their voices: "After the murderer! Don't let him get away!" One person grabbed a pike, another a battle-axe; everyone grabbed what he could. And they ran about wildly, breaking open houses and monasteries wherever they thought they might find him. They poked around with their bare swords in beds and straw so that everybody at the fair came running by. There came also respectable visitors who were well-acquainted with the friar. And when they heard him being named, they stepped forward and told the crowd they were making a mistake about him—he was a very pious person who would not in the least be willing to commit such an outrage. Since they did not find him, they gave up the search and led the companion captive before the village magistrate who had him locked up in a cell.

All this dragged on until daybreak. The servant knew nothing about this sorry affair. And when he thought it was time for a frugal breakfast,[93] assuming that his companion had gotten thoroughly dry by the fire, he wandered in planning to have a bite to eat. When he came into the inn, they started telling him the unfortunate story and how it had turned out. Terrified, he raced to the house where the companion and the magistrate were and begged that his companion be released. The magistrate said that this was impossible and that he intended to throw him into the tower because of his misbehavior. This seemed severe and intolerable to the servant, and he hurried here and there seeking help. But he did not find anyone willing to help. When he had pursued this for a long time in deep shame and bitterness, he finally brought it about at his own great expense that the lay brother was released.[94]

With this he imagined the sorry business was over, but it had just begun. Only after he got free of the civil authorities with much unpleasantness and at great cost did the danger to his life really begin. When he left the magistrate about evening, it had been spread about among the common people and young riffraff that he was a poisoner. They screamed at him that he was a murderer, so that he did not dare leave the village. They pointed at him and said, "Look, there's the poisoner! He has escaped us all day. He has to be killed. Money won't help him at all with us as it did with the magistrate." When he tried to escape and slip away into the village, they screamed all the louder at him. Some of them said, "Let's drown him in the Rhine!" It flowed past the village. Others said, "No, the filthy murderer will pollute all the water. Let's burn him!"

A horrible-looking peasant in a sooty jacket took hold of a pike, pushed his way to the front, and shouted, "Listen to me, all of you! We can't put this evil heretic to death in a more humiliating way than if I run this long spear right through his middle, just as one does to a poisonous toad that one is goring. Let me run the poisoner through naked with this pike, hoist him up from the back, slam him against this strong fence, and tie him to it so he won't slip down. We'll let his filthy body dry up in the wind so that everyone going by can look at him and curse him after his degrading death. Then he'll be even more doomed in this world and in the next. This is what the contemptible fiend deserves."

The hapless servant listened to this, quivering bitterly and sighing deeply, so that in his fear large tears ran down his face. All who were standing around and looking at him began to weep bitterly. Some beat their breasts in pity and others clapped their hands over their heads. But no one dared to say anything to the unruly crowd fearing that then they would be attacked as well. When it began to grow dark and he was going back and forth begging with tears in his eyes that someone for the love of God have pity on him and take him in, they drove him away roughly. Some kind-hearted women would have liked to offer him lodging, but they did not dare.

As the unfortunate sufferer was thus in mortal distress and bereft of all human assistance, and when they were just waiting to attack and kill him, he fell down next to the fence in grief and fear of death. Lifting his unhappy, swollen eyes to his heavenly Father, he said, "O Father of all mercies, when do you intend to come to my aid in my great need? O kind Heart, how you have forgotten kindness with regard to me! Alas, Father, devoted kind Father, help me in my great misfortune and distress. In my already numbed heart I cannot decide whether it would be more bearable to be drowned, burned or die run through with a spear. One of these deaths I will have to accept. I commend to you now my unhappy spirit. Pity my deplorable death, for those who plan to kill me are near me!"[95] This sad lament was heard by a priest who ran up and pulled him out of their hands. Taking him to his house, he kept him for the night so that nothing happened to him. Early in the morning he helped him escape from his troubles.

CHAPTER 26

The Murderer

Once he was traveling from the Netherlands and going up the Rhine. He had a young companion who was a strong hiker. One day it happened that he could not keep up with his companion because he had become quite tired and weak. The companion went on ahead of him a good couple of miles. The servant looked behind him to see if there was anyone with whom he might pass through the forest he was then approaching. It was late in the day. The forest was large and a cause for concern since many people had been murdered there. He stopped at the edge of the forest and waited for someone. Along came two people walking quite briskly. One was a pretty young woman, the other a very tall, forbidding man with a pike and a long knife, wearing a black jacket. He took fright because of the hideous appearance of the man, and he looked around to see if anyone else was approaching. No one was in sight. He thought, "Dear God, what kind of people are these? How am I going to make it through this forest today? How are things going to turn out for me today?" He made the sign of the cross over his heart and gave it a try.

When they had gotten far into the forest, the woman came up to him and asked who he was and what his name was. He told her and she said, "Sir, I recognize the name. I beg you to hear my confession." She began her confession saying, "Good sir, I must admit that things have gone very badly with me. Do you see the man following us? He is a real murderer and murders people here in this forest and elsewhere, taking their clothes and their money. He never spares anyone. He tricked me and got me away from my respectable family, and now I have to be his wife." This news so frightened him that he almost fainted, and he looked around very sorely distressed to see whether he could see or hear anyone, or whether he might somehow escape. He saw and heard no one in the dark forest except the murderer following him. He thought to himself, "If you try to flee now, as tired as you are, he will quickly catch up to you and kill you. And if you cry out, no one will hear you in this solitude and you are dead anyway." He looked up full of misery and said, "O God, what is going to happen to me now? O death, death, how close you are to me!" When the woman had finished her confession, she went back to the murderer and, begging him privately, said, "Dear one, go on ahead and make your confession, too. My people at home believe that whoever confesses to him, no matter how sinful, God will never forsake him. And so, go on! Maybe because of him God will help you at your last gasp." As they were whispering, the servant came completely undone and thought, "You have been betrayed!" The murderer said nothing and came up to him. When the unfortunate man saw the murderer striding toward him with the pike, he was utterly afraid and trembled all over, thinking, "Now you are lost!" He did not know what they had been talking about. Now it so happened that the Rhine flowed there next to the forest. There was a narrow path along the edge, and the murderer so arranged it that the friar had to walk on the water side, while he himself walked on the forest side. As he was walking along with trembling heart, the murderer began to confess, recounting all the killings and murders he had ever committed. One murder especially that he confessed was so hideous that his heart stopped. The murderer said, "I was once coming through this forest—just as I am doing now—bent on murder. A respected priest joined me and I made my confession. He was walking along beside me just as you are doing now. When I had finished my confession, I pulled out this knife that I carry with me, stuck it through him, and shoved him away from me and over the edge into the Rhine."

At this story and behavior of the murderer, he turned white and was so deathly afraid that a cold sweat ran over his face and down his chest. Panic-stricken and struck dumb, he felt all his senses numb. He kept looking over in expectation of the moment when this same knife was going to be thrust into him and he was going to be shoved over the edge. Since he had almost collapsed in anguish and could go no farther, he looked around very wretchedly, like a person who would very much like to escape death. The girl caught sight of his forlorn face, ran up, and caught him under the arms as he was sinking down. She lifted him up smartly, saying, "Dear sir, don't be afraid. He won't kill you." The murderer said, "I've heard a lot of good things about you and today you shall enjoy the benefit of it. I

118

am going to let you live. Pray to God that on my final journey he help me, a wretched murderer, because of you."

Meanwhile they had come out of the forest. His companion sat there at the edge of the forest under a tree waiting for him. The murderer and his girlfriend went on ahead. He crept up to his companion and fell down upon the ground, his heart and whole body shivering like someone shaken by fever. He lay there quiet for a long time. When he had regained his composure, he got up and continued on the path, praying to God earnestly and with interior sighs for the murderer, that God might allow him to reap the benefit of the confidence he had put in the servant and that God not let him be damned as he drew his last breath. He received such an answer from God that left no doubt that he would be one of the saved and, because of his faith, would never be separated from God.

CHAPTER 27

Danger on the Waters

Once after journeying to Strasbourg, as he often did, and as he was returning home, he fell into one of the treacherous tributaries of the Rhine. He had with him his recent little book, which the evil Enemy detested very much.[96] As he was being swept helplessly downstream and was in mortal danger, God ordained in his goodness that at this same time a young new member of the Teutonic Knights chanced to come along who daringly came out after him into the turbulent and muddy waters and helped him and his companion escape a dreadful death.

Once during cold weather he undertook a journey under obedience. And after he had ridden on a wagon the whole day in the cold and wind without food until it was quite late, they came upon a muddy river that was both deep and flowing swiftly because of heavy rains. The driver of the wagon somehow did not notice that he was driving too close to the edge and overturned. The friar fell out of the wagon and into the water where he ended up lying on his back. The wagon followed behind and landed on top of him in such a way that he could turn neither this way nor that and could not help himself. And so both man and wagon were somehow carried

119

some distance downstream toward a mill. There was nothing he could do. And so the driver and others ran in that direction, jumped into the water, and grabbed hold of him. They wanted to help him get free, but the heavy wagon was lying on top of him and pressing him down. When after much struggling they got the wagon off him, they dragged him out dripping onto the land. And when he came out, his clothes froze on him quickly because of the severe cold. He was shivering with frost and his teeth were chattering. He stood there a while, silent in his woeful state. Then looking up to God, he said, "Help me, God. What should I do? How should I begin? It is late at night and there is no town or village nearby where I can get warm or recover. Am I going to have to die like this? It is certainly a miserable way to die!" He turned this way and that. In the distance on a hill he saw a small group of houses. He crept there wet and cold as he was, it being late at night besides. He went all around looking for shelter in God's name, but he was driven away from the houses. Nobody wanted to take pity on him. He began to be afraid and called upon God in a loud voice, "Lord, Lord, you could just as well have let me drown. Then I would have been better off than I am now—having to freeze to death on the street." A peasant who had earlier driven him away now heard his laments and took pity on him. Supporting him he led him back into his house. And thus, though in distress, the servant made it through this night also.

CHAPTER 28

The Short Period of Rest That God Once Granted Him

God had gotten him used to this: Whenever one affliction was over, another one soon took its place. God dealt with him thus constantly, but once he granted him a period of relief, though it did not last long. During this period of relief he came to a nuns' convent, and his spiritual children asked him how things were going for him. He said, "I am afraid things are going quite badly for me, and this is why. It has been four weeks now since I have been attacked by anyone, either physically or with regard to my reputation, and this is quite unusual for me. And so I am afraid God has forgotten about me."

When he had been sitting there with them for a short time at the grille,[97] a fellow friar came along and, after asking him to come outside, said, "Recently I was at a castle and the lord asked very angrily where you were. He raised his hand and swore in the presence of many people that he would run you through with his sword when he found you. Some of his hot-headed soldiers, those closest to him, did the same and they have been looking for you in some of the monasteries around here in order to turn their evil intentions regarding you into deeds. And so be forewarned and take precautions if you value your life!"

He became frightened at these words and said to the friar, "I wish I knew what I have done to deserve death." The friar answered, "This lord was told that you caused his daughter and many others to take up a strange mode of life that is called 'spirit,' and those who thus live are called 'men and women of the spirit.'[98] It was explained to him that this is the most perverted group of people on earth. Further, another untrustworthy man was there and said this about you: 'He stole a very dear lady from me. Now she has put on a veil and won't look at me anymore. She only wants to look inward. He has to pay for this!' " When he had heard these stories, he said, "God be praised!" And he hurried back to the grille and said to his daughters, "Farewell, my children! God is thinking of me and has not forgotten me!" And he told them the unpleasant stories of how one was planning to repay with evil the good that he had done.

CHAPTER 29

A Dear Reckoning He Once Had With God

During the same period of suffering and in the places where he then lived, the servant sometimes went to the infirmary to allow his weak body some comfort. As he was sitting there at a meal silently, as was his custom, he was assailed with derogatory remarks and unkind words, which at first caused him much distress. He felt so sorry for himself that often hot tears would roll down his cheeks and mix in with what he was eating and drinking. And so he silently raised his eyes to God, sighing within himself, and said, "O God, isn't the distress I suffer day and night enough for you? Does the food I eat at meals have to be mixed with great disgust as well?" This happened to him very frequently.

121

Once as he was leaving the table, he could not restrain himself any longer. He went to his place of privacy and spoke to God thus: "Dear God and Lord of the whole world, be generous and kind to me, a poor man, because I have something to settle with you that cannot be passed over. And even though you do not owe anything to anyone, and in your exalted state are not at all bound, still it accords well with your immeasurable goodness that by your grace you allow a burdened heart to be lightened by talking to you, a heart that has no one to hear its complaints or console it. Lord, I swear before you, because you know all things, that I have always had a gentle heart since my mother bore me. Never have I noticed anyone in suffering or sadness without having heartfelt sympathy with that person; and I have always been saddened to hear anything that could cause anyone sorrow, whether it was said behind one's back or in one's presence. All who know me have to admit that they have scarcely ever heard a fellow Dominican or anyone else bad-mouthed by my words, either in the presence of superiors or otherwise, but rather that I have improved the situation for everyone as best I could. If I could not do so, I held my tongue or left quickly so as not to hear anything. I sought the intimate company of people whose honor was injured so that they might more readily regain their honor. I was called the father of the poor. I was the special friend of the friends of God. All the people who ever came to me sad or burdened always found help and left me cheerful and well-consoled. For I wept with those weeping; with those sorrowing I sorrowed until, like a mother, I had brought them around.[99] Never did anyone cause me such great interior suffering that it did not completely disappear, as though it had never happened, if he but smiled at me afterward. Lord, quite apart from what I have done for men— whenever I saw or heard of little animals, birds and other of God's creatures in want or suffering, it went straight to my heart. If I was not able to help them, I sighed and asked the kind and most exalted Lord to help them. Everything that lives on earth has found me to be merciful and kind. And yet you, gentle Lord, allow some concerning whom our dear St. Paul speaks calling them his false brothers[100]—O Lord, my complaint is that they have displayed such great cruelty toward me, as you, Lord, very well know and is obvious enough. Gentle Lord, look upon it and reward me for it with yourself."

When he had thus relieved his heart to God for a good while, somehow he entered into a state of calm repose, and he was enlightened by God thus: "Your childlike reckoning you have presented me with arises from your not being always aware of the words and conduct of Christ in his suffering. You should know that God is not satisfied with the kind heart that you possess. He wants more from you. He expects this from you also: When you are mistreated by someone's words or conduct, you must not just suffer it patiently. You must forget yourself so utterly that you do not go to bed until you have approached those who mistreat you and, as far as you are able, calm their raging hearts with your sweet and humble words and actions. By means of such meekness and humility you take the swords and knives out of their hands and render them powerless in their malice. Look, this is the old way of perfection that Christ taught his disciples when he said, 'Behold, I send you as sheep among wolves.' "[101] When the servant came to himself, this counsel of perfection seemed too onerous to him, and he found it difficult to think about it and still more difficult to carry it out. Nevertheless, he gave in and began to learn it.

It happened once thereafter that a lay brother, a shoemaker, spoke very arrogantly to him and publicly mistreated him. He kept silent very patiently and wanted to let that be the end of the matter. But he was admonished from within that he would have to do more. When it was evening and this same brother was eating in the infirmary, the servant went and stood in front of the infirmary waiting for the brother to come out. When he then came out, the servant fell down in front of him and humbly begged, "Dear virtuous father, honor God in your conduct toward me. If I have caused you distress, forgive me completely for the love of God!" The brother stood there quietly, looked at him in amazement and said with a sob, "Alas, what strange thing are you doing? You never did anything bad to me, or to anyone else. It was I who publicly caused you distress with my malicious words. I beg you to forgive me." Thus was his heart calmed and peace attained.

Once when he was sitting at a table in an inn, a brother abused him with a malicious tongue. He turned toward the brother very kindly and smiled at him as though he had given him something especially valuable. At this the brother was inwardly abashed. He became silent and turned his face with a pleasant expression toward the servant. After the meal the brother told of the incident in the town saying, "Today while eating I was made to feel as much ashamed in public as I have ever been. When I publicly treated the servant very badly during the meal, he inclined his head toward me with such great friendliness that I turned red in shame. The experience will always be valuable for me!"

CHAPTER 30

How He Was Once on the Point of Death
in His Suffering

It happened once that several times at night he would wake up with a start and there would somehow be intoned within him the psalm of our Lord's passion: "God, my God, look down upon me."[102] This is the psalm Christ spoke in his anguish, as he was deserted by the heavenly Father and by many on the cross. Because of this constant intoning, immediately upon awakening he was startled and afraid. Weeping bitterly, he called to the person on the cross and said, "Alas, my Lord and my God, if I am supposed to and must suffer a new crucifixion with you, let your pure and guiltless death receive honor through me. Stay with me and help me overcome all my suffering." When the cross came, as it had appeared to him, terrible sufferings began for him that cannot be told here. They grew quite strong, increasing from day to day and finally became so severe, and afflicted the weakened man so relentlessly, that they brought him to the point of death.

One evening when he lay down to sleep, being away from the friary, such a feeling of weakness came over him that he thought he would collapse from faintness and that this must be the end of things. He lay there so still that not a muscle of his body moved. When the devoted and kind person who was taking care of him noticed this—a person whom the servant had drawn to God and won over with great difficulty—he ran over to him bitterly afflicted and felt around his heart to determine whether life was still present. But the heart had stopped and it beat as little as it does in a dead person. And so he sank down in great grief and, with tears streaming down and with doleful laments, he began to speak: "Alas, God, for this noble heart that for many a day bore you, dear God, so lovingly within itself and that so enthusiastically spoke words of encouragement and wrote them as well to many a confused person in all the lands. Tonight it has passed away! And yet it is a greater evil that this noble heart will decay and not live any longer to praise God and console many a person." And so with pitiable laments and weeping eyes, he leaned forward feeling his heart, his mouth and arms to see whether he was still alive or already dead. There was no movement. His face was drained of color, his mouth black, and all signs of life were gone, as in the case of a dead person that has been laid out on a bier. This lasted about as long as it would take one to walk several miles.

As he was lying there thus absent, the attention of his spirit was focused on nothing else but God and the Godhead, the true and truth according to its eternal indwelling unity. This probably started before he began to feel weak and lose consciousness. Then he began in some manner to speak intimately with God within himself and said, "Eternal Truth, whose deep abyss lies hidden for all creatures, I, your poor servant, realize that things are at an end with me as my ebbing strength makes clear. I am now speaking with you on my final journey, mighty Lord, whom no one can delude or deceive because everything is clear to you. And so you alone know how things stand between us. Therefore, I seek your mercy, faithful heavenly Father, and if ever I have at all broken away from perfect truth, O dear God, I am sorry and regret it with all my heart. And I ask you to blot it out with your precious blood in accordance with your mercy and my need. Remember that I have always exalted this pure innocent blood with praise and glory as far as I could, and this will wash away all my sins on my final journey. All you saints and especially my gracious lord St. Nicholas,[103] I beg you, kneel down and extend your hands and help me ask the Lord for a good end. O pure, tender, gentle Mother Mary, give me today your hand, your merciful hand, and in this final hour receive my soul mercifully into your protection, for you alone are the joy and consolation of my heart. Lady and Mother mine, *'In manus tuas commendo spiritum meum*—into thy hands I commend my spirit.'[104] Dear angels, remember that I always laughed in my heart, even when I just heard your names mentioned; and how often during my earthly exile have you caused me heavenly joy and protected me against the enemy. O gentle spirits, now I am really approaching my final struggle and need help. Now help and protect me against the horrible sight of my enemies, the evil sprits. O Lord of heaven, I praise you for allowing me, as I die, to be so clearly conscious and to have knowledge of the end. I leave now with full Christian faith without any doubts or fear. Forgive all those who have ever done me harm as you forgave on the cross those who were killing you.[105] Lord, Lord, your divine body, which I received today at mass, weak though I was, must be my guard and my companion on the journey to your divine countenance. And my final request, which I now make as I die, gentle Lord of heaven, concerns my dear spiritual children who have come to me with special trust or in confession as intimate friends in this exile. Merciful Christ, as you in loyal devotedness commended your dear disciples to your heavenly Father at your final departure, so may they be entrusted to you in this same love, that you may grant them a good and holy end.[106] Now I turn away freely from all creatures and turn toward the naked Godhead and into the primal origin of eternal blessedness."

When he had finished saying these and similar things within himself, he lost consciousness and the aforementioned weakness came over him. Although he and others thought that he had passed away, he then somehow regained consciousness. His lifeless heart began to beat again and his weak limbs began to revive. And he recovered so that he was alive as he had been before.

CHAPTER 31

How a Person Should Offer Up His Sufferings to God
in a Praiseworthy Manner

Once when the suffering servant thought over this grueling struggle in deep contemplation and discovered also God's hidden marvels therein, he turned to God with a deep sigh and said, "O gentle Lord, these sufferings just described can be viewed externally as sharp thorns that pierce flesh and bone. Therefore, gentle Lord, besides the sharp thorns of suffering, let some sweet fruit of good teaching spring forth so that we poor struggling men might bear our suffering with more patience and can better offer up our afflictions for the praise of God."

After he had been seeking this from God for quite some time, it happened that he was transported into himself and beyond himself. And in a state of withdrawal from his senses something spoke sweetly within him thus: "I want to show you the lofty nobility of my suffering and how a man in his suffering should offer up his afflictions in a praiseworthy manner to his dear God." At these sweet words spoken within him his soul dissolved in his body and, with his senses absent, out of the unfathomable fullness of his heart, the arms of his soul somehow stretched forth to the far ends of the world in heaven and on earth. Thanking and praising God with immense longing in his heart, he said, "Lord, up till now I have praised you in my writings, using everything in creatures that can be delightful and attractive. But now I must burst forth joyfully in a new song of unusual praise that I have hitherto not known but have now become familiar with in this suffering. This is how it is: I desire from the boundless abyss of my heart that all the sufferings and grief that I have ever experienced, and, in addition, the painful suffering of all hearts, the pains of all wounds, the groans of all the sick, the sighs of all sad people, the tears of all weeping eyes, the insults suffered by all those oppressed, the needs of all poor indigent widows and orphans, the dire wants of all the thirsty and hungry, the blood spilled by all the martyrs, the breaking of their selfish wills by all the joyful and blossoming youth, the painful practices of all the friends of God, and all the hidden and open suffering and sorrow that I or any other afflicted person ever experienced with regard to their bodies, possessions, reputation, friends and relatives, or depression, or whatever any man shall suffer up to the last day—I desire that all this may praise you eternally, heavenly Father, and honor your only-begotten suffering Son from eternity to eternity. And I, your poor servant, desire to be today the devoted substitute for all suffering people who do not know how to bear their suffering in patient and thankful praise of God, so that I might offer up to you in their place today their sufferings, however they may have suffered. I offer it to you in their stead, just as if I myself alone had suffered it all physically and in my heart as I desired. And I present it today in their place to your only-begotten Son, that he may be praised by it forever and that those suffering may be consoled, whether they are still in this vale of lamentation or in the other world in your power.

"Oh, all you people suffering with me, look at me and listen to what I tell you. We poor members should console ourselves and rejoice in our noble Head; that is, in the beloved only-begotten Son who went before us in suffering and on earth never experienced a day without it. Note well, if in a poor family there were only one

127

rich and respected man, the whole family would rejoice because of him. O worthy Head of all us members, be merciful to us and, where we lack true patience in any adversity arising from human weakness, make this good for us to your dear heavenly Father! Remember that you once came to help one of your servants. As he was about to turn cowardly in suffering, you said to him, 'Take courage and look at me. I was noble and poor. I was gentle and miserable, born from all joys and yet full of suffering.' Hence we, the seasoned knights of the imperial Lord, do not turn cowardly; the noble followers of our respected leader, we take courage and are not unhappy to suffer. For if there were no other advantage or good thing in suffering except that we become much more like Christ, our fair shining model, it would be well worth it. One thing seems true to me: If after this life God wanted to reward equally those who had suffered and those who had not, then certainly we should still choose suffering just because it makes us like Christ. For love makes love like itself and inclines itself to love wherever at all it can.

"But what boldness allows us dare to presume that our suffering makes us like you, noble Lord? Alas, suffering and suffering—how completely unlike (each other) you are! Lord, Lord, you alone are the one who suffered without reason or guilt. But who can claim that he never gave cause for suffering? If he is without guilt regarding his present suffering, then he has reason to do penance because of something else. Therefore, all of us who have ever suffered, let us all sit down in a gigantic circle all around. And you, gentle, intimate, innocent Beloved, sit down in our midst in this circle of suffering people. Our thirsting interiors shall burst wide open out of deep desire for you, O Fountain of grace rushing forth. Behold a marvel! The earth that is most marked by drought absorbs the most storm-floods of rain. And the more guilty we weak men have become, the more we embrace you within us in our wounded hearts and want you, as your divine mouth itself has said: in joy or in sorrow, washed in your painful bleeding wounds and made innocent of all evil in all things—because of this you shall have eternal praise and honor from us, and we shall receive grace from you, for in your mighty power all dissimilarity is put aside."

After the servant had sat there very quietly for a good while until all this became clear in the innermost part of his soul with great intensity, he got up in good spirits and thanked God for his grace.

CHAPTER 32

How God Compensates a Suffering Person for His suffering on Earth

Once, on a joyous Easter Day, when the servant was in a jubilant mood, he was sitting there resting as he usually did. He asked God to tell him what reward people receive on earth who for his sake have undergone much suffering. And in a state of contemplation this enlightenment came from God: "Rejoice in your hearts, all you suffering forsaken men, for your patience shall be highly praised. And just as on earth there are many people to be pitied, so are there many who will eternally rejoice in God in the possession of worthy praise and eternal glory. They have died with me; in joy they shall also arise with me. Three special gifts I shall give them which are so precious that no one can estimate their value. The first is that I shall give them the power of wishing in heaven and on earth so that everything they ever wish for comes true. Second, I shall grant them my divine peace that neither angels nor devils nor men nor any other creature can take from them. Third, I shall kiss them so intimately and embrace them so lovingly that I am they and they are me, and we two shall remain a single one forever and ever.[107] And since long waiting causes pain to restless hearts, this joy shall not be put off at the present time for a single moment. It shall begin now and be enjoyed eternally to the degree that mortal men, each according to his capacity, can bear more or less of it."

These happy words delighted the servant and, when he had come to himself, he jumped up and laughed so heartily that it resounded throughout the chapel where he was. And he said cheerfully to himself, "Whoever has suffered, let him step forward and complain about it. God knows I can claim regarding myself that it seems to me that never on earth have I suffered. I don't know what suffering is, but I do know what bliss and joy are. The power of wishing has been given to me, which many a confused heart must do without. What more can I want?"

Afterward he turned in his mind to eternal Truth and said, "O eternal Truth, instruct me in this hidden secret to the extent that one can express it in words. The truth is so completely unknown to many a blind person." He received instruction from within thus:

129

People who are successful in the breakthrough,[108] which one must anticipate by withdrawing from oneself and all things—not many succeed—such people's minds and hearts are so completely lost in God that they somehow have no consciousness of self except by perceiving self and all things in their first origin. Therefore, they take great pleasure and enjoyment from anything that God does, as though God had nothing to do with it and had turned it over to them to deal with as they saw fit. Thus they have attained within themselves the power of wishing. Heaven and earth serve them, and all creatures are obedient to them in the sense that everything does what it does or leaves undone what it leaves undone.[109] Such people feel no sadness in their hearts regarding anything, because sorrow and suffering in one's heart happens only if one's will, after carefully considering the matter, would want to be released from it. Externally, such people do indeed feel pleasure and pain like other people, and it affects them even more than others because of their refined spirit of gentleness. However, there is no place for it to remain within them. Outwardly, they remain steadfast in turmoil. Because they have withdrawn from self, they are lifted up, as far as this is possible, so that their joy is whole and constant in all things. For in the divine being, where their hearts have lost themselves, there is no place for suffering or sadness, but only for peace and joy. To the degree that your own weaknesses draw you into sinning and this is why everyone who commits sins deservedly experiences suffering and sadness—to that degree this blessedness is still lacking in you. But to the extent that you avoid sin and thereby withdraw from yourself and pass on to where you can have neither suffering nor burdens, because for you suffering is not suffering nor sorrow sorrow but rather all things exist in true peace, then you are progressing rightly in truth. And this all comes about through losing one's own will, for such people are driven out of themselves by a terrible thirst for the will of God and his justice. And the will of God tastes so good to them, and they attain such majesty from it, that everything that God has ordained for them is so welcome to them that they neither want nor desire anything else. One should not construe this to mean that a person thereby no longer needs to beg and pray to God. It is God's will that one pray to him. Rather, it is to be understood as the ordered withdrawal from selfhood in favor of the will of the exalted Godhead, as has been said.

Now there lies hidden in this matter an obstacle that confuses many people. It is as follows. They say, "Who knows whether this is God's will?" Look, God is something above being that is more interior and present to each thing than the thing is to itself. And nothing can come about or continue in existence for an instant contrary to his will. Therefore, all who constantly strive against God's will and who would gladly carry out their own will, if they could, have to be in suffering. Such people have peace as it exists in hell because they are constantly distressed and sad. On the other hand, a liberated spirit has God and peace always present to it both in repugnant and in pleasant situations because God is truly there doing everything and being everything. How can the sight of suffering be difficult for them when they see God in it, find God in it, carry out God's will, and know nothing of their own will? I will say nothing about the dazzling consolation and heavenly enjoyment with which God often secretly supports his suffering friends. These people are somehow just as though they were in heaven. Whatever happens to them or doesn't happen, whatever God does in his creatures or doesn't do, all works for the best in them.[110] And so a person who knows how to suffer well is partly rewarded for his suffering on earth because he attains peace and joy in all things. And for him following upon death is eternal life. Amen.

Part Two

The Servant's Spiritual Daughter

"Confide, filia!"[112] At this same time the servant about whom we have been speaking had a spiritual daughter, a Dominican living in a cloistered convent in Töss.[113] Her name was Elsbeth Stagel.[114] Externally she led a very holy life, and within she possessed an angelic disposition. The noble striving that she had for God in heart and soul was so intense that all those vain concerns, which cause many to forfeit eternal happiness, dropped away from her. All her efforts were directed toward spiritual teaching with which she could be instructed in the blessed life of perfection, which all her desires fastened upon. Whenever she discovered something pleasing that could help her and others to practice holy virtues, she wrote it down. She did what the industrious bees do that collect sweet honey from various flowers.

In the convent, where she lived among the sisters as a model of all virtues, and despite failing health, she completed a very good book. In it, among other things, one can read about the departed holy sisters, how blessed their lives had been, and what marvels God had worked through them. This stimulates rightly disposed persons to devotion. This blessed daughter made the acquaintance of the servant of eternal Wisdom. She was drawn by God to his life and teachings with great devotion. She unobtrusively drew out of him the story of his breakthrough to God and wrote it down, as it is written above and as follows.

At the beginning of her religious life lofty intellectual matters

132

were imparted to her by someone,[115] things that were very high-flown: the naked Godhead, the nothingness of all things, losing oneself in the nothingness (of God), the inadequacy of all images,[116] and other similar teachings that were well-expressed and that one finds very pleasing. However, there was a hidden danger lurking behind them for simple people and neophytes. For such people lack completely the necessary discernment, with the result that they apply the words to nature or spirit, whatever they feel like. This teaching was good in itself but was of no help to her. She wrote to the servant that he be of assistance to her in this matter and get her onto the right path. Still, she had found the aforementioned teaching attractive and therefore thought he should omit basic instruction and write her about these previously mentioned lofty concepts.

The servant wrote her the following in reply: "Good daughter, if you are asking me about these exalted ideas out of curiosity, so that you may become familiar with them and learn to speak well about the spirit, then I can quickly set you straight in a few words. But there is no need for you to be very happy about it, because you can thereby enter upon a dangerous false path. True blessedness does not consist in fine phrases. It consists in good actions. But if you are asking about such things in order to put them into practice, then give up asking about such lofty notions and take up such questions as are appropriate for you. You appear to be still a young and inexperienced nun. Thus it is more useful for you and those like you to know, first of all, how one should begin, ascetic practices, good saintly models—how this or that friend of God also made a holy beginning; how they, first of all, practiced living and suffering with Christ; what they, like him, suffered; how they conducted themselves inwardly and outwardly; whether God drew them to himself by sweetness or sternness; and when and how mere images dropped from them. This is how a neophyte is urged on and directed to go on further to perfection, although it might be that God could give all this to a person in one instant. But he usually does not do that. It must generally be attained by struggle and toil."

The daughter wrote and responded thus: "My desire is not for clever phrases but for a holy life. And I have the determination to achieve it honestly, as I should, however painful it may be. Renunciation, suffering, death, or whatever reaching perfection might entail, one must persevere. And do not waver because of my poor health. Whatever you dare to command that is painful for human nature, I shall dare to carry it out with the aid of God's strength. Begin at the lowest level and lead me forward, as one teaches a young pupil that is still a child, bringing it along bit by bit until it becomes itself a master of the branches of knowledge. A single request I make of you that you must grant me for the love of God, so that I not just be instructed by you, but rather that I also be strengthened in any reversals that I may encounter." He asked what the request might be. She said, "Sir,[117] I have heard it said that it is the nature of a pelican to bite itself and feed its young in the nest with its own blood because of its love as a father.[118] Sir, in like manner, I think, you should treat me and nourish me, your thirsty child, with the spiritual food of your good teaching, not seeking things too far off but finding them close to yourself; for the closer it is to your own experience, the more attractive it shall be to the longings of my soul."

The servant wrote to her in reply, "You recently described to me some high-sounding notions, which you had collected for yourself from the sweet teachings of holy Meister Eckhart, which you treated, as is only right, very tenderly. I am amazed that after drinking such noble draughts from the sublime master you can be thirsty for the swill of the insignificant servant. But if I see things correctly, I joyfully feel your good sense in the matter—that you ask with great persistence what the beginning of a sublime and secure life is, or through what basic practices a person shall reach it."

CHAPTER 34

The First Steps of a Beginner

"Daughter, the beginning of a holy life can differ from one person to another. But the beginning you are inquiring about is what I shall discuss. I know a person in Christ who, when he began, first cleared his conscience with a general confession of his whole life. All his efforts were directed toward confessing correctly by presenting all his misdeeds to a discerning confessor so that he might depart from the confessor, who takes the place of God, pure and clean with all his sins forgiven, as was the case with Mary Magdalene when she washed the divine feet of Christ with a repentant heart and eyes flowing with tears, and God forgave her all her sins.[119] This is how this man started toward God."

The daughter took this example much to heart and wanted to do what was required quickly. She eagerly decided that this servant himself would be the best person to hear her confession and that by making her confession to him she would become his spiritual daughter and be better entrusted to him in loyalty to God. Now the confession could not be made orally. When she considered her whole life, which was actually pure and innocent, and what in her opinion she had done involving guilt, she wrote it all down on a large wax tablet and sent this to him sealed, asking him to give her absolution for her sins. When he came to the end of the list on the tablet, the last thing written there was this: "Gracious sir, I fall at your feet, a sinful person, and ask you that by your heart, rich in love, you bring me back into the heart of God and that I be called your child now and forever." He was deeply moved by his daughter's pious devotion. Turning to God, he said, "Merciful God, what should I, your servant, say to this? Should I send her away? Lord, I could not do that to a puppy. Lord, if I did that, it would probably reflect badly on you, my Lord. She is looking for the abundance of the Lord in his servant. My gentle Lord, now together with her I fall at your sacred feet. Generous God, I beg you to hear and answer her. Let her reap the benefit of her good faith, the trust in her heart, for she cries out after us.[120] How did you treat the pagan woman? O generous divine heart, your unfathomable goodness has been eagerly praised to us. Even if the offenses were much greater, you should forgive them. You who are mercy itself, turn your merciful eyes toward her. Say but a word to her. Say, 'Courage, daughter, your faith has restored you to health![121] Your good faith has preserved you.' Do this, taking my place. I have done what I could and have wished for her complete release from all her sins."

He wrote back to her by the same messenger, "What you asked for from God through the servant has been granted. You should know that all of this was previously revealed to him by God. On this very morning he had sat down after praying for a short period of rest. His external senses receded and he was in the presence of many divine mysteries. Among them he was somehow enlightened as to how God separated the angels according to their form and how he gave to each its own particular characteristic according to its special difference in the orders, but he cannot put it into words.[122] When he had spent some time in celestial conversation with angels and his heart was full of joy from this superabundant marvel that his soul had experienced, there was present to him in this same vision how you came and stood before him as he was sitting among the angelic hosts. With great solemnity you knelt down before him and pressed your face to his heart, so kneeling there with your face pressed to his heart for some time that the angels present witnessed it. The friar was amazed at your boldness. And yet it was appropriate for you because of your devotion, and so he good-naturedly let you do it. You were well aware of what favors the heavenly Father granted you, pressed to the heart of another. One could tell this by looking at you. After some time you straightened up, and your face was so full of joy and so radiated by these favors that one could clearly tell that God had granted you some special favors and will continue to do so through that same heart,[123] that God will thereby be praised and you will be comforted."

This same thing was experienced also by a holy person, an unmarried noblewoman named Anna living in a castle. Her whole life was pure suffering. Through her, God brought about many marvels from the time she was young until her death. Once, before she knew the servant or had even heard of him, when she was rapt in devotion, she saw the saints in the court of heaven enjoying the sight of God and praising him. She asked of her dear lord and patron, St. John, to whom she had special devotion, if he would hear her confession. With great kindness he said to her, "I shall give you a good confessor in place of me. God has given him all power over you and he well knows how to comfort you in your many kinds of sufferings." She asked who this person was, or where, or what his name was. And he gave her all this information. She thanked God and got up the next morning and came to the friary to which God had directed her, and she asked for him. He came to her at the entrance and asked her what she wanted. She told him everything and confessed to him. When he had listened to the divine message, he submitted to it and carried it out.

This same holy daughter told him that once in the spirit she had seen a beautiful rosebush covered grandly with red roses, and upon the rosebush the Child Jesus appeared with a garland of red roses. Sitting there under the rosebush she saw the servant. The Child broke off many of the roses and showered them upon the servant so that he was covered with red roses. When she asked the Child what the roses meant, it said, "This multitude of roses are the many different sufferings God intends to send him. He should accept them cheerfully from God and endure them in patience."

CHAPTER 35

The First Models and Teachings for a Beginner and What Practices He Should Discreetly Undertake

When the servant had made a beginning and through confession had been well-cleansed, in his thoughts he drew three circles, inside of which he enclosed himself for his spiritual protection. The first circle was his cell, his chapel,[124] and the choir. Whenever he was inside of this circle, he thought himself quite secure. The second circle was the whole friary, except for the gate.[125] The third and outermost was the gate, and here he had to be careful. Whenever he went outside these three circles, he thought of himself as an animal in the wilds that has left its lair and, surrounded by hunting dogs, needs its wits about it to protect itself.

Even at the beginning he had sought out a private place, a chapel where he could practice his devotions surrounded by pictures. In his youth he had had eternal Wisdom painted on parchment, with heaven and earth in her power, and surpassing in her lovely beauty and pleasing form the beauty of all creatures. This is why he had chosen her in his burgeoning youth as his loved one. He carried this lovely image around with him in his years of study, putting it in front of him on the windowsill of his cell and gazing at it lovingly with longing in his heart. He brought it back home with him and installed it in the chapel with thoughts of love.

What other models he had as objects of devotion, as is proper for him and other beginners, could be determined by noticing the painted images and good sayings of the old fathers. Their sayings are in part reproduced here as they were inscribed in the chapel, and have the following sense in German:

> The old father St. Arsenius asked an angel what he should do to be saved. The *angel* said, "You should flee, keep silent, and remain composed."

137

THE EXEMPLAR

Later, in a vision, the angel read aloud to the servant the following from the *Book of the Ancient Fathers:*[126] The origin of all blessedness is to retain one's composure and unity.

Theodorus: Keeping oneself pure gives one more knowledge than studying diligently.

The *Abbot Moses:* Sit in your cell. It will teach you all things. Keep your outer self composed and your inner self pure.

The *Abbot John:* The monk outside the monastery is like a fish out of water.

Anthony: Chastising the body, fervor of the heart, and fleeing men bring about a pure life. You should not wear any garment that suggests vanity. The first struggle of a beginner is boldly to oppose gluttony.

Pastor: You should not get angry at anyone until he wants to tear out your right eye.

Isidor: An angry man is displeasing to God no matter what great marvels he works.

Ipericius: It is less of a sin to eat meat when it could be avoided than to talk evil about one's neighbor behind his back.

Pyor: It is very evil to point out the failings of others and to hide one's own failings.

Zacharias: If a person is ever to succeed, he has to suffer great disgrace.

Nestor: To possess divine wisdom you must first become an ass.

Senex: You should stand immovable in pleasure and pain, just as the bones of the dead do.

Helias: A pale complexion, an emaciated body and a humble manner of acting are apt adornments of a spiritual person.

Hilarion: One should deny food to an undisciplined horse and an incontinent body.

Senex: One of the fathers said: "Put the wine away from me. The death of the soul is lurking within it."

Pastor: Never has someone become a spiritual person who continues to complain and who does not know how to suppress anger, impatience and talkativeness.

Cassian: Our conduct should be modeled on that of Christ dying on the cross.

Anthony said to a fellow monk: "Brother, help yourself. Otherwise neither I nor God will ever help you."

Arsenius: A woman asked a desert father to remember her to God. He said: "I beg God to blot out your image from my heart."

Macarius: I subject my body to severe discipline because it is the cause of many of my temptations.

John: One of the desert fathers said: "I have never clung to my own will nor taught anything by word that I have not carried out in deed."

Senex: Many beautiful words without deeds are as empty as a tree with many leaves and no fruit.

Nilus: He who must live in the world must also receive many wounds.

Senex: If you can do nothing else, you should keep to your cell for the love of God.

Ipericius: The person who remains pure shall be honored on earth and crowned by God in heaven.

Apollonius: Aim at the head of the serpent. Resist at the start.

Agathon: A desert father said: "I have kept a stone in my mouth for three years so that I might learn to keep silent."

Arsenius: I have often regretted speaking, but never remaining silent.

Senex: A disciple asked an old father how long he should observe silence. He answered, "Until you are asked a question."

St. Syncletica: If you get sick, rejoice because God has remembered you. If you become weak, do not blame that on your fasting because those who do not fast also get sick. If you are being tried by temptations of the flesh, rejoice. You can become another Paul.[127]

Nestorius: A good monk said: "The sun has never shone on me while eating."

John: A second monk said: "Nor on me while I was angry."

Anthony: The greatest virtue is to know how to be moderate in all things.

Paphnutius: It is not enough to begin well unless you bring it to a successful conclusion.

Abbot Moses: Whatever can separate you from a pure heart must be avoided no matter how good it appears.

Cassian: The goal of perfection is reached when the soul with all its powers is taken into the simple One, which is God.

The servant sent these models and teachings of the desert fathers to his spiritual daughter. She took this to heart and interpreted it to mean that he thought that she, too, should chastise her body in the severe manner of the desert fathers. And she began to subjugate herself and to torture herself with hair shirts, ropes and terrible bonds, with pointed iron nails and many other things.

When the servant became aware of this, he sent her the following message: "Dear daughter, if you intend to order your spiritual life according to my teachings, as you had requested of me, then put aside such exaggerated severity because it is out of keeping with your weakness as a woman and your physical well-being. Dear Christ did not say, 'Take up *my* cross,' He said, 'Everyone should take up *his own* cross.'[128] You should not aim at achieving the severities of the desert fathers or the austere practices of your spiritual father. You should choose only a part of all this that you can successfully accomplish, given your frail constitution, so that wickedness might die in you but that you might live a long time. This way of life requires endurance and is for you the best."

She asked him to tell her why he had practiced such severe austerities and yet did not want to advise them for her or others. He referred her to holy writings saying, "One finds written down that formerly many of the old fathers led a life of inhuman and incredible austerity. Some faint-hearted people of more recent times find it horrible even to hear about it. They do not realize what fervent resolve to act or suffer for God's sake can bring about with God's mighty help. A person with such fervor finds it possible in God to achieve all impossible things;[129] as David says, he would break through a strong wall with God's help.[130] One can also find in the *Book of the Ancient Fathers* that some of them did not subject themselves to such severe austerities, although all of them wanted to achieve the same goal. St. Peter and St. John were drawn (to Christ) in different ways. Who can fully explain this marvel except by saying that the Lord, who works wonders in his friends,[131] because of his great majesty wants to be praised in many different ways? This is also why we are all different. What is good for one person is not good for another. Thus one should not assume that if, perhaps, this person did not practice such austerity he could not achieve perfection. But less robust people should not condemn such strict practices in others or judge them with spiteful minds. Each one should look to himself and see what God expects of him. This is enough. Let everything else be.

"In general, austerity practiced in moderation is better than immoderate practices. But if one finds it difficult to find a middle road, it is still more sensible to remain a little on the easier side than to venture too far in the other direction. For it often happens, when a person deprives his nature of too much, that he also has to concede to his nature too much later on. Many great saints overlooked this because of their fervent zeal. Such a severe way of life and the examples that have been given can be useful for people who are too easy on themselves and arbitrarily give in to their insubordinate natures to their eternal ruin. But this does not apply to you or people like you. God has many kinds of crosses with which he chastens his friends. I expect that God will place a different kind of cross on your back that will cause you greater pain than all possible austerities. When this cross comes, accept it in patience."

A short time later God afflicted this spiritual daughter with an extended illness that kept her sick in body and in need of help until her death. She sent him the message that exactly what he had foretold had happened to her. He wrote thus in reply: "Dear daughter, God has struck not only you with this. By striking you he has struck me as well. I have no one else who has been as helpful with such industry and devotion to God, as you were while still in good health, in bringing my books to completion. And so the servant has asked God steadfastly that, if it be his will, he might restore you to health. And since he did not want to answer his prayers quickly, he chided God in friendly anger and claimed he would not write any more books about how lovable God is and would also omit his usual morning greeting because of his discontent, if he did not make you healthy again. When he sat down again, as was his custom, in his chapel with a troubled heart, his senses somehow faded and it seemed to him that a host of angels came into the chapel before him. To console him they sang a heavenly song because they knew that he was at that time suffering most especially, and they asked him why he was acting so sad and did not join in the singing. He then admitted to them his insubordination to God because God had not answered his prayers about your health. They said he should not continue in this because God had ordained sickness for you for the best of reasons. This was to be your cross in time. With it you should gain great graces here and abundant reward in heaven. Therefore, be patient, my daughter, and accept it simply as a gift of friendship from our beloved God."

CHAPTER 36

The Childlike Devotion of a Young Beginner

Once, when the servant had come and wanted to visit his spiritual daughter in her illness, she asked him to tell her about spiritual matters that were not so deadly serious and yet would cheer up a religious person hearing them. He told her the following about his devotion when he was young.

When the servant was yet a spirited and burgeoning youth, he had for a period of time the custom, after having been bled,[132] of turning immediately to his beloved God on the cross and, holding out his pierced arm, he would say with a deep sigh, "O dear Friend of my heart, remember that the lover usually goes to his beloved after being bled for good blood. Now you know, dear Lord, that I have no other love but you alone. And so I come to you that you might bless my wound and generate good blood for me."

During the same period of his youth, when he at times had his hair cut and when his face still had a fresh rosy color, he would go before his handsome Lord and say, "O gentle Lord, if my appearance and my mouth were as bright red as the rosy radiance of all roses, your servant would wish to preserve it for you and give it to no one else. And since you alone look into the heart and care little for one's external appearance, beloved Lord, I offer you my heart as a sign of love, that I shall turn with it only to you and to no one else."

When he would put on a new coat or cowl, he would then go immediately to his accustomed place and ask the Lord of heaven, who had provided him with the new apparel, to wish him good luck and health while wearing it and to help him wear it according to his dearest will.

Previous to this in his childhood he had the following practice. When summer came with its beauty and the tender little flowers began to spring up, he refrained from picking or touching any flowers until he was able to remember with his first flowers his spiritual Beloved, the gentle rose-colored Maiden adorned with flowers, the Mother of God. When the time seemed right, he picked some flowers with many loving thoughts and, carrying them into his cell, wove them into a wreath. He would then go into the choir or into the chapel of our Lady and kneel humbly before our dear Lady. And he would crown her statue with the lovely wreath with this in mind: Since they were the most beautiful flowers and were the summer joy of his young heart, she would not reject these first flowers from her servant.[133]

Once, when he had thus crowned her, it seemed to him in a vision that the heavens were open and he saw clearly the bright forms of angels going back and forth in splendid garments. He heard the most exquisite singing ever heard in the court of heaven by the joyous members of the court. They sang especially a song of our Lady. It sounded so sweet that his soul dissolved in great pleasure. It was like the song sung of her in the sequence on the feast of All Saints: "*Illic regina virginum transcendens culmen ordinum*, etc."[134] The sense of the song is that the pure Queen soars above the whole heavenly host in honor and dignity. He joined in with the court of heaven. In his soul there remained much of the taste of heaven and longing for God.

Once afterward, at the beginning of May, as was his custom, he had placed a garland of roses on the head of his dearest Lady of heaven with great devotion. That same morning, since he had come back from somewhere and was tired, he wanted to allow himself enough sleep and not greet his Lady at this hour. When the time came when he was usually supposed to get up, it seemed to him as though he were in a heavenly choir and they were singing the *Magnificat* in praise of the Mother of God. When it was finished, our Lady stepped forward and bade him begin the verse "*O vernalis rosula*," which means, "O you delicate rose of summer." He wondered why she wanted this, but he wanted to be obedient to her and, in a joyful mode began, "*O vernalis rosula.*" Immediately three or four youths of her heavenly retinue standing in the choir joined in, and then the whole group with much spirit. They sang the song with warmth, so that it sounded very fine, as though all the strings of the world were being played. His mortal nature could no longer hear such refined sound, and he came to himself.

On the day after the feast of the Assumption he was again shown great joy in the court of heaven. No one was to gain entrance who arrived unworthy. As the servant was trying to get in, a young man came up, grabbed him by the hand, and said, "Friend, you do not belong in there at this time. Stay outside. You have incurred guilt, and before you may hear the heavenly singing, you have to make up for your misdeed." And he led him somewhere down a crooked path into a hole under the earth. There it was dark and barren and wretched. He could go neither this way nor that, like someone who lies captive where he can see neither sun nor moon. Finding this painful, he began to sigh and feel miserable because of his imprisonment. Soon the messenger came and asked how he was doing. "Poorly, poorly," he replied. Then the young man said to him, "You should know that the exalted Queen of heaven is angry with you for that failing because of which you are a prisoner here." The servant became very frightened and said, "Alas, wretched me! How have I offended her?" He said, "She is angry with you because you do not like to preach about her on her feast days. And yesterday on her great feast you refused, against the wish of your superior, to preach about her." The servant replied, "Dear friend and lord, I think she is worthy of such great honor that I feel unequal to the task, and I leave it to the more mature and worthy (friars) because it seems to me that they can preach about her more worthily than a poor man like me." The youth said, "Know that she would like you to do it, that she considers it a pleasing service from you. And so do not refuse anymore." The servant began to weep and said to the young man, "Dear messenger, reconcile me to the pure Mother. I give you my word that it will never happen again." The young man looked at him amicably, consoled him kindly, and led him out of the prison and back home. He said, "I could tell by the look on the friendly face of the Queen of heaven and by her words when she speaks of you that she forgives you. She is no longer angry with you and wants always to be like a mother to you."

It was usually his custom, when he left his cell or came back up to it, to pass through the choir before the Blessed Sacrament. He thought to himself: If someone has a dear friend living somewhere on his street, he gladly extends his way a little for the sake of some friendly conversation.

A person once asked for a carnival gift from God because he did not want to receive it from any creature. And as his senses withdrew from him, he saw our dear Savior entering in the form of a thirty-year-old. He told the servant he wished to fulfill his wish and give him a celestial carnival. He took a cup of wine in his hand and offered it to the three women who were also sitting at the table, to one after the other. The first woman sank down faint. The second also became a bit weak. The third, however, paid no attention to him. And he explained to the servant the difference between a person beginning a spiritual life and one progressing and one who is perfect, and how they differ in their response to divine goodness.

With these and other similar pious stories the conversation was at an end. The nun secretly wrote it all down and sent it somewhere to have it kept hidden in a locked chest. Once a good sister came to the one keeping it and asked, "Dear sister, what kind of divine marvels do you have in that chest? I dreamed last night that there was a young boy from heaven in your chest. He had a delightful stringed instrument in his hand that is called a rebec.[135] And he played spiritual melodies on it that were so charming that many drew spiritual pleasure and joy from it. I ask you, take out what you have locked up so that the rest of us can read it, too." The other sister remained silent and did not want to tell her anything about it because she had been forbidden to do so.

CHAPTER 37

How He Drew Frivolous Persons to God and
Comforted Those Suffering

Once a long time had passed without the servant's having sent any message to his spiritual daughter. Then she wrote him a letter saying that she needed him to send her some message that would raise up her suffering spirits. She wrote: A miserable person receives a little consolation from seeing people who are more miserable than he is. And a suffering person finds some encouragement from hearing that his neighbors are in even greater distress and that God had helped them out of it.

And so he wrote to her: So that you may be more patient in your suffering, I shall tell you for the praise of God something about suffering. I knew a man whose good name in the world was struck down openly by a decree of God. This same man's honest desire was always to love God from the depths of his heart and to make all men find it pleasant to love as he loved and make them withdraw from all vain love. He accomplished this with many, both men and women. Because he was taking from the devil what was his and was giving it back to God, this troubled the evil spirit greatly. And he appeared to good people and confided in them that he wanted to get revenge on this man.

Once he came to a monastery of an order in which the monks had their living area and the nuns of the order also had their own living area.[136] In this monastery were two members of the order, very important people—a man and a woman—who were attached to each other in great love and destructive intimacy. The devil had so blinded the hearts of them both that they viewed this immorality as though it were no fault or sin, but that God had permitted it to

145

them. When the servant was asked in confidence whether this situation could truthfully go on in God's sight, he said, "No, in no way!" And he told them that such an illumination was wrong and against Christian doctrine. And he brought it about that they gave it up and afterward kept themselves pure.

While he was thus engaged, a holy person named Anna was at her devotions and was transported in spirit. She saw above the servant in the air a great army of demonic spirits gathering who were screaming all together: "Kill, kill the evil monk!" They abused and cursed him because he had driven them by his good counsel from their comfortable dwelling, and they all swore with terrifying gestures that they would always lie in wait for him and would get their revenge on him; and if they were not able to get at him physically or at his goods, they would in any case severely damage the high estimation people had of him. They intended to attribute disgraceful deeds to him. No matter how he avoided any cause for such as best he could, they intended nevertheless to bring about his ruin with clever deception. This caused the holy woman to become terribly afraid, and she asked our Lady to come to his aid in the trials to come. The dear Mother said to her kindly, "They cannot do anything to him without my dear Son's permission. Whatever he ordains for him will happen and will be the best and perfect thing for him. Hence tell him to take courage."

When she told this to the friar, he became very much afraid of the menacing gathering of evil spirits and, as he often did in time of trial, he went up onto a mountain where a chapel stood dedicated to the glory of the holy angels. As was his custom, he walked around the chapel nine times, praying in honor of the nine choirs of heavenly hosts and begging them earnestly to be his helpers against all his enemies.[137] When the dawn came, he was led in a spiritual vision onto a beautiful field. He saw around him a very great gathering of angelic young knights who wanted to help him. They consoled him and said, "God is with you and will never forsake you in any of your afflictions. And so do not cease drawing worldly hearts to the love of God!"

After this he was strengthened, and he went out eagerly to bring back to God both the rebellious and the meek. With kind words he was trying to help a renegade man who had not been to confession for eighteen years. The man gained confidence in him through God's help and made his confession to him with such sorrow that they both wept. He died soon afterward and had a blessed end. The servant once converted twelve women, public sinners, from their sinful lives. What he suffered because of them cannot be put into words. Only two of them remained constant.

There were here and there in the country a number of women, both those living in the world and nuns, who because of the weakness of their dispositions had openly fallen into sinful ways. Because of their shame these poor daughters had no one to whom they dared open their grief-stricken hearts, so that often they were driven by panic to the temptation of wanting to take their own lives. When these people heard that the servant had a generous heart for all those who were suffering, they plucked up their courage and came to him, each of them at a time when she was in great distress. They lamented to him the fears and troubles that held them captive. When he saw these poor souls in their pitiful afflictions, he wept with them and comforted them kindly. He helped them and put his reputation at great risk to aid them regain both respect and the salvation of their souls. He did not concern himself about what might happen through the gossip of evil tongues.

Among these one came to him, a woman of noble birth, and told him in confession that when she felt great sorrow because she had fallen, our Lady appeared to her and said to her, "Go to my chaplain. He shall help you." She said, "Dear Lady, I don't know him." The Mother of mercy said, "Look beneath my mantle. I have him under my protection. Look carefully at his face so that you can recognize him. He is a helper in need and a comforter of all those who suffer. He shall console you." She came to him in a foreign country and recognized his face as she had seen it before in spirit. She asked him to pardon her and told him what had happened. He received her kindly and helped her with all his might, as the Mother of mercy had requested.

CHAPTER 38

The Pitiful Affliction That This Caused Him

Thus did he come to the aid of many in their suffering. But these good and virtuous actions had to be paid for most bitterly with torturous suffering that befell him. God showed him these future sufferings beforehand in a vision as follows: He came one evening to an inn and, when it was getting on toward morning, he was led in a vision to a place where mass was about to be sung. He himself was supposed to sing the mass since the lot had fallen to him. The choir began singing the mass of the martyrs: "*Multae tribulationes justorum,* etc."[138] This tells of the many afflictions of the friends of God. He did not like what he heard and would have preferred to avoid it. He said, "Why all the commotion about martrys? Why are you singing about the martyrs today since it is not the feast of a martyr that we are celebrating?" They looked at him and, pointing their fingers at him, said, "God will find his martyr today as he has always found them. Prepare yourself and sing for yourself!" He turned the pages of the missal lying in front of him, back and forth, and would have liked to sing of the confessors or anything else but the suffering martyrs. Wherever he opened the book or whatever he turned to, he saw only things referring to the martyrs. When he saw that it could not be otherwise, he sang with them and his song sounded mournful indeed. After a little while he began again, saying, "This is certainly strange. One could much rather sing, 'Let us rejoice,' and sing of joyful things for the martyrs rather than of sad things." They said, "Dear friend, you still don't understand. This hymn to the martyrs precedes. Sometime later, when it is time, then comes the joyful song, 'Let us rejoice!' "

When he came to himself again, his heart trembled because of what he had experienced and he said, "O God, must I again suffer torments?" When he acted very sad on the way down, his companion said, "Father, what is wrong with you that you are acting so sad?" He said, "Dear companion, I must now sing the mass of the martyrs." He meant that God had given him to understand that he was going to have to suffer great torments, but his companion did not understand this. He, too, fell silent and kept it to himself.[139]

When he came into the town—it was at the time of the dark days before Christmas—he was as usual in bitter suffering so severe that it seemed to him, in a human way of speaking, that his heart would burst in his body, if that had ever happened to anyone. For afflictions were then so besieging him that nothing other was happening to him than the immediate pitiful loss of everything that was useful, or comforting, or that brought honor to a person during his stay on earth and could console him. This was the nature of the bitter affliction: Among the people that he would have liked to have drawn to God, there came to him a woman deceiving and cunning. She had the heart of a wolf beneath a kind exterior. She hid this so carefully that for a long time the friar did not notice anything. Previously she had fallen into serious sin and disgrace with a man, and had increased her wrongdoing by claiming that someone other than the one responsible was the father of the child. The real father declared himself innocent in the matter. The servant did not hold this daughter's misdeeds against her and heard her confession. She was helpful to him, more so than the others, in those necessary and honorable services in the land done by those called *terminarii*.[140] When this had been going on for a long time, he and other honest people became aware that she was secretly conducting herself in the same wicked manner as she had before. But he kept silent about it and did not want to inform on her. He did, however, break off from her and discontinue her services. When she realized this, she sent word to him that he should not do it and that, if he were to discontinue the advantages she had from him, he would pay for it. She would claim that the child she had conceived by a man in the world was his, that it had to be his. She would so disgrace him by means of the child that he would everywhere be in disrepute.

Hearing this he was terrified and stood glued to the spot. Sighing deeply he said to himself, "Oppression and distress beset me on all sides and I don't know where to turn. I'm damned if I do and damned if I don't. I am so surrounded by anguish and distress from all directions that I could go under in them."[141] Thus he waited with a terrified heart to see what God would allow the devil to do with him. He took counsel with God and with himself and decided that of the two miserable choices it was better for him, both body and soul, to break with this base person, no matter what this meant for his reputation on earth. And this is what he did.

Because of this she became so enraged at him in her perfidious heart that she ran here and there, to clergy and laity, with the intention of bringing deep shame upon herself from superhuman wickedness in order to cause a crisis for his poor heart. She told many people that she had given birth to a child and that the father was this very friar. Because of this there was very much scandal among all who believed what she said, and the scandal was the greater the farther his reputation for holiness had spread. This pierced him to the center of his heart and soul, and he went about preoccupied with himself and oppressed with his misery and distress. The days were long and the nights difficult. His brief periods of repose were interrupted by anguish. He looked up pitifully to God and said with a deep sigh, "O God, my hour of misery has come. How should or can I any longer endure this affliction of heart that makes me an outcast? Alas, God, if only I were dead and neither saw nor heard about this sorry business! Lord, Lord, I have honored your worthy name all my days and have caused others far and wide to love and honor it. And now you intend to subject my name to dishonor? This is my greatest complaint: The respected Order of Preachers has to be compromised in me. I shall never cease to lament that. My heart's anguish is great. All the good people who used to consider me a holy person and held me in honor, which was a great encouragement for me, now consider me the most malicious deceiver alive. This is what wounds and pierces my heart and soul."

When the poor suffering man had been lamenting for some time, and health and life were ebbing away from him, a (different) woman came to him and said, "Dear sir, why are you ruining yourself so pitifully? Pull yourself together. I shall give you advice and help so that, if you do as I say, you shall lose nothing of your honor. And so, buck up!" He looked up and said, "How can you accomplish that?" She said, "I shall stealthily put the child under my coat and at night bury it alive or stick a needle through its brain so that it will surely die. Once the child is gone, the wicked talk will quit completely and your honor remains intact." With his voice full of rage he said, "You wicked murderess! What a bloodthirsty heart you have! So you wanted to kill the innocent child! What difference does it make that his mother is an evil woman? So you wanted to bury it alive! No, no, God forbid that a murder take place because of me! Look, the worst that can happen to me is that I am robbed of my earthly honor. Even if the honor of a whole country rose or fell with me, I would rather offer it all up to our worthy God than that I would let innocent blood go to ruin." She said, "Well, after all, it's not your child. Why are you making such a fuss about it?" And she pulled out a sharp pointed knife and said, "Just let me carry it away from your sight and I'll slit its throat, or I'll stick this knife into its tiny heart. Then it will quickly die and you will have your peace." He said, "Silence, you filthy evil devil! Whatever it is on earth, it is still formed in the image of God and very dearly redeemed with the precious innocent blood of Christ. This is why I will not allow its young blood to be spilled like that." Impatiently she said, "If you don't want to have it killed, at least have it secretly brought early some morning to the church so that it might be treated like other rejected orphans; otherwise you will have great expense and trouble with it until the little boy has been brought up." He said, "I have trust in our powerful God of heaven who alone has been my help up till now. He will certainly give me help for us both." He said to her, "Go and bring me the child secretly so I can see it."

When he put the child on his lap and looked at it, it laughed. But he gave a deep sigh and said, "Am I supposed to kill a pretty child that smiles at me? I certainly cannot! Rather shall I gladly suffer everything that may come my way." He turned to the child tenderly and spoke these words, "Alas, you poor homeless child! What a poor little orphan you are! Your own faithless father has denied you. Your murderous mother wanted to throw you away like a repulsive cast-off dog. Now God's decree has given you to me so that I shall have to be your father. And that I shall gladly be. I have you from God and from no one else.[142] Oh, child of my heart, you sit on my miserable lap and look at me. You don't know how to speak. I look at you with my heart wounded. My weeping eyes and the kisses of my mouth pour over your childlike face in the stream of my hot tears." When the copious tears of the weeping man ran over the little eyes of the pretty child so steadily, it also began to cry hard along with him. And so they both cried together. When he saw the child crying so, he pressed it lovingly to his heart and said, "Hush, my joy! Child dear to my heart, should I kill you because you are not my child and because I must pay for you dearly? Oh pretty, dear and tender child of mine, I really cannot do you any harm, because you have to be my child and God's. As long as God supplies me with a single mouthful (of food), I shall share it with you for the praise of our dear God and shall suffer everything in patience that may ever befall me, dear child of mine."

When the heartless woman who previously wanted to kill the child saw and heard this weeping and fondling, she was so moved in her heart to great pity that she broke out in such weeping and wailing that he had to quiet her. For he was afraid that someone might come and notice it. When she had cried herself out, he held out the child to her again, blessed it, and said, "May dear God bless you now and the holy angels protect you from all evil." And he ordered that it be supplied with all the food it needed.

Sometime after this the evil woman, that is, the child's mother, came by and, as she had maliciously slandered the friar, now she continued to do so in whatever way could harm him. Because of this many pure and virtuous hearts felt pity for him, and for her they wished that a just God would remove her from the earth. It happened once that one of his relatives came to him and said, "Sir, that was a terrible crime that this evil woman committed against you. God knows I want to take harsh revenge on her for you. I shall stand surreptitiously on the long bridge that goes across the river and, when she walks across, I'll shove the blasphemer off it and drown her so that this terrible crime against you is avenged." "No, dear cousin," he said, "God does not want any living person to be killed on my account. God, who knows all things hidden, knows that she committed an injustice against me with this child. I put the matter in his hands, that he let her live or quickly die, whatever he wills. And I tell you, even if no harm came to my soul by her dying, I would still honor the name of all pure women in her and let her live." The man responded maliciously, "I would kill a woman who wanted to ruin me, just as I would a man." The servant said, "No, that would be senseless brutality and illicit savagery. Give up such ideas and let justice prevail. Let all the suffering come that God wants me to endure!"

When the suffering quickly grew, he was once overcome by a moment of weakness. His distress was so great that he wanted to create for himself a bit of relief and contentment in the midst of his troubles. He went out and sought comfort especially from two friends who, while he was sitting on top of the wheel of fortune,[143] had conducted themselves toward him as though they were his true friends and companions. From them he sought encouragement for his suffering heart. But through these two God let him realize that you can never completely count on creatures. He was openly mistreated by them and their company, worse than he had ever been by common folk. One of the friends received the poor friar harshly, turning his face away from him with a look of repugnance and causing him much shame with his cutting remarks. Among other wounding remarks that he made against him, he said he no longer wanted to be friends with him because he was ashamed to be seen in his company. Oh, how this tore through his heart! His voice filled with misery, he replied, "Dear friend, if by God's decree you had been thrown into a dirty puddle, as I have been, I certainly would have jumped in after you and as a friend helped you get out. But now it's not enough for you that I lie deep in a puddle before you. You also want to step on me! This I shall complain about to the lonely heart of Jesus Christ." The friend told him to shut up and said to him with a sneer, "Now you are finished. Not only your sermons but also the books that you have written shall be rejected." He responded with good grace and, looking up to heaven, said, "I trust dear God in heaven that, when the time comes, my books shall become more valuable and loved than they ever were." This is the kind of consolation he received from his closest friend.

Up to this time in this same town, life's necessities had always been provided him by kindhearted people. But after he had been thus maligned by these lying stories, those who believed what these gossipers said against him withdrew their help and friendship until they had been told by divine truth to restore their usual relationship to him.

Once, when he had sat down for a quiet period of rest and his active senses somehow faded from him, it seemed to him that he were being brought to a realm above the senses. Something in the ground of his soul said, "Listen to these comforting words that I shall read to you." He leaned forward and listened intently. It began to read the words in Latin of the chapter from nones[144] on Christmas eve: "*Non vocaberis ultra derelicta*"; in German: "You shall no longer be called the one whom God has forsaken, and your land shall not be called the devastated country. You shall be called 'God's will is in her,' and your land shall be cultivated because the heavenly Father himself has found you pleasing."[145] When the reading was finished, it began again, reading the same words over and over, four times. Puzzled he said, "My beloved, what is the meaning of your reading these words aloud to me over and over?" He received the answer: "I do this so that I might strengthen your trust in God, who shall supply his friends' country, that is, their mortal bodies, with their needs. And what they lack in one area he shall make up in another. Thus as a father shall God treat you also." All this actually happened so clear for all to see that many a heart, whose eyes had previously wept in pity, laughed for joy and praised God.

This suffering man was treated like a skinned carcass that has been torn to shreds by wild animals and still exudes a stench. Finally the hungry insects fall upon it in hordes and completely strip the bones that the animals had gnawed on, and they fly away with what they have sucked in. Thus was he carried away piece by piece into distant lands by these seemingly good people. And they did this with well-turned phrases and well-considered words of complaint, as a sign of friendship where really trust was lacking. In the midst of all this a terrible thought struck him: "Dear God, if one were only being mistreated by Jews or pagans or public sinners, one could put up with it. But these people who are causing me such terrible grief appear to be your intimate friends. This makes it all so much worse." But when he came to himself and viewed things with objectivity, he did not blame them. Rather, it was God who was acting through them, and he thus had to endure it. God often prepares what is best for his friends through his friends.

Once, especially, a voice spoke thus within him as he reflected on his suffering: "Remember that Christ did not just want his dear disciple John and loyal St. Peter in his chaste presence. He also wanted to allow evil Judas near him. And you long to be a follower of Christ, but do not want to endure willingly your Judas?" Immediately another thought raced through his head in reply: "Lord, if a suffering friend of God had but one Judas, it would be tolerable; but nowadays there is a Judas in every nook and cranny. And when one Judas leaves, four or five take his place." He received within the following reply: "For one who sees things rightly, Judas will not be Judas—as he considers it. Judas should be seen as someone cooperating with God, one through whom a person is to attain what is best for him. When Judas betrayed Christ with a kiss, Christ called him his friend and said, 'My friend, etc.' "[146]

After this poor man had thus suffered so miserably for a long time, he still held fast to one small consolation, which was his sole support—that the burden oppressing him had not yet come to the attention of the authorities of his order. But God pulled this small consolation out from under him, too. The general of the order and the provincial of his province, Teutonia, came together to the town where the evil woman had slandered the good man. When the poor man, who was living elsewhere at the time, heard the news, his heart stopped beating within him and he thought, "When these superiors hear what that wicked woman has to say about you, it will be the death of you. They will impose such a huge penance on you that you would be better off physically dead." This painful anxiety lasted twelve days and nights, one after the other, as he waited to see when the terrible punishment might come.

One day in a moment of human weakness he broke out in a

demonstration of unseemly conduct because of the trials he was experiencing, and in his wretched internal and external state he went alone away from everyone to a secret place where no one could see or hear him, and there he groaned again and again from the depths of his being. Tears stood in his eyes and then ran down his cheeks. Because of his restless anguish he was not able to remain still. First, he would abruptly sit down, then he would jump up and pace back and forth in the chamber like a person struggling against fear and oppression. Then a thought would pierce him in the heart and he would say to himself with his voice quaking, "O God, what do you have in store for me?" While he was in this wretched frame of mind, something from God spoke within him thus: "Is this your detachment? Is this the steadfastness in joy and sorrow that you have so often brought others to appreciate—that one should leave oneself for God in patience and have no other support?" In response he answered very tearfully, "You ask me what happened to my detachment? Well, you tell me what happened to God's infinite mercy toward his friends! Here I am waiting, and am as ruined as a man condemned to lose his life, goods and honor. I thought that he was generous; I thought he was an honorable Lord, merciful to all those who risked turning themselves over to him. Poor me! God has failed me! O Fountain of mercy that never runs dry, it has dried up for me! Alas, the generous heart, whose graciousness the whole world proclaims, has left me with nowhere to turn! He has turned his beautiful eyes and gracious countenance away from me. O kind Face, o generous Heart, I never would have thought that you would so utterly reject me. O endless Abyss, come to my aid or I am lost! You know that all my consolation and trust is in you and in no one else on earth. Listen to me today, all you suffering hearts, for God's sake! No one should take offense at my improper conduct, because the whole time I was speaking about detachment and nothing else it was pleasant for me to talk about it. But now my heart has been completely pierced, and the marrow of my bones, my very blood and brain are immersed (in suffering) so that there is no part of my body that has not been tortured and wounded. How, then, can I be detached?"

When he had been in this unfortunate state for a good half day and had so tortured his brain, he sat down calmly and turned away from himself and toward God. Surrendering himself to God's will, he said, "If it cannot be otherwise, your will be done!"[147] As he sat there bereft of his senses, it seemed to him in an apparition that one of his saintly spiritual daughters came and stood before him. She had often told him when she was alive that he would have to suffer much, but that God would help him through it. She appeared to him and consoled him kindly. But he treated all this as something of no value and questioned the truth of what she said. Then she laughed, came up to him, gave him her saintly hand, and said, "Take my word as a Christian as though it were God's (word) that God will not desert you. He will help you overcome this suffering and all your suffering." He said, "But look, daughter, I am being so greatly oppressed that I cannot believe you unless you give me a clear sign." She said, "God will make you free of blame in all good, pure hearts. Evil hearts respond to things according to their own evilness, so that a prudent friend of God pays no attention to that. And the Order of Preachers, which you are so worried about, shall be more pleasing to God and all right-thinking men because of you. Take this as a sign of the truth of this. God will quickly avenge you and will stretch out his angry hand over the evil heart that has caused you such sorrow and will let her die. In addition, all those who helped her in the affair with their malicious talk will also soon have to experience vengeance. Be sure of it." The friar was deeply consoled by this and waited steadfastly to see how God would bring the matter to an end.

Very shortly thereafter it really all turned out as she had said. The malicious woman who had caused him so much pain died inexplicably. Many of the others who had abused him most harshly were plucked by death from this life, part of whom died of unknown causes, and some departed without confession or communion. One of these persons was a superior who had inflicted much pain on him. This man appeared to the servant in a vision after he died and told him that God had ended his life and his prestige because of what he had done, and that he would have to languish in punishment and suffer thirst for a long time because of it.

When people who knew the truth and were favorably inclined toward him saw the unusual vengeance and even deaths which God visited upon his malingers, they praised God and said, "Truly God is with this good man and we see clearly that he has been treated unjustly. In our eyes and in the eyes of all people of discernment he should by rights be more respected from now on for his spiritual blessedness than if God had not ordained this suffering for him."

After this God in his mercy helped bring to a gracious end the tempest of suffering, just as the saintly daughter had said in the vision to console him. He often thought, "Dear Lord, how true that phrase is that one speaks of you: No one can harm the person whom God wishes well."

Also, his friend, who had treated him poorly in the affair and whom God took from the earth a short time later, appeared to him after he died and when all the obstacles keeping him from enjoying the pure sight of God had fallen from him. He was clothed in shining, golden finery. Embracing the servant affectionately and pressing his face to his cheek kindly, he begged him to forgive him for having so misjudged him and asked that an intimate heavenly friendship might exist between the two of them forever. The servant heard this with great joy and embraced the friend warmly. Then the friend disappeared from sight and entered into divine joy.[148]

Sometime afterward, when it seemed time to God, the sufferer was compensated for all the suffering that he had endured by interior peace of heart, calm repose and radiant grace. He praised God ardently because of the suffering caused by love and said that he would not take the whole world for what he had suffered. God clearly let him know that he had been more nobly removed from self and placed into God by this misfortune than from all the many different sufferings that he had endured from his youth to that time.

CHAPTER 39

Interior Suffering

When his spiritual daughter read the above account of his pitiful suffering and had wept much out of compassion, she asked him to explain to her the nature of interior suffering. This is what he answered: Concerning interior suffering I shall tell you two things. There was once in a religious order a fine person for whom God had ordained an interior affliction. In this suffering the friar's disposition and heart were so oppressed that day and night he would go about weeping, wailing and carrying on dejectedly. This friar came to the servant of Wisdom with ardent devotion, told him of his sorry condition, and begged him to pray to God about him that he be helped. Early one morning, when the servant was interceding for him and was sitting in his chapel, it seemed to him in a vision that the evil spirit himself came and stood before him. In the form he had assumed he was an ugly Moor with fiery eyes. He presented a hellish, terrifying sight and had a bow in his hand. The servant said to him, "I beseech you by the living God to tell me what you are and what you want here." He answered diabolically, "I am the spirit of blasphemy, and you know very well what I want."[149]

The servant turned around to the door of the choir. The suffering friar was just then coming to that same door and wanted to enter the choir to go to mass. The evil spirit pulled out his bow and shot a fiery arrow into the friar's heart so that he nearly fell over backward and was not able to enter the choir. This troubled the servant and he scolded the devil for it harshly. Because of this the arrogant devil became angry with him and pulled out the bow with the fiery arrow, as he had before, and was about to shoot him in the heart as well. The servant quickly turned to our Lady for help and said, "May the pious virgin Mary, together with her Son, bless us."[150] The devil lost his power and disappeared. When morning came he told the suffering friar of the incident. He consoled him and told him what would help against such a condition. This was nothing other than what he wrote in one of his sermons, which begins: "Our bed is covered with blossoms."[151]

Among the many other suffering people a layman once came to him from a distant country who said to him, "Sir, I am experiencing the most severe affliction that anyone ever suffered and no one can help me. Recently I despaired of God and was so despondent that I wanted to save myself from additional suffering by taking my own life physically and spiritually.[152] Whenever in my anguish I was about to jump into raging water and, taking a run for it, was recklessly about to drown myself, I heard a voice above me saying, 'Stop, stop! Don't kill yourself so shamefully! Go find a Dominican!'" And it named for him the servant's name, which he had never heard before, and said, "He shall help you get straightened out." He was happy and did not kill himself. He began asking around for the servant, as he had been commanded. When the servant saw what a wretched condition the man was in, he turned to the poor sufferer kindly and comforted him. He lightened his heart and taught him what he should do so that, with God's help, he never fell into such temptations again.

CHAPTER 40

Which Sufferings Are the Most Beneficial for Man and
Give God the Most Praise

His saintly daughter asked, "I would like to know which among all the kinds of sufferings are most beneficial for man and give God the most praise." He answered and said, "You should realize that one finds many kinds of sufferings that prepare a person and point the way to blessedness, if one knows how to use them properly. God sometimes ordains harsh suffering for a person without his being at all responsible. Through such suffering God either wants to test how firmly the person stands, or what he is really made of, as one frequently reads in the Old Testament; or God simply intends his own divine praise and honor, as is narrated in the gospel of the man born blind whom Christ said was innocent and then made him able to see.[153]

"Some suffering is very much the result of guilt, like the suffering of the good thief who was crucified with Christ and whom Christ made blessed because of the sincere conversion he experienced in his suffering.[154] Some suffering is not the result of being guilty of something directly connected with the suffering then being undergone. Rather, the person has some other failing because of which God ordained suffering for him. So it often happens that God punishes mindless arrogance and shows a person the way to him by a terrible catastrophe for his pride in a situation where he is completely blameless. Some afflictions are given people by God out of love, so that a person be spared still greater suffering, as happens to people to whom God gives their purgatory here on earth in the form of sickness, poverty, or the like, so that they are exempt from later sufferings. Or God will allow diabolical persons to try them so that they will be spared such an experience in the face of death. Some people suffer from true fervent love, like the martyrs who wanted to show dear God their love by their various ways of dying physically or interiorly.

"One also finds in this world much pointless suffering for which there is no comfort, as those suffer who live totally for the world for worldly reasons. They must earn their hell very bitterly, while a person suffering for God can very well help himself by suffering. Thus there are some people whom God frequently cautions to turn their path to him because he would like to be on intimate terms with them, but they resist by their apathy. God sometimes attracts them by suffering. Wherever they turn to escape God, God is there in temporal worldly misfortune and lifts them up by the hair so that they cannot escape him.

"One also finds people who experience no suffering except to the extent that they cause themselves suffering by considering of great moment things that should not be considered so. So, for example, a man oppressed by affliction was once walking by a house where he heard a woman carrying on in great distress. He thought, "Go in and console this person in her suffering." He entered and said, "Dear lady, what is happening to you that you are lamenting so?" She replied, "I dropped a needle and can't find it." He turned around and left, thinking, "You silly woman, if you had to carry one of my burdens, you would not be weeping for some needle!" Thus do some oversensitive people create suffering in various situations where none exists.

"The noblest and best suffering, however, is suffering in conformity with Christ. I mean that suffering that the heavenly Father gave his only-begotten Son and still gives to his dear friends. This should not be understood to mean that anyone is completely without guilt, except Christ who never committed a sin. Rather, just as Christ showed patience and acted in his suffering like a meek lamb among wolves, so he sometimes gives some of his dearest friends great suffering so that we, who have little capacity for suffering, might learn patience from these blessed persons and constantly to conquer evil with good with a cheerful heart.

"You should consider all this, my daughter, and should not suffer unwillingly, because wherever suffering comes from it can be beneficial for a person if he knows how to accept it all from God, bring it back to God, and together with him overcome it."

The daughter said, "This noblest suffering, which you mentioned last, that one suffers though innocent—that suffering is one few people experience. I would like to learn how a guilty and weak person can with God overcome his suffering because such a person has a twofold suffering: He has made God angry and he is outwardly tormented."

He said, "I shall tell you. I knew a man who had the following practice: Whenever out of human weakness he had committed some fault that required penance, he did what a good washerwoman does who, after wringing out her laundry and letting it soak, takes it to pure water and there, by washing it, gets everything clean and spotless that was previously dirty. Thus he would not give up before he had received the innocent flowing blood of Christ, which had been poured out in indescribable love for all sinners, so that in a spiritual manner he might have this blood pouring over himself. In this warm blood he would wash himself and remove spots. He bathed in the salutary bath of blood, just as one bathes a baby in warm water, and he did this with such heartfelt devotion and with such trusting Christian faith that it was supposed to and actually did wash away all his sins and cleanse him of all guilt with its almighty power. Thus, whatever turn things took, whether it was his fault or not, they all ended in like manner in our kind God."

CHAPTER 41

How He Drew Some Loving Hearts From Earthly Love to Love of God

At the time when the servant was still seriously pursuing the task of attracting people away from earthly love to God, he noticed that in some convents there were people who gave the appearance of being religious but beneath it had worldly hearts. Among these there was a woman who had set her heart intensely on a kind of transitory love called flirtation, which is a poison to spiritual happiness. He said to her that if she wished to lead a calm spiritual existence, she would have to give this up and take eternal Wisdom as her beloved in place of her present love. This was difficult for her to do because she was young and lively and was already engaged in such a relationship. He finally got her to the point where she was willing to break things off. But when this good will was nullified by some around her, he said to her, "Daughter, give it up! If you don't do so cheerfully, you will do it without cheer." Since she did not want to heed his well-intentioned words, he prayed to God earnestly for her, that God might draw her away either through what is pleasant or through pain. One day he went into the pulpit under his crucified Lord and, as was his custom, scourged his bare back so that the blood ran down it; and he begged God that she be tamed. And this happened in the following manner: When she returned home, a misshapen hump quickly grew on her back, making her ugly; and she had to give up of necessity what she did not want to give up for love of God.

In this same uncloistered convent there was a young and beautiful woman of noble birth who for many years occupied her heart with this same snare of the devil, passing her time vapidly with companions of all kinds. She was so blinded by it all that she constantly avoided the servant of Wisdom like a wild animal because she was afraid that he would forbid her the kind of life she was living. Now the blood sister of this girl asked him to try his luck with her to see whether he could not draw her away from her ruinous way of life to God. This seemed to him an impossible request, and he said that it seemed more possible to him that heaven come down to earth than that she change. Death would have to take her kind of life from her. She begged him with tears saying that she was convinced that God would not refuse him in whatever matter he approached him earnestly. With this kind of talk she persuaded him to promise to do it.

Since she avoided him constantly and he had no opportunity to speak with her, he noticed one day about the feast of St. Margaret that she had gone out onto the field to pick flax.[155] He sneaked out and went around the field to approach her tactfully. When she saw him getting close to her, she turned her back on him rudely, her face burning in anger, and she yelled impatiently at him, "My dear monk, what do you want from me? I advise you to get away from me. Rather than go to you to confession, I would rather have my head chopped off! Rather than follow your advice and give up my flirting, I would prefer to be buried alive. So mind your own business because you'll have no luck with me!"

The companion who was standing closest to her calmed her and scolded her, saying that he was only acting that way out of kindness. She raised her head defiantly and said, "Look, I don't want to mislead him. I want to show him by my words and conduct exactly what I have in my heart." The servant was frightened by these menacing words and unseemly behavior, blushing in shame, so dumbfounded that he could say nothing. The other sisters who had heard her screaming at him felt sorry for him and showed their disapproval. He quickly went off alone beating his retreat from her. Looking up he sighed deeply and wanted to give it all up, except there remained a certain inner urging from God that told him:

THE LIFE OF THE SERVANT

Whoever wants to attain something, be it with God or in the world, he is not allowed to give up so soon. This occurred in the afternoon.

When evening came and after supper the sisters all went out into the courtyard to dress the flax and this same girl went with them, they had to pass by the guest house where the servant was. He asked one of her companions to bring the daughter to him on some pretext or other and then to leave. This then came about, but it was not easy.

When she had come in and sat down next to him at the window, he began to sigh deeply from a full heart and said, "Alas, beautiful, gentle, chosen maiden of God, how long do you intend to leave your beautiful, lovely body and your sensitive, dear heart in the power of the hated devil? You have really been fashioned so very graceful in your whole being that it would be unfortunate if such an angelic, fine looking, noble person should be given to anyone as a beloved but to him who is noblest of all. Who should more rightfully pluck the beautiful delicate rose than he to whom it belongs? No, dear lovely maiden, open your bright falcon-like eyes and think of the beautiful love that begins here and goes on forever. Consider also what worry, unfaithfulness, sorrow and suffering in body, possessions, soul and honor those people must undergo, whether they like it or not, who pursue a worldly life, unless the sweetened poison so blinds them that they forget for a time the loss that pursues them both in time and in eternity. And so, angelic being, lovable, noble heart, direct your natural nobility to eternal nobility and give up your present way of life. I promise you by my faith that God will take you as a beloved and will always offer you trust and true love here and in eternity."

The time was ripe. These ardent words shot right through her heart and softened her so completely that she immediately raised her eyes and sighed deeply. With recklessly bold words she said to him, "Sir and dear father, I surrender myself today to God and to you. I shall say goodbye to my undisciplined and frivolous way of life this very hour and with your advice and help shall give myself to God to be his possession, serving him alone till my death." He said, "This is a happy moment. May our kind Lord be praised, who shall joyfully receive all those who come back to him!"

While the two of them were speaking so intimately to each other of God, her forsaken companions were standing outside the door

163

and were irritated by this lengthy conversation because they were afraid that she would desert their frivolous company. They called to her to hurry and finish. She got up a completely different person and, going out with him, said to them, "Dear friends, may God bless you. Let me say goodbye to you all, you and all our companions with whom I have unfortunately spent my time idly. Now I want to possess God alone and let everything else go."

The daughter began avoiding all harmful company and keeping herself detached. No matter how often one tempted her after this to return to her old way of life, it did not succeed. She preserved herself firmly and constantly with praiseworthy honor and saintly virtue, remaining with God until her death. Once later the servant went out to strengthen his new daughter in her holy life and to see whether she were suffering in any way, so that he might console her kindly. Traveling was painful for him then in his weakened condition. As he thus stepped through the deep mud and walked up the steep hills, he often raised his eyes to God, saying, "Merciful God, remember the pitiable way you made on foot to save mankind and preserve my child for me!" His companion on whom he was leaning said out of pity, "It is fitting to God's goodness that many souls be saved through you."

As he went on until he simply could not go farther and was completely exhausted, the companion said, "Father, God should see you in your weak condition and should send you a little horse to ride until you come to where people live." He answered, "Since we have both approached God, I am confident that God will let me reap the fruits of your virtue and it will happen." The servant looked around and saw on his right coming out of the woods a pretty little horse saddled and bridled and all alone. His companion cried out in joy, "Look, dear Father, look how God does not forsake you!" He said, "Son, look all over the large field. Is anyone passing by to whom it might belong?" He looked all around and saw no one but the horse trotting along and said, "Father, God has sent it to you. Mount it and ride." He answered, "Now if the horse stands still when it gets to us, then I am sure that God has sent it here to us in our need." The little horse came meekly up and stood still in front of them. He said, "Welcome, in God's name." Then his companion helped him up and let him ride, walking at some distance from him until he stopped to rest. When they came close to a village, he dismounted and put the bridle back on the horse's neck and told it to go back the way it had come. Where it then went or whose it was he was never afterward able to find out.

When the servant came to the place he had set out for, it happened one evening that he was sitting there with his spiritual children dissuading them from transitory love and urging them on to eternal love. After they left him, his heart was, as it were, on fire from his eager speech on love of God. It seemed to him that his Beloved, the object of all his thoughts and whom he urged others to love, was clearly better than all objects of love in this world. And when, while he was thus contemplating, his senses somehow faded away from him, it seemed to him in a vision that he was led onto a beautiful green meadow. A fine young man from heaven was walking with him and leading him by the hand. The young man began a song in the friar's soul and it resounded so joyously that it chased away all mere sense impressions by its overwhelming, sweet sound. It seemed to him that his heart was utterly full of ardent love and desire for God, as though it were moving out of control in his body, as though it were about to burst from being so full; and he had to put his right hand over his heart to help himself.[156] His eyes were so full that tears welled up and ran down. When the song was over, a picture was put before him in which one wanted to teach him the song, so that he might not forget it. He looked at it and saw our Lady pressing her child, eternal Wisdom, to her motherly heart. The beginning of the song was written above the head of the Child in beautiful flowery letters. But the writing was so secret that not many could read it. But those who had learned it with an abundance of feeling read it well. The writing was thus: "My heart's beloved." The servant read the writing easily. Then he looked up and looked at the young man affectionately, and he somehow had the feeling that it was quite right that the Child alone was the tender "heart's beloved" in whom one had joy without sorrow. He pressed him to the ground of his heart and then began the song again with the young man, singing it through again and again. And in the midst of this fervent heartfelt love he came to himself and found his right hand lying over his heart just as when he had placed it on his heart to protect against the wild motions.

Once he had walked very far and had thus become very weary. In the evening he came to a settlement of beguines in a distant town where he (and his companion) wanted to spend the night. There was no wine, either in the village or in the (beguine) convent. One of the good daughters came forward and said she had a small bottle of wine, about a half liter but, she said, what help would that be among so many. For there were a good twenty people including those who had come because they desired to hear God's word from his mouth. He said that the bottle should be brought to the table, and they asked that he bless it. He did this in the exalted power of the dear name of Jesus, and he started drinking because he was thirsty after walking. He passed it on and they all drank. The little bottle was placed in plain sight where all saw it without anyone pouring any water or wine into it, because there was no other wine there. Again and again they drank big swallows out of this bottle and were so desirous to hear God's word from him that no one noticed the divine miracle. When at last they came to themselves and recognized the mighty power of God in the increase of the beverage, they began to praise God and wanted to attribute the event to the sanctity of the servant. But he did not want to allow this and said, "Children, this is not my work. God has allowed this pure group to enjoy the fruits of its good faith and has satisfied both its physical and spiritual thirst."

CHAPTER 42

Some Suffering Persons Who Followed the Servant
With Special Loyalty

In a certain town there were two persons of superior holiness who knew him well. The spiritual paths of these two friends of God were quite different. The one woman was of a high social class and blessed by God's sweetness. The other was not of a high social class, and God visited constant suffering on her. When they both died, the servant would have liked to know from God how different their reward was in the other world since their lives were so dissimilar on earth. One morning the one who had been of high social rank appeared to him and told him that she was still in purgatory. When he asked how that could be, she said she thought that she had acquired no other guilt except that, because of her social superiority, some bit of spiritual arrogance had entered into her and she had not rid herself of it quickly enough; but her suffering should soon be at an

166

end. The other woman, who had been oppressed and in anguish, went straight to God.

The servant's mother had also experienced much suffering all her days. This came about because of the vexing dissimilarity between her and her husband. She was full of God and hence would have liked to live in a religious manner. He was full of the world and opposed this with unrelenting severity. From this arose the suffering. She had the custom of attaching all her sufferings to the bitter sufferings of Christ and thereby overcoming her own sufferings. She confessed to her son before her death that for thirty years she had not attended mass without weeping bitterly because of the sincere compassion she had for the torments endured by our Lord and his devoted Mother. She also told him that she had once become ill with longing from the immense love she had for God and that she lay in bed a good twelve weeks so pitifully and so intensely pining for God that the doctors became aware of it and were edified by her good example.

Once she went into the cathedral at the beginning of lent where the descent from the cross stood carved in wood over an altar. In front of this piece of art she somehow felt the intense pain that the gentle Mother had felt beneath the cross. Because of this anguish the good woman suffered so much pain out of sympathy that her heart palpably burst, as it were, within her, so that she sank down to the ground in a faint and could neither see nor speak. After she had been helped home, she lay sick until three o'clock on Good Friday when she died as the passion was being read.

At this same time her son, the servant, was studying in Cologne. She appeared to him in a vision and said with great joy, "My child, love God and trust in him completely. He will never, ever forsake you in any adversity. Look, I have departed from this world but am not dead. I shall live forever in God's presence." She gave him a motherly kiss on the mouth, blessed him lovingly, and disappeared. He began to weep and called after her, "O dear saintly mother of mine, be true to me before God." And thus weeping and sighing he came to himself.

When he was young and was still in his studies, God provided him once with a dear, holy companion. Once, as they were talking heart to heart about spiritual matters, the companion asked him for the sake of their friendship to show him and let him see the beloved name of Jesus that he had engraved over his heart. He did not want to do this, but seeing the companion's serious piety, the request was enough for him. He opened his clothes over his heart and let him see the precious sign, as he had wished. But this was not enough for his companion. When he had seen it visibly present there on his body right over his heart, he ran his hand over it and then his face, touching it with his mouth. He wept from his heart with devotion, and the tears welled up and flowed over the servant's heart. After this he kept the name hidden and never wanted to let anyone see it except for one chosen friend of God to whom God allowed it. He gazed upon it with the same devotion as the other person had.

When the two dear companions had spent several years together in spiritual harmony and were supposed to go separate ways, they gave each other their blessing in friendship and made a pact between them that whoever died first, the other one would remain his loyal friend after his death. He would celebrate two masses for him every week for a year—on Mondays a *requiem* and on Fridays a mass of the passion of our Lord. Many years later the friend of the servant died first, and he forgot about the promise of the masses just mentioned. However, he remembered him (in prayers) faithfully otherwise. One morning, as he sat in his chapel recollected, the friend came and stood before him in a vision. He said, scolding severely, "Friend, you have been unfaithful. Oh, how you have forgotten me!" The servant replied, "But I remember you every day in my masses." The friend said, "That is not enough. Fulfill your promise about masses so that the innocent blood (of Christ) might rain down over me and extinguish the terrible fire. Then I shall quickly be freed from purgatory." The servant did this then with great loyalty and regretted very much his forgetting, and the friend was quickly helped.

CHAPTER 43

How Christ Appeared to Him in the Form of a Seraph and Taught Him How to Suffer

Once when the servant had turned to God very earnestly and begged that he teach him how to suffer, there appeared to him in a spiritual vision the likeness of the crucified Christ in the form of a seraph. This angelic seraph had six wings. With two wings it covered its head; with two it covered its feet; and two it used for flying. On the two bottom wings was written: "Receive suffering willingly." On the middle ones: "Bear suffering patiently." On the top ones: "Learn to suffer as Christ did."[157]

He told a saintly friend about this delightful vision. She was a person of great holiness. She replied, "Know this for certain. New suffering is again being prepared for you by God and you must endure it." He asked what kind of sufferings these would be. She said, "You will have to be raised to the rank of superior so that those who hold you in disfavor can better strike you and drag you down. Therefore, arm yourself with patience, as is shown to you by the seraph." He sighed and was on the lookout for the new storm coming. And it really happened, as this holy person had said.

It happened at this very time that they were having years of austerity,[158] and the priory in which he lived was not receiving any bread or wine and had accumulated large debts. The friars decided all together to choose the servant as prior during the great austerity, no matter how irksome or repugnant he found it. For he knew very well that new suffering was thus being readied for him. On his first day he had a chapter meeting called and urged them to call upon St. Dominic because he had promised his friars, if they called upon him in times of need, he would come to their aid. In the chapter meeting two friars sitting next to each other were whispering to each other. The one said to the other derisively, "What a foolish man this prior is, to order us to go to God in our need. Does he think that God will open up heaven and send food and drink down to us?" The other friar said, "He is not the only fool. All of us are fools for choosing him as prior. We all knew beforehand that he is incapable in earthly matters and can only gape up at heaven." There were many scoffing judgments made about him.

The next morning he had the mass of St. Dominic sung, that he might bring them supplies. As he was standing in the choir deep in thought, the porter came and called him out to a rich canon, with whom he was particularly good friends.[159] The canon said to him, "Dear sir, you are not well-versed in temporal matters and I was inwardly admonished by God last night to help you in his stead. For a start I am bringing you twenty pounds of Constance pennies. Trust in God; he will not forsake you." The servant was happy, took the money, and had grain and wine bought. And God helped them, as did St. Dominic, all the time he was prior, so that supplies were always there. He paid everything up, so that nothing was left of the debts.

This same canon already mentioned, as he lay on his deathbed, willed large amounts of money for the good of his soul to this place and that where he wished to be generous. Then he sent for the servant, who was then prior, and handed over to him a number of florins to be distributed at other places among poor friends of God who had used up their strength in austere practices. The servant did not want to take them because he was afraid of destructive consequences, which then actually occurred. Finally he was persuaded to take it. He went abroad and distributed the money as he had promised, here and there, where he was sure it would be most beneficial for the benefactor's soul. He did this with careful accountability and with his superiors checking it all. Because of the affair he experienced much suffering.

The canon had an illegitimate son, who had not turned out well. He had used up what the canon had given him, and in his perversity he took up things that were ruinous for him. He would have liked to have that money. Since he could not get it, he called the servant his enemy and let him know by a sworn oath that when he met up with him he would kill him. No others could hinder this disconcerting enmity, no matter how often they tried. He simply wanted to kill him. The poor servant was long in anguish and distress and did not dare to venture forth here or there for fear of being murdered by this ruthless man. He often raised his eyes to God and said with a sigh within, "O God, what wretched death do you have in store for me?" His anguish was the more intense because a short time earlier in another town a respected friar had been brutally murdered in a similar situation. Because of the ruthlessness of this savage man, the poor friar had no one who wanted or dared to protect him from this anguish. He turned to his highest Lord who freed him from the ruthless man by cutting short his young and violent life, and he died.

To this trial there was added another bitter suffering. There was a whole parish that the canon had remembered very generously. But it was not enough for them and they all harbored great dislike for the friar because he had not seen that they got all the money. He was miserably persecuted by them for this and was brought before civil and church authorities. His reputation was carried by misrepresentation of his guilt far into the country, and in the eyes of men he was dishonored in matters of which he was innocent before God. As soon as this miserable affair had been put to rest for a while, it would be brought up again and again. This went on for many years until the poor man had been well-purified because of it.

In this same period this same departed canon appeared before him in a vision wearing a beautiful garment, green and full of red roses all over. He said to him that things were well with him in the other world, and he asked the servant to endure patiently this great injustice for which he was being blamed, because God intended to repay him for it all. The servant asked him what the beautiful garments meant. He said, "The red roses on a green field—that is your patient suffering. You have clothed me with it and because of this God wants to clothe you eternally with himself."

CHAPTER 44

How Steadfastly One Must Fight Who Would Attain the Spiritual Prize

Immediately after beginning,[160] it was the intention and sincere wish of the servant to be found pleasing in God's eyes in an especially noble way, but without suffering or hard work. It once happened that he went out preaching across the land. And he got on board a public boat on the Lake of Constance where there sat among others an imposing young knight wearing courtly attire. He went over to the squire and asked him whose vassal he was. He answered, "I go forth on quests and gather the lords together for courtly activities. There they engage in swordplay and tournaments and serve beautiful ladies. Whoever succeeds in this the best is given honor and is rewarded." He asked, "What is the reward?" The knight said, "The most beautiful lady present puts a gold ring on his hand." Then he asked, "Tell me, dear sir, what does one have to do to attain the honor and the ring?" He said, "The one who suffers the most blows and sallies and does not falter but rather displays boldness and manliness, who sits firmly (in the saddle) and lets the blows rain on him—he receives the prize." He then asked, "Now tell me: if someone were bold during the first encounter, would that be enough?" He said, "No, he has to stand firm through the whole tournament, even if he is struck so that fire shoots out of his eyes and blood pours out of his mouth and nose. All this he must endure if he is to win praise." He asked further, "Dear friend, does he dare weep or act sad when he is so severely struck?" He answered, "No, even if his heart sinks within him, as happens to many, he can do nothing of the kind but must act as though nothing were wrong. He must act in a cheerful and elegant manner; otherwise, he would be mocked and would lose honor and the ring."

The servant was deeply affected within himself by this conversation. Sighing from the heart within him he said, "Noble sir, if the knights of this world have to take such sufferings upon themselves for so small a reward, which is nothing in itself, dear God, how just it then is that one must suffer many more trials for the eternal prize! O gentle Lord, if only I were worthy of becoming your spiritual knight. Beautiful, comely, eternal Wisdom, whose riches of grace find no equal in all the lands, if only my soul could receive a ring from you! Indeed, for that I would be willing to suffer whatever you wanted." And he began to weep because of the intense emotion that had come over him.

When he came to the town that was his destination, God visited him with so much serious suffering visible to all that the poor man almost gave up on God, and many an eye was wet out of pity for him. He forgot all about venturesome knighthood and the promises he made to God in his resolve about spiritual knighthood. He became sad and irritable with God, asking what he was blaming him for and why he was sending him such suffering. When the next morning arrived, calm entered his soul and with his senses withdrawn something spoke thus within him: "How is it now with your outstanding knightly endeavors? What good is a knight of straw and a man made of cloth? Great daring in good times and then giving up in bad times—no one has ever won the ring you long for that way." He answered and said, "O Lord, the tournaments that one has to endure for you are much too long and difficult." He received the answer: "But the praise, honor and ring of the knights that are honored by me are constant and last forever." The servant was deeply struck by this and said very humbly, "Lord, I was wrong, but allow me to weep in my misery, for my heart is so full." He said, "You miserable creature! Are you going to weep like a woman? You are disgracing yourself at the court of heaven. Wipe your eyes and act cheerful so that neither God nor man notice that you have wept because of your suffering." He began to laugh, but tears still ran down his cheeks, and he promised God that he did not intend to weep anymore, so that he might win the spiritual ring.

Once, when the servant was preaching with great zeal in Cologne, a beginner was sitting there listening who had just recently turned to God. When this suffering woman looked at him intently, she saw with her inner eyes that his face began to take on a pleasing brilliance. Three times it became like the dazzling sun when it shines its brightest. His face became thereby so limpid that she saw herself in it. This apparition comforted her very much in her suffering and confirmed her in her holy way of life.

CHAPTER 45

The Beloved Name of Jesus

The servant of eternal Wisdom once made a journey from the high country down to Aachen to our Lady.[161] When he returned home, our Lady appeared to a very holy woman and said to her, "Look, the servant of my Child has come and has zealously spread the sweet name of Jesus far and wide, just as my Son's disciples spread it in their time. And just as they had the desire to proclaim this name to all men in faith, so too he works diligently to enkindle with new love all cold hearts with this same name of Jesus. Therefore after his death he shall receive with them eternal reward." Later this same holy woman looked at our Lady and saw that she had a beautiful candle in her hand. It burned so nicely that it shined through the whole world. And written all around on the candle was the name JESUS. Our Lady said to this person, "Look, this burning candle signifies the name *Jesus* because he truly illumines all hearts that receive his name with devotion, honor him and zealously carry him with them. And my Child has chosen the servant for the task of enkindling with desire many hearts through his name and leading them to their eternal happiness."

When this aforementioned holy daughter noticed repeatedly that her spiritual father had such great devotion to and firm faith in the beloved name of Jesus, which he carried over his heart, she developed a special love for it; and she piously sewed this same name of Jesus in red silk onto a small piece of cloth in this form, IHS, which

173

she herself intended to wear secretly. She repeated this countless times and brought it about that the servant put them all over his bare breast. She would then send them all over, with a religious blessing to his spiritual children. She was informed by God: Whoever thus wore this name and recited an Our Father daily for God's honor would be treated kindly by God, and God would give him his grace on his final journey.

Such austere practices and the divine example of Jesus Christ and his dear friends formed the beginning for this holy daughter.[162]

CHAPTER 46

Clear Distinction Between True and False Reasoning
In Some People

"Just like the eagle urging its young to fly, etc."[163]

After this holy daughter had been formed according to the good teaching of her spiritual father in every kind of holiness based on examples for the exterior man, just like a soft piece of wax near the fire that is able to take on the form of the seal, and had imitated for a long time the exemplary life of Christ, who is the surest way, her spiritual father wrote to her as follows:

Dear daughter, it is now time that you lift yourself out of the nest of consoling examples suited for a beginner and proceed to something more perfect. Do as the young maturing eagle does: With your well-developed wings, that is, the higher powers of your soul, raise yourself aloft to the heights of contemplative nobility of a blessed life of perfection. Do you not know that Christ said to his disciples, who were too firmly attached to his physical presence, "It is beneficial for you that I leave you if you are to become capable of receiving the spirit"?[164] The exercises mentioned already were good preparation for proceeding through the wastes of a brutish existence, which one does not reflect upon, to the promised land of a pure and peaceful heart in which blessedness begins here and continues eternally in the other world. And so that the lofty path of intellect be the more familiar to you, I shall light the way for you with the light of correct judgment. If you grasp well how to judge, you cannot go astray, no matter how high you soar in your thoughts.

Now remember: One finds two kinds of persons who appear

good. Some lead a life based on reason, and others one not based on reason. The first kind are persons who direct their reason in such a way that all their thoughts, actions and omissions are governed by judgments considered correct by holy Christianity for the praise of God and the tranquil peace of all other people. They are careful with their words and conduct so that they do not thereby give anyone offense, unless someone does so because of some fault in himself, as often happens. By conducting themselves so carefully and living so blessedly, they demonstrate the nature and name of reason. Theirs is a praiseworthy, godlike reason because it shines back into them with hidden truth, as heaven shines in its brilliant stars. But the people appearing to be good, but who do not live according to reason, are those who aim only at themselves with their nature unbroken, using their reason only to look at things— probingly inspecting them—and then speak arrogantly about them in front of uninformed people, completely ignoring the fact that unbefitting words or deeds might be the consequence. The light of reason in these people is directed outward but not inward, just like rotten wood that in poor light looks like something that it really is not. The inner light and external conduct of these people show themselves everywhere to be unlike him whom they should claim to be like.

These people can be recognized to some extent by their free and careless manner of speaking. Let us take just one of their sayings according to which one can evaluate all the others. One of them has stated in writing: "The just man does not have to avoid obstacles."[165] This saying and others like it appear to mean something for some people who view things perversely, but for those seeing them rightly they are not praiseworthy, not for those who correctly perceive what is contained in them. And this is evident in the above-quoted saying, which states that the just man does not need to avoid any obstacles. Now what is a just person, or what is an obstacle? A just person, as it is generally understood in speaking, is a just person understood according to his nature. "Just" does not exist as a separate entity; it must reside in some substance, which is in this case the just *person*. What is an obstacle? It is sin, which separates man from God. Should then a just person not shun or avoid an obstacle, that is, a sin? Such a saying is purely wrong and utterly contrary to reason. Certainly it is in some sense true for a just person and for everything else insofar as they are all the same with no formal

175

difference in their eternal uncreatedness in God's intellect, which is above being.[166] However, in this simple ground, which is above being, the just person is not a person of flesh and blood because there is no corporality in the Godhead. There is also no obstacle there. But everyone discovers that outside of this ground he is this or that person. Here, one is mortal; there, one is not. Here one is always in one's frail created (human) nature where one indeed has to avoid all damaging obstacles. If I were to be annihilated in my consciousness and thus were to know nothing of myself, and if I wanted to perform all my material actions[167] with no distinction between God and myself, as though uncreated Being were performing them, that would be a mistake to end all mistakes.

And thus one can note that such a saying really contains no true rationality. One does not thereby intend to reject rational teaching or rationally well-considered sayings or writings, which refine a person and show him in well-ordered fashion the path to intellectual truth, even if there are not many who understand them. For it is a well-known fact that faced with crass blindness and the unenlightened animal nature (in a human being) one cannot be careful enough in speaking.

The daughter said: God be praised for this valuable distinction! I would like to hear the distinction between true reasoning and capricious reasoning, and between false and true detachment.

The servant said:

CHAPTER 47

The Distinction Between Well-ordered and Capricious Reasoning

After the first battles that arise when one checks the flesh and passions, a person comes to a deep pool in which many go under. This is capricious reasoning. How is this to be understood? I call that capricious reasoning when a person is freed from crass sinfulness and is released from images to which he was attached, and freely lifts himself above time and place, which previously bound him so that he could not at all enjoy his inborn nobility. But when the eye of the intellect begins to open and a person is searching to fulfill a different and better kind of pleasure, namely, (knowledge of) the truth, enjoyment of divine blessedness, the sight of the

176

present "now" of eternity, and the like, and when the created intellect begins to understand a bit the eternal uncreated intellect in itself and in all things, it then in some strange way happens to a person that he looks at himself—what he was before, and what he now is—and he realizes that before he was miserable, godless and in need, completely blind and far from God. But now it seems to him he is filled with God and there is nothing that is not God; further, God and all things are a simple one. He grasps things too quickly, not taking enough time, and he becomes unstable, like fermenting cider that has not yet settled. He rushes to that which he understands or what is presented injudiciously to him by someone who is in the same situation. He is supposed to listen to this person alone and to no one else.[168] Then he views everything as it pleases his thinking; and things elude his grasp as they really are in themselves, be it hell, heaven, devil or angel,[169] because such persons have only grasped God in things and have not penetrated the things with knowledge that distinguishes them in their ground, things according to their permanence or transitoriness. These people are like bees making honey. When they mature and, for the first time, storm out of the hive, they fly confused this way and that and do not know where to go. Some fly off wrong and are lost, but others return to the hive in proper fashion. This is what happens to these people. When they see God with their unformed intellect as all in all according to their undeveloped intellect, they want to leave this or that but do not know how.[170] It is certainly true that everything must be removed from people if they are to become perfect, but they do not yet understand how this ridding self of everything is to take place.

Inappropriately, they want to abandon this and that and perceive themselves and all things as God. They want to act as God, without distinction. This mistake arises either because of unschooled simplicity or because of a duplicity that has not been completely rooted out. And so many a person thinks he has grasped everything when he can leave and abandon himself, but this is not the case, because he has only crept over the moat of the as-yet-unstormed fortress and is hiding behind the protecting wall in secret and still cannot withdraw further through the proper abandoning of his spiritual nature to a true poverty in which all foreign objects somehow disappear. Even the ever-existing, simple Godhead disappears through one's undisturbed quietude, as shall be explained below with careful distinctions.[171]

Notice, this is the point at which many people are secretly stalled for many a year, so that they cannot move in either direction. But I shall show you the way to good judgment, so that you cannot go astray.

CHAPTER 48

The Right Distinction Between True and False Detachment

You should know that there are three kinds of withdrawing.[172] The first kind is complete withdrawal, as when a thing so ceases to exist that there is nothing more of it, like a shadow passing away and becoming nothing. This is not how the spirit of a man withdraws when it departs.[173] By spirit here we mean a rational soul. It remains forever because of the nobility of its godlike intellectual powers, for God is an intelligence above being according to which the soul has been formed. Therefore it is impossible for it to cease to exist, as our mortal body does when it ceases to exist.

A second kind of withdrawal is called half-withdrawal, which requires its own place in time, as happens when a person is transported in contemplation into the naked Godhead, like St. Paul,[174] or even differently, as when a person in a manner that cannot be imagined is freed and withdraws from himself. But this is not permanent. When Paul returned, he found himself to be the same Paul, a man as he always had been.

One speaks also of a borrowed withdrawal, when a person by giving up his free will surrenders himself to God in every moment where he finds himself, as though he knew nothing of himself and God alone is the Lord. This withdrawal also cannot be permanent as long as body and soul are together; for when a person has forsaken himself completely and believes he has withdrawn into God as to his individuality, never to be restored to himself, at that moment he and his knavish servant suddenly return to themselves.[175] And he is the same as he was before and must forsake himself again and again. Anyone who intended to act from this weak detachment would be very wrong. This much is certainly true: To the extent that a person becomes a stranger to himself and is engaged in withdrawing, he is standing firm in genuine truth.

One should know further that there are two kinds of detachment.

178

One is called preceding detachment, the other is called subsequent detachment. Note what these are by this example. A thief has in him an urge to steal because he is evil by nature. His good sense contradicts this: You should not do it; it is wrong. If the thief were to go out from himself and turn himself over to his good sense, this would be preceding detachment, which is the noblest kind because he would remain innocent. But when he does not want to abandon himself in the matter and gives the evil in him free rein, afterward when he is caught and sees that he will have to hang, then subsequent detachment arises in that he goes to his death resigned because he cannot do anything else. This detachment is also good and leads him to heaven, but the other kind was incomparably nobler and better.

Therefore one should not take all risks and remain in wrong behavior, as some foolish people claim: that a person who wants to achieve perfect detachment must wade through all forms of wrong. That is wrong because a person who out of bravado throws himself into a dirty puddle thinking that he will become more beautiful afterward is a fool. This is why the most prudent of the friends of God keep this resolve, that they forsake themselves completely and remain constantly in preceding detachment and never take it back, as far as human weakness allows. When this is not what happens, they are distressed. Certainly they are ahead of other people in that they are more adept at ridding themselves of obstacles, because from this very distress there arises subsequent detachment, which quickly restores a person where he should be; that is, where a person finds himself to be still a human being and puts up with himself as such for the glory of God. And this subsequent detachment is sometimes also beneficial because of being recognized for what it is. And then the distress as such disappears, and (a person) simply gives birth to himself again into the same thing and becomes the same thing as he always was from the beginning.

If it were to happen that some such imperfect person through duplicity wanted to make an excuse for himself and were to say, "What does it matter if a person were to return to his earlier condition accidentally and commit some sins externally? Does not the substance of the person remain the same in spite of such a return?" I would then say that this person does not understand himself and does not realize what he is saying. All learned professors, if they can understand anything, have a knowledge of what the name "accident" means. Accident is that which arises and passes away in the essence of a substance without destroying the substance, like color on a board. This is not the case here because body and soul, which they in their ignorance call accidents, are both essential parts that give man being and are not just part of him as accidents. Therefore, everyone has the ability to practice virtue or vice by knowing how to leave himself or take himself back. For the annihilation of the spirit, with its withdrawal into the simple Godhead, and all its nobility and perfection, is not to be understood as a changing of its own nature or what it is into that same thing that God is, but which man, because of his insufficiency, does not realize (is happening): nor (does it mean) that man becomes God and ceases to exist as a separate being; rather, it is due to his being carried off in rapture and to forgetting himself in contemplation. And thus in a rapture the spirit does really withdraw, and here the spirit comes into its own because God has become all things for it and all things have somehow become God for it. All things respond to it in the manner they are in God and yet each thing remains what it is in its natural essence. But an ignorant blindness or an untrained mind cannot or will not let this correct explanation come to its confused attention.

On the basis of this clear explanation you are now able to understand the following insightful sayings and teachings that direct man away from his coarseness and toward his highest blessedness.

CHAPTER 49

A Sensible Introduction for the Outer Man
to His Inwardness

Keep your conduct discreet and do not be impetuous in word or deed.

Satisfy the truth simply; whatever happens, do not always be ready to help yourself, for a person who is too intent on helping himself will not be helped by the truth.

When you are with other people, let whatever you see or hear go unheeded and concentrate only on what has been revealed to you.

Strive to give your reason prominence in your actions because all evil comes from the overhasty impulsiveness of the senses.

One should not judge pleasure according to the senses. One should judge it according to truth.

God does not want to rob us of pleasure. He wants to arouse in us the desire for infinity.

In the most resolute submission one is elevated the most.

Whoever wants to be part of what is most interior must rid himself of all multiplicity. One must resolve to disregard everything that is not the One.[176]

Wherever human nature works on its own, there is toil, suffering and a darkening of reason.

When I find myself to be one, as I should be and the everything I should be, what could cause more joy?

A person should live free of images and possessiveness. This results in the most joy.

What is the spiritual practice of a completely detached person? Losing self.

Whenever a person loves an image or an individual, then accident is loving an accident.[177] This is wrong. Still, I should persevere in this until it fades away. There is something simple within, and there one does not love the presence of an image; rather, there man is one with himself and all things. And that is God.

He who forsakes himself with respect to impulsive desires of the senses has achieved conquest of self. Otherwise one is furthering the senses.

Endure in joy and suffering because a person holding himself in check progresses more in one year than an impulsive person does in three.

If you want to be of benefit to all creatures, turn away from all creatures.

A person cannot grasp things. Be patient and things will grasp you.

Strive to avoid impulsive actions, which are not in accord with your model.

One should be on the alert for inclination that goes out toward all things and undermines simple truth.

If you do not want to bear yourself in simplicity, you shall have to bear yourself in multiplicity.

Live as though there were no other creature on earth but you. Say, "As you are to me, I cannot be to you." Nature loves nature and considers only itself.

THE EXEMPLAR

The nature of some people has not been broken enough, and in this case the outer man remains present outside.

The power to renounce gives one more power than to possess things.

One disorder calls forth another.

See to it that your nature is not weighed down and that the outer man conforms to the inner man.

Be attentive to the inner man. This is important for the exterior and the interior life.

For inner detachment it is important always to have nature under rein.

One should always stay aware so that nature does not go astray.

You complain that you are still too caught up in external acts and are too far from true detachment and true patience. Do not give up. The nearer you come, the better.

A root of all sin and a clouding of all truth is transitory love.

The defeat of the senses means the ascent of truth.

When the powers (of the soul) are freed and the elements are purified, the powers somehow find themselves in their eternal goal because they have been directed there by their capacities. All powers have only one purpose and one function: to satisfy eternal Truth.

Nothing gives pleasure except that which conforms to the inmost ground of divine nature.

One finds people who have had an inner urge and have not followed it. Their inner and outer selves are far apart, and this is the weakness of many people.

Nature always has rich possibilities. The more it goes away, the farther it is. The more it enters within, the closer it is.

He who has discovered his own abundance performs all external functions the better for it.

If one connects nature to truth while nature is still pure, then it is in a better position to give direction outwardly. Otherwise, it withdraws into time and cannot give direction to anything.

Purity, understanding and virtue make one rich in the natural realm. It sometimes happens, when those having such qualities withdraw, they become less before all creatures; and when this turns out well, they are directed to what is more perfect.

What is it that drives a person to seek evil ways? It is the search for satiety. This one finds only in forsaking, not in evil ways.

THE LIFE OF THE SERVANT

Some people fall into culpable sadness because they are not always carefully alert to their selves in order to guard themselves against punishable deeds in all areas.

For a friend of God to be without victory is to have conquered.

Remain in yourself. Going out after other things presents itself as a necessity, but it is really an excuse.

It is wrong to begin many things and not bring any to completion. One should stop completely until one has determined whether God or nature is the cause.

Strive to let nature perform its works out of its own ground and not from other causes.

A truly detached person should strive for four things. 1. To be completely upright in his conduct so that things flow from him without his activity. 2. To be proper and calm in his senses and not casting about—that causes images to be drawn within one—so that the inner senses might have a leisurely journey. 3. Not to be attached. One should be careful not to allow anything mixed with impurity to arise. 4. Not to be quarrelsome, but kind to those through whom God wants to help one withdraw.

Remain firm in yourself until you are taken out of yourself without your doing it yourself.

See whether intimate contact with good people arises from whim or simplicity. The first is too often the case.

Do not press yourself on anyone too much. Where the most importunity is, there one is sometimes the least pleasing. A humble and restrained manner of conduct is proper for you. Whenever someone does not act in accordance with what sort he is, it does not well suit him.

Blessed the man who is simple in word and behavior. The more complicated one's behavior and words are, the more they are unessential.

Keep yourself within and be like the (divine) Nothing. Otherwise you shall suffer.

Some people act from their feelings in good times and bad, but in so doing one should not consider oneself.

In resignation all things are accomplished. When Christ said, "Into your hands (I commend my spirit),"[178] there followed immediately, "It has been accomplished."[179]

God and the devil are in man. Wanting to lead oneself or giving up one's own will determines the difference.

THE EXEMPLAR

Whichever person would want to have constant peace would get caught up in that just as he would in other things.

Whoever has inwardness in outward affairs, his inwardness will become more inward than someone's whose inwardness is only in inward matters.

It is good that a person not lead himself in anything, and one is progressing well for whom things correspond to the images in the highest part (of the soul).

There are many more rational people than simple people. People are called rational if reason leads them, but the multiplicity of things as they are in themselves disappears for simplicity because of simplicity's quiet nature. Its manner of seeing is different. Simplicity becomes somehow the very being of the simple person. And he is an instrument and a child (of God).

Whoever wants to have all things should become utter nothing to himself and all things.

Alas, how blessed is the person who remains steadfast in the face of multiplicity. What an intimate contact (with God) he must experience!

A good opinion (of self) often hinders true union.

The eye should not look outward unless it carries images forth.

The part (of us) that is from Adam should be borne as readily as that by which we are blessed.

A detached person forms no unhappiness within himself.

That a man still complains and is sad arises completely from sin. One must drive it out.

All who use freedom wrongly take themselves as a model.

To want to be free of a just obligation is the most dangerous freedom one can have.

A detached person must be freed from the forms of creatures, formed with Christ, and transformed in the Godhead.

Whoever takes himself in Christ leaves all things in their (proper) order.

When a man becomes a man in Christ and has lost himself to himself, he is doing well.

When a person wants to dwell in the truth, his self-abandonment lights up his interior and he notices that a creature is still within him he wanted to have gone. He bears himself in patience and sees that he is really not yet free of things. To endure oneself thus is to become simple. Withdrawing causes weariness; in turning away it disappears.

What is the goal of a truly detached person in all things? It is to sink away from self, and with the self all things sink away.

What is the smallest obstacle? A thought. What is the greatest obstacle? When the soul remains under the control of its own will.

For a detached person no hour should pass unexamined.

A detached person should not constantly be looking to see what he needs. He should look to see what he can do without.

When a detached person wants to become submissive to the truth, he should strive to restrain his senses, for God is a spirit. 2. He should see whether he has put obstacles in his own way. 3. He should determine whether he has been led by some encroachment on the part of his self. 4. And in this light he should realize the presence of the whole divine being in him and that he is simply its instrument.

To the extent that a person turns away from himself and from all created things, he will become one and blessed.

If you want to be a detached person, strive to be constantly the same in abandoning what is yours, no matter how God treats you with regard to himself or with regard to creatures, in joy or in sorrow.

Close your senses to all forms you encounter.

Free yourself from everything your external judgment chooses, which binds your will and causes pleasure to your memory.

Persist in nothing that is not God.

When you are present where someone is committing a sin or an impropriety, neither add anything of your own nor retain anything of it.

Who dwells always by himself gains a rich fortune indeed.

The enjoyment of nature by a detached person should be a limited necessary use in spiritual works, which bring about a liberating rejection of things.

The degree to which a person is detached determines to what extent he is saddened by things passing him by. The following happened to a half-detached person: When he was too attached to his own moods, he was told, "You should be more concerned about me and not about yourself. If you know that I am fine, you should not care how you are feeling."

A detached person, when he has locked himself within his inner fortress with his senses turned inward—the less support he finds within himself, the worse will be his experience within. Thus he will more quickly die (to himself) and more swiftly pass through.

Letting one's senses wander about far and wide removes a person from inwardness. See to it that you take up no business that carries you outward. When such business is looking for you, do not let it find you. Turn quickly inward to yourself.

Natural life manifests itself in movement and the activity of the senses. For anyone forsaking himself and losing himself, supernatural life begins in stillness.

Some people ascend without difficulty, but they do not long remain there.

Put yourself in the state of utter detachment. Immoderate desire for this, in being too much, could be a hidden obstacle to this end.

A detached person should so tame all the powers of his soul that, when he looks within himself, the (divine) majesty appears.

A detached person remains unconcerned about himself, as though he knew nothing about himself; for because God is there in him, all things are very well-ordered.

Show concern also for your outer man, that he be united to the inner man with all sensual appetites in subjection.

A return to detachment is often more pleasing to God than selfish constancy (in this state).

Recollect your soul from the outer senses when these have scattered themselves upon the diversity of external things.

Enter within yourself again, turn again back to your oneness of purpose and let God be your pleasure.

Remain steadfast and never be content until, though still on earth, you have struggled through to the everpresent now of eternity, to the extent this is possible for frail human nature.

CHAPTER 50

*Sublime Matters About Which the Well-versed Daughter
Inquired of Her Spiritual Father*

After this rational introduction for the outer man to what is within, the sublime powers in the spirit of the daughter were stimulated, and she wondered whether she should yet dare to ask about these same sublime powers. He said, "Certainly you should, because you have correctly been drawn past the actual obstacles, and therefore your highly refined intellect is now permitted to ask about sublime matters. Ask whatever you want." His daughter said, "Tell me what is God or where is he or how does he exist. That is to say, how is he one and yet three?"

He said: God knows, these are sublime matters. As to the first question—what God is—you should know that all the learned theologians that ever were cannot explain this completely because he is above all thought and intellect. And yet a diligent person does gain some knowledge of God by studiously searching, but (it is) knowledge quite distant in its manner from God himself. Knowing God comprises man's highest beatitude.[180] In this manner some virtuous pagan thinkers sought him in earlier times; foremost among these was the great mind of Aristotle. He pondered the course of nature and who that might be who is the Lord of nature. He sought him diligently and found him. He proves from the order found in nature that there must necessarily be one single Ruler and Lord of all creatures, and we call him God.

Concerning this God and Lord, we have the knowledge that he is a subsisting being, that he is eternal, without a before or after, that he is one, immutable, non-corporeal, essentially a spirit whose being is his living and acting, whose subsistent intellect knows all things as they are in him and with him, whose delight and joy is his own unfathomable being, and who, for himself and for all those who shall enjoy him in the beatific vision, is a supernatural, ineffable, bliss-bringing happiness.

His daughter looked up and said, "This is certainly a delight to hear. It touches the heart and raises the spirit up beyond itself. More, dear father, tell me more of this!"

He said: Note this. The divine being we have been describing is subsisting intellect that cannot be seen by mortal eye as it is in itself. One can see it very well in its effects, just as one recognizes a good master by examining his work. As Paul said, "Creatures are like a mirror in which God is reflected."[181] And this knowledge is called speculating.[182]

Now let us stay a while here and let us speculate on the exalted worthy Master in his work. Look beyond you and around you to the four corners of the earth, how far, how high the beautiful heavens are in their swift course, and how nobly their Master has adorned them with the seven planets,[183] each of which, except for the moon, is much greater than the whole earth, and how he is glorified by the countless number of bright stars. Oh, the beautiful sun, when it arises cloudless and bright in the summer, what fruits and other good things it gives evenly to the earth! How beautifully the meadow turns green, how leaf and grass surge forth. The pretty flowers laugh. Forest, heath and meadows echo the delightful songs of the nightingale and tiny birds. All the animals that had crept away from the nasty winter come forth, rejoice and join together, just as among humankind young and old are happy with delightful cheerfulness.[184] O gentle God, if you are so lovely in your creatures, how utterly beautiful and lovely you are then in yourself!

Look further, I ask you. Examine the four elements—earth, water, air and fire—and the utter miracle that in them are all sorts of different men, animals, birds, fish and wonders of the sea. Whatever is contained in them all calls out together: "Glory and honor to the unfathomable, marvelous immensity that is in you. Lord, who guards over all this, who gives it to eat? You furnish it all, to each in its own way, great and small, rich and poor. You, God, do this. You, God, are truly God!

Now, daughter, you have found your God for whom your heart has long been searching. Now look up with eager eyes, with smiling face, with your heart leaping up. Look at him and embrace him with the arms of your soul and heart reaching out infinitely. Thank him and praise him, this noble Ruler of all creatures. From the "speculating" there soon arises in a sensitive person a heartfelt jubilation.[185] Jubilation is a joy the tongue cannot describe, yet it rushes mightily through heart and soul.

Look, I am experiencing it in myself, whether I like it or not, that the mute mouth of my soul opens for you and must tell you for the glory of God an intimate secret that I have never told anyone. I knew a Dominican friar[186] who, after his beginning, for a good ten years received from God such grace pouring into him twice a day, mornings and evenings; and it lasted as long as two vigils.[187] During this time he sank so completely in God into eternal Wisdom that he was unable to speak of it. Sometimes he held an intimate conversation with God, sighed in lament, wept with longing, or sometimes smiled quietly. He often felt as though he were floating in the air and swimming in the deep flow of God's boundless marvels between time and eternity. From this his heart became so full that he would sometimes put his hand on his raging heart and say, "Ah, heart of mine, how you shall fare today!"

One day he felt as though the heart of the Father was tenderly inclined toward his heart somehow inexpressibly, in a spiritual manner with no obstacles intervening, as though his heart were opened in longing to the heart of the Father. It seemed to him that the Father's heart, eternal Wisdom, spoke lovingly and immediately into his heart. He began to speak joyfully in spiritual jubilation: "Come now, my dear Loved One, I shall uncover my heart, and in this simple nakedness of all createdness I embrace your bare divinity.[188] O you Love surpassing all love! The greatest love of a temporal lover for his beloved does not overcome the separation and difference of lover and beloved. But you, infinite Fullness of all love, flow into the heart of the beloved; you pour yourself into the being of the soul, you who are simply all in all, so that not a single particle of the lover remains outside, but is lovingly united to the beloved."

His daughter said, "O God, what a great grace it is that a person is thus by jubilation transported into God! Now I would like to know whether this is perfection or not." He replied, "No, it is only an enticing preview of entering into a genuine union."[189]

She said, "How do you define 'genuine' or 'not genuine?'"

He answered: I call that person "genuine" who by means of constant good exercises has by struggling attained virtue so that it has become a pleasure and constant presence for him in its highest and most noble form, just as brilliance is constantly with the sun. By "not genuine" I mean when the light of virtue shines in a person as something borrowed, as something transitory and imperfect, as shining light exists in the moon. The aforementioned gratuitous pleasure lures the spirit of a person who is not genuine into wanting to have it all the time. And just as its presence gives him joy, so its absence causes him inordinate sadness; and it becomes repugnant for him to devote himself to anything else, as I shall now make clear to you.

It once happened, as the servant was in the chapter house, that his heart was full of the holy joy of jubilation. The porter came and asked him to go to the door of the cloister to a woman who wanted to make her confession. He did not like to interrupt his interior delight and received the porter harshly, saying that she should ask for someone else and that he did not care to hear her confession. Her heart was burdened with sin, and she said she had special trust in him that he could comfort her, and she did not want to confess to anyone else. When he still did not want to come, she began to weep with heart saddened and, feeling miserable, she went off to a corner to sit where she wept intensely. Meanwhile God suddenly withdrew this joyous gift from him. His heart became as hard as a pebble. And when he would have liked to know what this all meant, God spoke within him thus: "Look, just as you drove from you the poor woman with her burdened heart without comforting her, so have I withdrawn my divine consolation from you." He heaved a sigh within himself and, striking his breast, ran quickly to the cloister door. Not finding the woman there, he behaved most miserably. The porter ran all around looking for her. When he found her where she was sitting and weeping and brought her back to the door, the servant received her kindly and consoled her calmed heart generously. Then he went back to the chapter and just like that, in an instant, our gentle Lord returned with his divine consolation just as before.

His daughter said, "That person could very well endure suffering to whom God gave the joy of jubilation." He replied, "Alas, afterward it all had to be bitterly earned by great suffering." But then finally, when it had all run its course and it seemed time to God, this same gift of jubilation came back again and remained somehow constant within him. Whether he was at home or away, with people or alone, often while bathing or eating, he experienced this grace. But it took place within him, not externally.

CHAPTER 51

Instruction Concerning Where God Is and How God Is

His daughter said, "Sir, I have now well understood *that* God is, but I would like to know *where* he is." He replied: You shall now hear about this.

The theologians say that God does not have a "where," that he is completely present in everything. Open the inward ear of your soul and listen. These same learned men also maintain in the branch of knowledge called logic that one sometimes learns something about a thing from its name. One teacher says that the name "being" is the first name of God.[190] Turn your eyes toward this being in its pure simplicity and let go of this or that which only participates in being.[191] Take being alone in itself, which is not mixed with nonbeing. For just as nonbeing negates all being, so being in itself is the negation of all nonbeing.[192] A thing that is yet to come about or which has already been is not at this moment really existing as being. Now one can only know mixed being or nonbeing by referring them to total being. It is not a divided being of this or that creature because divided being is all mixed together with some otherness of potency to receive something.[193] Therefore the nameless divine being must be in itself complete being that supports all divided beings with its presence. It is a strange blindness of the human intellect that it cannot examine this without being unable to know or understand (anything else). The same thing happens to it as to the eye: When it is seriously engaged in seeing a variety of colors, it does not perceive the light by means of which it sees everything else; or if it sees the light, it is not aware of it. This is also how it is with the eye of our mind. When it directs its attention to this or that being, it fails to see the being which exists above all this as pure simple being, through the power by which it perceives the other beings. It is unaware of this (highest being). Therefore, a wise teacher says that the eye of our intellect, because of its weakness, takes as its object that being which in itself is best known of all, like the eyes of a bat toward the bright light of the sun. The divided beings distract and blind the mind so that it is not able to see the divine darkness, which in itself is the brightest of all splendors.

Now open your inward eyes and behold, if you can, this being as it is in its simple purity. You can quickly see that it derives from no one, has neither a before nor an after, and that it is immutable both within itself and from without. It is simple being. Then you notice that it is entirely in act, completely present, and most perfect. In it there is nothing lacking or any otherness. It is a simple one in utter nakedness. This truth is so clear to illumined minds that they cannot think otherwise because one statement proves and leads to the next. Because it is simple being, it must of necessity be the first, derive from no one, and be eternal. And because it is the first, eternal and simple, it must be completely present. It has the highest perfection and simplicity. Nothing can be added to it or taken away from it.

If you can understand what I have told you about the naked Godhead, you are to a large degree instructed about the incomprehensible light of hidden divine truth. This simple pure being is the first and highest cause of all caused beings and, in its unchanging presence, it embraces all becoming in time as the beginning and end of all things. It is completely in all things and completely apart from all things. For this reason a teacher says: God is like a circle whose center is everywhere and whose circumference is nowhere.[194]

His daughter said, "Praised be God! I have been instructed, as far as it is possible for me, that God is and where God is. Now I would like to know how, since he is utterly simple, he can also be three."

He began anew, saying: Every being, the more simple it is in itself, the more manifold it is in its potential capabilities. That which has nothing gives nothing. That which has much can give much. Now we have already mentioned the inward-flowing and overflowing goodness that God is in himself. His immeasurable natural goodness forces him not to keep it all for himself. He distributes it freely both within himself and outside. Now it must of necessity be that the highest good has the highest and most perfect emanation of itself. And this cannot be unless this emanation is present, interior, substantial, personal, natural and not forced, and is endless and complete. All other outpourings (of goodness) that are in time or in a creature come from the reflection of the eternal outpouring of the boundless divine goodness. The theologians say that at the outflowing of the creature from its primal origin there is a circle-like bending back of the goal toward the beginning. For just as the flowing out of the Persons from God is a formal image of the origin of creatures, it is also a prelude of the creatures' flowing back into God.

Now pay close attention to the difference between the flowing out of creatures and of God. Because a creature is a divided being, its giving and its flowing out are also by participation and limited. A human father gives his son by birth a part of being, but not completely that which he is because he is himself only a partial good. Now since it is well-known that the divine outpouring is so much more intense and more noble according to the greatness of the goodness that God himself is—he infinitely surpasses all other good—it must necessarily be that the outpouring is equal to the being. And this is only possible through the outpouring of his being as a separate Person.

If now with a purified eye you can look inside and see the utterly pure goodness of the highest Good, which is there in its being as an ever-present, active beginning of loving itself naturally and freely, you will see the exuberant, supernatural outpouring of the Word out of the Father in whose generation and being spoken all things are uttered and given. And you also see that in the highest Good and in this highest pouring forth there necessarily arises the divine Trinity: Father, Son and Holy Spirit. And since this first pouring out springs forth from the highest subsistent Goodness, in the flowing forth of the Trinity there must be the highest and most perfect sameness in being, the most exalted equality and individuality of being that the Persons have in the outpouring which yet remains within in the undivided substance and undivided omnipotence of the three Persons in the Godhead.

His daughter said, "Look! I am soaring in the Godhead like an eagle in the air!"

He said: How the Trinity of divine Persons can exist in a oneness of being no one can express in words. St. Augustine said as much as anyone is able to say: that the Father is the source of all the divinity of the Son and the Spirit, as Persons and as being.[195] Dionysius says that in the Father there is an outflowing or a spring of the Godhead, and this spring pours itself forth naturally in the Word as he sprouts up. He is a Son by nature. And he pours himself forth also in loving abundance of the will, and this is in the Holy Spirit.[196]

Dear St. Thomas, the teacher, unlocks the secret meanings for us and points us toward the bright light, saying this: When the Word pours forth from the heart and intellect of the Father, it must happen that God in his radiant knowledge of himself looks at his divine being in the manner of reflection. If the object of the intellect of the Father were not the divine being, then the conceived Word would not be God, but would be rather a creature.[197] This would be wrong, but as just explained it is divine being from being. And the reflecting upon the divine being by the intellect of the Father must take place in a way that forms the (Son's) equality (with the Father) by nature. Otherwise, the Word would not be the Son. Thus there is oneness of being and distinction of Persons. In bearing witness to this way of distinguishing, the high-soaring eagle, St. John, said, "The Word was in the beginning with God."[198]

Concerning the emanation of the Spirit, one should realize that the substance of the divine intellect is knowing, and it strives of necessity to its end, toward the form that is received in the intellect. This striving is the will, whose desire it is to seek pleasure of the highest and best kind.[199] Now note also that the object (of the be-)loved is in the one loving not according to its form existing in nature, as is also true of the object of the intellect in the light of knowledge. And when the Word flows forth from the sight of the Father as a natural form and a distinct Person, this pouring forth from the Father is called a birth. However, since this is not the manner of flowing out from the will and from love, the third Person, who pours forth in the flow of love from the Father and also from the image formed from his innermost abyss,[200] can be said neither to be Son nor "born." And because love as something intellectual or spiritual is present in the will as a tendency or as a bond of love within the one loving toward that which he loves, therefore it is proper that the third Person be called Spirit because its origin is according to the manner in which the will loves. Here man is transformed by the divine light with an intimacy no one can understand who has not felt it.

His daughter said, "Ah, sir, what a richly overflowing Christian teaching this is! But one finds some intelligent people who deny everything that has just been said about God and who are of the opinion that God is a harmful obstacle for anyone striving to achieve perfection. Such a person must be made rid of God; he must also be made rid of spirit and must reject all visions, turning alone to the truth shining within which this person is himself."[201]

He said: This line of thought is wrong according to the common opinion (of theologians). Therefore, be free of it and listen to what Christian truth says about it. According to the common way of speaking, God is conceived of as the Lord of the whole world. He suffers no evil to go unpunished and no good work to go unrewarded. Now if someone commits a sin, God is a God to be feared by that person; as pious Job said, "I have always feared God as sailors fear the big waves."[202] He who serves God with an eye to a great reward has a great God who is able to reward him greatly. But a person well-versed in religious practices and sensible, one who rids himself of the sinfulness, which God hates, through many kinds of mortification and who serves God constantly full of fervent love, such a person does indeed have God in his heart, but not God in the sense just mentioned; he is certainly rid of that God. He has God as his deeply desired beloved since servile fear, mentioned by Paul, has fallen away from him.[203] Thus, for a truly religious person God certainly remains God and Lord, but he is rid of God as he is crassly imagined, because he has comprehended something more perfect.

Now concerning the sense in which a person should be rid of spirit, listen to this distinction. When a man who is beginning first notices that he is a creature of body and spirit, and that the body is mortal while the soul is an everlasting spirit, he says farewell to the body and all its animal urges and holds fast to the spirit, subjecting the body to the spirit. All his activity is directed inward through contemplation toward the spirit, which is above being, as he finds this spirit, as he comprehends it, and as he unites his spirit to this spirit. Such people are called spiritual or holy. And when a person fares well, exercising himself this way for a long time with the spirit that is above being constantly showing him the way but without his ever being able to grasp it, then the creature's spirit begins to consider its own powerlessness and through a sinking of itself it abandons itself utterly to eternal divine power and turns away from itself, disregarding anything it can call its own and turns toward the immensity of the highest Being. And dwelling within it, the human spirit somehow forgets and loses itself. As Paul said, "I live, no longer I,"[204] and Christ said, "Blessed are the poor in spirit."[205] Thus the spirit remains according to its being but is rid of everything that belongs to it in its own right.

I shall also tell you how to distinguish between pure truth and dubious visions originating in sense knowledge. Direct sight of the naked Godhead: this is pure genuine truth without any doubts. And every vision, the more intellectual and free of images it is and the more like this same pure seeing, the nobler it is.[206] Some prophets had visions rich in fantasy, such as Jeremiah and the others. God's intimate friends often experience such vivid visions, sometimes while awake, sometimes while asleep, in the calm repose and detachment of the outer senses. One teacher says that the presence of angels is more frequently experienced by some people while they sleep than while they are awake. The reason is that while asleep a person is more at rest and more separated from the various external activities than while awake.

But how can one check the truth of a vision a person has in his sleep, if this can or should be a prophetic vision—as when in the Old Testament Pharaoh dreamed of the seven fat cows and the seven gaunt cows,[207] and in other similar dreams mentioned in sacred scripture? How can one come to the truth since such dreams often deceive and yet without a doubt they are sometimes prophetic? You should know that St. Augustine said of his saintly mother that she told him she had this gift from God: When she experienced something from God either while completely asleep or half asleep, the ability to distinguish was given her within, so that she recognized whether it was just an ordinary dream and should be disregarded, or whether it was a vision using images and was to be taken seriously.[208] And the person to whom God has given this same gift can better find his own way in this matter. No one can explain this to another just with words. One knows it by experiencing it.

CHAPTER 52

The Most Sublime Flights of a Soul
Experienced in Spiritual Things

The wise spiritual daughter said, "There is nothing I would rather find out from learned writings than the rich material they provide about where and how the knowledge of a person experienced in spiritual matters is supposed to reach its most sublime goal in the deep abyss (of the Godhead). (I would like to know this in such a manner) that the opinions given in these writings achieve the same results as the feelings one experiences." He excerpted from such writings a sensible response, and it goes as follows in its hidden sense:

Such a noble person hearkens in simple meditation to the significant words the eternal Son spoke in the gospel: "Where I am, my servant shall also be."[209] The person who has not avoided following the harsh "where" that the Son took upon himself in his humanity in dying on the cross—according to Christ's commandment it is certainly possible that such a person experiences the delightful "where" of the naked divinity of the Son, enjoying it in spiritual joy both in time and in eternity, either more or less, to the extent this is possible.

Now where is this "where" of the pure divinity of the Son?[210] It is in the brilliant light of divine unity, and this is according to his nameless name a nothingness; according to one in rapture a stillness in being; according to one returned to himself the single nature of the Trinity; according to his own individuality a light of himself, as

196

he is as uncreated cause: the *is-ness* giving being to all things. And in the darkness beyond distinct manners of existing, all multiplicity disappears and the spirit loses what is its own. It disappears with regard to its own activity. This is the highest goal and the "where" beyond boundaries. In this the spirituality of all spirits ends. Here to lose oneself forever is eternal happiness.

So that you remember this better, you should know that in this brilliant light of divine unity the continuous coming-forth of the outpourings of Persons out of the omnipotent, eternal Godhead takes place; for the threeness of Persons is based on the unity of their nature; and the unity in nature is based on the threeness of Persons. The effect of the unity is the threeness, and the possibility of threeness derives from the unity, as St. Augustine says in his book on the Trinity.[211] The threeness of Persons has embraced the unity within itself as its natural being. Hence each Person is God, and because of the unity of nature it is the Godhead. Now the unity shines in the Trinity in different ways; but, when one reflects on it, the Trinity shines simply in the unity as the Trinity has embraced it within itself simply.

The Father is the origin of the Son. The Son is his welling over, having flowed out from the Father from all eternity, flowing out as a Person and remaining within him as to being. The Father and the Son pour forth their Spirit. And the unity that is the being of the primal origin is the same being of all three Persons. But how the Trinity is one, and how the Trinity in its unity of nature is one and yet is also outside of unity, cannot be expressed in words because of the simplicity of the deep ground (of the Godhead).

Here in this region beyond thought the (human) spirit actively soars, sometimes rising aloft because of the limitless heights and then hovering in the measureless depths because of the sublime marvels of the Godhead. And still the spirit remains here as spirit in the enjoyment of these equally eternal, equally powerful, equally immanent and yet outflowing Persons, being detached from the mist and bustle of lower things, gazing at the divine marvels. For what can be more marvelous than the naked unity into which the Trinity of Persons plunges in oneness and where all multiplicity loses itself? This must be understood in the sense that the flowing out of the Persons who have poured forth is at the same time a returning to the unity of this same being. And all creatures according to their immanent flowing out[212] are eternally in the One, as

197

they exist living for God, knowing God, according to God's being, as the gospel says, "In the beginning: whatever came about is in him eternally his life."[213]

This naked unity is a dark stillness and a restful calm that no one can understand but one into whom unity has shined with its essence. Out of this calm rest true freedom without any evil shines because it (freedom) gives birth to itself being born again in renunciation. There hidden truth shines forth free of all error, and it gives birth to itself by uncovering the nakedness that had been concealed. Here the spirit is stripped of the murky light that, because of its being human, had followed it when these things were revealed. It is divested of this light because it finds itself to be someone else in a more real sense than as it knew itself in the manner of the previous light. As Paul says, "I live, no longer I." It is stripped and bared of all limited modes of being in the simple divine being that has no limited modes.[214] This illumines for itself all things in simple stillness. Here the remaining distinction of Persons according to their individuality is disregarded in a simplicity that excludes modes of being. For, as this treatise says: The Person of the Father alone does not give happiness, nor the Person of the Son alone, nor of the Holy Spirit alone. Rather, the three Persons subsisting in the unity of being is happiness. And this is the being of the Persons according to nature, giving being to all creatures as grace. This being has the image of all things contained within it in simplicity and in being. Because this brilliant light contains being, the things in it exist according to *its* being and not in the manner of accidents. And because it illumines all things for itself, it has the characteristic of light. Thus all things shine in this being in the calm existing within it according to the simplicity of this being.

This same spiritual "where" previously mentioned, where a tried and true servant should dwell with the eternal Son, one can call the nameless existing nothingness.[215] Here the spirit encounters the nothing of unity. This unity is called a "nothing" because the spirit can find no human manner of saying what it is. Instead, the spirit clearly feels that it is being preserved by something other than itself. Therefore, what is preserving it is more properly a something than a nothing, but for the (human) spirit it is rather a nothing according to *how* it exists.

Now when the spirit, unconscious of itself, really begins to dwell in this transfigured resplendent darkness, it becomes free of all obstacles and all that is its own, as St. Bernard says.[216] And this happens according to the extent that the spirit is in the body or has withdrawn from the body, out of itself into that (resplendent darkness). This losing of self is something divine that somehow becomes all things for him, as the treatise says. In this losing of self the spirit withdraws, but not completely. It takes on certain qualities of the Godhead although, of course, it does not become God by nature. What happens to the spirit happens by grace because it is a something created out of nothing that remains forever. One can say this much: that in this withdrawal, as the soul is taken in, it is freed from doubt as it becomes lost when it is separated from its individuality and is joined to what is divine while being unconscious of itself. It is generally believed that, through the power of the resplendent divine being, the spirit is pulled upward beyond its natural capacities into the nakedness of this nothing because it is bare of creatures of any kind. What is more, in itself it has its mode (of being) in accordance with its essence. This manner (of being) without manner is the being of the Persons. They have taken hold of it as their nature after grasping it with their direct way of knowing. This knowledge, as has been said, sets the spirit apart (from itself). This happens in the nothing of unity in accordance with the unfathomable knowledge that the nothing has. The spirit loses its own knowledge because it loses itself, lacking any awareness of self and forgetting all things. And this happened when the spirit in itself turned away from the created nature of its self and all things toward the naked uncreatedness of nothingness.

In this wild mountain region of the "where" beyond God there is an abyss full of play and feeling for all pure spirits, and the spirit enters into this secret namelessness (of God) and into this wild, foreign terrain. This is a deep, bottomless abyss for all creatures and is intelligible to God alone. It is hidden for everything that is not God, except for those with whom he wants to share himself. And even these must seek him with detachment and in some manner must know as he knows. As the scripture says, "There we shall know as we are known."[217] The spirit does not have this knowledge from itself. Unity draws it from the Trinity to itself, that is, to its rightful supernatural dwelling place, where it dwells beyond itself in that which had drawn it there. Here the spirit dies, living utterly in the marvels of the Godhead. The spirit dies because, in its withdrawal, it is not aware of the distinction of its real being.[218] When it returns to itself, it holds to the distinction according to the Trinity of Persons and respects the differences and separate existences of things, as the servant explained through distinctions in the *Little Book of Truth*.[219] And note one further point: that, in the rapture which preceded, a simple light shines out of the unity, and this light beyond manner is shined by the three Persons into the purity of the spirit. At the sight of it the spirit sinks away from itself and from everything belonging to it. It also sinks away from the activity of its powers, becoming inactive and unaware. This is due to the spirit's being transported, when it withdraws from itself, into that which is foreign to what is its own and is lost in accordance with the stillness of the transfigured, resplendent darkness in the naked, simple unity. And in this "where," bereft of mode, there lies the most sublime happiness.

His daughter said, "Oh, how wonderful! How does one enter here?" He said: To answer this I shall let the illustrious Dionysius[220] speak, who says this to his disciple: If you desire to enter the hidden mystery, step boldly upward. Let go of the outer and inner senses, the activity of your own intellect, everything visible and invisible, and everything that is being and not being. Step upward to the simple unity, into which you shall press with no awareness of self, into the silence above all being and above all the learning of the professors. Do this by a pure transport of the unfathomable, simple, pure spirit into the brilliant radiance of the divine darkness. Here one is released from all bonds, all things are left behind, because in the superessential Trinity of the Godhead above God, in the mysterious, more-than-unknown, blinding bright, highest pinnacle, by remaining wordlessly silent one hears wonders—wonders! One senses there new, detached, unchanging wonders in the resplendent, unlit darkness. This is a brilliant radiance above all revelation in which everything shines back and floods the sightless intellect with unknown, invisible, dazzling lights.

CHAPTER 53

Conclusion to This Book in Short, Simple Words

His daughter said, "Sir, you have spoken from your own thinking and from sacred scripture very knowledgeably and in keeping with Christian teaching about the mystery of the naked Godhead, about the flowing out and the flowing back in of the spirit. Could you outline for me the hidden meanings, as you understand them, by concrete comparisons, so that I might better understand? I would also like you to give me a summary in brief, concrete form of all the sublime thoughts that were extensively treated earlier, so that they might stick longer in my poor mind.

He said: How can one form images of what entails no images or state the manner of something that has no manner (of being), that is beyond all thinking and the human intellect? No matter what one compares it to, it is still a thousand times more unlike than like. But still, so that one may drive out one image with another, I shall now explain it to you through images and by making comparisons, as far as this is possible, for these same meanings beyond images—how it is to be understood in truth, and thus conclude a long discussion with few words.

Now listen. A wise teacher says that God in his Godhead is like a very large circle whose center is everywhere and whose circumference is nowhere.[221] Now imagine someone vigorously throwing a heavy stone into an undisturbed body of water. A circle would form in the water, and this circle with its force would make another circle, and this yet another and, in proportion to the power of the first throw, the circles will go out farther and farther. The power of the throw could be so great that it spreads over the whole body of water. Now consider the first circle to be an image of the might of the divine nature in the Father. This immeasurable power produces a second circle like itself in the form of a Person which is the Son, and these two produce a third which is the Spirit of them both, equally eternal, equally omnipotent. This is what the three circles mean—Father, Son, Holy Spirit. In this deep abyss the divine nature is present in the Father speaking and giving birth to the Son as the separate Person who, while remaining within (the Father), assumed a human nature.

Now if you want to imagine this, think of the form of a man. Out of the innermost depths of his heart there springs forth this same form in such a way that it constantly gazes back upon it.[222] This spiritual birth taking place beyond being is the complete cause, which leads all things and spirits forth into their natural existence. The highest Spirit above being has ennobled man by illuminating him with his eternal Godhead. And this is the image of God in his intellect, which is everlasting.[223] Therefore, out of this large circle, which signifies the eternal Godhead, other small circles, as it were, flow. These signify the sublime nobility of the intellect.

Now there are those who to their harm turn away from this nobility of intellect. They cover over the shining image[224] and turn to the bodily pleasures of this world. And when they think they possess joy, grim death comes and makes an end of it. But a man of insight turns back because of the bright spark of the soul to that which is eternal and from which he flowed forth. He says farewell to all creatures and keeps himself close to eternal Truth.

Now notice, too, how the return of the spirit, as it can be explained through image, takes place in its proper order. The first image is a liberating rejection of worldly pleasures and of sinful weaknesses, enabling one to turn toward God in earnest prayer with detachment and prudent virtuous exercises in order to make the body subject to the spirit. The second image is: to offer oneself freely and patiently to suffer the countless amounts of adversity as they might befall one from God or creature. The third image is that one should form the suffering of Christ crucified within oneself, his sweet teachings, his gentle conduct, and his pure life, which he led as an example for us to follow, and thus through him press farther within. Afterward, as exterior preoccupations disappear, one should sit in the stillness of one's spirit in vigorous detachment, as though one is dead to oneself, never leading oneself or being one's own goal, but having Christ alone and the honor and glory of the heavenly Father as one's goal. Toward others, both friends and enemies, one should act humbly and friendly.

After this an experienced person achieves liberation from the outer senses, which earlier were much too eager to break loose, and his spirit achieves a fading away of its highest powers as to their capricious nature and it becomes sensitive to what is supernatural. Then the spirit, losing the creatureliness adhering to it, presses on into the circle, which signifies the eternal Godhead, and attains spiritual perfection. The most sublime richness of spirit in its own form consists in its swinging itself, aloft with no faults to weigh it down, and with God's strength (swinging itself) into his refulgent intellect where it experiences the constant inward flow of heavenly consolation. Such a person can see things in their secret natures and deal with them prudently with careful discernment. And he stands in his proper place—free—through the Son and in the Son. But he acts yet as one returning from deep contemplation, perceiving things as they are in their own nature. One can call this a crossing-over of the spirit because it is here above time and place and, rich in loving contemplation, it is withdrawn into God.

The person who at this point can still progress further and to whom God wants to give much extraordinary help by lifting him out of himself, as he did to Paul,[225] and as can still happen according to the words of St. Bernard,[226] such a person's created spirit is drawn by this spirit that is above being up to where it could not come by its own power. This rapture takes from him images, forms and multiplicity; he loses all awareness of himself and all things. In its abiding simplicity it is carried forth again with the three Persons into the abyss where it delights in its blessedness in highest truth. Here, there is no longer any struggle or striving because beginning and end, as we have described it by representations, have become one, and the spirit has become one with him (God) by losing itself. But concerning withdrawal, as it happens to a person at the present time, whether it happens in a permanent or transitory manner, or how a person in time is taken up beyond time and placed outside himself and transported into the One beyond images, all that has been treated above with careful distinctions.

Noble daughter, now note that all these images I have developed, and these thoughts distorted by images I have explained, are as far removed from the truth, which is beyond images and as unlike them, as a black Moor is unlike the beautiful sun. And this arises because of the truth's simplicity, which is beyond ideas and knowledge.

His daughter looked up fervently and said, "Praised be eternal Truth, that by your wise and vivid words I have been so well-instructed about the first steps of a beginner, about the proper order of renunciation, suffering, and the exercises of someone making progress, and in the proper way of judging the mysterious ways of the most perfect and bare truth. For this may God be eternally praised!"

When this holy daughter had been nobly instructed by her spiritual father in a Christian spirit about truth, with prudent discernment on all the paths that lead to sublime blessedness, and when she grasped it well, to the extent one can here on earth, he wrote her in his last letter, among other things, the following:

And so, daughter, say farewell to creatures and let your questions be. Listen rather to what God says within you. You can certainly be happy that you have experienced what has been withheld from many people, even though it became very arduous for you. All of that passes in time. There is nothing left for you to do than enjoy divine peace in calm repose and joyfully to wait for the hour of your withdrawal from time into perfect eternal happiness.

Shortly after this the saintly daughter died, leaving the world blessed, just as her whole life had been blessed. She appeared to her spiritual father after her death in a spiritual vision and shone in garments white as snow: She was well-adorned with luminous brilliance and was full of heavenly joys. She approached him and showed him how nobly she had entered into the naked Godhead. He saw and heard this with delight and joy, and because of this apparition his soul became full of divine consolation. When he came to himself, he sighed within and thought, "Ah God, how blessed is the person who seeks you alone! One can suffer willingly if you shall thus reward one's suffering." May God help us to profit from this holy daughter and from all his dear friends, so that we may enjoy eternally the sight of his divine countenance. Amen.

Little Book
of
Eternal Wisdom

(Here begins the second little book:)

A Dominican friar[1] was once standing before a crucifix after matins and was complaining keenly that he was not able to meditate on his (Christ's) torment and suffering (as it deserved), and that he found this especially trying because he had been very deficient in this to that very hour. As he was standing there lamenting, his inner senses were carried off in an unusual manner, and suddenly he was clearly illumined within thus: "You should perform a hundred *veniae*,[2] each one with its own special meditation on my suffering and join to each meditation a petition. Each suffering shall be spiritually impressed upon you, with you repeating this same suffering to the extent you are able." And as he stood there in this illumination and wanted to count them, he found no more than ninety. Then he prayed to God thus: "Dear Lord, you spoke of a hundred, and I can find no more than ninety." Then ten more were pointed out to him, which he had previously practiced in the chapter room before following, as was his practice, his (Christ's) anguished path to death and arriving under this very crucifix.[3] He found that the hundred meditations covered his bitter death very exactly from beginning to end. And when he had begun to practice them as he had been instructed, his previous insensitivity was transformed into heartfelt sweetness. Then he asked whether perhaps anyone else was experiencing this same difficulty of insensitivity and aridity while meditating on (Christ's) dear suffering, the source of all blessedness, so that such a person might also be helped by engaging in this practice and persevering in it until he too might be cured. This is why he wrote down the meditations and did it in German, because this is how they came to him from God.

In connection with this he experienced many a bright infusion of divine truth whose source was the meditations that occasioned in him intimate conversations with eternal Wisdom. This did not take place in the manner of physical conversations or with responses perceptible through the senses. It took place only in meditation, in the light of sacred scripture whose answers can never deceive. Thus the responses are taken either from the mouth of eternal Wisdom— responses it spoke itself in the gospels—or from the most sublime teachers. They include either the very words or the same meaning, or such truth as is in accord with the sense of sacred scripture, out of which source eternal Wisdom has spoken. The visions that follow are not actual physical events. They are simply allegory.[4] The words of our Lady's lament were taken from the sense of St. Bernard's words.[5]

The author presents his instruction in the form of question and answer in order to make it more interesting, and not because he is the one it pertains to or because he himself spoke it all about himself. He intends to present here common teaching in which both he and everyone else can find what applies to them.

As a teacher should, he takes on the roles of all persons, now speaking as a sinner, now as someone perfect, now as an example of the loving soul, and then, according to the demands of the material, in the figure of a servant with whom eternal Wisdom speaks. Almost everything is explained symbolically. Much is present here for instruction that a serious person can choose for himself for his devotions. The thoughts expressed here are simple; their expression simpler still, because they come forth from a simple soul and are spoken to simple people who still have failings to rid themselves of.

When this same friar had begun to write about these three subjects—the suffering and imitation (of Christ) and all the rest contained here—and had come to the part about sorrow, which says, "Courage, my soul," etc.,[6] he felt a certain resistance. He had leaned back in his chair in the middle of the day and, lightly napping, he seemed to see quite clearly two guilty persons dressed as religious sitting in front of him. He scolded them quite severely for just sitting there at leisure and not doing anything. He was then given to understand that he should thread a needle for them that had been put in his hand. The thread had three strands,[7] two of them quite short but the third a bit longer. And when he tried to twist them together, he could not quite make it work. Then he saw our dear Lord standing next to him on the right, (looking as he did) when he came from being scourged at the pillar. He stood before him looking so kind and fatherly that he wondered whether he was his father. Then he noticed that his tender body had a completely natural color. He was not really white, though partly white; rather, red and white mixed,[8] which is the most natural color. He saw that his whole body was covered with wounds that were fresh and bloody. Some were round and others wedge-shaped. Some were long where the scourge had torn into him. And as our Lord was standing before him so lovingly and looking at him so kindly, the friar raised his hands and stroked them over his bleeding wounds back and forth. Then he took the three strands of thread and quickly twisted them together. He was then given the power, and he understood that he was to complete it (the book) and that God intended to clothe in eternal splendor, with a rose-colored garment beautifully fashioned from his wounds, those who spent their time with this book.

One should be aware of one thing. Unlike as it is to hear for oneself the melody of sweet strings being played rather than merely to hear someone describe it, just so dissimilar are the words that are received in pure grace and flow out of a responsive heart through a fervent mouth to those same words written on dead parchment, especially in the German tongue. They somehow grow cold and lose their color, like a plucked rose. The pleasant melody, which touches the human heart more than anything else, then fades, and it is received in the dryness of parched hearts. Never were strings so sweet that they did not lose their tone when stretched over a dry piece of wood. A heart void of love can understand a tongue rich in love as little as a German can understand an Italian. And so an eager person should hasten to the outflowing streams of these sweet teachings and learn to see them according to their source where they existed alive and in attractive beauty: This was the source of present grace in which they can bring dead hearts back to life. And if one has so seen these streams, he cannot really ever read through this without his heart being deeply moved, either to fervent love or to fresh illumination or to painful longing for God and to repugnance for sin, or to some other spiritual desire in which the soul is made new in grace.

This is the end of the *prologus*, that is, the foreword to this book.

Part One

CHAPTER 1

How Some Men Are Drawn by God Without Their Knowing It

"Hanc amavi et exquisivi a iuventute mea, et quaesivi mihi sponsam assumere."[9]

These words are written in the Book of Wisdom and refer to beautiful, lovely eternal Wisdom. In German they are: "I have loved her and sought her out from my youth and have chosen her for my bride."

An undisciplined spirit, as it first ventured forth, strayed onto the paths of error. There, eternal Wisdom in an indescribable spiritual form confronted him and drew him by means both pleasant and unpleasant until it brought him to the right path of divine truth. And, when he reflected deeply on how wondrously he had been drawn, he addressed God thus:[10] "Dear gentle Lord, since I was a child, my spirit has been searching with unslaked thirst for something. And what this was, Lord, I have never yet fully grasped. For many a year, Lord, I have pursued it feverishly, yet could never attain it because I never really knew what it was; and yet it is something that draws my heart and soul to itself and without which I cannot ever really find peace. Lord, in the early days of my childhood I would search for it as I saw others do before me—in creatures. And the more I sought, the less I found; and the closer I came, the farther away I got. Concerning every form that I looked at I heard an inner voice, and before I would occupy myself with it completely or devote myself to it in peace, it would say: 'This is not

211

what you are searching for.' Always I have had this force driving me away from all things. Lord, my heart is raging to possess it because it wants it. It certainly has more than once sensed what it is *not*, Lord; but it is still uninstructed about what it *is*. Alas, beloved Lord of heaven, what is it, or what is the nature of that which so mysteriously moves within me?"

Response of *eternal Wisdom:* Don't you recognize it? It has, after all, lovingly embraced you and has often stood in your path until it gained you for itself alone.

The *servant:* Lord, I never saw or heard it at all. I don't know what it is.

Response of *eternal Wisdom:* That is not surprising. It was caused by your intimacy with creatures and your unfamiliarity with it. But now open your inner eyes and see who I am. It is I, eternal Wisdom, who chose you for myself in eternity with the embrace of my eternal providence. I have blocked your path whenever you would have been separated from me if I had let you be. You always found something repugnant in all things. This is the surest mark of my chosen ones, that I want them for myself.

The *servant:* Tender loving Wisdom, is it you that I have been so long searching for? Are you what my spirit has ever and again struggled to attain? O God, why have you waited so long to reveal yourself to me? How very long you put it off! How many a wearisome way have I plodded![11]

Response of *eternal Wisdom:* If I had acted earlier, you would not have recognized the value of my treasures as intensely as you do now.

The *servant:* O infinite Good, how sweetly have you now poured out your goodness in me! When I did not exist, you gave me being. When I left you, you would not leave me. When I tried to escape you, you so gently took me captive. O eternal Wisdom, my heart would now like to burst into a thousand pieces and, embracing you in its bliss, consume all its days with you in constant love and full praise. This is the desire of my heart. That person is truly blessed whose desire you so lovingly anticipate that you never let him rest until he seeks his rest in you alone![12]

O exquisite, lovely Wisdom, since I have found it is you whom my soul loves, do not despise your poor creature. Look how numb my heart is to the whole world, in joy and sorrow. Lord, is my heart ever to remain mute to you? Permit, beloved Lord, permit my wretched soul to speak a word with you, for my fully laden heart can no longer carry on alone. It has no one in this wide world with whom to share its burden except you, tender, beloved Lord and Brother. Lord, you alone see and know the nature of a heart filled with love. You know that no one can love something he cannot at all know. Therefore, since I shall now love you alone, let me get to know you better so that I can learn to love you completely.

Response of *eternal Wisdom:* According to the order of nature, the loftiest flowing forth of all beings from their primal origin proceeds from the highest beings to the lowest; but the return to the origin proceeds from the lowest beings to the highest. And so, if you want to see me in my uncreated Godhead, you should learn to know and love me here in my suffering humanity. This is the quickest way to eternal happiness.

The *servant:* Lord, I shall remind you today of the boundless love that brought you down from your lofty throne, from the royal abode in the heart of the Father, into exile and misery for thirty-three years. And this love you had for me and for all men you show most clearly in that most bitter suffering of your brutal death. Lord, be mindful of this: that you revealed yourself to my soul in the most lovely spiritual form that your immense love ever assumed.

Response of *eternal Wisdom:* The more exhausted, the closer to death from love I am, the more lovely I am to a well-ordered spirit. My boundless love reveals itself in the deep bitterness of my suffering just as the sun reveals itself in its splendor, as the rose does in its fragrance, and as fire does in its searing heat. And so listen attentively to how intense was the suffering on your behalf.

CHAPTER 2

The Events Before the Crucifixion

After the Last Supper, when on the mountain[13] I surrendered myself to the throes of a cruel death and discovered that I was about to confront it, because of the fear in my gentle heart and the distress of my whole human body, a bloody sweat began to pour out of me. I was treacherously taken captive, tightly bound and led off to agony. All through the night I was shamefully mistreated with blows, spat upon and blindfolded. In the morning, before Caiaphas, I was slandered and condemned to death. One could see the indescribable heartbreak of my pure Mother from the time she first saw me in distress until I was executed on the cross. I was brought before Pilate ignominiously, falsely accused and condemned to death. With their cruel eyes they stood opposite me, powerful as giants, and I stood before them like a gentle lamb. I, eternal Wisdom, was scorned as a fool in white garments before Herod. My fair body was painfully torn open and marred by the wanton blows of the scourge. My gentle head was pierced and my loving countenance dripped with blood and spit. Thus was I condemned in misery and shamefully led forth with my cross to death. They screamed at me so cruelly that the air rang with their cries: "Crucify him! Crucify the evil fiend!"

The *servant:* O Lord, the beginning is so completely terrible. How will it end? If I were to see a wild animal thus treated before my eyes, I could scarcely endure it. How right it is that your suffering pass through my heart and soul! But, Lord, my heart is greatly confused. Beloved Lord, I seek always your divinity, but you show me your humanity. I seek your sweetness, but you stress what is bitter. I wish always to suckle, but you teach me to struggle. O Lord, why are you doing this?

Response of *eternal Wisdom:* No one can reach the heights of the divinity or unusual sweetness without first being drawn through the bitterness I experienced as man. The higher one climbs without sharing the path of my humanity, the deeper one falls. My humanity is the path one takes; my suffering is the gate through which one must pass who will come to what you are seeking. And so, away with faint-heartedness and enter with me the lists of knightly steadfastness. Indulgence is not fitting for the servant when the lord is practicing warlike boldness. I shall clothe you with my armor because all my suffering has to be endured by you as far as you are able.

Stir yourself to boldness, because your heart must often die before you overcome your nature and must in fear pour out bloody sweat because of much painful suffering in which I shall make you ready for me. I want to dung your spice garden with red blossoms. Against your old ways you must be taken captive and bound. My enemies will often secretly dishonor you and cause you public shame. People will make many wrong judgments about you. And you shall constantly carry my torment in your heart with the intense love of a mother. You will have many an evil judge of your religious life. Your divinely motivated way of life will often be scorned as foolish by the all-too-human. Your untried body will be scourged by a harsh and severe way of life. You shall be derisively crowned by the suppression of your spiritual life. After this you shall be led out with me along the desolate way of the cross, as you withdraw from your own willing, give up yourself and all creatures, and become as truly free of all creatures in things that can interfere with your eternal salvation as a dying person when he is about to leave and has nothing more to do with the world.

The *servant:* O Lord, this will be a dreadful path for me! My whole being shudders at these words, Lord. How shall I ever endure it all? Gentle Lord, I must say something. In your eternal wisdom could you find no other way to keep me and show me your love? Could you not spare yourself this great suffering and spare me having to share this bitter suffering? How very strange your judgments seem![14]

Response of *eternal Wisdom:* No one should try to probe the unfathomable abyss of my mysterious being, in which I ordain all things in my eternal foreknowledge. No one can grasp it. Here, both this and many other things were a possibility, and yet they will never happen. Still, you should know that in the present order that has flowed out (from God) there can be no better way. The Lord of nature does not consider what he can accomplish in nature. Rather, he looks to what is most fitting for each individual creature and acts accordingly.

How, then, can a person better know the mysteries of God than in the humanity he assumed? How can a person who because of improper pleasures lost eternal joy be more properly instructed about this joy? How could the untried path of an austere and scorned way of life be better traveled than that it be traveled by God himself? If you had been condemned to death and someone allowed himself to be executed in your place, how could he show you more faithfulness and love, or better move you to love him in return? If my infinite love, my indescribable mercy, my shining Godhead, my congenial humanity, my brotherly devotion and my intimate love cannot move someone to intense love, what could then soften a stone-hard heart? Ask all creatures in their fine order: Could I restrain my justice, show my boundless mercy, ennoble humanity, pour forth my goodness and reconcile heaven and earth in a more delightful way than by my bitter death?

The *servant:* Lord, I now really and truly begin to see that this is true. And if a person has not been blinded by ignorance and reflects on this as he should, he must admit it to you and praise your loving way of acting above all other ways. And yet, following you is painful for a sluggish body.

Response of *eternal Wisdom:* Do not be afraid to follow me in suffering. He who possesses God so intimately that suffering becomes easy has no reason to complain. No one has more benefit from my extraordinary sweetness than those who stand with me in deepest bitterness. No one complains more about the bitterness of the husk than he who has not experienced the inner sweetness of the kernel. The battle is half won if you have an able companion.

The *servant:* Lord, your consoling words have given me such courage that I think I can accomplish and suffer all things in you. And so I beg you to open up for me completely the treasures of your suffering and tell me more about them.

CHAPTER 3

What His Condition Was on the Cross With Regard to the Outer Man

Response of *eternal Wisdom:* When I had been stretched out on the high branch of the cross for you and for all men out of boundless love, my whole form was very pitiably disfigured. My fair eyes grew dim and turned askew. My divine ears were filled with cries of scorn and insult. My refined sense of smell was assaulted with foul odors, my fair mouth with a bitter drink. My tender sense of feeling suffered from heavy blows. There was no place on this whole earth for me to find a little rest. My divine head was bowed in discomfort and distress. My tender throat was cruelly abused. My fair face was defiled by spit. My pure complexion was devoid of color. Look, my fine figure died away as utterly as though I were a leper and had never been fair Wisdom.

The *servant:* O you charming Mirror of all graces in which heavenly spirits refresh their eyes lovingly, if only I had your dear countenance here as it was when you were dying that I might wash it with the tears of my heart and might contemplate your beautiful eyes, your fair cheeks, your tender mouth, now so pale and deathly, and might thus relieve my heart by bitterly lamenting them.

O dear Lord, your suffering affects some hearts very deeply; they can lament for you earnestly and weep for you sincerely. O God, if only I knew how and were able to represent all loving hearts in my lamenting! If I could only shed the radiant tears of all eyes and speak the words of grief of all tongues, then I would show you now how deeply your pitiable anguish moves me!

Response of *eternal Wisdom:* No one shows better how deeply my suffering affects him than he who bears it with me through the evidence of deeds. I prefer a free heart, untroubled by any transitory love, that pursues perfection through constant efforts by imitating my exemplary life rather than that you should constantly mourn for me and weep as many tears in grieving for my torment as there are drops of water that ever fell from the skies. That it be imitated was the reason why I endured my bitter death, however dear and touching I may find such tears.

The *servant:* O gentle Lord, since a loving imitation of your meek way of life and your suffering from love is so very pleasing to you, I shall spend all my efforts from now on to imitate you joyfully rather than to lament with weeping, though I should do both according to your words. And so teach me how to become like you in this suffering.

Response of *eternal Wisdom:* Break off your pleasure in looking at wantonness and in hearing frivolous things. In your love (for me) find pleasure and enjoyment in those things that you used to find repugnant. For my sake give up pampering your body. You should seek all your rest in me, should love bodily discomfort, should willingly endure evil from others, should desire humiliation, and should diminish your desires and kill all your pleasures. In the school of wisdom this is the beginning that one reads from the open, outstretched book of my crucified body. But consider! If a person does all that he can, still—is there anyone in this whole world who is for me what I am for him?

THE EXEMPLAR

CHAPTER 4

That His Suffering Was a Loving Commitment

The *servant:* Lord, even when I am not mindful of your dignity, your gifts (to me), the benefits and everything else, one thing still affects me very deeply. And this is when I truly reflect not just on the manner of our salvation, but on what an infinite loving commitment (to me on your part) it shows. Lord, when one person gives something to another, the love and devotion involved is often more apparent in the manner of giving than in the gift itself. A small gift given with true sincerity is often worth more than a valuable gift without it. Lord, your gift is not only large. The manner also seems to me immeasurably loving. You did not just suffer death for me. You also sought out the most extreme, the most perfect and the most mysterious of all love in which one can and may choose to suffer. You acted as though you were saying, "Look, all you hearts, was there ever a heart so full of love? Consider this. If all the parts of my body were the most precious one, namely, the heart, I would be willing to have them be pierced, killed, torn apart and ripped to shreds so that there would be nothing left of me that had not been offered up that you might know my love." O Lord, how did you feel, or what were you thinking? You will, I hope, allow me to press further?

Response of *eternal Wisdom:* Never did a thirsting mouth so ardently long for cold spring water or any dying man long for another cheery day of life as I longed to help all sinners and to endear myself to them. It would be easier to bring back the days gone by, to breathe fresh life into withered flowers, and to gather together all the raindrops than it would be to measure my love for you and all men. As a result, I am so completely covered with tokens of my love that a person could not touch me anywhere on my tormented body with the point of a needle without finding his own special token of love.[15]

See how my right hand was transfixed with a nail, my left hand stabbed through, my right arm disjointed and my left arm distended. My right foot was gored through and my left foot savagely pierced. I hung there powerless, my divine legs exhausted. All my delicate limbs were forced to remain motionless on the cramped space of the cross. My warm blood frequently burst forth uncontrollably, covering my dying body with gore—a pitiable sight. This was something to lament about: My body, so young, fair and full of life began to lose its color, to dry out and to waste away. My weary, tender back was pressed roughly against the coarse cross. My heavy body sank down; my whole body was permeated with wounds through and through—all this my dear heart endured for love.

CHAPTER 5

*How the Soul Beneath the Cross Achieves Sincere Sorrow
and Generous Forgiveness*

The *servant:* Courage, my soul, recollect yourself completely from what is outside to (enter) the still silence of the true interior life, so that you can set out with all your strength and rush in and lose yourself completely in the wild desolation of infinite suffering of the heart. Climb the lofty crags of well-pondered misery and shriek with your wounded heart that, over mountain and valley, high in the air, it might penetrate heaven and come before the heavenly hosts. With your plaintive voice say, "O living stones, wild borders of the fields, bright meadows, who shall give me the power to make the raging fire of my full heart and the warm flow of my mournful tears awaken you, so that you help me mourn the immeasurable suffering, the suffering of heart, that my poor heart so secretly harbors? The heavenly Father had adorned me more beautifully than all other corporeal creatures and had chosen me for his tender and lovely bride. Now I have run off from him! Oh, I have lost him. I have lost my only chosen Love. Alas for my poor miserable heart! What have I done? What is it I have lost? Myself and the hosts of heaven. Everything that brings joy and delight—that has forsaken me! I sit here naked; for my false lover, my true deceiver—oh, the foulness of the deed—has left me deceived and wretched and has stripped me of all the belongings with which my only true Love had clothed me. Alas honor, alas joy, alas all comfort, I have been completely robbed of you! Grief and pain shall be my comfort from now on. Where shall I turn? This whole world has forsaken me because I have forsaken my only Love. Oh, how could I have done it? What a miserable hour that was! All you red roses and white lilies, look at me, a late-blossoming, stunted daffodil, a blackthorn bush, and see how utterly faded, wilted and withered is

219

the flower that this world plucks. From now on I shall, living thus, die; blossoming, thus wither; thus young, grow old; and thus healthy, grow sick.

O gentle Lord, all this that I suffer is to be considered insignificant in comparison with the fact that I have caused your fatherly countenance to grow angry. For me this is hell and a suffering beyond all suffering. Oh, how you have so lovingly anticipated my every wish, have so gently admonished me, so delicately drawn me (to you). Oh, that I so utterly forgot all this! Oh, I should die! Oh, heart of man, what you are able to endure! Oh, my heart, you are like steel if you do not burst apart in suffering. I used to be called his dear bride. Now, alas, I am not worthy to be called his poor washerwoman. In my deep shame I no longer even dare to raise up my eyes. My mouth must ever more remain dumb toward him in joy and sorrow. How stifling I find it in this wide world. O God, if I only were in a wild forest where no one could see or hear me, that I might cry myself out to my heart's content, that my poor heart might be thereby relieved. No other comfort is available to me. O sin, where you have led me! O deceiving world, what does one get for serving you! You have so given me my deserts that I am and shall remain a burden to myself and all the world. Oh, if God were to look upon the majestic queens, majestic souls, that have become prudent through the misfortunes of others and have retained their first innocence and purity of body and spirit. How blessed they are in their ignorance. O pure conscience, free and detached heart, how oblivious you are to what it is like to have a sinful, burdened and despondent heart! Oh, poor woman that I am, how well off I was with my husband and how little I appreciated it! Who shall give me the expanse of heaven for my parchment and the depths of the sea for my ink, leaf and grass for my pen, that I might describe to the full the suffering of my heart and the irreparable desolation that this bitter separation from my Beloved has caused me? Oh, that I was ever born! What is left for me to do but cast myself into the abyss of bitter despair?

Response of *eternal Wisdom:* You should not despair. After all, I came into this world for your sake and that of all sinners, to bring you back again to my Father in heaven as radiantly and purely adorned as you could possibly be.

The *servant:* Oh, what is that which so softly rings in my dead and worthless outcast soul?

Response of *eternal Wisdom:* Don't you recognize me? Have you sunk so low? Or are you faint from your immense sorrow? My dear child, it is I, gentle merciful Wisdom, who, while remaining hidden to all the saints in my innermost depths, have opened up wide the abyss of my mercy to receive you and all penitent hearts kindly. It is I, dear Wisdom, who became poor and outcast, so that I might return you to your true dignity. It is I, who suffered a bitter death in order to let you live again. I stand here now pale, bloody and loving, as I stood on the high gallows of the cross mediating between you and the stern judgment of my Father. It is I, your Brother, your Husband. I shall forget everything that you have ever done to me, as though it had never happened, if only you will completely turn to me alone and never again leave me. Wash yourself in my loving, rose-colored blood. Lift up your head. Open your eyes. Take courage. Receive as testimony of our perfect reconciliation this wedding band, your former dress, shoes for your feet, and the dear name of my bride that you shall be called and shall be eternally.

See how I have struggled to bring you back. Therefore, if the whole earth were a raging fire and in the middle of it there lay a handful of hemp, it would not be as quick to catch fire, given its natural characteristics, as the depths of my measureless mercy (are quick to welcome) someone who returns.

The *servant:* O my Father, my Brother, oh my everything that gladdens the heart, shall you show mercy to my unworthy soul? What generosity, what mercy! Because of it I shall fall at your feet, heavenly Father, and thank you from the depths of my heart, and I ask you to look upon your dear only-begotten Son, whom you out of love sent to a bitter death, and forget my great wrongdoings. Remember, heavenly Father, what you promised to Noah, and say, "I shall stretch my (rain)bow in the air; I shall look at it and it shall be a sign of reconciliation between me and the earth."[16] Now look at him, gentle Father, how he is so stretched out and torn apart that one could count his bones and his ribs. See how love has turned him red, green and yellow.[17] Now look upon the hands of your dear, gentle, only-begotten Child, heavenly Father, and his arms and feet so terribly twisted. Look at his fair body, so rosy-red and martyred, and forget your anger toward me. Remember, why are you called merciful Lord, Father of mercy, if you don't forgive? That is your name. To whom have you given what you hold most dear? To sinners! Lord, he is mine! Lord, he is truly ours! I receive today the embrace of his arms, bare and exhausted, with a tender response from the depths of my heart and soul, and I never want to be separated from him again in life or in death. And so, show him honor today in me and graciously forget that I ever made you angry. It seems more possible for me to endure death than, heavenly Father, that you should ever again be seriously angry with me. Any suffering and oppression—be it hell or purgatory—there is nothing I lament so much or that causes my heart such pain as that I might anger you, my Creator, my Lord, my God, my Redeemer, all my joy and heart's delight, or that I might cause you dishonor. If I could cry out the sorrow of my heart through all the heavens so that the heart in my body burst into a thousand pieces, I would gladly do it. And the more completely you forgive me my wrongdoing, the more sorrow my heart feels that I have been so ungrateful for your great goodness.

Response of *eternal Wisdom:* You should surrender yourself and all that you have to me freely, and never take it back. Everything that is not a necessity should remain untouched by you. Then your hands are truly nailed to my cross. Embark upon good works joyfully and persevere in them steadfastly. Then your left foot is fastened. Make your capricious spirit and distracted mind constant and firm in me. Then your right foot has been placed on my cross. Your spiritual and bodily powers should not be paralyzed in tepidity. With my arms as a model they should be stretched out and twisted in my service. In praise of my divine body your frail body should often grow weary and be powerless to fulfill its own desires. Many an unexpected suffering will press you to me in the narrow confinement of my cross. From this you will become lovable and the color of blood, as I am.

The fall of your nature shall make me fresh again. Your willingly endured hardships shall provide a bed for my weary back. Your vigorous opposition to sin shall cheer my spirits. Your heart's devotion shall relieve all my pain, and its flames shall ignite my loving heart.

The *servant:* Eternal Wisdom, bring now my good will to completion for your highest praise according to your dearest will. For truly your yoke is gentle and your burden is light.[18] All those who have felt it at all and have ever been overburdened with the heavy load of sin know this.

CHAPTER 6

How Deceiving Wordly Love Is and How Lovable God Is

O lovable Goodness, whenever I turn ever so slightly away from you, I feel like a fawn that has lost its mother and is being harried by the hunt. It flees, turning this way and that, until it escapes back to its lair. Lord, I flee and chase after you with ardent zeal as does the stag to living waters.[19] Lord, one hour without you is a whole year. One day away from you is a thousand years for a loving heart. And so, you branch of happiness, bough of springtime, blossoming red rosebush, open your arms. Open and stretch out the blossoming branches of your divine and human nature. Lord, your countenance is so full of grace, your mouth so full of living words. Your whole manner is a pure reflection of all refinement and gentility. O sight pleasing to all the saints, how truly happy he is who is worthy to have you as his sweet spouse.

Response of *eternal Wisdom:* Many are called to this, but few of them are chosen.[20]

The *servant:* Dear Lord, are they rejected by you or are you rejected by them?

Response of *eternal Wisdom:* To learn of this, open your interior eyes and take in this sight.

The *servant* looked up and shuddered. With a deep sigh he said: Alas, beloved Lord, that I was ever born. Am I sane or am I dreaming? I saw you before so richly adorned and attractive in your gentleness. And now I see nothing but a poor, outcast, helpless pilgrim standing there piteously hunched over his staff in front of the ancient ruins of a town. The moats are caved in and the town wall is in ruins, except that here and there the lofty towers of the old structure rise up. In the town there are great multitudes, and among them are very many who seem like wild beasts in human form. The wretched pilgrim goes all around looking for someone who will offer him a hand. Alas, I see that most of them drive him away in scorn and, because of their preoccupations, hardly give him a glance. Some of them, but only a few, do offer him their hand. Then the others come, the wild beasts, and pull them apart. And I hear how the poor pilgrim sighs forlornly from his depths and says, "O heaven and earth, be moved to pity, that I have saved this town by struggling grimly and am received here so shamelessly, while those who never had to struggle on its behalf are received here so warmly." Lord, this is what I see. Alas, dear God, what does it mean? Am I seeing rightly or not?

Response of *eternal Wisdom:* This vision is a view of pure truth. Listen to something sad and let it move your gentle heart to pity. I am the wretched, outcast pilgrim that you see. Once I enjoyed great respect in the town. Now I am a poor stranger and rejected.

The *servant:* O dear Lord, what town is it and who are the people in it?

Response of *eternal Wisdom:* The town in ruins is serious religious life, in which formerly I was served uniformly by all. Here one used to live in holiness and security. Now in many places this is beginning to go completely to ruin. The moats begin to cave in and the walls collapse. This means that eager obedience, voluntary poverty and detached purity in holy simplicity are beginning to disappear, though one still sees that the lofty structures yet maintain outward strength in how they appear. But most people, the wild beasts in human form, have worldly hearts beneath their religious habit and drive me out of their hearts by their frivolous preoccupation with fleeting concerns. That there are some who offer me their hand and are pulled away by the others means that the good will and beginning of some are perverted by the advice and example of the others. The staff I was leaning on, as I stood before them, is the cross of my bitter suffering, which I constantly use to warn them to reflect seriously, and with the love of their hearts to turn to me alone. But the terrible shouting you heard means that my death began to call out and continues to lament for those whose hearts can be touched neither by boundless love nor my bitter death. I am simply jostled and driven out by them.

The *servant:* O gentle Lord, how this cuts through my heart and soul—that you are so lovable and yet in many hearts, despite your offers, you are actually despised. Dear Lord, what shall you offer those who with true loyalty and love offer their hands to you in the wretched form you have as you are driven out by the crowd?

Response of *eternal Wisdom:* Those who leave transitory love for my sake, and receive me alone with true devotion and love and remain steadfast in this, I shall make my bride here on earth with my divine love and sweetness, and at their death I shall offer them my hands, and in the presence of the heavenly hosts shall raise them onto the throne of my eternal glory.

The *servant:* Lord, there are many who think they want to love you and yet do not relinquish transitory love. They want to please you but nonetheless want to have transitory love as well.

Response of *eternal Wisdom:* That is as impossible as it is to crumple the heavens and squash them into a small nutshell. Such people beautify themselves with fine words; they build upon the wind and the rainbow. How can what is eternal be together with what is temporal when one temporal love cannot endure another one? He is obviously fooling himself who thinks he can settle the King of kings in a common inn or in a separate servants' quarters. Whoever wants to receive this esteemed guest properly must preserve himself in pure detachment from all creatures.

The *servant:* O sweet Wisdom, they must be completely under a spell not to realize this.

Response of *eternal Wisdom:* They are completely blind. They engage in many a serious contest for joys that they will never find to their pleasure or complete satisfaction. Before something good happens to them ten bad things will befall them. And as they pursue their desires more and more, they are led further astray to what is unfulfilling. Consider that godless hearts must live in constant fear and trembling. Even the brief small joy they experience will turn sour for them because it only comes to them through toil; they hold onto it with much fear, and they lose it and are bitter. The world is filled with disloyalty, deception and inconstancy. When no more advantage is to be gained, friendship is over. To be brief: No heart ever achieved true pleasure or complete joy or constant peace of heart through a creature.

The *servant:* O gentle Lord, what a sorry fact that is! So many noble souls, so many loving hearts, so many who were very wonderfully formed in the image of God, who were destined to be queens and empresses wedded to you, who could have been powerful in heaven and on earth—that they so foolishly go astray and debase themselves. Alas, gentle God, how can they so willingly throw themselves away? According to your own true words, the terrible separation of the soul from the body would be better for them than that you, eternal Life, would have to depart from their soul because you find no room there.[21] Oh, stupid fools! Your great ruin is growing. Your great loss is increasing. You are letting the beautiful, valuable and pleasant time slip by and you can scarcely or not at all bring it back! How happy you act in all this, as though it all made no difference! O kind Wisdom, if they only knew and might recognize this for themselves!

Response of *eternal Wisdom:* Hear strange and sad things. They know this and experience it all the time, and still they cannot stop. They know and do not want to know. They decorate completely the insubstantial ground with shining lights that have no resemblance to unadorned truth, as many of them ultimately find out when it is too late.

The *servant:* O gentle Wisdom, how can they be so senseless? What does it mean?

Response of *eternal Wisdom:* They want to escape trouble and suffering (which comes) from me and (yet) they fall into the middle of it. And because they do not want to carry me, eternal Good, and my sweet yoke, they are overwhelmed by the decree of my stern justice with many a heavy burden. They fear the frost and fall into the snow.[22]

The *servant:* O tender, kind Wisdom, remember that no one can do anything without your strength. I see no other way but that they raise their helpless eyes to you and fall at your merciful feet with bitter tears from their heart, begging that you illumine them and free them from the heavy shackles with which they are bound.

Response of *eternal Wisdom:* I am always ready to help. If *they* were only ready for me! I do not desert them. They desert me.

The *servant:* Lord, it is painful for a lover to leave his beloved.

Response of *eternal Wisdom:* That would be true, if I could not and would not lovingly replace all love in the heart of the lover.

The *servant:* But, Lord, it is so difficult to abandon old habits.

Response of *eternal Wisdom:* It will be much more difficult to endure the sufferings to come.

The *servant:* Lord, maybe they are so disciplined in themselves that it does them no harm.

Response of *eternal Wisdom:* I was the best disciplined of any, yet the most empty of earthly love. How can that be disciplined which by its very nature disorients the heart, confuses the spirit, distracts one from what is within and robs one of peace of heart? It breaks open the gates behind which the divine life lies hidden, that is, the gates of the five senses. It takes away modesty and brings in insolence, absence of grace and godlessness, as well as lukewarmness of the inner man and sloth for the outer man.

The *servant:* Lord, it does not seem to them that they are so impeded if the one they love wears the habit of a religious order.

Response of *eternal Wisdom:* A clear eye is sometimes as quickly blinded by white flour as by gray ashes. Look, was ever the company of any person as free from harm as mine with my dear disciples? There were no idle words, no inappropriate behavior. There was no beginning high in the spirit and ending in the pit of countless words. There was nothing but true seriousness and full truth without any deception. And yet my physical presence had to be denied them before they were able to receive the spirit.[23] What obstacles then will (merely) human company cause! Before they are led within by one person, they will be led without by a thousand. Before they are once soundly instructed, they will be misled by bad example. To put it briefly: Just as the cold frost in May destroys and withers the lovely blossoms, so does transitory love destroy all zeal for God and spiritual discipline. And if you still have any doubts about this, then look around you at the beautiful, thriving vineyards that used to be in their first bloom.[24] See how faded and barren they are, so that one scarcely notices fervent zeal and great devotion anymore. This is what causes irreparable damage, that everything becomes mere habit and religious formality. This is what so secretly destroys all religious happiness. The less harmful it appears the more harmful it is. Many a delightful herb garden[25] that was decorated with fine gifts and was a celestial paradise in which God was pleased to dwell has been turned into a garden of weeds by transitory love. And where roses and lilies used to grow there are now thorns, nettles and thistles. Where the holy angels were accustomed to dwell pigs are now wallowing. Alas, the hour comes when one shall have to account for all one's idle words, all wasted time, all neglected goods; when one shall read before God and the whole world all frivolous words, whether spoken, thought or written, whether secret or public, and their meaning will be clear, with nothing kept secret!

The *servant:* O Lord, these words are sharp indeed. Any heart not moved by them must be made of stone.

Dear Lord, some hearts are of such a tender nature that they are more quickly attracted by love than by fear. And since you, the Lord of nature, are not a destroyer of nature but rather fulfill nature, so, dear Lord, make an end to this depressing talk and tell me that you are a Mother of wonderful love and how sweet your love is.

CHAPTER 7

How Lovable God Is

The *servant:* Lord, I am reflecting on the call of love as you speak of yourself in the Book of Wisdom: "*Transite ad me omnes*, etc.—Come to me all who desire me. You shall be filled with my fruits. I am the mother of fair love. My spirit is sweeter than honey and my inheritance is sweeter than honey and the honeycomb. Noble wine and sweet song make the heart rejoice, and above them both is the love of wisdom."[26] Gentle Lord, you can show yourself to be so lovable and tender and all hearts could take pleasure in you and could have an aching longing for your love. The words of love flow so ardently from your sweet mouth that they so powerfully wound many hearts in their days of blossoming that all transitory love is totally extinguished in them. O gentle Lord, my heart longs for this and my spirit is saddened by its absence. I would like to hear you speak of it. So, my only true Comfort, speak but a single word to my soul, to your poor servant girl, because I have fallen softly asleep in your shadow but my heart is awake.[27]

Response of *eternal Wisdom:* Now listen, my daughter, and look. Incline your ears to me.[28] Turn within with all your strength and forget yourself and all things.

I am in myself the incomprehensible Good that always was and ever is, that has never been (fully) expressed and never will be. I can let the heart feel me within itself, but no tongue can really express what I am or describe me. And yet, when I, supernatural and unchanging Good, give myself to a creature according to its capacity to receive me, I wrap up the brightness of the sun in a cloth and in human words give you spiritual meaning about me and my sweet love thus: I place myself tenderly before the eyes of your heart. Now clothe and adorn me in a spiritual manner, putting finery on me as you wish. Give me everything that can move your heart to special love (for me), delight, and full joy of heart. And this is absolutely everything that you, together with all men, can think up: form, adornment, grace; but in me all this is more lovely than anyone can describe. And these are the words in which I reveal myself.

Now listen to me: I am highborn, of a noble family. I am the lovable Word of the Father's heart. There, because of the abundance of love in the abyss of my being the Son by nature, the loving eyes of his pure fatherhood find exquisite delight in the sweet flaming love of the Holy Spirit. I am the throne of delight. I am the crown of happiness. My eyes are bright, my mouth so tender. My cheeks shine the color of red roses. My whole form is as beautiful and delightful as it can be. And if a person were to be in a glowing furnace until the day of judgment and were granted the sight of me only for an instant, he would still not have earned it. Look, I am so finely arrayed with bright garments, with a flowery mix of colors of fresh flowers, with red roses, white lilies, pretty violets and flowers of all kinds, that the beautiful, rich burgeoning of May, the green foliage of sunny meadows, and all the delicate blossoms of the fair heath are, in comparison with my adornment, like a coarse thistle.

In the Godhead I play the game of joy that gives the host of angels such joy that a thousand years are for them like a short hour. The whole army of heaven gazes upon me and contemplates me in wonder. Their eyes are drawn to mine; their hearts are inclined to mine. Their soul and spirit are ever bowed to me. Happy is the one who shall enter the game of love, the dance of joy in heavenly bliss at my side, holding my fair hand, eternally secure. A single word sung so lively by my sweet mouth surpasses the song of all the angels, the strains of all harps, all dulcet strings. Oh, look, I am so lovely to love, so delightful to embrace, and so tender for the pure loving soul to kiss, that all hearts should break, longing for me. I am gentle, devoted, and attend the pure soul always. I am secretly present to it at meals, at prayer and on all its journeys. I turn this way and that. There is nothing in me that displeases. I possess everything that can please a wishing heart, a longing soul. I am utterly pure Good. Whoever on earth experiences a single drop of me will find all the joy and pleasure of this world to be bitter, all possessions and honor to be worthless trash.[29] These dear ones will be surrounded by my love and swept into the single One with love inexpressible and beyond our imaginings. And they will be liberated and flooded into the Good from which they flowed out. My love can also relieve the hearts of beginners of the heavy burden of sin, giving them a free and contented pure heart and a clean conscience free of guilt. Tell me, what is there in this whole world that can equal this one thing? The whole world is not the equal of such a heart. For who gives his heart to me alone, he lives joyfully and dies securely, has heaven here on earth and hereafter forever.

Consider now. I have said a great many words to you, yet in my delicate beauty I am as untouched by them as the firmament is by your little finger,[30] because eye has never seen it nor ear ever heard it, and it could never enter into any heart.[31] But let this be a vague description, so that you can distinguish my sweet love from false transitory love.

The *servant:* O you delicate Flower of the field,[32] Love of the heart in the embrace of a pure loving soul, how well all this is known to one who has really felt you, and how seldom is it to be heard from one who does not know you, whose heart and spirit are still of the flesh. O beloved incomprehensible Good, this is a dear time, a delightful "now" in which I must reveal to you a secret wound my heart still bears from your sweet love. Lord, sharing someone's love is like fire and water. Dear Lord, you know that really ardent love cannot endure any twoness.[33] O gentle, sole Lord of my heart and soul, this is why my heart so intensely desires that you have a special inclination and love toward me and that your divine eyes take a special pleasure in me. O Lord, you have so many dear hearts that love you and have much favor with you. Alas, gentle, beloved Lord, where do I then stand?

Response of *eternal Wisdom:* I am the kind of lover who is not lessened in exclusivity or increased by sharing. I am always as completely concerned with and intent on you as if I were trying to make you alone love me, and I do everything that concerns you as though I were free of all other concerns.

The *servant:* "My soul welled up as my beloved spoke."[34] Help, where are you taking me? How very confused I am! How my soul dissolves at the sweet and intimate words of the Beloved! Turn your radiant eyes from me, for they have put me to flight. Where was there ever a heart so hard, where was there ever a soul so cold and so tepid that, on hearing your sweet, living and loving words so intensely on fire, it did not grow soft and warm in your sweet love? Alas, a marvel and a wonder above all wonders if one looks at you with the eyes of his heart without his heart utterly dissolving from love. How blessed is the lover who is called and is your spouse! What tender comfort and intimate love he can receive from you! O sweet, tender maiden, St. Agnes, lover of eternal Wisdom, how happy you could be with your dear bridegroom when you said, "His blood has colored my cheeks rosy."[35] Gentle Lord, if only I were worthy that my soul might be called your lover! If it were possible that all pleasure, all joy and love that this world can offer were deposited in one person, I would freely give him (that person) up for this. Blessed is he born in this world who is called and is your lover! If a person had a thousand lives, he should risk them all to be able to win you. Oh, all of you friends of God, all you heavenly hosts, and you dear virgin, St. Agnes, help me beg, because I never really knew what his love was. Oh, my heart, throw off all sloth, put it aside and see whether before you die you can reach the point that you feel his sweet love! How sluggishly and lukewarmly you have lived up to now!

O tender, fair Wisdom, my Chosen One, you certainly know how to be an endearing Love above all love of this world. How unequal are your love and that of a creature. Everything in this world that appears lovable and seems valuable turns out to be deceptive as soon as one begins to know it intimately. Lord, wherever I have set my eyes, I always found a *nisi*[36] and an "if it were not for this." If something had a beautiful form, it lacked grace. If it was beautiful and desirable, it lacked refinement. And if it had this, too, I always found something, either within or without, that repelled the overtures of my heart. Through contact and acquaintance with it I found that it harbored a certain dissatisfaction with itself. But you, Beauty boundlessly attractive, Grace wedded to form, Word joined to melody, Nobility to virtue, Riches to power, internal Freedom with external brilliance—something I never found on earth: a proper balance satisfying the capabilities, capacities and the longing of the will of a truly loving heart. The better one knows you, the more one likes you. The more contact one has with you, the more desirable one finds you. You are certainly a measureless, whole, pure Good. Look, all you hearts, how deceived those are who place their love somewhere else. Oh, you false lovers, flee far from me! Never come near me again! For I have chosen the one Lover of my heart who alone can satisfy heart, soul, desire and all my faculties with an intense love that never grows faint. O Lord, if I could only inscribe you on my heart! If I could only melt you into the innermost depths of my heart and soul in gold letters so that you could never be erased in me! It is my regret and distress that I did not ever and again busy my heart with this. What have I retained from all my lovers except lost time, misdirected words, an empty hand, few good actions and a conscience weighed down with sin? Gentle Lord, kill me if you will in your love, because I shall never again depart from your dear footsteps.

Response of *eternal Wisdom:* I run to meet those who seek me, and I receive with joy and delight those who seek my love. Everything that you can feel of my sweet love on earth is like a drop in the ocean when compared to love in eternity.

CHAPTER 8

*An Explanation of Three Things a Lover Might Find
Most Repelling About God.
The First Is: How He Can Appear So Angry
and Yet Be So Lovable*

The *servant:* O gentle Lord, there are three things I find very strange. The first is that you are utterly lovable in yourself, but that you are also such a terribly stern judge of wrongdoing. Lord, when I reflect upon your relentless justice, my heart cries out with a voice of longing: Too bad for those who ever sin! If they knew the strict justice you exact silently and without discussion for every single sin, even from your dearest friends, they should tear out their own teeth and hair rather than ever arouse your anger. Oh, your angry countenance is so terrible, your contemptuous turning away is so unbearable, and your fierce words are so fiery that they cut through heart and soul. O Lord, protect me from your angry face and do not delay your vengeance against me until the next world. When I have even a suspicion that you have turned your countenance from me in contempt because of the failings of which I am guilty, Lord, I find it so unbearable that nothing in the whole wide world is so bitter. O my Lord and devoted Father, how shall my heart ever bear your grim countenance! When I reflect on your face distorted by anger, my soul becomes so utterly terrified and my faculties tremble so that I can find nothing like it except when the sky begins to darken and turn black. And the fire in the clouds rages and powerful thunder rips through the clouds that the whole earth quakes; then you shoot down a fiery flash at a man. Lord, let no one rely on your silence, because, truly, your calm silence ultimately turns into horrible thunder. Lord, the wrathful countenance of your fatherly anger is a hell beyond all hells for someone who fears to arouse your anger and to lose you—I shall not mention the terrible countenance that the damned on the day of judgment must face with hearts full of pain. Alas, and again alas, for those who have this terrible thing awaiting them. Lord, this is a great puzzle in my heart, and yet you say that you are so lovable?

Response of *eternal Wisdom:* I am immutable Good, always remaining the same. That I seem to change is caused by the varying viewpoints of those looking at me according to whether they have sinned or not. By nature I am full of love, but a fearsome judge of wrongdoing as well. I expect childlike fear and gentle love from my intimate friends, so that fear may always hold them back from sinning and love may unite them with me in complete devotion.

CHAPTER 9

*The Second Thing: Why He Often Withdraws Himself
From His Friends As He Sees Fit,
and How One Knows When He Is Really Present*

The *servant:* Lord, all this seems as the heart should wish it except for one thing. Lord, when the soul consumes its strength searching for you and the sweet intimacy of your presence, it indeed happens, Lord, that you are silent, uttering not a single word that one can hear. O dear Lord, should that not cause pain when you, gentle Lord, have been chosen as the only Love of one's heart and then act so strange and remain completely silent?

Response of *eternal Wisdom:* And yet all creatures proclaim that I am.[37]

The *servant:* But, Lord, for a soul filled with longing this is not enough.

Response of *eternal Wisdom:* Every word that I utter is a message of love to their hearts, and every word of sacred scripture that I have written is a sweet love letter, as though I had written it especially for them. Should this not be enough for them?

The *servant:* O my gentle chosen Love, you know quite well that for a loving heart anything other than what is its only love, its only comfort, is not enough. Lord, you are such a dear, exquisite, boundless Loved One. See how the tongues of all the angels speak to me of you and how immeasurable love continually surges forth, struggling to reach the one it desires. A soul in love would prefer you to heaven because you are its heaven. O Lord, if I dare say so, you ought to be a bit more true to these poor loving hearts that languish and consume themselves with desire for you, that send up so many deep sighs to you, their only Love, that look up toward you in their misery and say in a trembling voice: "Come back, come back!"[38] Speaking to themselves, they say, "Do you think you have made him angry and he wants to get rid of you? Do you think he will ever again let you enjoy his dear presence so that you may embrace him with the arms of your heart and press him into your heart, making all sorrow disappear?"

Lord, you hear this and see it, and yet you remain silent?

Response of *eternal Wisdom:* I know about it and see it, and it brings joy and desire to my heart.

Wisdom asks: Now answer a question for me since you are pondering such mysteries. What is it of all things that the highest created spirit finds most pleasing?

The *servant:* O Lord, I wish to learn this from you. The question is beyond me.

Response of *eternal Wisdom:* Then I shall tell you. The highest angel likes nothing better than to satisfy my will in all things. And if it knew that my glory depended on pulling out nettles and other weeds, this would be what it would most desire to do.

The *servant:* O Lord, you confound me with this question. You mean to say that I should keep myself free and detached in my desires and should seek to praise you alone in difficulty as in sweetness?

Response of *eternal Wisdom:* It is detachment above all detachment to be detached in one's detachment.

The *servant:* But, Lord, that is very painful.

Response of *eternal Wisdom:* Where does virtue prove itself if not in adversity? But you should know that I often come and desire to enter my house and I am not allowed in. Often I am received like a homeless foreigner, mistreated and quickly driven out. But I come to my beloved Self and find a desirable place to stay in it. However, this happens so mysteriously that it is completely hidden from all men except for those who are completely detached and perceive my paths, who always stand ready to comply with my grace. For in my

Godhead I am a pure subsisting spirit and am received spiritually in pure spirits.

The *servant:* Gentle Lord, it seems to me that you are a very secret lover. And so I beg that you give me some signs of when you are truly present.

Response of *eternal Wisdom:* You can recognize my actual presence in no better way than this: When I hide myself and withdraw what is mine from the soul, only then do you become aware of who I am or who you are. I am eternal Good without which no one has any goodness. And so, when I, eternal Good, pour myself forth so generously and lovingly, everything I enter becomes good. This is how one can detect my presence, as (one detects) the sun by its brightness since one cannot see its essence. If you have ever found anything of me, then enter into yourself and learn to separate the roses from the thorns and to gather flowers from the grass.

The *servant:* Lord, truly I seek and find within me great unevenness. When I feel forsaken, my soul is like a sick person to whom nothing tastes good and everything is repugnant. The body is sluggish; my disposition is sullen. Within there is harshness, and sadness without. Then I find everything I see or hear or know a bother, no matter how good it is, because all sense of proportion deserts me. I am then vulnerable to faults, weak in opposing these enemies, and cold and apathetic with regard to all good things. Whoever approaches me finds a deserted house because the owner, who imparts good advice and keeps the whole household in a good mood, is not at home.

But when, Lord, the bright star of morning bursts forth in the middle of my soul, all sadness dissolves, all gloom disappears, and bright cheer is there. Lord, then my heart laughs, my spirits become light, my soul is full of joy, just like on a festive occasion. And everything in me and about me turns to praise you. Whatever was difficult, irksome or impossible becomes easy and a delight: fasting, keeping vigils, praying, suffering, renouncing and any austerity— all are as utter nothing in your presence. I become quite daring, which I then lose when left deserted. My soul is drenched with brightness, truth and sweetness, so that it forgets all hardships. My heart can contemplate in sweetness; my tongue speaks of lofty things; my body approaches everything as though it were easy. One has only to seek to find valuable help for whatever one desires. It then seems as though I have passed beyond time and place, and I stand at the antechamber of eternal happiness. O Lord, who will make it last for me? For quickly, in an instant, it is all snatched away and I am again naked and forsaken, sometimes as completely as though it had never happened. But then, after intense sadness, it returns again. O Lord, are you the cause of this? Or am I? Or what is going on?

Response of *eternal Wisdom:* You are and have from yourself nothing but weakness. I am causing it, and it is the game of love.

The *servant:* Lord, what is the game of love?

Response of *eternal Wisdom:* As long as love is together with love, love does not know how dear love is. But when love departs from love, then truly love feels how dear love was.

The *servant:* Lord, this is a tiresome game. Lord, does anyone ever lose this instability while on earth?

Response of *eternal Wisdom:* In the case of only a very few. Changelessness is a quality of eternity.

The *servant:* Which are these people?

Response of *eternal Wisdom:* Those who are most pure and who most resemble eternity.

The *servant:* Lord, which are they?

Response of *eternal Wisdom:* Those persons who have most resolutely removed from themselves all obstacles.

The *servant:* Gentle Lord, teach me how, in spite of my imperfection, I should conduct myself in this matter.

Response of *eternal Wisdom:* On good days you should consider the bad days, and on the bad days not forget the good days.[39] Then neither exuberance at my presence nor despondency when you feel forsaken can harm you. If, because of your limitations, you cannot yet renounce me when you want to, then at least wait for me in patience and seek me lovingly.

The *servant:* O Lord, waiting a long time is painful.[40]

Response of *eternal Wisdom:* He must bear good times and bad who wants to have any joy on earth. It is not enough that one give me a certain period of the day. One must constantly remain within (himself) if one wants to find God within, hear his familiar words and be sensitive to his secret thoughts.

But you! How you let your eyes and your heart wander about so thoughtlessly, though you have the blissful eternal image present before you that never for an instant turns away from you! And how you let your ears run off, though I am speaking many a loving word to you! You clearly forget yourself, though surrounded by the presence of eternal Good. What is the soul searching for in something or other outside, since it carries within itself so mysteriously the kingdom of heaven?[41]

The *servant:* Lord, what is this kingdom of heaven that is in the soul?

Response of *eternal Wisdom:* It is justice, peace, and joy in the Holy Spirit.[42]

The *servant:* Lord, I can tell from your words that you work in the soul in many mysterious ways, which are unknown to it, and that you draw it secretly and direct it diligently to the love and knowledge of your exalted Godhead, while previously it was only concerned with your sweet humanity.

CHAPTER 10

The Third Thing: Why God Allows His Friends to Have
Such a Bad Time of It on Earth

The *servant:* I have a concern in my heart. May I speak to you about it? O dear Lord, if only I might dare, with your leave, to argue with you as the holy Jeremiah did.[43] Gentle Lord, do not be angry, and listen patiently. Lord, people say: No matter how intensely sweet your love and intimacy are, still you often allow things to go quite badly for your friends, who endure much bitter suffering that you send them: the contempt of the whole world and much opposition, both internal and external. After a person had entered into friendship with you, the next step is that he prepare himself and firmly resolve to accept suffering. Lord, by your goodness, what sweetness can they enjoy in that? Or how can you allow all this in the case of your friends? Or is it something I am not allowed to know?

Response of *eternal Wisdom:* As my Father loves me, so do I love my friends.[44] I treat my friends now as I have from the beginning of the world until this very day.

The *servant:* Lord, that is exactly what people complain about. This is why they say that you have so few friends: because you let things go so badly for them in this world. Lord, this is why so many people, when they are trying to gain your friendship and are supposed to prove themselves in suffering, desert you and, I must say with a sorrowful heart and bitter tears, they return again to that which they had left for your sake. My Lord, what do you say to this?

Response of *eternal Wisdom:* This complaint comes from people of weak faith, little good works, lukewarm lives and undisciplined spirit. But you, beloved, press on courageously! Get out of the mire and deep pool of bodily pleasures! Open your inner senses; open up your spiritual eyes and look! Realize what you are, where you are and where you belong. Look! Then you can understand that I am treating my friends most lovingly.

In your natural being you are a reflection of the divinity; you are an image of the Trinity and a model of eternity. And just as I, in my eternal uncreatedness, am that Good, which is infinite, so you are boundless in what you desire. Just as a small drop can add little to the great depths of the sea, so everything that the world can offer adds little to the fulfillment of your desires.

Thus do you live in this miserable valley of sorrow in which pleasure is mixed with suffering, laughter with weeping, joy with sadness, in which never a heart attained perfect joy. It is false and lying, as I shall explain to you. It promises much and gives little. It is short, unreliable and changeable. Today there is much pleasure, tomorrow a heartful of grief. See, that is the game of the world.

CHAPTER 11

The Never-ending Pains of Hell

Alas, my chosen one, now look at this sorry state of things from the depths of your heart. Where now are all those who have settled down here in the world pampering themselves and seeking the comfort of the body? How does all the joy of the world help them, which passed on as quickly in this short life as though it had never been? How quickly the pleasure is gone, while the suffering bound to it must last forever and ever! Oh, you silly fools! What good is it now that you said so cheerfully, "Come now, stouthearted fellows, we should say goodbye to sadness and give ourselves to fine enjoyment."[45] What help to you now is all the enjoyment you ever had? You can well cry out in a sad voice: "Alas, that we were ever born! How this short time has deceived us! Death has sneaked up on us! Is

238

there still someone on earth who is being deceived as we poor wretches have been deceived? Or is there anyone who wants to learn a lesson from harm coming to someone else? If a person had the sufferings of all men for a thousand years, it would be like an instant compared to this. Oh, that person is very blessed who never sought pleasures contrary to God, who for God's sake never had a good day on earth. We fools imagined such people had been forsaken and forgotten by God.[46] But now he has lovingly embraced them in his eternity and in honor before the whole host of heaven. What harm was all that suffering and insult able to do them, which turned out to bring them such great joy? But all our pleasure has completely vanished. Oh, our grief and distress! And it has to go on forever. Oh, forever and ever, what is that? End without end, dying beyond all dying, dying all the time and yet never being able to die completely. O father and mother and all those we loved, may God be merciful to you forever and ever. We shall never have the joy of seeing you again. We shall be separated from you forever. Separation, separation lasting forever, how painful you are! Oh, the wringing of hands, the gnashing of teeth, groaning and weeping! Constant howling and calling out, and never being heard!

"Our miserable eyes can never look upon anything else but affliction and oppressive fear. Our ears can hear nothing but sighs and groans. O all hearts, let this lamentable 'forever and ever' move you to pity. Let this pitiable 'forever and ever' move your hearts. O you mountains and valleys, what are you waiting for? What is keeping you? Why do you put up with us? Why do you not fall upon us at the miserable sight of us? O suffering here and hereafter, how unequal the two of you are! O present moment, how you blind one! How deceiving you are! That we, when we were in the bloom of youth, in our fair and joyful days, did not notice this and used them up so wastefully. Alas, they shall never more return! Oh, if we still had but a single short hour in all those long misspent years that is denied us by God's justice and must forever be denied us without any hope. Oh, the sorrow, distress and grief forever and ever in this forgotten land, where we shall be forevermore separated from everything dear, with no comfort or hope. We would desire nothing else but that if there were a millstone as wide as the whole earth and with such circumference that it touched the sky all over, and if a tiny bird would come once in a hundred thousand years and peck away from the stone a piece as large as the tenth part of a millet seed—and again a hundred thousand years later, so that after ten times a hundred thousand years the equivalent of one millet seed had been pecked away from the stone—we poor wretches would beg nothing more than that our eternal torment be at an end when the stone no longer existed! Yet this cannot be!" This is the song of woe that follows for the friends of this world.

The *servant:* O stern Judge, my heart is utterly terrified. My soul sinks down, its strength ebbing away out of grief and pity for these poor souls. Who in the whole world is so callous that, on hearing this, he would not tremble at this terrible fate? O my only Love, do not leave me! My one beloved Consolation, never depart from me thus! If I were to be separated from you forever and ever, my only Love—I shall not mention anything else—oh, what grief and torment! I would rather be tortured a thousand times a day! Just thinking about the separation could make me collapse in fright. O my Lord, tender Father, treat me here as you will. You have my freely given permission for this. Just spare me this terrible separation. I simply could not endure it.

Response of *eternal Wisdom:* Do not be frightened. What is united on earth remains undivided in eternity.

The *servant:* O Lord, if only all those might hear this who are so foolishly wasting their pleasant days, so that they might have their eyes opened and reform their lives before this happens to them, too!

CHAPTER 12

The Immeasurable Joy of Heaven

Eternal Wisdom: Now, open your eyes and look up to where you belong. You belong in the fatherland of eternal paradise. On earth you are a stranger, a homeless pilgrim. And so, just as a pilgrim hurries back to his homeland where his dear friends are looking for him to come and are waiting in sadness, you also should hurry to the fatherland where people would like to see you and with intense longing look forward to your cheerful presence. They will greet you lovingly, receive you tenderly, and unite you to their merry company forever. And if you knew how they thirst for you, how they want you to struggle bravely in suffering and conduct yourself with valor in all the adversity that they have overcome, now that they reflect back on the difficult years they had—(if you knew all this) all your suffering would be more endurable. The more bitterly you have suffered, the more worthily you will be received. How wonderful the honor feels, how joy races through heart and spirit when a soul receives honor, praise and glory from me in the sight of my Father and all the heavenly hosts because it suffered so much on earth in its time of struggle, because it struggled and conquered so much that is unknown to many who have been without suffering. How wonderfully the crown will shine forth that you gained through grim battles here on earth. How the wounds will flame bright that you received here for love of me. In the fatherland you are among such intimate friends that the one in this countless number who knows you the least loves you more dearly than any father or mother ever loved an only dear child on earth.

The *servant:* O Lord, imposing on your kindness, might I now dare expect of you that you tell me still more about the fatherland, that I may more ardently long for it and may more readily endure all my suffering now? My Lord, what kind of country is it, or what does one do there? Are there many of them, and do they know how we down here are getting along, as your words seem to indicate?

Response of *eternal Wisdom:* Now set out with me. I shall take you there in contemplation and shall let you look at it from a distance by means of a rough comparison.

Look, above the ninth heaven, which is countless times more than a hundred thousand times more extended than the whole earth, there is another heaven, which is called *coelum enpyreum,* the fiery heaven, so-called not because of fire, but because of the unsurpassed shining brightness that it has from its nature. It is immovable and indestructible. This is the glorious court where the heavenly host dwells and where the morning stars praise me all together and all the children of God rejoice.[47] There, surrounded by ineffable splendor, stand the eternal thrones from which the evil spirits were cast down and which now belong to the elect. Look how this wonderful place glitters with hammered gold, how it glows with precious pearls, adorned with jewels and translucent as crystal, alive with the sparkle of red roses, white lilies and all kinds of fresh flowers. Now look at the beautiful celestial fields. Here are the complete joys of summer. Here are the meadows of sunny May. Here is the valley of true joy. Here one sees lovers' glances dart joyfully back and forth. Here are the strains of harps, the tones of violins, singing, dancing of all kinds and the constant enjoyment of perfect joy. Here all wishes are fulfilled; here there is joy without sorrow, and it will go on with complete certainty forever.[48] Look around you now at the countless multitudes as they drink from the living, gushing spring to their hearts' content. Look how they gaze upon the pure, bright mirror of the naked Godhead in which all things are known and revealed.

Creep quietly forward and see how the sweet Queen of the heavenly country, whom you love so intensely, hovers above the whole heavenly host in dignity and joy, bowing in tenderness to him whom she loves,[49] surrounded by roses and lilies of the valley.[50] Look how her wondrous beauty gives delight and joy to the whole heavenly host and astonishes them. Now take a look—it will elate your heart and spirit—and see how the Mother of mercy has her eyes, gentle and merciful eyes, turned kindly toward you and all sinners and how she powerfully protects them and reconciles them to her beloved Child.

Now turn with the eyes of pure intellect and see also how the exalted Seraphim and the loving souls of this choir of angels flame up ardently toward me constantly; how the bright Cherubim and their company flow radiantly in and out of my eternal and incomprehensible light; how the lofty Thrones[51] and their host have pleasant repose in me and I in them. Look then at the trinity of the second hierarchy, the Dominions, Virtues and Powers, how they in turn bring about the wonderful eternal order in the natural universe. See, too, how the third order of angelic spirits[52] carries forth my messages from on high and announces my decrees in the various parts of the world. See how splendidly this great multitude is arrayed, each with its own individuality. What a beautiful sight this is!

Turn your eye and look at how my chosen disciples and my dearest friends sit in such great peace and honor upon the revered seats of judgment, how the martyrs are resplendent in their rose-red garments, how the confessors shine in ever-fresh beauty, how the tender virgins sparkle in their angelic purity, and how the whole court of heaven is drenched with divine sweetness. What a community! What a joyful country! Happy is he that he was ever born who is destined to live here forever!

Out of exile, to dwell in this fatherland I bring in my arms my dear bride along with her lavish bridal gift.[53] I adorn her internally with the beautiful garment of the light of glory. This raises her above all her natural powers. Externally she will be clothed with her transfigured body, which shall shine seven times brighter than the sun, be quick, agile and incapable of suffering.[54] I shall put on her a crown and on top of this a golden wreath.

The *servant:* Gentle Lord, what is the bridal gift and what is the crown and the fine wreath?

Response of *eternal Wisdom:* The bridal gift is a clear seeing of what on earth you only believe, an immediate grasping of what on earth you only hope for, and a loving and intense enjoyment of what you love on earth. The beautiful crown is your essential reward, and the pretty wreath is your accidental reward.[55]

The *servant:* Lord, what is that?

Response of *eternal Wisdom:* Accidental reward consists in the special joy the soul gains because of the specific praiseworthy actions through which it conquered here on earth, as did the actions of the venerable doctors, the steadfast martyrs and the pure virgins. Essential reward, however, consists in the contemplative union of the soul with the naked Godhead, because it never rests until it is led beyond all its powers and capacities and is directed into the natural substance of the Persons and into the simple nakedness of Being. Face to face with this it then finds fulfillment and eternal happiness. The more the soul freely goes out of itself in detachment, the freer is its ascent; and the freer its ascent is, the farther it enters into the wild wasteland and deep abyss of the pathless Godhead into which it plummets, where it is swept along, and to which it is so united that it cannot want otherwise than what God wants. And this is the same Being that God is: They become blessed by grace as he is blessed by nature.

Now, raise up your face in joy. Forget for a while all your sorrow. Ease your heart in this shadowy solitude with this pleasant company that you gaze at so intimately, and notice how rosy and fair those faces shine that on earth so often turned red with shame for my sake. Lift up your cheerful heart and say, "Where are you now, O bitter shame, that so permeated these pure hearts? Where are you now, you bowed heads, you eyes cast down, you heartfelt grief, deep sighs and bitter tears? And you, pallid face, deep poverty and want, and the wretched voice crying, 'O Lord, O God, how sick at heart I am!' Where are all those who despised and oppressed you (saints in heaven)? One no longer hears night and day: 'To the struggle, to war, to the fight!' as when one fights against the heathens. And what you thousands of times said through the workings of grace, 'Are you firmly prepared to remain forsaken?' One no longer hears the plaintive sorry call that you uttered, 'O Lord, why have you deserted me?'[56] I hear rather the lovely words in your ears, 'Come to me, my beloved; take possession of the eternal kingdom that has been prepared for you from the beginning of the world.'[57] Where is all the suffering, sorrow and distress that you experienced on earth? O God, it has all vanished as quickly as a dream, as though you never had any sorrow. O gentle God, how completely mysterious are your judgments to the world![58] O you elect, it is no longer a question of slipping into a corner and hiding from the senseless raging of others. If all hearts were but one heart, they still could not comprehend the great honor, the enormous dignity, the praise, the glory that you shall have forever and ever. O princes of heaven, you noble kings and emperors, you eternal children of God, your faces are so fair, your hearts so joyous; you feel exhilaration and your voices sing so joyfully this song: 'Amen. Praise and glory and wisdom and thanksgiving and honor be given to him from eternity to eternity from the depths of our hearts.[59] From his grace we have possessed all this eternally!' This is the fatherland, this is complete rest, great jubilation and boundless everlasting praise!"

The *servant:* O wonder of wonders! O unfathomable Good, what are you? Truly, gentle dear Lord, it is very good to be here.[60] Oh, my only Love, let us stay here always!

Response of *eternal Wisdom:* You cannot remain here yet. You still have to struggle through many an encounter. This sight was only shown you so that you might learn to turn quickly (to it) in all your suffering—then you can never lose heart—and might forget all your sorrow and have an answer to the complaint of those senseless people who say that I let things go badly for my friends. Consider the difference between friendship with me and with the world and how differently I order things for my friends, if the truth be known. I shall not mention the great worry, the toil and the suffering in which they are immersed and guard against day and night. They are so blinded that they do not realize this. It is, after all, my eternal order that a disordered spirit is a torment and a severe punishment to itself. My friends experience physical distress but have peace of heart. The friends of the world, however, seek physical comfort and attain distress of heart, soul and spirit.

The *servant:* Lord, those people are without sense and insane who compare your true friendship with the false friendship of the world on the basis of your having few friends. This is due to their utter blindness. They are always complaining about some suffering. Oh, how fatherly and loving is your rod! Happy is he on whom you did not spare it![61] Lord, I now see clearly that suffering does not come from your severity. It comes from your loving tenderness. Let no one ever say that you have forgotten your friends. You forget those—because you lose hope with them—for whom you have omitted suffering here on earth. Lord, those should by rights never have a good day, never gain pleasure or comfort, whom you hereafter shall keep from eternal affliction and to whom you intend to give everlasting joy. O Lord, grant that these two visions[62] may never depart from the eyes of my heart so that I may never lose your friendship.

CHAPTER 13

The Incomparable Nobility of Earthly Suffering

Gentle Lord, tell me, which suffering do you think is extremely useful and good? And I beg you from my heart that you also tell me if you are sending it to me, so that I might accept it with love and good cheer as coming from your fatherly hand.

Response of *eternal Wisdom:* I consider every suffering good, whether it be willingly taken on or befalls one unexpectedly when a person then makes a virtue of necessity, as long as he would not want to be free of it against my will and with loving and humble patience directs it to my eternal praise. The more he does this willingly, the more noble it is and the more pleasing to me. Hear now more about such suffering and inscribe it into the ground of your heart and keep it as a sign for the spiritual eyes of your soul.

I dwell in the pure soul as in a paradise of all pleasures. This is why I cannot bear that in love or pleasure it turn to any (other) thing. By nature the soul is inclined toward harmful pleasure. And so I cover its path with thorns. I fill all the gaps with adversity, whether it likes it or not, so that it not escape me. I strew all its paths with suffering so that it cannot take one step to pursue its heart's desire except in the heights of my divine nature. If all hearts were but one heart, they could not bear on this earth the smallest reward that I intend to give in eternity for the slightest suffering that a person suffers for my sake. This is my eternal decree, which I never depart from in all of nature: Whatever is noble and good must be earned through hardship. Whoever wants to stay behind, let him do so. Many are called and few are chosen.[63]

The *servant:* Lord, it may well be that suffering is an immeasurable good as long as it is not without moderation, not cruel and terrible. Lord, you alone know all things hidden and have created all things in their number and size.[64] You know that my suffering is beyond all measure, that it is beyond my strength. Lord, if there is anyone in this whole world who has more intense and constant sufferings than I, it would be hard for me to believe. How shall I bear them? Lord, if you were to give me ordinary sufferings, I could endure them. I do not see how I can ever bear the extraordinary sufferings, which you alone really see, that secretly oppress my soul and my spirit.

Response of *eternal Wisdom:* Every sick person imagines that he is the worst off of all, and every needy person thinks that he is the poorest. If I had given you other sufferings, the same thing would happen. Surrender yourself freely to my will in all suffering that I want from you, without excepting this or that suffering. Don't you know that I only want the best for you as much as you yourself do? But I am eternal Wisdom and know better what is best of all for you. You may have felt this—that for a person handling them well, sufferings from me are more penetrating and go deeper, driving one on more vigorously than any other suffering one accepts. Why, then, are you complaining? Say rather to me: "My very devoted Father, treat me in all things as you want!"[65]

The *servant:* O Lord, this is quite easy to say, but the reality of suffering is very hard to bear. It is painful indeed.

Response of *eternal Wisdom:* If suffering were not painful, it would not be called suffering. Nothing is more painful than suffering, and nothing is more of a joy than to have suffered. Suffering is a short affliction and a long joy. What causes suffering to suffer is that for suffering there is no suffering.[66] If you had so much spiritual sweetness, divine consolation and pleasure that you constantly overflowed with dew from heaven, this would not in itself be as worthy of reward (as suffering). I would not have as much reason to be grateful to you for all of this taken together, and it would not put me in your debt as much as suffering out of love or being forsaken in hardship when you suffer this for love of me. For every person who vacillates (about undertaking a truly religious life) because of constant suffering and adversity there are ten who do so because of (a life) of great enjoyment and pleasant sweetness. If you had as much knowledge as all astronomers, and if you could speak as eloquently of God as the angelic tongues of all men and had the wealth of learning of all the professors, this could not help you progress toward a good life as much as if you knew how to surrender and abandon yourself to God in all suffering. The former things are common to good and bad alike,[67] but the latter is a characteristic of my chosen ones alone. Whoever could rightly weigh time and eternity would rather be for a hundred years in a fiery furnace than do without the smallest reward in eternity for the slightest suffering. The time in the furnace has an end; this never has any end.

The *servant:* O sweet, loving Lord, this is like the music of sweet strings to a suffering person. Lord, if only you would play such songs for me in my suffering, I would gladly suffer. Then I would feel better with suffering than without it.

Response of *eternal Wisdom:* Now, listen to the music from the taut strings of a person suffering for God (and see) how rich it sounds and how sweet the tones are:

In the eyes of the world suffering is repugnant, but in my sight it is something immeasurably valuable. Suffering quenches my anger and wins my favor. Suffering makes a person worthy of my love because a person in suffering resembles me. Suffering is a hidden good that no one can buy. If someone knelt before me for a hundred years asking to suffer well, he would not deserve it. It turns an earthly man into a heavenly man. Suffering estranges one from the world, but it affords constant intimacy with me. It decreases (the number of one's) friends, but it increases grace. If I am to become someone's friend, he must be completely rejected and forsaken by the whole world. This is the safest and shortest path, and the most perfect. Look, the person who really knows how advantageous suffering is should accept it from God as a valuable gift. Indeed, how many there are who were children of eternal death and who had fallen into a deep torpor, and suffering revived them and encouraged them to a good life! How many wild beasts and untamed birds there are who are held in check by constant suffering, as though it were a cage. And if they were given time and room enough, they would run away from their eternal happiness. Suffering preserves one from serious falls. It forces a person to know himself, to be self-reliant and to believe his neighbor. Suffering keeps the soul humble and teaches it patience. It is a guardian of purity and brings the crown of eternal happiness. There is hardly anyone[68] who does not receive something good from suffering, whether he is in sin, or a beginner, or one progressing or perfect. For it cleanses iron, purifies gold and is an adornment to precious jewelry. Suffering removes sin, shortens purgatory, repels temptations, causes faults to vanish and renews the spirit. It brings true confidence, a pure conscience and a constant positive feeling. Know that it is a healthful potion and a healing herb above all the herbs of paradise. It chastens the body, which after all will rot, and it feeds the noble soul, which shall remain forever.

Look, a noble soul thrives in suffering as beautiful roses do in the sweet dew of May. Suffering gives one wisdom and makes one a tested person. A person who has not suffered—what does he know?[69] Suffering is a (punishing) rod of love, a fatherly chastening for my chosen ones. Suffering draws a person up and forces him to God, whether he likes it or not. One who stays cheerful in suffering is served by joy and sorrow, friend and foe. How often you have smashed in the iron teeth of your snarling enemies and rendered them powerless with your joyous praise and meek suffering! I would prefer to create unnecessary suffering rather than let my friends go without suffering, because in suffering all virtues prove themselves, a person is adorned, one's neighbor is improved, and God is praised. Patience in suffering is a living sacrifice. It is a sweet fragrance of precious balsam before my divine countenance. It is a marvel springing up in front of the whole heavenly army. Never was there as great astonishment at a knight performing well in a tournament as the astonishment of the whole heavenly host at a person suffering well. All the saints are the cupbearers of a person suffering because they have tasted it already and call out with one voice that it is free of any poison and is a health-bringing potion. Patience in suffering is greater than raising the dead or performing other marvelous signs. It is the narrow path that gloriously reaches the gates of heaven. Suffering makes one the equal of the martyrs. It brings praise, and victory over all enemies. Suffering clothes the soul in a rose-colored garment, in purple.[70] It wears a garland of red roses and a scepter of green palm branches.[71] It is the sparkling ruby on the clasp (on the robe) of a virgin. In eternity it leads the singing of a new dance song with a sweet voice and free spirit, a song that the angelic hosts could never sing because they never experienced suffering. Put briefly: In the world those who suffer are called poor, but by me they are called the blessed because they are my elect.

The *servant:* Truly, it becomes very apparent that you are eternal Wisdom because you know how to bring truth out into the open so vividly that no one is able to have the slightest doubt about it. No wonder that the person for whom you make suffering such a joy can endure suffering. Lord, by your sweet words you have brought about not just that I shall find all suffering much more bearable and shall endure it in joy, my Lord and devoted Father; but also, I kneel before you today and praise you earnestly for my present suffering and for severe past suffering as well, which seemed so immense to me because it appeared so menacing.

Eternal Wisdom: What, then, is your opinion now?

The *servant:* Lord, this is what I really think: When with loving eyes I look at you, a joy for my heart to gaze upon, all the severe sufferings, with which you, like a father, have tried me, and at the sight of which your saintly friends shuddered, were like the sweet dew of springtime.

When this same Dominican father began to write about suffering, it seemed to him in the same manner as mentioned above that these same two persons[72] who had been caught up in suffering and despondency were sitting in front of him, and one of them asked that he play a tune on the psaltery.[73] This he felt was undignified, considering it not something religious. He was told that their desire for this music was not irreligious. And immediately a young man appeared who got a psaltery ready and, this done, stretched two threads crossways over the strings and put it into the friar's hands. Then he (the friar) began to speak of suffering:

<h3 style="text-align:center">CHAPTER 14</h3>

*The Inexpressible Good Arising From the
Contemplation of God's Suffering*

The *servant:* Lord, the unfathomable benefit that a person finds in your suffering, if he takes the opportunity, is truly hidden from all hearts. Indeed, the path of your suffering is a sure path through the way of truth to the highest pinnacle of all perfection. O Paul, noble light among the stars in the heavens, how fortunate you were to be drawn up so high and led deeply into the hidden mysteries of the naked Godhead where you heard those profound words than no one can utter. And yet this same (divine) suffering so deeply penetrated your heart more than any of this, so that you could say, "I know nothing but Jesus Christ, and him crucified."[74] Blessed are you among all teachers, dear St. Bernard. Your soul was so transfused by the pure light of the eternal Word, and from a full heart your sweet words endeared to us the suffering of his humanity. Your loving soul said: "I have lovingly placed between my breasts the blossoming myrrh branch of the bitter sufferings of my dear Lord and have pressed it tenderly to my heart. I do not seek as a bride where he rests at noon whom I embrace in my heart. I do not ask where he eats in the middle of the day whom my soul gazes at lovingly on the cross. The former is certainly more sublime, but the latter is sweeter and more accessible.[75] From this dear suffering I am completely recompensed for my small service. In this lies my complete justification. I consider contemplating this to be eternal wisdom, the fulfillment of all knowledge, the richness of all salvation, complete abundance of all reward. In good times it keeps me in check; in adversity it supports me. It provides the right balance between the joy and sorrow of this world and preserves me from all evil in complete safety. I have sometimes received from it a drink of his bitter suffering. Sometimes, too, I have experienced a drink of divine consolation and spiritual sweetness."[76] Therefore, dear St. Bernard, it is right for your tongue to overflow with sweetness because your heart had been so sweetened by this dear suffering.

Eternal Wisdom, in this I see that he who desires a great reward and eternal salvation, who desires sublime knowledge and profound wisdom, who wants to remain the same in joy and sorrow, be totally safe from all evil, and receive a drink of your bitter suffering and of extraordinary sweetness should keep you, Jesus crucified, constantly before the eyes of his heart.

Response of *eternal Wisdom:* You do not really know what great benefit is contained in this. Look, constant contemplation of my dear suffering turns a simple person into a highly learned master. It is a living book where one discovers all things. That person is truly blessed who keeps it always before his eyes and studies from it.

What great wisdom and grace he can gain, comfort and sweetness, the loss of all his faults and my continual presence! Now listen to something concerning this:

Many years ago, when he was a beginner, a Dominican friar experienced the bitter affliction of immoderate despondency that sometimes so overwhelmed him that no one could comprehend it who had not experienced it. Once, when he was sitting in his cell after collation, this affliction so overwhelmed him that he could neither study nor pray nor do anything useful, but only sat there sad in his cell with his hands in his lap, as though he were keeping to his cell for God's glory since he was unfit for any other spiritual activities. And as he was sitting there so disconsolate, it seemed that these sensible words were spoken to him: "Why are you sitting here? Get up and become absorbed in my suffering. Then you will overcome your suffering!" He got up quickly because it seemed to him that the words had resounded from heaven, and he focused on the suffering (of Christ); and in this suffering he lost all his suffering and never again in such a manner experienced such despondency.

The *servant:* O my sweet Wisdom, since you know all hearts, you know that above all things I desire that your anguished suffering would deeply affect all men and that it might make of my eyes a flowing spring of bitter tears day and night. Alas, my soul very much regrets that it does not affect me as deeply at all times and that it cannot contemplate it as lovingly as you, my tender Beloved, deserve. And so, teach me how I should act.

Response of *eternal Wisdom:* The contemplation of my torment should not be undertaken with hasty superficiality when one happens to have time and opportunity for it. Rather, it should be done with tender love and sorrowful reflection. Otherwise the heart remains unaffected by devotion, as the mouth does by unchewed candy. If you cannot with eyes weeping reflect upon the suffering of the bitter distress I underwent, then you should meditate on it with a laughing heart because of the joyous benefit that you discover in it. If you can neither laugh nor cry, you should think it through to my praise in the dryness of your heart. In so doing you will not have done less than if you were melting in tears and sweetness, because you are then acting out of love of virtue without advantage to yourself. That it affect you ever more deeply, listen to this:

My stern justice requires that in all of nature any injustice, be it great or small, has to be atoned for and corrected. Now how should a great sinner, who perhaps has committed more than a hundred serious sins—and, according to theological writings, each serious sin requires seven years of atonement or else the unaccomplished atonement has to be performed in the scorching furnace of grim purgatory—alas, when should this miserable soul have finished its penance? When should its long period of anguish be over? How long this would last! Yet look! It can easily do penance and make amends through my innocent and noble suffering. The soul can simply reach into the precious treasure of the merit I earned and draw on it for itself. Even if it were supposed to burn in purgatory for a thousand years, it has removed its guilt and done its penance in a short time so that it enters into eternal joy without any purgatory.

The *servant:* O my tender, eternal Wisdom, in your goodness teach me. How can I accomplish this trick?

Response of *eternal Wisdom:* It is accomplished as follows: 1. A person considers with a sorrowful heart very carefully and often the seriousness and number of his offenses, for which he has so clearly deserved angry looks from his heavenly Father. 2. He should then consider as nothing his own acts of atonement because, compared to his sins, they are a drop in the ocean. 3. He should then joyfully consider the immensity of my atonement because the smallest drop of my precious blood that flowed abundantly all over out of my loving body could atone for the sins of a thousand worlds. And yet each person draws this atonement to himself only to the extent that he identifies himself with me by suffering along with me. 4. Finally, a person should humbly and beseechingly sink his small self into the immensity of my atonement and cling to it.

Put briefly, you should realize that all mathematicians and geometricians could not measure the immense good that is hidden in the diligent contemplation of my suffering.

The *servant:* O gentle Lord, for this reason let there be an end to such talk. I have completely lost my way. Open up for me further the hidden treasure of what you suffered for love.

CHAPTER 15

After the Intimate Conversation the Soul Engaged in
With God Beneath the Cross, It Again Turns to His Suffering

The *servant:* You have revealed to me the immense distress your outer man experienced on the high gallows of the cross—how he was thoroughly tormented and surrounded with the bonds of a miserable death. But, Lord, what was going on beneath the cross? Was there someone present who was deeply affected by your wretched death? What was your relation to your sorrowful Mother in your distress?

Response of *eternal Wisdom:* Listen to something sad, and let yourself be moved by it.

When, as you have heard, I was hanging there miserably in the sight of them all in great distress and deathly anguish, they stood there facing me and very scornfully called out to me with their voices. They wagged their heads at me contemptuously, and in their hearts they despised me completely, just as though I were a repulsive worm. But I remained inwardly steadfast and interceded for them lovingly with my dear Father.[77] Look, I, the innocent lamb, was made equal to those who were guilty. By one of them I was mocked, but the other one called on me (for help). I immediately received him and forgave him all his sins. I opened up for him the paradise of heaven.[78]

Now, hear a sorry thing: Looking all around me I found myself wretchedly forsaken by everyone. Even those friends who had followed after me stood far from me.[79] My dear disciples had fled from me. I hung there naked, robbed of all my clothes. I had become the one who was powerless and conquered. They treated me mercilessly, but I behaved meekly, like a silent lamb.[80]

I was engulfed in deep sorrow and bitter anguish wherever I turned. My sorrowful Mother stood beneath me. Her maternal heart suffered in its ground everything that I suffered physically. My gentle heart was deeply moved by this because I alone really understood the great sorrow in her heart, saw her gestures of longing, and heard her sorrowful words. I consoled her very kindly as I departed in death and entrusted her to my beloved disciple to be loved as a mother, and I entrusted the disciple to her to be loved as a child.[81]

253

The *servant:* O my gentle Lord, who can here refrain from sighing deeply or weeping bitterly? My fair Wisdom, how can they be so terribly cruel to you, a sweet lamb, these raging lions, these murderous wolves, that they treated you so? Alas, gentle God, if only your poor servant had been there taking the place of everyone else and standing there before my Lord; or if only I would have gone with my only Love into bitter death; or, if they would not kill me together with my Love, if only I might have embraced the hard rock at the foot of the cross with the arms of my heart in misery and grief so that, when it burst in pity,[82] my wretched heart might burst as well for my Beloved!

Response of *eternal Wisdom:* It was my eternal decree that I bear alone at that time the cup of my bitter torment for all men. But you and all those who want to follow me and who deny themselves, take up your own cross now and follow me.[83] Such dying is as pleasing to me as though such people had gone with me to bitter death.

The *servant:* Gentle Lord, teach me then how I am to die with you and which cross is mine, for truly, my Lord, I should not continue living since you are dead for me.

Response of *eternal Wisdom:* When you strive to do the very best you know how and then, because of this, you receive from people words of scorn and contemptuous shrugs, and when they consider you in their hearts as nothing at all and think that you neither know how to nor dare to seek revenge—and if you not only stand firm and unshaken by all this but also pray lovingly to the heavenly Father for them and pardon them before him out of love—as often as you thus die to yourself out of love, just so often does my death turn green and bloom in you. When you keep yourself pure and innocent and yet your good actions are so suppressed that you are counted among the evildoers and your heart is joyful at this, and when you are so ready to forgive completely those who cause you anguish or seek your pardon for all the misery they ever caused you, as though it never happened, and, in addition, are ready to help them and render them service in word and deed in imitation of me forgiving those who crucified me, then you truly stand next to your crucified Love. When you withdraw from human advantage and comfort, except for the bare minimum you need, then your renunciation of these joys and pleasures makes up for all those who then deserted me.

When you are so free of attachments to your friends for my sake, as though they did not concern you in all things where an obstacle can occur, then I have a disciple and brother standing beneath the cross who helps me bear my suffering. The undisturbed freedom of your heart clothes and adorns my nakedness. When, in all the adversity that befalls you because of your neighbor, you are overcome for my sake and you accept the chaotic anger of all men as meekly as a silent lamb—no matter where it comes from or how quickly it arises or whether it is your fault or not—and when you thus overcome the evil of others with a good disposition, mild speech and a kind expression on your face, then the true image of my death is being fashioned in you. Truly, when I find this likeness, what pleasure and joy my heavenly Father and I experience!

Bear my bitter death in the ground of your heart, in your prayers and in the manifestation of your actions. Then you experience fully the suffering and loyal love of my pure Mother and my dear disciple.

The *servant:* O dear Lord, my soul desires you to fashion the image of your pitiful death on my body and soul to your highest praise and dearest will, whether I like it or not. Also, I desire especially that you touch a bit more upon your sorrowful Mother's grief of heart and tell me what she did beneath the cross.

Response of *eternal Wisdom:* Ask her this yourself.

CHAPTER 16

Fitting Praise for the Pure Queen of Heaven

The *servant:* O sublime Abundance of divine knowledge and wisdom, how incomprehensible are your judgments and how unknowable your ways![84] How strange are many of your paths to bring back poor souls. What were you thinking, or how well you must have been feeling in your eternal unchanging Being when you so gloriously created this pure, tender and noble creature above all pure creatures![85] Lord, you could rightly say, "*Ego cogito cogitationes pacis*—I think thoughts of peace."[86] Lord, from the abyss of your subsistent goodness there shines forth from you in her the One[87] in whom you lead back to the origin all beings that have flowed forth. Truly, heavenly Father, how would a sinful person dare approach you if you had not given us your only beloved Son, eternal Wisdom, as our guide? O eternal Wisdom, how would a poor sinful person ever muster the boldness to expose his lack of purity in the presence of such purity if he could not take the Mother of all mercy as his protection? Eternal Wisdom, if you are my Brother, you are my Lord as well. If you are true man, you are also true God and, alas, a very strict judge of wrongdoing.

And so, when our poor souls are in the narrow confines of boundless suffering and we cannot move this way or that, we have no other choice but to raise our eyes to you, dear Queen of heaven. O you refulgent Mirror of the eternal Sun's splendor, you hidden Treasure of endless, divine mercy, greetings today from me and from all sinful penitent hearts! O you sublime spirits, you pure souls, step forward. Honor, praise, revere and glorify the charming paradise of all pleasure, the lofty Queen, because I am not worthy to do so, unless she sees fit to permit it out of her goodness.

O chosen Beloved of God, you beautiful golden Throne of eternal Wisdom, allow me, a poor sinner, to chat a bit with you about my shortcomings. My soul prostrates itself before you with modest eyes, with blushing countenance, and with eyes cast down. O Mother of all grace, I somehow feel that neither my soul nor any other sinful soul needs any permission or any intercessor with you. You are a direct intercessor for all sinners. The more sinful a soul is, the more rightfully it thinks that it may approach you. The more wrong it has done, the more rightfully it crowds forward in front of you. And so, my soul, go forward freely. If your great wrongdoing drives you away, her boundless kindness invites you.

And so, you sole Comfort of all sinful hearts, you sole Refuge of guilt-ridden men, to whom many a damp eye, many a wounded and lonely heart is raised up, be a gracious intercessor and reconciler between me and eternal Wisdom. Remember, kind and beloved Queen, remember that you have all your dignity from us sinful men. What made you the Mother of God, a shrine in which eternal Wisdom sweetly slumbered? Lady, the sins of us poor men did all this. Why would you be called the Mother of grace and the Mother of mercy except because of our misery that requires your grace and mercy? Our poverty made you rich; our weakness ennobled you above all pure creatures.

And so, turn toward me, a poor mortal, your eyes of mercy that your kind heart never averted from any sinner, from any disconsolate person. Take me under your protection. My comfort and trust are in you. How many sinful souls there are who have clung to you when they have bidden farewell to God and all the host of heaven, have denied God, despaired of God, and been separated from him in misery. And they were so kindly supported by you until through your favor they again found favor. What sinner is there that committed so many crimes and evil deeds who, upon thinking of you, does not gain courage? Chosen single Comfort of us poor sinners, the boundless goodness of God has made you such a joy for all sinners that we must long for him because of your overflowing goodness. When my soul seriously reflects on you, my spirit is elated and it seems fitting to me, if it were possible, that my heart with its weeping eyes might spring out of my mouth in joy. Your name dissolves like honey in my soul. You are called, after all, the Mother, the Queen of mercy. O tender Mother, O generous Queen of boundless mercy! O your name! How immense that being is whose name is so rich in grace. Did strings ever sound so pleasant in a restless heart as this pure name does in our penitent hearts? All heads should by rights bow to this exalted name, and all knees should bend. How often you have made the hostile hands of the evil spirits withdraw from us! How often you have arrested the angry justice of our stern Judge! How often you have gained favor and comfort from him for us! And we poor sinful men, what can we say to all this? How should we ever show our gratitude for this great kindness? If the tongues of all angels, all pure spirits and souls, heaven and earth and everything contained in them, their excellence, their attractiveness, their charm and their boundless glory cannot praise it as it deserves, then what should our sinful hearts do? Let us do what we can and express our good will and gratitude because her great humility does not consider the smallness of the gift but rather the fullness of the will.

O sweet Queen, how fitting it is for all women to rejoice in you! Can one really say: Cursed be Eve for eating the fruit? Blessed be Eve for bringing us the sweet fruit of heaven! Let no one still regret (the loss of) paradise. We lost one paradise and have gained two. Or is she not a paradise in whom the fruit of the tree of life grew, in whom all bliss and joy are contained together? Or is that also not a paradise above all others in which the dead live again when they taste of the fruit from whose hands, feet and side the living spring of inexhaustible mercy, unfathomable wisdom, overflowing delight and ardent love pours over the whole earth, which is the spring of eternal life? Truly, Lord, he who has tasted of this fruit and drunk from this spring knows that these two paradises surpass by far the earthly paradise.

O esteemed Queen, you are also the Gate of all grace, the Portal of mercy that has never been closed. It is more likely that heaven and earth would pass away[88] than that you would let someone depart from you without help, if he sought it in earnest. Look, this is why you are the first thing my soul gazes upon when I arise. You are the last thing I see when I go to bed. What your pure hands bring to God's sight, though it be small in itself, because of the dignity of the messenger how can that be rejected which you, O Pure One, offer to your dear Child? And so, gentle Beloved, take my insignificant works and present them, that they might seem of some value in your hands before the eyes of God almighty. You are, after all, the pure vessel of red gold, permeated with mercy, inlaid with precious emeralds and sapphires and all virtues. In the eyes of the King of heaven the sight of this surpasses the sight of all pure creatures. O Beloved, charming Bride of God, if King Ahasuerus' heart was taken with the beauty of lovely Esther, if she found favor in his eyes above all other women, if she was found pleasing before all, so that he did what she desired,[89] alas, you who surpass red roses and all lilies, how utterly then may the King of heaven be taken by your spotless purity, by your meek humility, by the fragrant store of all your virtues and graces! Who but you captured the wild unicorn?[90] What abundant favor in his eyes does your delicate, charming beauty have, surpassing that of all humanity, and in comparison with which all beauty is extinguished like the light of a glowworm in the glaring radiance of the sun! What overflowing grace you have found in his sight for yourself and for the rest of us unfavored ones. How should or can the King of heaven deny you anything at all? You can rightfully say, "My beloved for me and I for him."[91] Oh, you who are God's and God yours, the two of you an eternal unfathomable courtship that no twoness can ever destroy! Remember and do not forget us poor needy ones who still wander so pitifully in worry and exile.

Now, O Lady of heaven and earth, arise and be a mediatrix, a bringer of grace from your tender Child, eternal Wisdom! O eternal Wisdom, how shall you deny me anything? In offering you to the eternal Father, I offer before your eyes the pure, tender, beloved Mother as well. O kind and beautiful Wisdom, now look at her. See those kind eyes that often looked upon you so lovingly. Look at those beautiful cheeks that she so often pressed so caressingly to your small face. Oh, see that sweet mouth that often covered you with kisses so tenderly. O you generous Kindness, how can you deny anything to her who suckled you so lovingly and carried you in her arms, putting you down and lifting you up, and raised you so gently?

Lord, I ask you to remember all the love that you enjoyed from her in the days of your childhood when, sitting on your Mother's lap, you smiled at her so very tenderly with your sparkling eyes, gently embraced her with the arms of a child in the immense love and affection you had for her above all (other) creatures. Remember also the great sorrow that her maternal heart alone helped you bear beneath the desolate cross, as she saw you dying and her heart and soul again and again died with you in misery and distress, and through her grant me the grace to renounce all obstacles, to seek to gain your favor and never to lose it.

CHAPTER 17

Her Indescribable Sorrow

Who shall give my eyes as many tears as there are letters that I might describe with bright tears the desolate tears and immense sorrow of my dear Lady? Pure Lady and noble Queen of heaven and earth, touch my heart of stone with one of the hot tears you shed at the bitter distress of your gentle Child (as you stood) under the cross, that it may be softened and become sensitive to you. It is the nature of sorrow that no one really knows it except whom it touches. Oh, touch my heart now, beloved Lady, with your sad words, and tell me briefly yet poignantly for my own improvement how you felt and how you conducted yourself beneath the cross as you saw your tender Child, fair, eternal Wisdom, die in such misery.

Response: You shall hear this in grief and sorrow. For even though I am now free of all suffering, that was not how things were then.

Before I came beneath the cross, I had already received many great and indescribable sorrows, beginning especially from the place where I had the first sight of my Child being beaten, shoved and mistreated. From this I lost my strength and, thus weakened, I was led behind my dear Son all the way to the foot of the cross. But what you were asking about—how I felt and how I conducted myself—listen, as far as it is possible to understand, for no heart ever born can grasp it completely.

Look, compared to the infinite depths of sorrow my motherly heart then experienced, all the sorrow that any heart ever had would be like a drop compared to the sea. And keep this in mind: The more loved a loved one is and the more delightful and sweeter he is, the more unbearable his loss and death are. Oh, where was ever born on earth someone more gentle or more lovable than my only dear Love? With him and in him I possessed completely all that this world could offer. I had died to myself and lived in him; and when my fair Love was killed, it was then that I died completely. Because my only Love was my only One and my Love beyond all love, my only sorrow was my only One and a sorrow beyond all sorrow ever uttered. His beautiful, friendly humanity was for me a joy to look upon; his revered divinity was a delight for my eyes. To think of him was the cheer of my heart. To speak of him was my pleasure. To hear his sweet words was like music to my soul. He was a mirror of my heart, bliss for my soul. Heaven, earth and everything therein I possessed in his presence. When I saw my only Love hanging there before me dying—what a terrible sight this was for my eyes! How my heart stopped within me! How my spirit died! I lost all strength and my senses grew faint. I looked up and was unable to help my dear Child. I looked down and saw with my very eyes those who were so terribly abusing my Child. How oppressive was the whole earth for me! I had lost my heart. My voice would not work. I had lost my strength entirely. And yet, when I came to myself, I raised my hoarse voice in misery and said to my Child, among other things, words like this: "O my Child, the Mirror of my heart's joy in which I have often looked at myself with elation, how pitiable do I see you before my eyes now! O Treasure more precious than this whole world, my Mother, my Father, and everything my heart can offer, take me with you! Or to whom shall you entrust your disconsolate mother as you go? O my Child, who shall allow me to die in place of you?[92] That I suffer this bitter death instead of you? Oh, the terrible distress of a mother who lost her love; how all my joy, love and comfort has been torn from me. O longed-for death, why do you spare me? Take me, take the poor mother to her Child. Life is more bitter to her than any death. I see him actually dying whom my soul loves. O my Child, my dear Child!"

And as I surrendered myself so to my grief, my Child comforted me kindly and said, among other things, that mankind could not otherwise be saved and he intended to rise on the third day and to appear to me and his disciples. He said, "Lady, stop your weeping. Weep not, my beautiful Mother. I shall not leave you forever." And when my Child had consoled me so gently and entrusted me to the disciple whom he loved and who was also standing there full of sorrow—his words entered my heart with such grief and sadness that they pierced through my heart and soul like a pointed sword— then even hard hearts took very great pity on me. I raised my hands and arms and would have liked to embrace my Love in the sorrow of my heart, but I could not. Overcome by my deep sorrow I sank there beneath the cross, I know not how often, and did not utter a word. When I came to myself and could not do anything to help, I kissed the blood flowing down from his wounds and my pale cheeks and mouth became covered with blood.

The *servant:* O infinite Meekness, what immense torment and distress this is! Where should I turn or to whom shall I raise my eyes? If I look at beautiful Wisdom, I see distress that should make my heart sink. Externally, he is being shouted at; internally, he struggles in combat with death. All his muscles are taut; all his blood spent. Nothing all around but pain and misery; a grim death with no hope of recovery. If I turn my eyes to his pure Mother, I see her tender heart deeply wounded, as though a thousand daggers were sticking in it, and I see her pure soul in torment. Never has one seen the like of her gestures of yearning or heard the like of this Mother's mourning. Her wasted body sank down in grief, her fair face covered with the dried blood. Oh, this is a grief and distress above all others! The torment of his heart is caused by the sorrow of his forlorn Mother. The torment of the sad Mother is caused by her dear innocent Child's death that is more painful for her than her own death. He looks at her and comforts her kindly. She lifts her hands up toward him and would gladly die miserably in his place. Oh, which of the two suffers more? Whose distress is greater? It is for both of them so immense that the like was never seen. The Mother's heart! The tender feelings of the Lady! How could your mother's heart ever bear all this immeasurable suffering? Blessed be this tender heart. All the sorrow ever described in word or writing is, when compared to all this sorrow, like a dream compared to reality. Blessed are you, red-rising Sun of the dawn, above all creatures; and blessed is the blossoming, rose-covered meadow of your fair face, which is adorned with the ruby blood of eternal Wisdom!

And you, friendly countenance of beautiful Wisdom, how you are dying! O fair body hanging there! O pure blood running down warm upon the Mother who bore you. O all you mothers, hear of this profound grief! All you pure hearts, be moved by this rosy-hued, pure blood that so drenched the pure Mother! Look, all hearts who ever felt sorrow, and see that never was there anything like this sorrow.[93] No wonder our hearts dissolve from grief and pity. This misery was certainly enough to split hard stones, make the earth quake and extinguish the sun, so that they might share their Creator's suffering.

CHAPTER 18

What the Condition of His Inner Man Was at This Time

The *servant:* Eternal Wisdom, the closer one approaches your immeasurable suffering, the more beyond all dimensions it becomes. Your distress was very great *beneath* the cross; it was greater still *on* the cross as to your exterior powers, which at this time were experiencing the throes of bitter death. O my gentle Lord, what was the condition of the inner man, of your noble soul? Did it experience some consolation or sweetness then, as other martyrs did, which then eased a bit the terrible suffering? Or when did it all end?

Response of *eternal Wisdom:* Hear of anguish beyond all the anguish that you have ever heard. Although the highest powers of my soul continued to see and enjoy the naked Godhead in accordance with its sublimity, the lower powers of the inner and outer man had nevertheless been so completely abandoned to themselves to the most extreme point of immense bitterness—suffering with not a bit of consolation—that no torment was ever its equal. And as I hung there utterly helpless and forsaken, with blood dripping from my wounds, my eyes weeping, my arms stretched out and the twisted tendons of all my limbs at the point of death, I raised my pitiful voice and called out in my abandonment to my Father saying, "My God, my God, why have you forsaken me?"[94] But in spite of this my will was united with his in the eternal order. And when my blood and all my strength had been completely poured out and drained away, I became terribly thirsty in my death agony; but my thirst for the salvation of all men was more terrible still. In my torment of thirst my mouth was offered gall and vinegar. And when I had accomplished the salvation of mankind, I said, "It is finished."[95] I offered my Father complete obedience to death.[96] I entrusted my spirit into his hands saying, "Into your hands I commend my spirit."[97] Then my noble soul departed from my divine body, both of which remained unseparated from my divinity. Afterward a sharp spear was jabbed through my right side. A stream of precious blood trickled forth and, along with it, a spring of living water.

See, my child, through such sad misery I won back you and all those chosen and redeemed from eternal death by the living sacrifice of my innocent blood.

The *servant:* O gentle, dear Lord and Brother, how terribly bitter was your regaining me! How dearly have you loved me and as a true friend redeemed me. O my fair Wisdom, how can I thank you for your love and great suffering? Lord, if I had the strength of Samson, the beauty of Absalom, the wisdom of Solomon and the riches and glory of all kings, I would want to use them all up in your service and praise you. But, Lord, I am nothing and can do nothing. O Lord, how shall I thank you?

Response of *eternal Wisdom:* If you had the tongues of all the angels, the good works of all men and the powers of all creatures, you could not show me (proper) gratitude for the least of the sufferings I ever endured for love of you.

The *servant:* Gentle Lord, grant me and teach me by your grace to win your favor since no one can repay you for the signs of your love.[98]

Response of *eternal Wisdom:* You should keep before your eyes my cross, bare of all comfort, and let my bitter torment penetrate your heart, modeling all your suffering on it. When I abandon you to comfortless suffering, let you languish unfeeling and dry up without sweetness, as my heavenly Father let me do; you should not go seeking comfort from others. Your lonely calls shall be directed to the heavenly Father in renunciation of self to please his fatherly will. See, the more bitter your external suffering and the more forsaken you are within, the more you resemble me and are pleasing to the heavenly Father, because in experiencing this pious persons are tested most severely. When you have a thirsting desire to find satisfaction and pleasure in something that would be very pleasant for you, you should renounce it out of love, and your thirsty mouth will share with me a drink of bitterness. You should thirst for the salvation of all men. You should direct your good works toward a life of perfection and carry through to the end. You should have a submissive will quick to obey your superiors, a soul surrendered into the hands of the heavenly Father with everything it calls its own, and a spirit that has left time behind for eternity after the model of your final departure. See, your cross is then modeled on my cross of anguish and shall thus be nobly brought to completion.

In my open side you should lovingly close yourself up next to my heart wounded for love and should seek to dwell there and remain there. Then I shall cleanse you with living water and adorn you in rose colors with my rose-colored blood. I shall attach myself to you and unite you to me forever.

The *servant:* Lord, never was there a magnet that drew hard iron to itself with such power as your exemplary and loving suffering joins all hearts to it. O dear Lord, now draw me through joy and sorrow away from this world to you on the cross; bring about in me the most perfect similarity to your cross so that my soul shall enjoy you in your most sublime glory.

CHAPTER 19

The Descent From the Cross

The *servant:* O pure Mother and gentle Lady, when did the great and bitter sorrow you felt because of your beloved child come to an end?

Response: Listen with grieving pity. When my gentle Child had departed and was hanging there before me dead, and my heart and mind had been drained of all strength, since I could do nothing else, I still kept looking up helplessly to my dear Child. And when they came and wanted to take him down, it seemed as though I were brought back from the dead. Oh, how like a mother I took hold of his lifeless arms! With what love did I press them to my blood-covered cheeks! And when he was down, with what deep love I embraced him, dead as he was, in my arms and pressed to my motherly heart my only dear and tender Love, kissing all his wounds still fresh with blood and his lifeless face, which, along with his whole body, had taken on an exquisite beauty beyond what all hearts could imagine. I took my tender Child onto my lap and looked at him.[99] Now he was dead. I looked at him again and again. There was no sign or sound of life. Then my heart died again and would have liked to burst into a thousand pieces from the mortal wounds it received. It sighed deeply and intensely again and again. My eyes let flow many a desolate and bitter tear. My whole appearance was sad indeed. My words of grief, as they came to my lips, were so distorted by pain that they remained broken. I said: "Oh, was ever anyone on this earth as maliciously mistreated as this innocent, beloved Child? O my Child, my Comfort and my only Joy, why have you abandoned me? You have become nothing but a source of sorrow for me! Where now is the joy I had from your birth? Where is the pleasure I had from your dear childhood? Where is the honor and respect I had from your presence? What happened to all the things that were able to bring joy to my heart? Oh, anguish, bitterness and sorrow! It has all become endless sorrow and deathly torment. O my Child, my Child, now I am without all love. My heart has been robbed of all consolation!" These and other laments I spoke over my dead Child.

The *servant:* O pure and fair Mother, permit me, let me once more bring relief to my heart at the sight of your Love and my Lord, dear Wisdom, before the parting must come and he is carried off from us to the grave. Pure Mother, no matter how profound your sorrow was and how very deeply it may move all hearts, it still seems to me that you should somehow have found joy in lovingly embracing your dead Child. O pure, gentle Lady, I now beg you to lay your tender Child on the lap of my soul, as he looked in death, that I might experience in spirit through contemplation, as far as I can, what you then experienced physically.

Lord, I turn my eyes to you in joyful elation and intense love. Never was a loved one so looked upon by his beloved. Lord, my heart opens to receive you, as does the delicate rose to receive the bright radiance of the sun. Lord, my soul stretches out wide toward you the arms of its immense desire. Dear Lord, in ardent desire I embrace you today with thanks and praise, and I press you to the innermost part of my heart and soul and bid you that this precious moment never be lost for me. And I beg that neither life nor death, joy nor sorrow ever separate you from me. Lord, my eyes gaze intently at your lifeless countenance. My soul kisses all your fresh, bloody wounds; my whole consciousness is nourished by this sweet fruit under this living tree of the cross. And this is as it should be. Lord, one person finds reassurance in his innocent life; another in his harsh penances and austere manner of living; yet another in this, and another in that. But all my comfort and hope are completely in your suffering, in the reconciliation you effected, and in the reward you earned. And so I shall always carry it with me joyfully in the depths of my heart and, as far as I can, display this same example outwardly in word and deed.

O delightful Splendor of the eternal Light, you have now been completely extinguished for my sake. Extinguish in me the burning desires of all vices. O pure, bright Mirror of the divine majesty, how befouled you now are! Cleanse away the blemishes caused by my misdeeds. O fair Likeness of the Father's goodness, how defiled and utterly disfigured you are! Restore the disfigured and faded picture of my soul.[100] Oh, you innocent Lamb, how poorly you have been treated! Do penance and atone for my guilt-ridden, sinful life. O King of kings and Lord of lords, my soul sees you lying here so wretched in death. As my soul now embraces you in sorrow and mourning at your abandonment, grant that it may be embraced by you with joy in your eternal glory.

CHAPTER 20

The Sad Parting From the Grave

The *servant:* Now, gentle Lady, bring your sorrow and your words to a conclusion and tell me how you parted from your beloved Child.

Response: It was a sad thing to hear and see. Oh, it was all endurable as long as I had my Child with me. But when they tore my dead Child from my deadened heart, from my arms embracing him and from my face pressed against him, and buried him, one can hardly imagine how wretched I then felt. When it was time to depart, what grief and anguish one saw in me! When they parted me from my buried Love, this parting was like death wrestling with my heart. Helpless, I walked supported by the hands of those leading me. I was utterly without consolation. My heart was grieving and longing again for its Love. My trust was unbroken. Among all people I alone showed him complete loyalty and true devotion to the grave.

The *servant:* Dear, gentle Lady, this is why all hearts greet you and all tongues praise you, for all the goodness the heart of the Father wanted to give us flowed through your hands. You are the beginning and the mediatrix.[101] You shall also be the end. O gentle, pure Mother, remember today that sorrowful parting. Think of the bitter departure you took from your tender Child and help me never to be separated from you or his joyous sight. O pure Mother, as my whole soul stands by you in kind pity, receives you with sincere desire, and, in contemplation with heart full of desire, in gratitude and praise, leads you back through the gate at Jerusalem to your house, I beg that on its final journey my soul might be guided by you, pure gentle Mother and Goal of all my comfort, to its fatherland and that it may be established in eternal blessedness. Amen.

Part Two

CHAPTER 21

How One Should Learn to Die and What a Death Unprepared for Is Like

Eternal Wisdom, if someone were to give me the whole earth as my own, that would not be as dear to me as the truth and profit I have found in your delightful teaching. And so I ask you from the depths of my heart, eternal Wisdom, to teach me yet more.

Lord, what is most important for a servant of eternal Wisdom, if he wishes to be yours alone? Lord, I would like to hear about the union of the naked intellect with the holy Trinity where, in the true reflection of the birth of the Word and also the birth of their Spirit, the intellect is taken from itself and is stripped of all obstacles.

Response of *eternal Wisdom:* A person standing at the bottom in his own (spiritual) life should not ask about the most sublime teachings. I shall teach you what can profit you.

The *servant:* Lord, what do you want to teach me?

Response of *eternal Wisdom:* 1. I shall teach you how to die. 2. I shall teach you how to live. 3. I shall teach you to receive me with love. 4. And I shall teach you to praise me ardently.[102] See, this is what is really most important for you.

The *servant:* Eternal Wisdom, if I could have anything I wished for, I do not know of anything else I should wish for but to know how to die to myself and all things, to live for you alone, to love you with my whole heart, to receive you lovingly, and to praise you as you deserve. O God, how blessed is the person who can do all this properly and who consumes his whole life in doing it! Lord, do you mean a spiritual dying, which your lonely death demonstrated so lovingly, or physical death?

Response of *eternal Wisdom:* I mean both of them.

The *servant:* Lord, why do I need instruction about the death of the body? It teaches itself quite well, when it arrives.

Response of *eternal Wisdom:* If one puts off learning about it until then, one is ill-prepared.

The *servant:* O Lord, right now I find it a bit unpleasant to hear about death.

Response of *eternal Wisdom:* See, this is the reason for the increase in deaths that are unprepared for and frightening, of which the towns and monasteries are now so full. Such a death has often secretly been lying in wait for you and was about to carry you off, as he (death) does to countless multitudes among whom I shall show you one in particular. Now open your inner senses. See and listen! See the figure of grim Death next to your neighbor. Listen to the doleful voice you shall hear.

The *servant* heard in his mind how the grim figure of a person dying unprepared screamed words full of regret like this:

"The groans of death surround me."[103] Oh, God in heaven, that I was ever born into this world! The beginning of my life was with screaming and crying, and now my departure is with bitter screaming and weeping. Oh, the groans of death have surrounded me. The pains of hell have surrounded me. Oh, Death! Oh, terrible Death, what a grim visitor you are for my young and carefree heart! How little have I been expecting you! And now you have fallen upon me from behind. You have quickly caught up with me. Oh, you are leading me away in your shackles as one leads off a condemned man to the place where he is to be killed. I clap my hands together over my head; I wring them together in grief because I would like to escape. I look around me to all corners of this world to see if anyone can help or counsel me, and there is no one. I hear death speaking deathly within me thus: 'Neither friend nor possessions nor ability nor intelligence are of any help. It has to be.' Oh, does it really have to be? Oh, God, do I really have to go? Is the parting now? That I was ever born! Oh, Death, oh, Death, what do you intend to do to me?"

The *servant* spoke: Dear friend, why are you behaving so badly? This is the common destiny of rich and poor, of young and old. Many more people go to their death before their time than at their time. Or did you imagine that you alone could escape death? That was a serious misunderstanding!

Response of the *man dying unprepared:* Oh, God, what bitter consolation this is! My conduct is not incomprehensible. Theirs is who have not lived for him (God) and are not being frightened by death. They are blind; they die like cattle, not knowing what awaits them. I am not complaining that I have to die. Alas, I complain that I must die unprepared! I mourn not just the end of my life. I wail and weep for the happy days that are so utterly lost and gone without any benefit. I am like one born before his time and cast away, like a May blossom torn off. My days passed by more swiftly than the arrow leaving the bow.[104] That I ever existed is as forgotten as the path that the bird makes through the air, which closes again behind it and is lost for all men.[105] This is why my words are full of bitterness and my speech full of pain.[106]

Oh, who will permit me, poor man, to be as I was before, that I still have the happy times before me, yet know what I know now. Oh, when I was living in those times, I did not rightly appreciate it. I let it pass by emptily and foolishly. Now it has been torn from me and I can bring nothing of it back again. I cannot catch up with it. No hour was so short that I should not have considered it more precious and been more thankful for it than a poor man who had been given a kingdom. This is why the bright tears wet my eyes— because they cannot bring this back again. Oh, God in heaven, that I have frivolously wasted so many days and that this is of no help to me now! Why did I not learn in all that time to die? Oh, you blooming roses, who still have your life ahead of you, look at me and learn something. Turn your youth to God and pass the time with him alone so that this does not happen to you. Oh, youth, how I wasted you! Lord of heaven, let me grieve about it to you forever. I did not want to believe anyone. My reckless spirit was not able to listen to anyone. Oh, God, now I have fallen into the trap of bitter death. The time is up, youth is over. It would have been better for me that my mother's womb had been my grave than that I so utterly wasted the happy time.

The *servant:* Turn to God; be sorry for your sins. All is well that ends well.

Response of the *man dying unprepared:* What kind of talk is that? I should be sorry? I should change my ways? Don't you see I am utterly terrified? My anguish is great indeed. My lot is like that of a wounded bird, held in a hawk's talons, that has been rendered senseless by its mortal distress. I can only wish to escape, yet cannot. Death and bitter parting press in on me. Alas, Sorrow and Free Conversion of a person still capable, you are such a certainty! Who loses you is lost. Oh, that I so long put off my amendment! Now it has become too long! Good will without actions, good intentions unfulfilled have been my ruin. I put God off until I fell into the night of death. Oh, almighty God, is that not a calamity beyond all calamities? Should that not cause me pain that I have thus lost my whole life, my thirty years? And yet I really do not know that I ever spent a day completely in accordance with God's will, as by right I should have if I ever gave God any acceptable service. Oh, this cuts through my heart. Oh, God, how shamefully I shall stand before you and all the hosts of heaven!

Now I shall depart. Now a single Hail Mary spoken with devotion would cheer me more than if someone would put a thousand gold marks in my hand. Oh, God, what a waste; I myself am the one who has harmed me. That I did not notice this while I could! How many hours escaped me! That I let such trivial things lead me away from such immense happiness! I would prefer, and it would bring me more eternal reward, that I had renounced, out of love (for God) the pleasure I had seeing my friend, which happened against God's will, than if this person had asked God for a reward on my behalf on his knees for thirty years. Listen, listen, everyone, to something lamentable: I went all around, since my time was short, and was begging for the small alms of the reward earned by good people as atonement for myself; and they turned me down because they were afraid that the oil in their lamps would not be enough.[107] Oh, God of heaven, feel pity at this. I could have earned such great reward and riches on many a day with my healthy body as I went around with nothing to do. And now this small alms, just for atonement, not as a reward, would make me grateful; but no one gives it to me. Oh, people young and old, let this move you deeply. Gather in the good times so that at this time you do not become beggars like me and be sent away.

The *servant:* Oh, dear friend, your distress affects me deeply. I ask you by the living God, give me some advice so that this same distress does not befall me.

Response of the *man dying unprepared:* The best advice, the greatest wisdom and foresight on earth, is to prepare yourself by a general confession and by renouncing everything you are attached to, and to keep yourself in this state, as though you were going to depart from here that same day or in a week at the most. Imagine now in your heart that your soul is in purgatory and is to be there for ten years because of its misdeeds and that this year alone is given to you to help it. Look at it often—how disconsolately it calls out to you and says, "Oh, my dearest friend, give me your hand. Have pity on me. Help me to escape this terrible fire right now. I am so alone that no one can help me with their loyalty but you alone. The whole world has forgotten me. Everyone is looking out for himself."

The *servant:* This would be well-chosen advice for one deeply concerned and experiencing this now, as you are. But although your words cut to the quick, people sit around and pay little attention to them. They have ears and do not hear. They have eyes and do not see. No one intends to die before his soul departs.[108]

Response of the *man dying unprepared:* Therefore, when they are dangling from the hook of bitter death and cry out in pain, they will not be heard. Look, not one person in a hundred wearing the religious habit—I won't even mention the others—pays any attention to my words to turn his life around and improve. And hence it has reached the point that under a hundred there is not one who does not fall unprepared into death's snare, just as I have done. Happy are those who do not die in complete ignorance and without insight. Vain honor, ease of the body, passing love and the selfish seeking of everyday needs blind most people. If you want to be among the few who avoid a miserable and unprepared death, follow my advice. The constant thought of death, the loyal support of your poor soul that calls to you in such misery, will quickly bring you to the point of not only not fearing death but even of welcoming it with the full desire of your heart. Reflect on me seriously and often every day. Engrave my words on your heart. Look at my bitter anguish that shall soon be yours. Look at what kind of night this is. Happy that he was ever born is the person who comes to this hour well-prepared. He is well-off even if his death is hard. Resplendent angels watch over him. The saints accompany him. The court of heaven receives him. His last journey is an entrance into his eternal fatherland. Alas, God, where shall my soul yet find shelter tonight in this strange, unknown land? Oh, God, how utterly my soul is abandoned! How lonely it is among all the lonely souls! Who is there to help it with complete devotion?

LITTLE BOOK OF ETERNAL WISDOM

Now I shall end my mournful lament. The hour has come. Alas, I see that it cannot be otherwise. Life is ebbing away from my hands. My face drains of color; my eyes are vacant. The onslaughts of heartless death struggle against my poor soul. I begin desperately to seek for breath. The light of this world begins to fade. I see a different world. Oh, God, it is a hideous sight! The ruthless forms of black Moors are gathering. The beasts of hell have surrounded me. They look at my poor soul to see if it shall belong to them. Oh, just Judge, stern judgment! How heavy you weigh the smallest things that no one paid any attention to because of their insignificance! In terror the chilling sweat of death penetrates my body. The angry look of the stern Judge! How strict are your judgments!

Now I turn in spirit to the other world where I am soon to be led—to purgatory, and I see in this land of torment terror and agony. Oh, God, I see the wild hot flames shoot up high over their heads. They bob up and down in the murky flames like sparks in a fire. They scream: "Oh, great is our suffering!" No heart can comprehend the variety and intensity of our afflictions. One hears many a sad cry: "Help, oh, help! Where is the help of our friends? Where are all the nice promises of our faithless friends? They have forsaken us. They have completely forgotten us. Oh, have pity, have pity on us, dearest friends of ours! We served you well. What we did love and how we have been rewarded! Now you are letting us burn in this hot stove! Oh, that we did not prevent this ourselves. We could have done so very easily. The slightest torment here is more than any martyr on earth ever suffered. One hour in purgatory lasts a hundred years! Now we are boiling, now we are roasting, now we cry for help! But above all else is the torment that we must for so long be without the joyful sight (of God). This drains heart, mind and spirit." And thus I die.

The *servant:* O eternal Wisdom, have you forsaken me? O God, how vivid death has become for me! O my soul, are you still in my body? Lord of heaven, do I still live? O Lord, I praise you and promise you improvement until my death. I am utterly terrified. I never realized that death was so close to me. Truly, Lord, this sight will be good for me always. Lord, every day I go forward looking for death's ambush, watching that it does not creep up on me from behind. I shall learn how to die. I shall direct my life toward the other world. Lord, I see that there is nothing permanent here.[109] Lord, I shall certainly not put off my sorrow and penance until

273

death. Help, I am so frightened at the sight of this that I am surprised my soul is still in my body. Away, away from me, comfortable repose, long sleeping, good eating and drinking, transitory honor, luxury and sensual pleasure. Here on earth a little suffering causes me such pain. How shall I ever endure that immense suffering? O God, if I were thus dead, if I were to die right now, how would I fare? I still have so much (guilt) upon me. Lord, today I shall consider my poor soul as a beggar and, since all friends forsake it, I shall be its friend.

Response of *eternal Wisdom:* Look, this is what you should constantly consider as long as you are young, as long as you are healthy and strong, and as long as you can make amends. But when you really come to the hour when there can be no more amendment, then you should look at nothing else on earth but my death and my infinite mercy so that your trust (in me) might remain intact.

The *servant:* O Lord, I fall before your feet with bitter tears and beg you to let me do penance here, however you want. Just don't put it off for me for there! O Lord, (I fear) purgatory and immense suffering. How uncomprehending I have been until now that I have considered this so little. And now I fear it so terribly!

Response of *eternal Wisdom:* Take heart! This fear is a beginning of all wisdom and a path to all happiness.[110] Or have you forgotten, as all of scripture cries out, what great wisdom there is in fear and the constant contemplation of death? You should forever praise God because under a thousand men not one has been given this insight as you have. Hear something that is a shame. They hear it being talked about and know about it beforehand, yet let it pass and ignore it until they are devoured by it. Then they call out; then they moan and weep. Then it is too late. But you, open your eyes, count on your fingers how many there are who have died in your time. Talk to them in your heart, place the old you beside them, as though he were dead, and ask them all. See how they speak with deep groans and bitter tears: "Oh, happy is he ever to be born who follows that sweet advice and learns from the harm that has come to others!" Prepare well for a journey because truly you are like a bird sitting on a branch and like a man standing on the shore watching the boat quickly sailing off, in which he, too, shall one day be sitting, and sailing to a strange land from which he shall never return. And so, put your whole life in such order that, when death comes, you are ready and depart joyfully.

LITTLE BOOK OF ETERNAL WISDOM

How One Should Live Inwardly

The *servant:* Lord, there are many (spiritual) practices. There are many ways of living, one like this, another like that. The modes are many and different. Lord, the writings about this are endless, and the teachings on this subject are beyond number. Eternal Wisdom, tell me in a few words out of the profundity of them all taken together: On what should I rely most in keeping to the path of true life?

Response of *eternal Wisdom:*[111] The truest, most useful, most effective teaching that you can find in all these writings, where with brevity you are richly instructed in all truth about the most lofty perfection of a pure life, is this: 1. Keep yourself apart from all men. 2. Keep yourself free of all images coming from outside. 3. Free yourself from everything that is accidental, binding or that brings worry. 4. Always direct your spirit to the intimate contemplation of God, keeping me constantly present before your eyes and never really turning them away from me. Direct all other exercises, whether poverty, fasting, vigils and all other types of chastisement, toward this as their goal, and make use of them to the extent that they further you to this end. Then you shall attain the summit of perfection that not one person in a thousand comprehends because they make these other exercises their goal and therefore wander about for years.

The *servant:* But, Lord, who can constantly remain with their uninterrupted sight on your divine presence?

Response of *eternal Wisdom:* No one can who now lives on this earth. You have only been told this so that you know what your goal is, where you should set your aim, and in what direction your heart and spirit should strive. And when you are deprived of this sight it should be like having your eternal happiness taken away from you, and you should immediately return to it so that you have it again; and you should keep a watch on yourself. For when you lose it, you are like a man in a boat whose oars have slipped from his grasp in heavy waves and he does not know where to turn. But if you cannot permanently remain in this contemplation, the great number of times you return to it and your repeatedly taking refuge there should take you toward permanence as far as this is possible.

Listen, my child, to the loving instruction of your devoted Father.[112] Pay heed to it now. Lock it up in the depths of your heart. Remember who it is who is teaching you this and how profoundly serious he is about it. If you wish to become ever more perfect, keep it before your eyes. Wherever you sit, stand or go, let it be for you as though I am present to you, admonishing you and saying, "My child, keep yourself inward, pure, free and directed upward." Then you will quickly become aware of my words. And you will also understand well what is yet quite hidden from you.

The *servant:* O eternal Wisdom, may you be praised forever! My Lord and my most faithful Friend, even if I did not want to do this on my own, you would force me to with your sweet words and gentle, dear teachings. Lord, I must and shall devote myself to this with all my efforts.

CHAPTER 23

With What Love One Should Receive God

Eternal Wisdom, if my soul could only enter the hidden shrine of your divine mystery, I would want to ask still more about love; and this is my question: Lord, in your sufferings for love you so poured out the abyss of your boundless love that I wonder if you would be able to give any more signs of your love.

Response of *eternal Wisdom:* Just as the stars in the heavens are beyond number, so the signs of my infinite love are countless.

The *servant:* O sweet Love of mine, gentle, dear, beloved Lord, look how my soul yearns for your love. Turn your loving face toward me, an outcast creature. See how everything within me fades and withdraws except for the one treasure of your ardent love, and tell me more about this precious secret treasure. Lord, you know that it is proper for love that it never has enough of what it loves. The more it has, the more it desires, no matter how unworthy it knows itself to be in this regard. This is the force of love working. O fair Wisdom, tell me, aside from the unfathomable sign of love your bitter death was, what is the greatest and dearest sign of love you gave in becoming man?

Response of *eternal Wisdom:* First, you answer a question for me:

Among all the things that pertain to love, what is it that a loving heart most desires from its beloved?

The *servant:* Lord, as I see things, nothing is more desirable to a loving heart than the beloved himself and his very dear presence.

Response of *eternal Wisdom:* This is true. Look, because I knew in advance the sorrowful longing many a loving heart would feel for me when my boundless love forced me to leave this world through my bitter death and return to my Father, this is why—so that nothing essential for true love would be lacking for those I love—I gave my very self and my dear presence to my disciples at the banquet of the Last Supper and continue to give this to my chosen ones every day.

The *servant:* O dear Lord, are you yourself really present?

Response of *eternal Wisdom:* In the sacrament you have me before you and with you as truly and really, as both God and man, body and soul, flesh and blood, as certainly as my pure Mother carried me in her arms and as truly as I am in heaven in perfect splendor.

The *servant:* Gentle Lord, there is something now in my heart. May I have your permission to speak to you about it? Lord, it does not arise from a lack of faith. I believe you can accomplish whatever you will to do. But, my gentle Lord, if I may dare to say it, I am puzzled how the beautiful, marvelously glorified body of my dear Lord can in its grandeur and fullness hide itself so mysteriously under the tiny form of the bread, which is so disproportionate to your greatness. Gentle Lord, do not be angry! Because you are my dearly beloved Wisdom, I would like, by your favor, to hear something about this from your own sweet mouth.

Response of *eternal Wisdom:* No tongue can say how my fair body and soul are truly present in the sacrament because no mind can grasp it. It is a work of my omnipotence. And so you should just simply believe it and should not pursue the matter much. Still, I must tell you a little about it. I shall drive out this marvel with another marvel. Tell me, how can it be in nature that a large house can be reconstituted in a small mirror, and in every piece (of the mirror) if it were divided? Or how can it be that the huge sky presses itself so small into the tiny eye, although they are so unlike in size?

The *servant:* Lord, I really don't know what to say. It is a strange thing. The eye is a point in comparison with the sky.

THE EXEMPLAR

Response of *eternal Wisdom:* Look, even though neither this nor any other thing in nature is like that and yet nature can make it happen, why couldn't I then, the Lord of nature, do many more things in a manner transcending nature? Now tell me, isn't it just as great a marvel to create heaven, earth and all creatures out of nothing as it is to change bread into me, though I remain invisible?

The *servant:* Lord, as I understand it, it is just as possible for you to change one thing into another as to create something out of nothing.

Response of *eternal Wisdom:* And the one thing puzzles you but the other doesn't? Then tell me, you believe that I fed five thousand men from five loaves of bread? Where was the secret material that served my words?

The *servant:* Lord, I don't know.

Wisdom: Or do you believe that you have a soul?

The *servant:* Lord, I don't believe it because I *know* it. Otherwise I would not be living.

Response of *eternal Wisdom:* But you can't see the soul with any physical eyes. Do you believe that no other being exists except what one can see and hear?

The *servant:* Lord, I know that there are many more beings that are unseen by all physical eyes than those one can see.

Wisdom: Now consider. Many a person has such an unsophisticated mind that he does not want to believe that something exists except what he can grasp with his senses, although learned persons have the knowledge that this is not true. The same relationship pertains here between human understanding and divine knowledge. If I had asked you, what are the entrances to the abyss like, or how are the waters placed above the sky, you might say: "That is too deep for me. I don't pursue such matters. I never came to the abyss or up to the sky." In this case I was asking you about physical things you see and hear, yet you don't understand them. How then do you expect to comprehend that which totally surpasses heaven, earth and all understanding? Or why do you want to ask about it? Look, such puzzlement and the occurrence of such thoughts arise because of the crudeness of the mind, which perceives divine and supernatural things as being similar to physical and natural things. But this is not the case. If a woman were to give birth to a child in a dungeon, and as it was being raised there, the mother would explain about the sun and the stars, the child would be greatly puzzled and would

278

think to be untrue and unbelievable that which is perfectly obvious to the mother.

The *servant:* Lord, I certainly can say nothing more because you have enlightened my faith that no puzzlement need ever again arise in my heart. Or how shall I pursue sublime matters if I cannot grasp what is ordinary? You are the Truth that cannot deceive. You are highest Wisdom that knows everything. You are the Almighty One who can do all things.

O dear, fair Lord, I have often wished in my heart that I could have received you, together with just Simeon, physically into my arms in the temple. O dear Lord, I could have pressed you with my arms into my soul and into my heart so that the spiritual kiss of your true presence would have been mine as truly as it was his. Lord, now I see that I receive you as truly as he, and in a more magnificent manner insofar as your tender body, which suffered so much, is now glorified and unable to suffer. O loving Lord, if my heart had the love of all hearts, if my conscience were as pure as those of all the angels, and if my soul had the beauty of all souls so that I were worthy of your grace, then, Lord, I would want to receive you today very endearingly and plunge you into the ground of my heart and soul so that neither life nor death could separate me from you.

O sweet, loving Lord and my chosen Love, if you had sent me only your messenger, I would not in the least know how to receive him properly. How then should I conduct myself toward him, the very One himself, whom my soul loves? You are, after all, the only One in whom everything is contained that my heart can wish for in time and in eternity. Or is there anything my soul desires besides you that is not you? I shall not mention what is opposed to you or what is without you because I would find such things repugnant. Certainly, you are the most fair object for all eyes, the sweetest for all mouths, the most tender to touch, and the most lovable for all hearts. Lord, I do not see or hear or feel my soul in all that exists without its finding each thing a thousand times more desirable in you, my Beloved. O dear Lord, how should I act in my astonishment and joy regarding you? Your presence inflames me, but your majesty terrifies me. My sense of propriety wants to honor my Lord, but my heart wants to love and warmly embrace its only Love. You are my Lord and my God, but you are my Brother as well, and, if I dare to say it, my beloved Spouse. Oh, what love, what bliss, what joy, what glory I have in you alone!

And so, sweet Lord, it seems to me that it would be the fulfillment of all my wishes if I were just to experience the grace of receiving in my mouth a single drop of blood from the open wound of the heart of my Beloved. Oh, dear, incomprehensible marvel, now I have not just received (blood) from his heart, or from his hands and feet and all his tender wounds; I have not received just one or two drops. I have taken into my heart and soul through my mouth all of his rose-colored, warm blood. Isn't this a wonderful thing? Should I not hold dear what is precious to all the exalted angels? Is this not something dear? Lord, I would like all my limbs and everything that I am and can do to be turned into an immense love in response to this token of your love. Lord, what is there still in all this world that could bring joy to my heart, that any heart could desire, if you give yourself to me to love and enjoy? It is well-named the sacrament of love. Where was ever anything heard or seen that bespeaks more love than to become love itself in grace? Lord, I see no difference except that Simeon received you when you were visible and I do so when you are invisible. But just as little as my physical eye can now see you as truly human, so little was his physical eye able to see your divinity except in faith, as I see you now. Lord, why should this physical seeing be important to me? If one's spiritual eyes are open, one does not consider physical sight very important. What the eyes of the spirit see is more real and more true. Lord, as long as I know in faith—to the extent one can know it—that I have you there (in the sacrament), what more do I want? Then I have everything my heart desires. Lord, it is a thousand times more beneficial for me not to be able to see you. How could I ever find a way in my heart to enjoy you this way if you were visible. But now that remains which is lovable, and what is not to be grasped by men falls by the way. Lord, when I consider how totally well, lovingly and orderly you have arranged everything, my heart calls with a loud voice. O sublime Abundance of the abyss of divine wisdom, what are you in yourself if you are so rich in your beautiful emanations!

Now, dear Lord, look upon the desire of my heart. Lord, never was a king or an emperor received with so much honor, never was a dear stranger so warmly embraced, never a bride so beautifully or tenderly led home and held in such honor as my soul longs to receive you today, my most glorious Emperor, most charming Guest of my heart, most beloved Bride of my soul, and to lead you into the best and most inward that my heart and soul can offer and present it to you as honorably as any creature ever did. And so, Lord, teach me how I should act toward you, how I should receive you with enough grace and love.

Response of *eternal Wisdom:* You should receive me with honor and enjoy me with humility. You should keep me with you earnestly, embrace me with the love of a spouse, and place me before your eyes in spiritual dignity. Spiritual hunger and intense devotion rather than habit should draw you to me. The soul that wants to experience me within, in the secret hermitage of a detached life, and wants to taste of my sweetness must first be cleansed of defects and be adorned with virtues, be draped with the will to suffer, be decked out with the red roses of ardent love, with the pretty violets of humble self-effacement, and with the white lilies of true purity. Such a soul should prepare me a bed of peace of heart because my dwelling place is peace.[113] It should embrace me in its arms through the exclusion of all other love because I shun and flee this as a free bird flees the cage. It should sing me the song of Sion, a fervent love song with endless praise.[114] Then I shall embrace the soul and it shall lean on my heart. There it will have calm repose, direct vision, extraordinary enjoyment, a foretaste of eternal delight and a feeling of eternal happiness. What it possesses it has for itself because an outsider senses nothing of it. With a deep sigh you should say, "Indeed, you are the hidden God,[115] the intimate Good that no one can know who has experienced nothing of this."

The *servant:* Oh, how blind I have been standing here till now! I plucked red roses and did not sense their fragrance. I walked among beautiful flowers and did not see them. I was like a dry twig in the sweet dew of May. I can never stop regretting that you were so close to me so many a day, and I was so far from you. O sweet Guest of a pure soul, how have I welcomed you until now? How often I have treated you badly! How apathetically I have acted toward the delectable food of angels! I held this precious balsam in my mouth and felt nothing. You are the joyous feast of all angels' eyes, yet I did not really rejoice because of you. If a human friend were supposed to come to me the following morning, I would be looking forward to it the whole night. Yet I never prepared for you as I should, honored Guest, whom heaven and earth glorify. Oh, how quickly I turned away from you. How quickly I drove you away from what was yours! O dear God, you are here yourself truly present, and the host of angels as well, and I have responded so negligently! Lord, to say nothing about you; truly, Lord, if I had known of some place miles away where I knew that the holy angels would be present, these sublime spirits who constantly gaze upon you, I would have willingly gone there. And even if I could not have seen them, within me my heart would still have felt joy because of them. O sweet Lord, you yourself, the Lord of all the angels, are present here, and with you many hosts of angels. Yet I never took better notice of this place. This must always be my regret. I should really have bowed to this place where I knew you to be, even if I could have done nothing else.

O God, how often I have stood at the place where you come to exist in front of me and near me in the sacrament without reflecting and without devotion! My body stood there but my heart was elsewhere. How often I have passed you by, worthy Lord, so thoughtlessly that my heart did not even make a devout bow to greet you. Lord, gentle Lord of mine, my eyes should have looked at you shining with joy. My heart should have thought of you filled with desire. My mouth should have praised you with fervent jubilation of the heart. All my strength should have been spent in cheerful service of you. Look what your servant David did before the ark. Inside it were only earthly manna and other material things. He leaped about full of joy with all his strength.[116] Lord, now I stand before you and before the holy angels, and with my heart's intense tears I fall at your feet. Remember, gentle Lord, you are here before me, my flesh and my Brother. Forget and forgive me today all the dishonor that I ever caused you. I am sorry for it and shall always have to regret it because only now does the light of wisdom begin to shine for me. And the place where you are not only as God but also as a fair and lovable man shall from now on forever be honored by me.

O delightful Good, honored Lord and dear Guest, my soul would very much like to ask a question: Gentle Lord, tell me, what do you bring to your beloved with your true presence in the sacrament when she receives you with love and desire?

Response of *eternal Wisdom:* Is this a proper question for a lover? What do I possess that is better than myself? If one has his love, what else can one ask for? Whoever gives himself—has he refused to give anything? I give myself to you and take you from yourself and unite you with me.[117] You lose yourself and are changed into me. What does the sun bring to the cloudless air in its beautiful, refulgent splendor? What does the rising brilliant star of morning bring to gloomy night? Or what kind of charming adornment does the fair bliss of summer bring after the cold and somber wintertime?

The *servant:* Lord, they certainly do bring an abundance of gifts.

Response of *eternal Wisdom:* They seem abundant to you because you can see them. Look, the least of the graces flowing from me in this sacrament is more brilliant in eternity than any physical radiance of the sun. It shines brighter than any morning star and enhances you more delightfully with eternal beauty than any summer decoration that ever clothed the earth. Or is my radiant Godhead not brighter than any sun? Does my noble soul not shine more than any star? Is my transfigured body that you have truly received today not more delightful than any of summer's delights?

The *servant:* O Lord, why then can your delights not be felt more? Lord, I often come (to the sacrament) with such a lack of feeling that all light, grace and sweetness, as I understand it, are as rare for me as they are for a man born blind who has never seen light. Lord, if I may dare say so: Regarding your true presence, I would much prefer that you had arranged that it give more evidence of itself.

Response of *eternal Wisdom:* The less evidence there is, the purer your faith is and the greater your reward. The Lord of nature brings delightful growth so mysteriously in so many beautiful trees, and yet no eye or mind is able to be aware of it before it is accomplished. I am not a light shining outward. I am not something good that brings about outward results. I am a good that works within. And the more spiritual this is, the more noble it is.

The *servant:* O God, there are so few people who consider deeply what they are receiving. They approach (the altar), as many do, hardly aware. And because they come to you so empty, they leave (the altar) without grace. They do not digest the food in order to benefit from what they receive.

Eternal Wisdom: For those well-prepared I am the living bread; for the poorly prepared dry bread; for the unprepared a blow of misfortune on earth, a mortal plunge and an eternal curse.

The *servant:* O Lord, this is such a frightening thing. O gentle Lord, which ones do you say are well-prepared and which unprepared?

Response of *eternal Wisdom:* Those are well-prepared who are purified, the poorly prepared are those hindered by obstacles. But the unprepared are the sinful people who with their will or their deeds persist in mortal sin.

The *servant:* But if, gentle Lord, a person is heartily sorry for his sins at that time and does his best to be rid of them according to the Christian dispensation?[118]

Response of *eternal Wisdom:* Then a person is no longer in sin.

The *servant:* Lord, it seems to me that this is one of the most important things that one can do on earth. Lord, who is there on earth who can prepare himself for you worthily enough?

Response of *eternal Wisdom:* Such a person was never born. Even if a man had all the natural purity of all the angels, the integrity of all the saints, and the good deeds of all men, he would still be unworthy of me.

The *servant:* O loving Lord, with what trembling should we useless men, lacking all grace, approach you?

Response of *eternal Wisdom:* When a person does what he can, nothing else is required of him. God brings to completion what remains unfinished. A sick person should cast aside all timidity and approach the physician whose work results in his being restored to health.

The *servant:* Dear Lord, is it better to receive you in this noble sacrament frequently or infrequently?

Response of *eternal Wisdom:* Those whose grace and devotion grow perceptibly because of it profit from frequently receiving it.

The *servant:* Lord, and when a person, as he experiences it, stays the same or is often in an unfeeling state?

Response of *eternal Wisdom:* As long as one does one's part, one should not let oneself be noticeably influenced by insensitivity because the salvation of the soul, which is in this state of insensitivity by God's decree, is often as nobly achieved in the light of pure faith alone as in consolation. I am the kind of good that increases when enjoyed and disappears when stored away. It is better to act out of love than to refrain out of fear. It is better to receive (the sacrament) once every week out of a deep sense of true humility than once a year arrogantly, feeling one has a right to do so.

The *servant:* Lord, when does the flow of grace from the sacrament occur?

Response of *eternal Wisdom:* The moment it is received.

The *servant:* Gentle Lord, what if a person is in a state of utterly painful longing for your physical presence in the sacrament but must do without you?

Response of *eternal Wisdom:* Many persons become filled with me though abstaining; others suffer a lack of me although they partake. The latter only digest me physically. The former enjoy me spiritually.

The *servant:* Gentle Lord, doesn't a person who receives you physically and spiritually have more than one who just has the benefit of you spiritually?

Response of *eternal Wisdom:* Who has more, the person who has me and my grace or the person who just has my grace?

The *servant:* Lord, how long do you remain physically present in a person when he receives you?

Response of *eternal Wisdom:* As long as the form and the outward appearance of the sacrament remain.

This is what you should say when you go (to the altar):

O living Fruit, delightful Jewel, delicious Pomegranate of the glorious heart of the Father, sweet Grape of Cyprus in the vineyard of Engedi,[119] who will enable me to receive you today so worthily that you find it pleasing to come to me, to remain with me and never to depart from me? O infinite Good that fills heaven and earth, mercifully incline toward me today and do not despise your poor creature. Lord, I am not worthy of you but I am in need of you. O gentle Lord, are you not the one who created heaven and earth with a single word? Lord, with a single word heal my sick soul. O gentle Lord, act toward me in accordance with your grace, your infinite mercy and not in accordance with what I deserve. You are, after all, the innocent Easter Lamb that is being offered up today for the sins of all men. O sweet, delicious Bread of heaven, which contains within it all the sweetness every heart desires, let the dry mouth of my soul enjoy you today. Give me food and drink; strengthen and adorn me; and join yourself to me in love! O eternal Wisdom, come into my soul today with such force that you drive out all my enemies, dissolve my failings and forgive all my sins. Enlighten my mind with the light of your true faith, inflame my will with your sweet love, brighten my thoughts with your joyful presence and give all my faculties virtue and perfection. Preserve me at my death so that I may enjoy you face to face in eternal happiness. Amen.

CHAPTER 24

How One Should Unsparingly Praise God Always

"Praise, my soul, the Lord; I shall praise the Lord in my life."[120] O God, who will grant that my full heart satisfy before my death its desire of praising you? Who shall let me praise worthily in my days the beloved Lord whom my soul loves? O gentle Lord, if only so many pleasant melodies would go forth from my heart as ever all others played on their strings and as many as there are leaves and blades of grass. All these strains should then be lifted aloft to you in the court of heaven so that from my heart such a blissful, unusual song of praise would arise that might be pleasing to the eyes of your heart and bring joy to all the celestial ranks. Dear Lord, though I am not worthy to praise you, still my soul wishes that the heavens praise you when they shine in their stunning beauty with the splendor of the sun and the countless multitudes of the bright stars in their lofty brilliance. And (let) the pretty meadows (praise you) when, in the delights of summer, decked out with flowers of all kinds, they reflect their natural nobility in beauty that brings pleasure, and (may you be praised by) all the tender thoughts and ardent desires which any pure loving heart ever harbored for you when it was surrounded by the cheerful summer joy of your radiant spirit.

Lord, I have just to think about sublime praise of you, and my heart would like to melt in my body. Thoughts fade away, words fail me and all manners (of expression) escape me. Something in my heart that no one can express shines when I want to praise you, my Good without manner.[121] If I go to the most beautiful of creatures, to the most sublime spirits, to the purest beings, you surpass them all indescribably. If I then go to the deep abyss of your own goodness, Lord, all praise disappears in its smallness. When I look at attractive living forms or see pleasing creatures, they say to my heart, "Oh, look how very pleasing he is from whom we flowed forth, from whom all beauty comes!" I traverse the earth and the heavens, the world and the abyss, forest and meadow, mountain and valley: They all cry out to my ears in rich tones of boundless praise of you. When I see how infinitely well and orderly you arrange all things, both evil and good, I am left without words. But when I consider that you are the praiseworthy Good that my soul has chosen and whom it has chosen for itself alone for its only Beloved, then, Lord, my heart could burst within from praise.

O gentle Lord, look at the eager desire of my heart and my soul, and teach me to praise you. Teach me how I might praise you worthily before I depart from here because the soul in my body thirsts for this.

Response of *eternal Wisdom:* Would you like to praise me?

The *servant:* O Lord, why are you provoking me? You know all hearts. You know that my heart would like to turn over within me from the sheer desire I have had for this since childhood.

Response of *eternal Wisdom:* It is fitting for the just to praise me.[122]

The *servant:* Alas, Lord, all my justice rests on your infinite mercy. Dear Lord, the frogs in the ditches praise you. And if they can't sing, at least they croak. O gentle Lord, I know quite well who I am. I know well that it would be more fitting for me to weep for my sins than to praise you. And yet, you infinite Good, do not despise in me, a repulsive worm, my desire to praise you. Lord, when the Seraphim and Cherubim and the large number of lofty spirits all praise you with all their might, how much better do they fare than the least of creatures in praising dignity that is immeasurable and cannot be praised rightly? Lord, you have no need of any creature, but one becomes more aware of your infinite goodness the more generously you give yourself.

Response of *eternal Wisdom:* Whoever imagines he is praising me as fully as I deserve is like one who chases the wind and wants to grab hold of a shadow. And yet you and all creatures are permitted to praise me as best you can. For there was never a creature so small or so great, so good or so bad, nor will there ever be one, that did not praise me or show that I was worthy of praise. And the more a creature is united with me, the more worthy of praise I am for it and the more similar your (a creature's) praise is to the praise in eternal glory.[123] And the more the praise (of a creature) is similar (to this), the more it is free from the impressions of all creatures and united with me in true devotion. Inward contemplation resounds better in my ears than merely praise with words, and a heartfelt sigh sounds better than a sublime chant. Humble contempt for self with real submission to God and all men by giving up one's own will is more pleasing to me than all other beautiful strains. On earth I never seemed so worthy of praise in the eyes of my Father as when I hung in death's agony on the cross. Some people only praise me with exquisite words while their heart is far from me.[124] This praise means nothing to me. Some praise me well as long as things go as they wish, but when things begin to go bad for them their praise ceases. Such praise does not please me. This is valuable praise in my divine eyes: when you praise me with your heart, words and actions as earnestly in sorrow as in joy, in all adversity as much as when things are going very well for you. Then I am really your goal, and not yourself.

The *servant:* Lord, I do not beg for suffering from you. And I do not want to give you any cause for sending me such things. But in the desire of my heart I surrender myself completely to your eternal praise since I could never really surrender myself on my own. Lord, if you were to ordain that I become the most despised man that the earth can bring forth, Lord, I would want to endure that out of love in order to praise you. Lord, I surrender myself today to your grace. And if one were to accuse me of the worst crime a man ever committed so that whoever looked at me would spit in my face, Lord, that I would want to suffer gladly in order to praise you as long as I remained innocent in your eyes. But if I were guilty, I would want to suffer it to praise your esteemed justice, whose honor is a thousand times more important than my own; for each insult I would give you special praise and would say with the (good) thief on the cross: "Lord, I am suffering justly, but what have you done? Lord, remember me in your kingdom!"[125] And if you wanted to let me die right now, and if that would mean praise for you, I would not look back for a minute's delay. However, I would desire this: If I were to become as old as Methuselah, that every year of this long period and every week of these years and every day of these weeks and every hour of these days and every second of each small hour might be praise to you from me as delightful as any saint ever praised you among the true splendor of the saints, that this praise be as beyond reckoning as the motes of dust in sunshine, and that my sincere desire be fulfilled as though I had actually accomplished all this while on earth.

And so, Lord, take me to yourself now or later. This is my heart's desire. Lord, let me say something more: If it were to your praise that I should depart from this earth at this moment and should burn in purgatory for fifty years, I would immediately bow to your praise at your feet and accept it willingly for your eternal praise. Blessed be purgatory, if there your praise is accomplished through me. Lord, you, not I; you are the very one that is the object of my thoughts, the one I love and search for, not I. Lord, you know all things and can see into all hearts. You know what my firm resolve is. Even if I knew that I would be in the depths of hell forever, I would not for that reason break with you, no matter how painful the loss of the marvelous sight of you might be for my forsaken heart. And if I could bring back the time lost by all men, make good their wrongdoings and all the dishonor you ever experienced, and could replace this completely with praise and honor, I would willingly do so. And if it were possible, a beautiful song of praise would have to burst forth from me from the lowest depths of hell and it would penetrate hell, the earth, the air and all the heavens before reaching your divine countenance. But if that were impossible, then I would wish to praise you here all the more so that I might enjoy you the more here.

Lord, act toward me, your poor creature, in a way that brings you praise. Come what may, I shall speak your praises as long as a bit of breath is in my mouth. And when I can speak no more, I ask that raising my finger might be the confirmation and finale of all the praise that I ever spoke to you. And yet, when my body has turned to dust, I would ask that from each little particle a resounding song of praise spring forth upward through the hard rock, through the whole heavens to your divine countenance and last till judgment day when body and soul are again united to praise you.

Response of *eternal Wisdom:* Remain constant in this desire till your death. This is for me endearing praise.

The *servant:* O dear Lord, since you now look with favor on praise from me, a poor sinful man, I ask that you instruct me in these things. Lord, the external praise one gives in word and song, is it of any value?

Response of *eternal Wisdom:* It is of value, especially to the extent that it can urge on the inner man, and he is often urged on by it, especially in the case of beginners.

The *servant:* Gentle Lord, since one likes to begin in time what one is going to be doing in eternity, I find within me a strong desire to achieve within a constant praising that would never be interrupted even for an instant. Lord, I have often spoken of this same desire: "O heavens, why such haste? You run so fast! I beg you: Stand still right here until I have thoroughly praised my only beloved, gentle Lord to my heart's desire!" Lord, when a short time passed without my actually turning to your praise and when I then came to myself, I said, "O Lord, it's been a thousand years since I have thought of my Beloved!" Now, dear Lord, teach me, as far as possible while the body is still together with the soul, that I might achieve a state of constant, undistracted praising.

Response of *eternal Wisdom:* Whoever has me as his goal in all things, keeps from sinning, and practices virtue earnestly, praises me at all times. And yet, if you are pursuing the highest act of praising, listen closely. The soul is like a light, fluffy feather. With nothing attached to it, it is very easily drawn upward toward heaven by its natural mobility, but when it is weighed down, it sinks. In the same manner, a spirit purified of the weight of its faults is raised aloft toward celestial things by its own nobility if helped slightly by spiritual contemplation. And so, whenever it happens that a person is freed from all sensual desires and attains a state of stillness so that his whole attention is fastened at all times without interruption upon the unchangeable Good—such a person successfully praises me constantly. For in purity, to the extent that one can express it, the human understanding is drowned and reconstituted out of its earthliness into something resembling spirits and angels. Whatever a person takes in from outside, whatever he does, whatever he accomplishes—whether it be eating, drinking, sleeping, being awake—all this is nothing but the purest of all praise.

The *servant:* O my gentle Lord, what a very delightful teaching this is! Lovable Wisdom, I would yet like you to instruct me about four things. The first is: Lord, where do I discover the most important reasons for praising you?

Response of *eternal Wisdom:* In the primal source of all good, and after that in the streams flowing out (from it).

The *servant:* Lord, the source is beyond my grasp and unknown to me. The high cedars in the Lebanon of heavenly spirits and angelic beings should praise you there. And yet I, too, as a coarse thistle, want to spring up in praise so that they, seeing the utter impotence of my desire, are reminded of their high dignity and are stimulated in their pure clarity to praise you zealously. Thus does the cuckoo cause the charming song of the nightingale.[126] But is it my task to praise well the good that flows forth from you? Lord, when I rightly consider who I was, what you have protected me from and how often, from what perils, bonds and snares you have freed me, O eternal Good, why does my heart not completely dissolve in praising you? Lord, how long you waited for me, how amiably you have received me, how tenderly you have in secret anticipated my needs, inwardly counseled me! How ungrateful I always was! But you never gave up until you had drawn me to you. Should I not praise you for this? Indeed, I should, Lord! My gentle Lord, I ask that abundant praise rise up before your eyes like the great joyous praise of the angels the instant they realized they had passed their test and that the others had been cast aside[127]; like the joy that the suffering souls have when they come out of the prison of terrible fire to you and for the first time look at your joyful, lovable countenance; and like the boundless praise that bursts forth from the streets of heaven after the Last Judgment when the elect are separated from those who were evil and attain security forever.

Lord, one thing about praising you I would still like to know is how I might use the goodness I have by nature for praising you.

Response of *eternal Wisdom:* Since no one on earth can really distinguish by clear knowledge between grace and nature, therefore— whether it be from grace or nature—when something pleasant, joyful or delightful arises in your spirit or person, turn quickly and offer it to God, so that it be made to praise me because I am Lord of nature *and* grace. Thus nature becomes for you supernature.

The *servant:* Lord, how can I turn even the incursions of the evil spirits to your eternal praise?

Response of *eternal Wisdom:* In response to the suggestions of an evil spirit, say: "Lord, as often as this evil spirit or any other sends unseemly thoughts into me against my will, let there be sent up to God from me in its stead by my deliberate will the most beautiful (hymn of) praise for everlasting eternity with which this same evil spirit would have praised you in everlasting eternity if it had passed the test. Now, since it is damned, let me take its place in praising you. And as often as it sends these hideous evil whisperings, may something good be sent up to you."

The *servant:* Lord, I now see that just as for good people all things work to the good,[128] so also the worst that an evil spirit can do can also be turned to good. Now tell me one thing more: Dear Lord, how do I turn all that I see or hear to your praise?

Response of *eternal Wisdom:* As often as you perceive a great number, as often as you behold something of exquisite beauty or rich variety, say from the bottom of your heart: "Lord, just so often and just so beautifully may the thousand times a thousand angelic spirits serving you greet you lovingly today in my stead, and may the ten thousand times a hundred thousand spirits standing before you praise you today for me and wish on my behalf for all the holy desires of all the saints, and in my place may the charming beauty of all creatures honor you."

The *servant:* Indeed, dear Lord, you have refreshed my spirit and made it feel welcome to praise you!

But, Lord, praising you in time has reminded my heart and made my heart desirous of a praising that goes on forever. O my beloved Wisdom, when shall this bright day begin? When shall the joyous hour come when, fully prepared, I can leave this foreign land and go to my Beloved and lovingly look upon you and praise you? Lord, truly I am beginning to pine away and to desire fervently the one bliss of my heart. Oh, when shall I ever get there? How time drags, becoming later and later for me to see face-to-face the sight that will satisfy the eyes of my heart and fulfill the desires of my whole heart! Oh, exile, how truly you are an exile for one who really feels like someone homeless! Lord, see, there is no one on earth who does not have someone he visits, who does not have some place to settle down and rest his feet awhile. Oh, you only One that my soul seeks and desires, you know that I am the one who has been left for you alone. Lord, whatever I see and hear, where I do not find you is a torment for me. The presence of all other persons is, except for your sake, bitter for me. Lord, what shall encourage me or what shall be my support?

Response of *eternal Wisdom:* You shall often walk in this fair, charming garden filled with the blossoms of my praise. There is nothing on earth that is more really a foretaste of dwelling in heaven than when one praises God with spirited joy. There is nothing that exhilarates one's spirit, eases suffering, drives out evil spirits, or makes sadness disappear as does praising joyfully. God is with such people, they are on intimate terms with angels, and they benefit themselves. It improves one's neighbor and gladdens the soul. The whole heavenly army is honored by spirited praise.

The *servant:* Dear Lord, my gentle eternal Wisdom, I ask that the moment my eyes open in the morning, my heart open as well and that there burst forth from it the flaming torch of your praise with the dearest love of the most insignificant, loving heart on earth, similar in its fiery love to the sublime spirit of the Seraphim in eternity and to the infinite love with which you, heavenly Father, love your beloved Child in the love that flashes forth in the Spirit of you both. May this praise sound as sweet in your fatherly heart as any sweet melody of this kind played on delightful strings ever sounded in a carefree spirit. And may as sweet a fragrance of praise be wafted aloft from the torch of love as if it were of herbs, spices and all the healing plants of virtue mixed together as an aromatic powder. And may its appearance be so beautifully adorned with the blossoms of grace that never a May in its charming blossoms was so fair, so that it might become a delight to see for your divine eyes and for the whole heavenly assembly. And I ask that this torch of love constantly shoot forth sparks in all my prayer, from my mouth, in song, in thoughts, words and deeds, that it drive away all my enemies, make my failings disappear, gain me grace and a holy end, and that the end of this praise in time may be the beginning of everlasting eternal praise. Amen.

Part Three

The Hundred Meditations and Petitions Briefly Stated
As One Should Recite Them Devoutly Every Day

Whoever wants to learn briefly, genuinely and ardently to meditate with the aid of the loving sufferings of our Lord Jesus Christ, who is our complete salvation, and whoever wants to show gratitude for his manifold suffering, should learn the hundred meditations that follow by heart, at least according to their briefly delineated senses. Such a person should go over them every day with devotion accompanied by a hundred *veniae*,[129] or however it works out best for him. With each *venia* he should recite an Our Father, or when the meditation has to do with our Lady, a Hail, Holy Queen or Hail Mary. God gave them, as they are here, to a Dominican friar one time after matins as he was standing before a crucifix and was seriously lamenting to God that he could not use the passion as a means of contemplation and that he found it a bitter subject for contemplation. Up to that time he had had great difficulties in this regard, but at this moment they all disappeared. The brief prayers of petition he added briefly afterward on his own so that each person himself might find something to ask for according to his disposition at the time.

1. O eternal Wisdom, my heart reminds you how, after the Last Supper, on the Mount you were drenched in bloody sweat because of the anguish of your tender heart.
2. And how you were taken captive by your enemies, roughly bound and led off in misery.

294

3. And how, Lord, during the night you were shamefully abused with harsh blows, were spit upon and blindfolded.
4. In the morning you were falsely charged before Caiaphas and bound over for death as a guilty person.
5. Your gentle Mother looked on in immense sorrow.
6. In shame you were brought before Pilate, falsely accused and condemned to death.
7. Eternal Wisdom, before Herod you appeared in white clothing and were scorned as a fool.
8. Your fair body was brutally torn open and mutilated by the frenzied lashes of the scourge.
9. Your gentle head was punctured by pointed thorns and blood ran down over your dear face.
10. You were thus condemned and with your cross led forth to death in misery and shame.

O my only Hope, remember all this so that as a Father you might come to my aid in all my distress. Free me from the heavy bonds of my sins. Protect me from secret sins and public crimes. Guard me against the deceiving counsels of the enemy and against the occasions of all sins. Let me feel in my heart your suffering and the sorrow of your gentle Mother. Lord, judge me with mercy on my final journey, teach me to have no regard for worldly honor and to serve you in wisdom. Let my failings be healed in your wounds, my reason be strengthened against all temptations and made fair in the pain of your head. Let me conform myself, as best I can, completely to your suffering.

1. Dear Lord, on the high branch of the cross your bright eyes were darkened and rolled.
2. Your divine ears were filled with the sounds of scorn and curses.
3. Your refined sense of smell was defiled by vile stench.
4. Your sweet mouth was assaulted with bitter drink.
5. Your tender sense of feeling was battered with cruel blows.

And so I ask today that you keep my eyes from wanton looking about and my ears from listening to empty words. Lord, take from

THE EXEMPLAR

me the taste for material things. Let me find no pleasure in the
things of time and take from me the softness of my own body.

1. Gentle Lord, your divine head was bowed by pain and
   anguish.
2. Your tender throat was roughly abused.
3. Your unblemished countenance ran with spit and blood.
4. Your clear skin was devoid of color.
5. Your whole fair form was dying away.

My Lord, make me love bodily pain and let me seek all rest in
you. Let me willingly suffer wrong from others, seek humiliation,
weaken my desires and kill all my pleasures.

1. Dear Lord, your right hand was pierced with a nail.
2. Your left hand was pounded through.
3. Your right arm was distended.
4. Your left arm wrenched out.
5. Your right foot was dug into.
6. Your left foot was hammered through.
7. You hung there powerless.
8. Your divine body was utterly exhausted.
9. All your tender limbs were held motionless to the confining
   anguish of the cross.
10. On many parts of your body warm blood was running down.

O dear Lord, I therefore ask that I be nailed motionless to you in
joy and sorrow, that all the faculties of my body and soul be
stretched out on your cross, and that my mind and my desires be
riveted to you. Make it impossible for me to find joy in the body,
and let me be quick to seek your praise and honor. I ask that there be
no part of my body that does not bear a special mark of your death,
and that in love each part show a likeness to your suffering.

1. Gentle Lord, your thriving body dried up and wasted away
   on the cross.
2. Your tired back leaned in pain against the rough cross.

3. Your heavy body sagged.
4. Your whole body was riddled with wounds and racked with pain.
5. And all this, Lord, your heart endured in love.

Lord, let your wasting away cause me to thrive again eternally. Let your painful leaning be a spiritual resting, your sagging a strong support. May all your pain ease mine and may your heart filled with love set mine on fire.

1. Dear Lord, in your death agony you were scorned with sharp words.
2. With mocking gestures.
3. You were utterly destroyed in your heart.
4. Through all this you stood firm.
5. And you prayed for them (your tormenters) to your dear Father lovingly.
6. An innocent Lamb, you were put among the criminals.
7. By the criminal on your left you were condemned.
8. The one on your right called upon you.
9. You forgave him all his sins.
10. And you opened for him the paradise of heaven.

Now, beloved Lord, teach your servant to suffer steadfastly for your sake all sharp words, mocking gestures and all destructiveness, and to forgive in your sight all my enemies with love. O boundless Gentleness, today I offer before the eyes of the heavenly Father your guiltless death for my guilt-ridden life. Lord, I call to you with the (good) thief, "Remember, remember me in your kingdom!" Do not damn me for my wrongdoing. Forgive me all my sins. Open for me your heavenly paradise.

1. Gentle Lord, in that hour you were forsaken by all men for my sake.
2. Your friends had withdrawn from you.
3. You stood naked, robbed of your clothes and all honor.
4. Your strength appeared conquered.

5. They treated you mercilessly, and you suffered it all quietly and meekly.
6. How your gentle heart suffered when you alone recognized the depths of sorrow your Mother's heart was enduring!
7. You saw her gestures of longing.
8. You heard her words of grief.
9. And in this separation by death you entrusted her to your disciple to be his mother.
10. And you entrusted him to her as a son.

O gentle Model of all virtues, take from me all harmful human love, all inordinate trust in friends. Strip me of all impatience. Give me constancy against all evil spirits and meekness in regard to all reckless men. Gentle Lord, put your bitter death into the ground of my heart, into my prayer and into the evidence my deeds give. O tender, lovable Lord, I entrust myself today to the lasting faithfulness and protection of your gentle, pure Mother and your dearly beloved disciple.

Hail, Holy Queen or Hail Mary.

1. O pure, tender Mother, I recall to you today the profound suffering of your heart at that first sight of your dear Child hanging there in his death agony.
2. You could not come to his aid.
3. You had to look in anguish upon the murderers of your Child.
4. You grieved for him most sorrowfully.
5. And he consoled you with great kindness.
6. His kind words wounded your heart.
7. Your gestures of grief softened hard hearts.
8. Your motherly hands and arms were raised in vain.
9. Your weakened body sank helplessly.
10. Your tender mouth lovingly kissed his blood as it ran down.

O Mother of all grace, protect me as a mother does in all of my life. Preserve me mercifully at my death. O gentle Lady, the hour that causes me to ask to be your servant all my days is that grim hour that makes heart and soul tremble. Then all begging and beseeching is futile. Then I do not know to whom I, poor wretch, should turn. And so, you limitless abyss of divine mercy, I now fall at your feet, my heart sighing deeply, (and beg) that I might become worthy of your gladdening presence. How can that person lose heart or come to harm whom you, pure Mother, intend to protect?

O my only Consolation, guard me from the terrible glances of the evil spirits. Help me and keep me from the hands of my enemies. Comfort my disconsolate groans and look kindly with your eyes of mercy upon my mortal helplessness. Offer me your kind hands and receive my wandering soul and, with your rosy countenance, lead me to my exalted Judge and establish me in eternal blessedness.

1. O beloved Delight of the heavenly Father, at that hour on the cross, besides the outward pain of bitter death you were also inwardly abandoned completely by any sweetness or comfort.
2. You called out to your Father in desperation.
3. You united your will completely with his.
4. Lord, your body parched, you thirsted terribly.
5. Out of love you thirsted in spirit.
6. You were given something bitter for your thirst.
7. And when everything had been accomplished, you said, "It is finished."
8. You became obedient to your beloved Father unto death.
9. You commended your spirit into his fatherly hands.
10. And then your noble soul left your divine body.

O dear Lord, in love I ask you to be gentle with me in all suffering, that you open your ears like a father to my entreaties, and that you grant me to unite my will to yours in all things. Lord, remove from me all thirst for material things. Give me a thirst for spiritual things. Gentle Lord, may your bitter drink turn all the adversity I encounter into sweetness. Let me remain in a proper attitude and perform good actions up to my death and never transgress your commands.

Eternal Wisdom, let my spirit be surrendered into your hands today so that, when it finally departs, it might be received by you in joy. Lord, let me live in a manner that pleases you, die well-prepared, and reach the goal that you have made secure. Lord, may your bitter death so permeate my insignificant deeds that in that final hour all guilt and punishment may have been completely put behind me.

1. O Lord, remember how the sharp lance was jabbed through your divine side.
2. How rose-colored blood spurted forth from it.
3. How living water ran out of it.
4. O Lord, and with what difficulty you redeemed me.
5. And how spontaneously you saved me.

Dear Lord, may your deep wound keep me from all my enemies. May your living water cleanse me from all my sins. May your rose-colored blood adorn me with all graces and virtues. Gentle Lord, may your afflictions and toil in redeeming me bind you to me and your freely saving me unite me eternally with you.

1. O exquisite Comfort for all sinners, sweet Queen, let me remind you today—when you stood beneath the cross and your Child had departed and was hanging dead in front of you—how often you looked up helplessly.
2. How his arms were taken by you, his Mother.
3. With what devotion he was pressed to your bloodstained face.
4. How his open wounds and his lifeless countenance were all kissed.
5. How often your heart was wounded.
6. How many times you deeply groaned.
7. How many bitter and desolate tears you shed.
8. Your words of grief were so very mournful.
9. Your attractive appearance was so very sad.
10. But your desolate heart could not be comforted by anyone.

O pure Lady, remember all this today so that you might constantly protect me throughout life and lead me faithfully. Always turn your eyes toward me in mercy. Receive me like a mother whenever I seek you. Keep me from all my enemies in your faithful and tender embrace. May your loving kissing of his wounds reconcile me to him. May your deathly wounds gain for me sincere sorrow. May your intense groans bring me constant zeal. And may your bitter tears turn my hard heart soft. May your words of grief make me avoid all empty speech. May your sad gestures make me throw off all gestures of abandonment. May your disconsolate heart cause me to disdain all transitory love.

1. O delightful Splendor of eternal light, as my soul in mourning and gratitude embraces you under the cross, dead on the lap of your sorrowful Mother—as I look at you, you are completely extinguished. Extinguish in me the burning desires of all vices.
2. O clear, pure Mirror of divine majesty, how defiled you have become for my sake. Cleanse away the large stains of my wrongdoing.
3. O bright, fair Image of the Father's goodness, how soiled you have become. Restore the disfigured image of my soul.
4. O innocent Lamb, how wretchedly you have been mistreated. Do penance and make amends for my guilt-ridden and sinful life.
5. O King of all kings and Lord of all lords, grant me that, as my soul now embraces you in sorrow and laments in your abandonment, it shall be embraced by you in joy in your eternal splendor.

1. Lovely, pure Mother, remember today how mournfully you conducted yourself when they tore your dead Child from your heart.
2. Remember your grieving departure from the place.
3. Remember your lonely footsteps.
4. Remember your lamenting heart wishing to have him back.
5. Remember the loyal constancy that you alone offered him in all his afflictions, even to the grave.

And so, in your sorrow and his suffering obtain for me from your tender Child that I may overcome my sorrow and suffering, that together with him in his grave I close myself up against all earthly worries, that this whole world cause me to be a stranger, that I have an immense yearning for him (Christ) alone, and that I remain

constant in praise of him and service to you, even to the grave.
Amen.

When all this was ready and had been written down on paper,
nothing further remained except to add a little of the part that
belonged to our dear Lady.[130] And for this purpose he had left some
space until God should enlighten him, because for a number of
months he remained in a state of insensitivity and could not finish it.
And so he came to our Lady, asking that she finish it. And then on
the eve of the feast of St. Dominic, at night after matins for his feast
had already been sung, it seemed to him in his sleep as though he
were in a room. And as he sat there, a handsome young man came
walking in with a wonderful harp and, along with him, four other
young men with shawms.[131] Then the young man with the harp sat
down next to the friar and began to pluck the harp and produce
beautiful tones. The friar found this pleasant indeed to hear, and he
said to him, "Why could you not come to the place where I live and
sometimes give me such an exhilarating feeling?" The young man
asked the friar whether he had a certain task that he had been
working on for some time. He said, "Certainly!" The young man
replied saying, "That is a hard piece."[132]

Then the young man turned to the four with the shawms and told
them to play. One of them answered that he thought it would be
enough if two played. But the young man did not consider it enough
and said they should all begin to play together and showed them some
melody that he knew well but that was unfamiliar to the friar. And so
they began to play. But in the midst of this he suddenly neither saw
nor heard any stringed music. Rather, what he saw was that the
young men held in their hands an incomparably beautiful picture of
our Lady, which had been embroidered on a cloth. The mantle of the
figure was red and purple, unusual work from the Muslim East that
had a marvelous appearance. The background was white as snow.
The friar was greatly astonished and enjoyed looking at it. He noticed
that they wanted to finish the picture. They began first to finish the
background. They said, "Look how it is coming along!" And he saw
how it was finished. Then one of them took a needle and thread and
on the front of the mantle made some very clever stitches crosswise.
They looked very fine, adorning our dear Lady charmingly. And
with that his eyes opened and he understood that he should entertain

no doubts. He was supposed to finish the background, namely, the empty space and the spiritual image that had for so long been closed off from him. For he was accustomed to the earlier sections all coming about well enough, one just like the other. And immediately the next morning it was finished to the very end.

This small volume called the *Little Book of Eternal Wisdom* has as its purpose to rekindle in some the love of God, which in most recent times is beginning to be extinguished in many hearts. Its subject matter from beginning to end is our Lord Jesus Christ's suffering from abundant love, how a devout person should imitate this model as best he can, and about the esteemed praises and indescribable sorrow of the pure Queen of heaven. In it mixed together in a hidden manner are ten subjects that are unusually valuable and useful:

1. How some people are attracted by God without their knowing it.
2. Concerning sincere sorrow and kind forgiveness.
3. How lovable God is and how deceiving worldly love is.

An explanation of three things that a lover could most especially find repugnant about God:

4. The first is: How he can appear so angry and yet be so lovable.
5. The second: Why he often withdraws himself from his lovers whenever he pleases, and how one can tell when he is present.
6. The third: Why God allows his friends to have such a bad time of it on earth. And this section has contained within it:
7. The everlasting pain of hell.
8. The immeasurable joy of heaven.
9. The immeasurable nobility of suffering on earth.
10. The indescribable benefit of contemplating divine suffering.

The second part of this little book:

1. How one should learn to die.
2. How one should live inwardly.

3. How one should receive God with love.
4. How one should praise God at all times beyond measure.

The third part contains the hundred meditations briefly stated as one should recite them every day with devotion.

Whoever intends to copy this book that has been written and arranged with care should write everything as to words and meaning exactly as it is here. He should neither add anything nor leave anything out nor change the words. Then he should go through it again carefully once or twice and should not excerpt any part of it except the hundred meditations at the end. These he may copy separately if he wishes. Whoever treats it in any other way should fear God's punishment because he robs God of valuable praise, men of their improvement, and the man who worked on it of his labor. Therefore, whoever still intends to misuse it shall be punished by eternal Wisdom.[133]

Little Book
of
Truth

(Here begins the third book[1])

Concerning Inner Detachment and True Discernment, Which Can Be Had in the Use of Reason

"Behold! You have loved truth, uncertain and hidden things of your wisdom you have shown me."[2]

There was a man in Christ who in his youth exercised himself in all the practices of the outward man in which beginners usually engage, yet the inner man remained without practice in perfect self-detachment. He clearly felt that something was missing but did not know just what. And after he had gone on like this for a long time—even many years—he suddenly experienced a turning-inward in which he was thrown back into himself. And it spoke within him thus: "You must realize that inner detachment leads one to perfect truth."[3]

Now this noble saying was as yet strange and unknown to him, but he felt a great affection for it and was very strongly drawn to this and similar things. Would he before his death come to the point of understanding it clearly and grasping it in its entirety? It came to the point that he was warned, and the accusation was made that hidden beneath the appearance of this revelation there lay concealed the perfidious abyss of unrestrained liberty, which causes great harm to Holy Christendom.[4] From this point on he became frightened and felt for some time a repugnance for the inner calling within him.

And then one time he experienced a powerful force within him and divine truth shined forth in him informing him that from then on he should not give in to any gloom, because it has always been

307

and ever will be the case that evil hides within what is good, and one should not reject what is good because of the evil. He was told that in the Old Testament, when God worked his true signs through Moses, the magicians mixed their false ones in between.[5] And when Christ the true Messiah came, others came too and falsely pretended they were the one.[6] So it is everywhere in all things, and therefore the good is not to be thrown out with the bad, but rather it is to be sorted out with keen discrimination, as the divine mouth does.[7] He was told that good intellectual perceptions that submit their lucid intelligibility to the opinion of holy Christianity should not be rejected, and that sensible ideas which bear within them the testimony of a life of perfection should not be shunned. For these things refine a person and reveal to him his own nobility, the incomparability of the divine being, and the nothingness of all other things. This more than anything else rightly spurs one on to true detachment. And thus he came back again to the way of life to which he had already been called—the way of true detachment.

And so he asked of eternal Truth that, as far as was possible, it give him the power to distinguish well between people whose goal is a well-ordered simplicity and those who, as they say, aim at unrestrained liberty,[8] and that it teach him what true detachment is, by which he might come to where he ought to be. He received an answer in bright clarity: All of this would take place in the manner of an explained allegory, as though the disciple were asking and Truth answering.[9] He was first directed to the core of holy scripture out of which eternal Truth speaks, that he might seek and gaze upon what the most learned and experienced human beings, to whom God has revealed his hidden wisdom, had spoken about it—as is written in the Latin quotation that begins this book—or what holy Christianity thinks about it, so that he might stay on the secure path of truth. As a result he was illumined as follows.

CHAPTER 1

How a Detached Person Begins and Ends in Unity

For all those who are to be led within, it is profitable to know their ultimate origin and that of all things, for in this same thing is also their final goal. And therefore one should know that all those who

308

have ever spoken of truth agree that something exists that is univer-sally the first and the simplest, and before which nothing is.[10] Now Dionysius gazed upon this unfathomable being in its nakedness and he states, as do other teachers,[11] that the aforementioned simplest being is not at all grasped by any name whatever. The science of logic states that a name is supposed to express the nature and the rational concept of the thing named. Now it is obvious that the nature of the aforementioned simple being is limitless and immeasur-able and cannot be grasped by the intellectual powers of any crea-ture. Thus it is clear to all learned theologians that this "being without mode of being" is also nameless.[12] Therefore, Dionysius says in *The Book of Divine Names* that God is nonbeing or a nothing. This is to be understood in relationship to the being and "some-thing" that we attribute to him, which we can understand only as it describes creatures. Whatever one can attribute to him in this man-ner is, in a sense, all incorrect, and its negation is true. Conse-quently one could call him an eternal nothing. And yet, if one is to speak of how unsurpassable or above comprehension something is, one still has to create names for it. The being of this calm simplicity is its life, and its life is its being. It is a living, existing, substantial intellect, which understands itself, exists and lives in itself and is this self.[13]

I simply cannot express it any more clearly, and I call it the eternal, uncreated Truth. All things are in it as in their primordial freshness and eternal source. This is where a detached person be-gins and ends—in well-ordered inwardness, as will be shown in what follows.

CHAPTER 2

Whether Any Difference Can Exist in the Highest Unity

The *disciple* asked, speaking as follows: Since it is true that this one being is so utterly simple, I am confused about whence arises the diversity that is attributed to him. One person clothes him with wisdom and calls him Wisdom. Another does this with goodness, yet another with justice, and so on. Basing it on faith, theologians speak of a divine Trinity. Why does one not let him be in the simplicity that he in himself is? It seems clear to me that this utterly

One has too much activity and too much diversity. How can it be an utterly pure One if there is so much multiplicity?

Truth spoke in response: All this multiplicity is, in its ground and foundation, one simple unity.

The *disciple* said: What do you call the ground and source, and what is not ground?

The answer of *Truth:* I call ground that which is source and origin from which the outflowings arise.

The *disciple:* Lord, what is that?

Truth: That is the nature and being of the Godhead. And in this limitless abyss the Trinity of Persons sinks into its oneness, and in a certain sense all multiplicity becomes lost. In this same sense nothing at all of outside activity can be perceived, but only a calm, hovering darkness.

The *disciple* said: Oh, tell me, dear Lord, what is it that gives this being its first impetus to act, especially to perform its most proper work, which is to give birth?[14]

Truth said: His enabling power does this.

The *disciple:* Lord, what is that?

Truth: That is the divine nature in the Father. In this very instant it becomes pregnant to bear fruit and to act; according to our capacity to understand, the Godhead springs across into God.[15]

The *disciple:* Dear Lord, is this not one and the same thing?

Truth said: Yes, the Godhead and God are one. And yet the Godhead neither acts nor gives birth; rather, God gives birth and acts. This arises solely because of the difference that is in the concept formed according to the way our intellect understands.[16] But it is one in its ground because in the divine nature there is nothing but being and the concomitant qualities, which nowhere add anything to being.[17] They are completely the same although they are differentiated in respect to that in which they exist, namely, in their object. Divine nature, understood in this same ground, is not the least bit simpler in itself than the Father is when conceived in this same nature, or any other Person. You are simply deceived in your way of imagining, which views all this according to how it exists in creatures. In itself it is one and pure.

The *disciple* spoke: I well see that I have come to the deepest ground of perfect simplicity beyond which no one can go who wants to attain truth.

LITTLE BOOK OF TRUTH

How Man and All Creatures Have Existed Eternally
and How They Came About and Proceeded

The *disciple:* Eternal Truth, in what manner have creatures existed eternally in God?

Answer: They have been there as in their eternal exemplar.

Disciple: What is this exemplar?

Truth: This is his eternal being according to how it gives itself universally to creatures so that they might come to be. And notice that all creatures eternally in God *are* God and have there no basic difference other than that already mentioned. They are the same life, being and power insofar as they are in God and are this same One and nothing less. But after their issuing forth, when they take on their own being, each has its own special being distinguished by its own form which gives it its natural being. For form gives being, separate and distinct both from the divine being and from everything else, as, for example, the natural form of a stone causes it to have its own being.[18] And this (being) is not God's being because the stone is not God nor God the stone, although it and all creatures are dependent on him for their being. And in thus flowing forth all creatures have gained their God, because when a creature finds itself to be a creature, it acknowledges its Creator and God.[19]

Disciple: Dear Lord, is the being of a creature nobler as it exists in God or as it exists in the creature itself?

Truth: The being of a creature in God is not a creature, but each creature's created nature is nobler and of more advantage to it than is the being it has in God. For how is a stone or a man or any creature more in its being as creature because it has eternally been God in God? God has ordered things well and rightly, for everything looks back to its primal origin submissively.

Disciple: Ah, Lord, where then does sin come from, or evil, hell, purgatory, the devil, or the like?

Answer: Because a rational creature is supposed to withdraw from itself and return to the One and yet remains turned outward, looking with unjustified possessiveness at its own self—this is where the devil and all evil come from.

311

THE EXEMPLAR

Concerning the True Return, Which a Detached Person Should Accomplish Through the Only-begotten Son

Disciple: I have grasped well the truth about the flowing-out and coming-to-be of creatures. I would now like to hear about the breakthrough—how a person through Christ is supposed to return again within and attain his happiness.

Truth: One must realize that Christ, God's Son, has something in common with all men and something special separating him from other men. What he has in common with all men is human nature— that he too was also true man. He assumed human nature but not (a human) person; that is to say, Christ took on human nature in the indivisibility of matter, which the teacher Damascene calls "in athomo."[20] Thus the pure blossom[21] in Mary's blessed body, from which he took his corporeal instrument,[22] corresponded to this common human nature, which he assumed.

And so human nature taken in itself can make no claim that just because Christ assumed it, and not human personality, every man therefore should or can be God and man in the same manner (as Christ). It is he alone to whom this unattainable dignity belongs, that he assumed this nature in purity so that the consequences of original sin or any other sin did not touch him.[23] Thus he alone was able to redeem guilt-ridden mankind.

Second, the meritorious works of all other men, which they perform in true detachment from themselves, actually direct a person to happiness, which is the reward for virtue. This happiness consists in the full enjoyment of the divinity when all means and otherness have been put aside.[24] But the union occurring in Christ's incarnation, because it occurs within one personal being, transcends this and is higher than the union of the spirit of the blessed with God. From the very beginning of his conception as man, he was truly the Son of God in the sense that he had no other way of existing than as Son of God. All other men, however, have their natural substance determined by their natural essence, and no matter how completely they withdraw from themselves or how purely they abandon themselves in truth, it never happens that they are transformed into the substance of a divine Person and lose their own.

Third, this man, Christ, is superior to all other men in that he is

312

the head of Christianity, just as one speaks of the head of a man in relation to his body,[25] as is written that all those whom he has foreordained, whom he has prepared, would become of the same form as the image of God's Son, that he is the firstborn among many others.[26] Hence, whoever wants to achieve a true return and become a son in Christ, let him in true detachment turn to him and away from self. Then he will come to where he should be.

Disciple: Lord, what is true detachment?

Truth: Take note with careful discrimination of these two words: *oneself* and *leave*. If you know how to weigh these two words properly, testing their meaning thoroughly to their core and viewing them with true discernment, then you can quickly grasp the truth.

Take, first of all, the first word—*oneself* or *myself*—and see what it is. It is important to realize that everyone has five kinds of *self*. The first self one has in common with a stone, and this is being. The second one shares with plants, and this is growing. The third self one shares with animals, and this is sensation. The fourth one shares with all other men, and this is that one possesses a common human nature in which all men are one.[27] The fifth—which belongs to a person exclusively as his own—is one's individual human self, both with respect to one's nobility and with respect to accident.[28]

Now what is it that leads a person astray and robs him of happiness? It is exclusively this last *self*. Because of it a person turns outward, away from God and toward himself, when he should be re-turning inward, and he fashions for himself his own self according to what is accidental.[29] In his blindness he appropriates to himself what is God's. This is the direction he takes, and he eventually sinks into sinfulness.

But whoever would really leave this self should have three insights. First, he should turn his thoughtful gaze upon the nothingness of his own self and see that this self, and the self of all things, is a nothing, removed and excluded from that something which is the sole productive force. The second insight is that it not be overlooked that in this state of utter detachment one's own self rests entirely upon one's own operative being, (as one realizes) after one becomes conscious of oneself again and is not utterly destroyed.[30] The third insight occurs as one becomes less and less, and freely surrenders oneself in everything in which one had become involved by looking to one's own creaturely existence in unfree multiplicity,[31] as opposed to divine truth. (One surrenders oneself) in happiness or

313

suffering, in action or omission in such a way that one loses oneself completely and utterly, withdrawing from oneself irreversibly and becoming one in unity with Christ, so that one always acts at his urging and receives all things and views all things in this unity. And this detached self becomes the same form as Christ about whom the scripture by Paul says, "I live, no longer I, Christ lives in me."[32] This is what I call a rightly valued self.

Now we shall concentrate on the other word spoken: *leave*. This means to surrender or to despise, but not in the sense that one can really so leave the self that it becomes absolutely nothing. One can only despise it. Then one has the right attitude.

Disciple: The truth be praised! Dear Lord, tell me, does anything (of this self) still remain in the happy, detached person?

Truth:[33] Without a doubt it happens that, when the good and loyal servant is led into the joy of his Lord,[34] he becomes drunk from the limitless overabundance of God's house. What happens to a drunken man happens to him, though it cannot really be described, that he so forgets his self that he is not at all his self and consequently has gotten rid of his self completely and lost himself entirely in God, becoming one spirit in all ways with him,[35] just as a small drop of water does which has been dropped into a large amount of wine. Just as the drop of water loses itself, drawing the taste and color (of the wine) to and into itself, so it happens that those who are in full possession of blessedness lose all human desires in an inexpressible manner, and they ebb away from themselves and are immersed completely in the divine will. Otherwise, if something of man were to remain in man of which he were not completely emptied, scripture could not be true in stating that God shall become all things in all things.[36] Certainly his being remains, but in a different form, in a different resplendence, and in a different power. This is all the result of his total detachment from self.

Regarding this same idea (of leaving self) he (St. Bernard) says: But whether anyone in this life is so detached as to reach completely the state in which he does not consider his own self in happiness or suffering but rather loves himself completely for God's sake and views things from the perspective of perfect understanding—on this point, he says, I cannot ascertain whether it really happens. Let those step forward who have experienced it. Speaking from what I know, it does not seem possible.[37]

From this line of thought you can discover an answer to your question. The true detachment of such an ennobled person while on earth is conceived and measured according to the detachment of the blessed (in heaven) about whom this text speaks of a "more or less" according to whether the persons are more or less united or have become one (with God). Note especially that he says they are removed from their selfhood and transformed into a different form, into a different splendor, and into a different power. What, then, is this other, different form if not the divine nature and the divine being into which they flow and which flows into them making them the same? What is this different splendor if it is not to be transfigured and illuminated in the subsisting light to which there is no approach?[38] What is this other power if not, in place of the self and unity with oneself, that one is given a divine force and a divine power to do and leave undone whatever belongs to one's happiness. Thus is a person divested of his humanity, as has been said.

Disciple: Lord, is this possible here on earth?

Truth: The blessedness that is spoken of here can be attained in two ways. One way is to the fullest possible degree beyond all (merely human) capabilities. This cannot come about here on earth because the body, whose various urges are contrary to this, is part of man's nature. But blessedness can also be understood as something communally participated in and in this sense it is possible, although many people consider it impossible. And this is certainly understandable because neither sense knowledge nor intellectual capacity can reach it. One text[39] states well that one finds a kind of person, set apart and proven, whose spirit is so purified and godlike that the virtues exist in him in a manner approaching the divine. Such persons have lost their own forms and have been transformed into oneness with the first Exemplar, somehow achieving complete forgetfulness of transitory and temporal existence; and they are changed into a divine image and are one with him. But the qualification is made that this state belongs only to those who have possessed this blessedness at its highest,[40] or to some people, few and most pious of all, who are still living on earth.

315

THE EXEMPLAR

CHAPTER 5

Concerning Lofty and Useful Questions
Into Which Truth Granted Him Insight
Through the Figurative Example[41] *of a Detached Person*

At this point the disciple felt a strong desire to find out whether there existed in any land such a noble, detached person who through Christ had really been taken up (into God). He wished dearly to make his acquaintance and have intimate talks with him. And when he was seriously desiring this, he retreated within himself and, as his senses faded, it seemed to him as though he were being led into a land of the intellect. And he saw there hovering between heaven and earth a symbolic figure, as though it were the kindly looking figure of a man next to a cross. Two types of persons wandered about but could not get there. The one type saw the figure only from inside and not from without. The other type saw it only from outside and not from within. Both types had an attitude of opposition and obduracy toward the figure. And it seemed to the disciple that the figure lowered itself like a real human being, sat down beside him, and bade him ask whatever questions he had and he would receive answers.

He began, heaving a sigh within his heart, and said: "Alas, eternal Truth, what is this? Or what is the meaning of this strange apparition?" This was the answer he received and the Word spoke thus within him: "This figure that you have seen signifies the only-begotten Son of God in the manner in which he assumed human nature. That you saw only one image, although there was countless multiplicity, signifies all the people who are his members, who have also become sons or Son through him and in him, as the number of many physical parts of one body. However, that his head appeared above all signifies that he is the first and only-begotten Son by his being preeminently taken up into the subsistence of the divine Person, while the others are changed only by taking on the form of the same image.[42] The cross signifies that a truly detached person should always be disposed, both outwardly and inwardly, to self-surrender in everything that God wants him to endure, no matter where it comes from; that he be inclined, dying to self, to accept it all for the praise of his heavenly Father. Such people are inwardly noble and outwardly attentive. That the figure next to the cross was

316

kind means that however much suffering such people have, they disregard it because of their own detachment. In whatever direction the head turns, so turns the body as well. This symbolizes the oneness of mind among the loyal followers of his exemplary life and good teachings. To these they turn and conform with all their might. Those people who saw him from inside and not from outside signify people who look upon the life of Christ with the intellect in a contemplative manner and not as a model for action; but they should be transcending their own nature through practices that imitate this image. They interpret everything from this point of view, which supports their enjoyment of natural pleasure and their exercising unrestrained freedom. Those who do not approve of this they consider unsophisticated and dense.

"Some others saw it only from the outside and not according to its inside, and these seemed hard and severe. Based on this perspective they engage in harsh practices, living carefully and presenting in public a respectable and holy manner of life; but they overlook the interior of Christ. His way of life was gentle and generous, but these people are destructive and judge others, assuming that everything not done their way is wrong. These people do not conduct themselves like the one who is, after all, the object of their intentions, and this is apparent because of this: Observing them closely, one finds they are not in a state of detachment from self nor have they withdrawn from their nature nor freed themselves from those things that defend self-will, such as likes, dislikes, and so forth. Because of this their own will is maintained and defended and, consequently, such persons do not attain divine virtues like obedience, patience in suffering, flexibility, and the like. Such virtues as these lead a person to the image of Christ."

The *disciple* began anew to inquire and said: Tell me, what do you call the manner in which a person attains his blessedness?

Response: One can call it a giving birth, as is written in the gospel of St. John that he gave the power and capacity to become God's Son to all those who are born of nothing else than of God.[43] This takes place in the same way that one conceives of giving birth in general. Now whatever gives birth to something else in such a manner forms it like itself and within itself and gives it sameness in being and acting. And therefore, since God alone is his Father, in a detached person nothing merely temporal is born in possessiveness. His eyes are opened. He becomes fully aware and, receiving his

317

blessed existence and life, is one with him; for all things are here one in the One.

The *disciple* said: But I see mountains and valleys, water and air, and all kinds of creatures. Why do you say that there is only one?

The pure *Word* answered, saying: I shall tell you still more. Unless a person is conscious of two contraries, that is, two things that contradict each other, seeing them as one with each other, then certainly without a doubt it is not at all easy to talk to him about such things. But even if he grasps this, he has only traveled half the way to the life I have in mind.

Question: What are these contraries?

Answer: An eternal nothing and its coming to be in time.[44]

Objection: Two contraries existing as one in any manner contradicts every branch of knowledge.

Answer: You and I do not meet on one branch or in one place. You make your way along one path and I along another. Your questions arise from human thinking, and I respond from a knowledge that is far beyond all human comprehension. You must give up human understanding if you want to reach the goal, because the truth is known by not knowing.[45]

During this same span of time he underwent a very great change. It happened sometimes that in the course of ten weeks more or less he was so powerfully carried off that, though fully conscious, in the presence of others and in their absence, his senses so lost their usual effectiveness that everywhere only the One responded to him in all things and all things were in the One without the multiplicity of this and that.

The *Word* began to speak to him: How are things going now? Did I tell you the truth?

He said: Yes! What I was not able to believe before has become for me now certain knowledge, but I do not understand why it faded away.

The *Word* said: That is perhaps because it has not yet sunk to its essential ground.

The *disciple* began again to question: How far does a detached person's capacity to understand reach?

Answer: Here on earth a man can reach the point that he sees himself as one in that which is the nothing of all the things that one can conceive or put into words. This nothing is called by common agreement "God" and is in itself a something existing to an incomparable degree. Here a person sees himself as one with this nothing, and this nothing knows itself without the activity of knowing.[46] But this is mysteriously hidden further within.

Question: Does some writing mention anything about that which you have called the "nothing," not because of his nonbeing but rather because of his unsurpassed incomprehensibility?

Answer: Dionysius writes of One that is nameless and that can be the nothing I have in mind, for whoever calls him Godhead or being—or whatever names one gives him—they are not appropriate to him in the way names are formed in a creature.[47]

Question: But what is it that is hidden further within this aforementioned nothing, which according to you excludes in its meaning everything that has come into existence? It is after all pure simplicity. How can that which is utterly simple have a "further within" or a "further without?"

Answer: As long as a person understands oneness or something like it as something that can be presented in words, he still has to go "further within." The nothing cannot go further within itself; it is rather a question of our understanding; that is, we must understand it apart from any illuminating form or image because no understanding based on forms or images can grasp it. And one cannot talk about it in the sense that one talks about a thing that can be clarified with words. Whatever one says about it describes not the least little bit what it is, no matter how many theologians and books there might be. To say that this nothing is intellect or being or fulfillment is certainly true according to what anyone can tell us about it. However, in true point of fact it is as far and farther from these things than if one were to call a fine pearl a chopping block.

Question: What does it mean to say that, when the birth-giving nothing that one calls God comes into itself, a person is not aware of any difference between it and himself?

Answer: As long as it is working such things in us, it is not the nothing in itself with respect to us. But when it comes into itself with respect to us, we know nothing of such things even with respect to ourselves.[48]

Question: Clarify this further for me.

Answer: Do you not realize that being powerfully transported from self into the nothing completely eliminates all difference, not of essences but rather in how we perceive, as has been said?

Question: Another statement made earlier disturbs me—that a person while on earth can reach the point of comprehending himself as one in that (being) which has always existed. How can this be?

Answer: One learned teacher defines eternity as life that is beyond time but includes within itself all time but without "a before or after."[49] And whoever is taken into the eternal nothing possesses all in all and has no "before or after." Indeed, a person taken within today would not have been there for a shorter period from the point of view of eternity than someone who had been taken within a thousand years ago.

Objection: It is only after his death that man can expect to be thus taken within, as the scripture says.

Answer: That is true regarding a continuous and complete possession (of such a state) but not regarding a partial foretaste.

Question: How do things stand with man's co-acting with God?

Answer: What has been said about this is not to be understood in the bare sense words have in ordinary speech. It is to be taken in the sense of transport in which the person does not remain for himself and has betaken himself into the One and has become one. Here man does not act as man. This is the reason it is to be understood that this person has within himself all creatures in oneness and all pleasures, even those he has in corporeal activities, but without the physical or spiritual activity, because it is he himself who exists in the aforementioned oneness.

And note here a difference. The ancient philosophers pursued the study of natural things exclusively in connection with their natural causes. This is how they talked about them and this is how they perceived them, and not otherwise. The holy Christian thinkers, and all theologians and saintly people as well, consider things as they have flowed out from God and how they bring man back within after his natural death if he is living here on earth according to his will. Now these people who are taken within, because of their boundless immanent oneness (with God), see themselves and all things as always and eternally existing.

Question: Is there no difference present?

Answer: Yes. He who sees things at all correctly knows this and recognizes himself as a creature, not in its frailty but rather as united

320

(with God). And when he did not exist, he was the same, and not united.[50]

Question: What does that mean; "When he did not exist, he was the same?"

Answer: This is the same as what St. John says in his gospel: "Whatever has come about or been created, that was life in him."[51]

Question: But how can this be true? It sounds as though the soul were two things, one created and one uncreated. How can this be? How can man be both creature and non-creature?

Answer: In our manner of speaking man cannot be creature and God. Still, God is three and one. So also can man be one (with God) in a certain sense when he loses himself in God, in losing himself while outwardly seeing, enjoying, and the like. I shall give an analogy of this. The eye loses itself while seeing because in the act of seeing it becomes one with its object, yet each remains what it is.[52]

Question: Whoever is familiar with the literature knows that in this nothing the soul must either be transformed or be annihilated in its being, and that is not the case here.

Answer: The soul always remains a creature. But when it is lost in the nothing, it is not at all aware of how it is a creature or how it is nothing, or whether or not it is a creature, or whether it is united or not. As long as one is operating according to reason, one perceives this quite clearly, and this remains for a person in any case.[53]

Question: Has such a person reached the best state?

Answer: Yes, in the sense that what he has is not taken from him, and something different and better is given him. He continues to understand all this better and more keenly, and this remains his. But he has not arrived at this state that we have described after he returns to himself. If he is to attain this, he must be in the ground that lies hidden in the previously mentioned nothing. There one knows nothing about anything. There nothing is. There is not even a "there." Whatever one says of it is sheer mockery. Nevertheless, such a person is his own nothing in which all this remains his according to what was said earlier.

Question: Explain this to me more thoroughly.

Answer: The professors say that the happiness of the soul consists before all else in this: When it sees God directly it takes its whole being and life, and it draws everything that it is—insofar as it is happy—from the ground of this nothing. As it is thus engaged in gazing, it knows nothing about knowing or love or anything else. It is at rest completely and exclusively in the nothing and knows nothing but being, which is God or the nothing. But when it knows and recognizes that it knows, sees and recognizes the nothing, this is a departure from and a reflecting upon the earlier state and a return to oneself in the natural order. And since being taken within comes forth from the same vein, you can understand how it is in its ground.

Question: I would like to understand this better from the truth of the literature.

Answer: Learned men say: When one knows a creature in itself this is called and is "evening knowledge," because then one sees a creature differentiated according to various forms. But when one knows a creature in God, it is called and is "morning knowledge," and one then sees the creature without any differentiation, free of all forms and similarity in the One that God is in himself.[54]

Question: Can a person understand this nothing while on earth?

Answer: I do not see how this might be possible for the (unaided) human mind, but as united (with God) it knows itself to be united with that with which this nothing enjoys itself and is giving birth. This (knowing) takes place when the body is, as they say, on earth but the person is beyond time.

Question: Is it the being of the soul that enters this union or is it (only) its powers?[55]

Answer: The being of the soul is united to the being of the nothing, and the powers of the soul with the activity of the nothing, that is, the internal activity of the nothing.

Question: When a person thus remains conscious of his being a creature, not in his weak human way of knowing but rather in his knowledge arising from union, do his failings drop away from him and can he afterward have any failings?

Answer: To the extent that a man remains himself he can engage in wrongdoing. St. John says, "If we assume that we are without sin, we deceive ourselves and there is no truth in us."[56] But to the extent that a man does not remain himself, he does not commit wrong. St. John says in his epistle that the person who is born of God commits no sin nor practices wrongdoing because the divine seed remains in him.[57] Hence a man for whom all goes as it should performs only one act because there is only one birth and one ground with respect to this union.

Objection: How can it be that a person performs only one act? Did not Christ perform two kinds of acts?

Answer: I maintain that a man who has an eye for no other act but that which the eternal birth performs carries out only one act. If God were not continually giving birth to his Son, Christ would never have performed a natural act. Hence I call it only one act, unless one is considering it according to (merely) human understanding.

Objection: But the pagan thinkers say that nothing can be separated from its effect.[58]

Answer: A person is not separated from what he brings about, rather he remains unaware of it.[59]

Question: Regarding those creaturely acts that remain to be performed—does this person do them or somebody else?

Answer: If a person is to attain the highest goal, he must be dead to the rebirth within him, but the rebirth must have taken place.[60] Note how this is to be. Everything that comes into us, wherever it is from, if it is not reborn in us, it is of no use to us. This rebirth is so strange and has so little to do with the body after it has taken place that nature performs in the person, as in a rational animal, such acts as belong to human life. And the person somehow has no more to do to bring about an effect than he had before his rebirth. Rather, it (nature) performs these acts as its own. Here is a comparison with brandy. It does not have less matter but rather a stronger and more calming effect than wine, which has remained in its first birth.

Question: Tell me the difference between the eternal birth and the rebirth that takes place in man.

Answer: I call "eternal birth" the unique force from which all things and the causes of all things have it that they exist and are causes. But I call "rebirth" that which is proper to man alone, a redirecting of each and every thing that happens back into its origin, taking it according to the nature of its origin without any regard for itself.

Objection: What do the essential natural causes bring about, which the natural philosophers describe?[61]

Answer: They bring about everything according to natural forces that the eternal birth by its giving birth brings about in man, but how this is in the ground cannot be said.

Question: When the soul, as it is taken within, loses its awareness and use of everything created, what is it that directs the use of external things?

Answer: All the powers of the soul are too weak to be able to enter into the nothing in the manner previously described. Nevertheless, when one has lost oneself in this nothing, the powers bring about that which is their origin.

Question: Describe how a person loses himself in God.

Answer: If you have been paying attention, it has actually already been completely described for you. For when a person has been so taken from himself that he knows neither anything about himself nor anything else and is in complete repose in the ground of the eternal nothing, then he is certainly lost to himself.

Question: Does the (human) will cease to exist in the nothing?

Answer: Yes, with regard to its actually willing, because however free the will is, it is only really free when it does not have to will anymore.

Objection: How can the human will cease to exist? Christ kept his will in the sense of continuing to will.

Answer: Such a person loses the actual willing that his will does in the sense that the will wants now this object and now that out of a desire to possess. Here one does not exercise the will in the imperfect manner just explained; rather, one's will has been set free so that it performs only the one act that it is itself in the union and performs it beyond time. What is more, whoever understands this in our sense never ever wants to work evil and wills all good things. Actually such a person's whole life, willing and activity are quiet, undisturbed freedom, which is certainly without a doubt his support. Then he lives and acts in the manner of the birth.

Objection: The will does not burst into action in the manner of the birth.

Answer: Such a will is united with the divine will and does not will anything but what he himself is to the extent that there is willing in God. And what was said before is not to be understood as an invasion of the self into God, as it is generally explained; it is to be understood as a divesting of the self because such a person is so completely united that God is his ground.

Question: Does a person keep his personal distinct being in the ground of nothing?

Answer: All of this is to be understood only as expressing human perception (of the experience) in which this thing and that go unnoticed after one has divested oneself of self and gazes intently (at God), not as expressing actual existence, in which each thing remains what it is. As St. Augustine says, "Reject in contempt this and that good. What remains is pure goodness pervading all in its boundlessness, and this is God.[62]

Question: Does the person who sees and enjoys himself as the nothing we have described remain always in this state?

Answer: Not in the state of enjoying it, but certainly he retains the experience and never loses it.

Question: Do not external events disturb what is internal?

Answer: If we were outside of time with our body, there would be fewer obstacles with respect to hunger, labor and other things; but intellectual awareness of external things does not disturb what is interior because it (this awareness) exists in freedom. Also, it sometimes happens, the more nature is set upon, the more richly divine truth is adorned.

Question: Where does despondency come from?

Answer: If such a thing comes only from natural causes and if a person remains inwardly free, pay no attention to it. It will pass as with all physical things. But if what is internal in the ground were to become involved, this would not be good.

Objection: In the Old Testament and the gospel we are told that a person on earth cannot attain what has been described.

Answer: This is true regarding possession of this state and full knowledge. What one has a taste of here is more perfect there, although it is the same thing; and though beyond human understanding it can occur on earth.

Question: What should a person do who begins to understand his eternal nothing, not from an overpowering force but just from hearing it talked about or, apart from this, from his own imaginings?

Answer: A person who is not to the point of understanding with supernatural help what the aforementioned nothing is, in which all things are extinguished as to their individuality, should let all things be as they are no matter what happens and should hold fast to the common teaching of holy Christianity, as one sees many a good, simple person do who achieves praiseworthy holiness but who is not called to this state. And yet the closer, the better. If he attains a secure position, he should keep hold of it. He is on the right path, because this position is in conformity with holy scripture. For him to do otherwise causes me concern, because if one goes astray on this point, one ends up either unfree or often in chaotic liberty.

THE EXEMPLAR

CHAPTER 6

In What Points Those People Fall Short
Who Live According to a Mistaken Idea of Freedom

One bright Sunday, as he (the disciple) was sitting withdrawn and deep in thought, there came to him in the calmness of his mind the figure of a rational being who was sophisticated in speech but inexperienced in deeds and who overflowed with rich ostentation.

He began speaking to the figure thus: Where do you come from?

It said: I never came from anywhere.

He said: Tell me, what are you?

It said: I am nothing.

He said: What do you want?

It answered and said: I want nothing.

And he said: This is very strange. Tell me, what is your name?

It said: I am called nameless wild one.

The *disciple* said: You are well named "the wild one" because your words and answers are completely wild. Now tell me something I shall ask you. Where does your wisdom take you?

It said: To unrestrained liberty.

The *disciple* said: Tell me, how do you define unrestrained liberty?

It said: When a person lives completely according to his impulses heedless of all else, without looking ahead or behind.

The *disciple* said: You are not on the path of truth. Such liberty leads a person away from all blessedness and robs him of his true liberty; for if one lacks the power of discriminating, one lacks order. And whatever is without correct order is evil and defective. As Christ said: "He who commits sin is the slave of sin."[63] But a person who with a pure conscience and a prudent way of life enters into Christ in true detachment from himself attains true freedom, as Christ himself said: "If the Son frees you, then you shall become truly free."[64]

The *wild one* said: How do you define "orderly" or "without order?"

The *disciple* said: "Orderly" is when everything pertaining to an issue, both interiorly and exteriorly, is not left out of consideration, including the consequences. "Disorderly" is when one of these things has been neglected.

The *wild one* said: Unrestrained liberty will transcend all this and scorn it all.

The *disciple* said: Such recklessness would be against all truth and accords well with false, unrestrained liberty because it is against the order that the eternal nothing bestowed upon all things in its giving birth.

The *wild one* said: The person who has become nothing in his eternal nothing knows nothing of such distinctions.

The *disciple* said: The eternal nothing that is meant here and as understood by all well-oriented intellects is not nothing because it does not exist but because of its unsurpassable abundance of being which has absolutely no differences within itself and from which, as birth-giving, all ordered differences in things arise. A person never becomes so completely annihilated in this nothing that his senses are not aware of the difference of their origin or his reason not aware of its free choice, even if all this is ignored in his primal ground.

The *wild one:* Does anyone perceive anywhere else but in this same ground and from this ground?

The *disciple:* A person would not perceive it correctly because it is not just in the ground. It is also in itself a created something outside the ground, and it remains what it is. And one has to understand it as such also. If a person were to lose his distinctness (from God) in being, as he does in how he perceives (himself and God), then one could agree with this view. But this is not the case, as has already been said. It is important always to keep this distinction in mind.

The *wild one* said: I have heard that there was a learned teacher who denied all distinctions.[65]

The *disciple* said: If you mean he denied all distinction in the Godhead, one could interpret this to mean a denial of each of the Persons in the ground where they are indistinct from each other, but not as they are contrasted to each other. In this sense they are certainly to be considered distinct as Persons.

If you take it to refer to the condition of a person lost (in God), enough has already been said to show that this describes human perception of the event but does not affect the mode of being. Note that there is a difference between separation and distinctness. As is obvious, body and soul are not separate because the one is in the other and no member that has been separated can remain alive. But the soul is distinct from the body because the soul is not the body,

327

nor the body the soul. In this sense, I take it that nothing truly exists that can be separate from the simple being (of God), because this gives being to all being. With regard to distinctness, however, the divine being is not the stone's being, nor is the stone's being the divine being, nor is one creature the being of another. This is why theologians say that this distinctness in a proper sense is not *in* God but rather *from* God. In interpreting the Book of Wisdom it is said: Nothing is more within (creatures) than God, just as nothing is more distinct (from them).[66] Thus the other explanation is wrong, and this interpretation is correct.

The *wild one* said: This same teacher said much that is beautiful about the Christlike person.

The *disciple* said: In one passage this teacher says the following: Christ is the only-begotten Son and we are not. He is the Son by nature because his birth corresponds to his nature, but we are not the son by nature and our birth is a rebirth because its goal is to be uniform with his nature. He is the image of the Father; we are formed in the image of the holy Trinity; and in this, he says, no one is his (Christ's) equal.[67]

The *wild one* said: I have heard that he said such a person accomplishes everything that Christ accomplished.[68]

The *disciple* answered: In one passage this same master says the following: The just man does everything that justice does. This is true, he says, because the just man is born from justice, as it is written: "What is born of flesh is flesh, and what is born of spirit is spirit."[69] This is true only of Christ, he says, and not of any other man because he (Christ) has no being but the being of the Father and no other progenitor than the heavenly Father. Therefore, he did everything that the Father does. But in all other men, he says, it happens that we co-act with him either more or less according to whether we are more or less born of him. This explanation directs you to the real truth.

The *wild one* said: His words proclaim that everything which is given to Christ is also given to me.[70]

The *disciple:* This "everything" that is given to Christ is the perfect possession of substantial blessedness. He said, "*Omnia dedit mihi pater*—the Father has given everything to me."[71] This same "everything" he has given to us, but in a different manner. And he (Eckhart) says in many places that he (Christ) has this "everything" through the incarnation, and we (have it) through conforming union with God. Hence he has it more nobly to the extent that he was able to receive it more nobly.

The *wild one* kept objecting and said that this teacher denied all mere similarity and union (between God and creature) and that he posited us, naked and freed from all (mere) similarity, in pure oneness.

The *disciple* answered, saying: Your problem is without a doubt that you do not understand the distinction previously mentioned about how a person should become one in Christ and yet remain distinct, and how he is united though perceives himself to be one and not just united.[72] The genuine light has not yet illumined you. Genuine light allows for order and distinction, while rejecting turbulent plurality.[73] Your sharp mind with its agility in reasoning employs with complete control the light of nature, which illumines much like the light of divine truth.

The *wild one* was silent and then begged him in pliant submissiveness to talk more about this valuable distinction.

He answered and said: The most prominent shortcoming that disorients you and those like you is the inability to distinguish correctly in matters of rational truth. Therefore, whoever wants to reach perfection and not fall into these shortcomings should give serious attention to this subtle doctrine. Then he will attain unimpeded a blessed life.

CHAPTER 7

How Nobly a Truly Detached Person Acts in All Things

After this the disciple turned again in all seriousness to eternal Truth and asked for the power to discern from indications of outward appearance a person who was truly detached. He asked thus: Eternal Truth, how does such a person act in his relationships with various things?

Answer: He withdraws from himself and all things withdraw along with this self.

Question: How does he conduct himself with respect to time?

Answer: He exists in an ever-present now, free of selfish intentions and perceives his perfection in the smallest thing as in the greatest.

Question: Paul says that no law is made for the just man.[74]

Answer: A just man, by becoming so,[75] conducts himself more submissively than other men because he understands from within in the ground what is proper outwardly for everyone, and he views all things accordingly. The reason that he is unfettered is that he himself does (freely) out of (an attitude of) detachment what ordinary people do under compulsion.

Question: Is not the person who has been transported to interior detachment freed from external exercises?

Answer: One sees few people reach the condition you describe without their strength being used up. The efforts of those who really achieve it affect them to the marrow. And so, when they realize what is to be done and left undone, they continue to practice the usual exercises, performing them more or less frequently as their strength and the occasion permit.

Question: Where do the pangs of conscience and other anxieties of seemingly good people come from, as well as the unrestrained latitude (of conscience) in other people?

Answer: Both types are focusing their attention on their own image but in different ways; the one group spiritually, the other bodily.

Question: Does a detached person remain unoccupied all the time, or what does he do?

Answer: A really detached person's activity is his becoming detached, and his achievement is to remain unoccupied because he remains calm in action and unoccupied by his achievement.[76]

Question: What is his conduct toward his fellowman?

Answer: He enjoys the companionship of people, but without their making a deep impression on him.[77] He loves them without attachment, and he shows them sympathy without anxious concern—all in true freedom.

Question: Is such a person required to go to confession?

Answer: The confession that is motivated by love is nobler than one motivated by necessity.

Question: What is such a person's prayer like? Is he supposed to pray, too?

Answer: His prayer is effective because he forestalls the influence of the senses. God is a spirit and knows whether this person has put an obstacle in the way or whether he has acted from selfish impulses. And then a light is enkindled in his highest power[78] which makes clear that God is the being, life and activity within him and that he is merely an instrument.

Question: What are such a person's eating, drinking and sleeping like?

Answer: Externally, and in keeping with his sensuous nature, the outward man eats. Internally, however, he eats nothing; otherwise, he would be enjoying food and rest like an animal. This is also the case in other things pertaining to human existence.

Question: What is his external behavior like?

Answer: He has few mannerisms, and he does not talk a lot; his words are simple and direct. He lives modestly so that things pass through him without his involvement. He is composed in his use of the senses.

Question: Are all detached people like this?

Answer: More so or less so depending on accidental circumstances. Essentially, however, they are the same.

Question: Does such a person come to a full knowledge of the truth, or does he remain in the realm of opinion and imagining?

Answer: Since such a person remains basically human, he continues to have opinions and imaginings. But because he has withdrawn from himself into that which is, he has a knowledge of all truth; for this is truth itself and the person is unaware of himself. But let this be enough for you. One does not arrive at the goal by asking questions. It is rather through detachment that one comes to this hidden truth. Amen.

Little Book
of
Letters

(Here begins the fourth little book)

The instruction given here has been selected from actual letters the servant of eternal Wisdom sent to his spiritual daughter[1] and other of his spiritual children.

Because the mind of a spiritual person cannot constantly remain extended in detached purity and yet should flee harmful amusements, to refresh your spirit you can read these letters.

LETTER 1

A Beginner's Turning From the World to God

"I have despised the kingdom of the world and all its adornment for the love of my Lord, Jesus Christ."[2]

When I heard this joyful refrain being sung over you and saw your maidenly departure (from the world) as a chosen bride of God, I was thinking: If one has found something better to devote oneself to, one can cheerfully leave what is pleasant. And this has truly happened to you today. And so you should freely bid the deceiving world farewell.

Look, all you lovers, at the way of the world. I had embraced a shadow, married an illusion, possessed a fantasy. Alas, where is the fantasy I imagined now? Where is the fulfillment of the dream? Lady World, even if I had possessed you for a thousand years, what would that be now? Like a fleeting moment! Proper to your nature is to pass away. I thought I could hold you in my embrace, but look how you have vanished before my very eyes.[3] If a person does not abandon you first, then you abandon him. You murderess, you! And so, farewell, farewell. May God be good to you today and always. Deceive those who do not know you. Me you shall never deceive again! "The kingdom of the world, etc."

My child in almighty God, remember that, after much reflection, you have given up all your friends and relatives, honor and possessions. Remain firm in this resolve. Do not be like some foolish virgins who act like wild, caged animals. When the gate closes behind them, they gape outward through the fence. Those who are half outside and half inside—they certainly waste arduous labor on insignificant things. For them, to serve God is to be in prison; religious discipline is a dungeon. And so, because they cannot have the apple, they are hooked on its fragrance.[4] Instead of a garland of roses, they put on flowery cloth. Since they can no longer wear bright red, they admire themselves in their white habit. In place of marriage (to Christ) they get involved with what wastes their time, carries off their heart and destroys their religious life completely: idle infatuation. They languish in desire and talk to their fantasies like a thirsty man dreaming of cold water. And as they turn this way and that, it all disappears and they find their hand empty, their heart sad and their soul without grace. They experience what the ancient desert father experienced when the devil sat down upon the mat that he had put on instead of a long coat. Mocking, the devil said, "Poor man! If you could put on more, you would!" Such is a miserable and lonely life, and is the antechamber of hell: not to be able to possess the world and to be without God, to be robbed of both worldly and divine comfort, to have lost both. How shamefully and pitifully shall they stand there on the day of judgment in front of friend and foe. But to serve God diligently is a secure and liberated existence, here and hereafter, because such people walk here on earth in their bodies and yet their dwelling is always in heaven. Truly this is a sweet yoke and a mild burden.[5] That they sometimes have to suffer should be ignored. Who does not suffer on earth? No one. Neither castle nor town can escape suffering. Neither a red coat nor colorful clothes offer deliverance from it. Often that which appears sound on the outside is fully devastated within. Hence, if a person also suffers as a free divine spectacle,[6] this is not to be taken seriously. Breaking free is painful at first, as it should be, but in the end one acts out of joy and it all disappears.

Remember the days before; examine the long years and see how long you have slept. Was not the whole thing like a dream, and you thought it all so fine? Arise, it is time.[7] The Lord whom you have so often driven off will not give up. It is not good to deny yourself to your friend too long. Open up your heart. Let the beloved in. Make up for the long time you have wasted. Whoever opens up for his love late should certainly do so in haste. You are not like many other people who are lukewarm and love neither God nor the world. God wants to possess your loving heart, spiritual in every way as it was worldly before. And so, put all your effort and wit that you used to use for transitory things—now you should turn them to what is lasting and eternal.

The Humble Subordination of a Religious-minded Person

"The wolf shall dwell with the lamb."[8]

When the Lord of nature came down and became man, he intended to work new marvels. And he made what was wild tame, what was fearsome gentle, as the prophet Isaiah had foretold.

My child, I once read a saying in a book that I am just now beginning to understand. It is this: Love makes unlike things alike.[9] This is why Venus is painted blind and without eyes—because seeing with the eyes of love she loses the ability to see objectively. And though this is true of transitory love, it is much more so concerning spiritual love. It has stripped many noble and worthy people of their lofty position. Some, who were exalted rulers in Rome, gave it all up and became servants of poor people so that they would be like their beloved divine Child. And so, my child, give up the arrogance hidden in your family's nobility and the illusory comfort of friends and relatives that until now were deceptively covered in you with a spiritual appearance, and bow down today to the Child in his crib, in his abasement, that he might raise you to his eternal dignity. If you sow sparingly, you shall harvest poorly. But if you sow lavishly, you shall harvest in abundance. Act in your own interest and bow down to the feet of all men as though you were a doormat.[10] A doormat does not get angry with anyone, no matter what is done to it, because it is a doormat.

True subordination in a person is a root of all virtue and happiness. From it there springs forth a meek calmness for true detachment from self with regard to things both insignificant and great. This causes pain: to have something to say but to remain silent, to receive insult and not to retaliate, as a capable and respected person to keep silent in front of a bungler of no repute. This is modeled on our noble Christ. What can be more useful for a person or give more praise to God? For this it is useful to hold one's tongue and not to open one's mouth to speak except with genuine mildness and well-ordered prudence, so that nothing is said except for the bare minimum necessary for the glory of God or the advantage of one's fellowman.

Notice that I am not demanding something terribly severe of you. You should eat, drink and sleep as needed, and be allowed dispensations that your frail physical constitution requires.

If you wish to be happy, you should put the things just mentioned into practice; and do not become discouraged if nothing happens immediately. How would it be possible to throw out so quickly all the rubbish that has been gathering in one place for twenty years? It will disappear little by little when it sees that there is no place for it. Pious contemplation, fervent prayer and spiritual industry will help. If you do not experience much consolation, you should not let it bother you. You should consider yourself unworthy of it. Lie at his (Christ's) gentle feet until you find his favor, and let God do as he pleases. You will have to experience many a storm before heavenly serenity has a permanent abode within you. Did things constantly go well for you before? Certainly not. It was joy and sorrow, sorrow and joy, as the wheel of Lady Fortune determined.[11] Accept the same from our dear God whom you serve, as well you should, and whose loving anger is better than false endearments. Overlook such treatment from him; he certainly has overlooked much from you. Trust God completely because he will not forsake you. He is so good that he could not find it in his generous heart to forsake a person who surrenders himself completely to him.

There once was a man who was detached from everything that could give him pleasure or comfort in an earthly manner. Once he had a good idea and thought, "Oh, my heart, why are you so very happy?" His interior responded, saying, "In this whole world there is nothing that gives me joy, neither possessions nor honor nor friends nor any pleasure of this world. My only joy is that God is so good and that this loving Goodness is my intimate friend. I am very confident of this."

My child, although there is hardly anyone who does not, sometimes more than others, fall into a condition of lukewarmness, still I must tell you something. The mountain is high and the path slippery. The goal cannot be reached with one burst. It is a question of trying again and again until the struggle brings success. That knight is certainly fainthearted who, having once yielded to the superiority of the enemy, does not boldly charge forward again. Struggle is part of being a good person on earth.

I know a Dominican friar. When he had been driven backward by many strong waves and, in his own thinking, was far removed from true resolve and devotion of the heart, he entered into himself and said, "O God, what has happened to me? How could I sink like this without knowing it? But courage! Try to gain a new goodness. The old one is completely gone." And he began again to mortify himself, to chastize the body, to avoid people's company, to conduct himself with earnestness, to put a watch on himself, to compose new prayers, to take on new exercises (of penance), and to block all the paths where he had previously fallen. He did this day and night until he was again on fire with a divine zeal and devotion in his heart. And this latter state was often much better than the earlier one had been. By contemplating in his heart he buried the old man, as though he had never existed; and he found many a way to guard himself that he had never thought of before. Thus he became wiser and wiser. When he again began to sink, he reacted as he had earlier. This may have happened to him countless times. Notice, eternal Wisdom teaches us this through the words of St. Bernard, who says: "This is the one factor separating the chosen from those not chosen. The latter remain lying down, while the chosen ones return again and again to the task."[12] On earth no one can just stay calmly where he is.

A beginner, before he is permanently established in God, can quite easily lose the way. To prevent this I can find nothing better than that, as far as possible, a person completely give up all things that take him outside himself, and that he make his way into himself and remain within himself. A person who without real necessity devotes himself to external matters gives up peace of heart. Albert the Great is supposed to have said, "I never go to the front door of the cloister without coming back a lesser person."[13]

One should always unite oneself with God with one's whole heart, and for this silence is necessary as well as lofty contemplation, few words and much hard work. Whatever suffering God gives a person should be cheerfully accepted, everyone's failings patiently overlooked, things that attract shunned, no one listened to very much, the senses held in check, little time and few words devoted to anyone, one's attention fastened assiduously on oneself, subordination of self to God and to all men practiced, everyone well spoken of and oneself despised, God cheerfully served and men given a good example. One should be vigilant in great things and small, have God as one's goal in all things and walk with God at all times. And thus can one become established in God, making up for time lost and gaining new treasures from God. Amen.

LETTER 3

How One Should Willingly Surrender Oneself to Suffering
After the Example of Christ

To Elsbeth Stagel in Töss.
  "I am black but beautiful."[14]

This is written in the Song of Songs about the soul in love. The daughters of Jerusalem marveled at the most beloved of all King Solomon's wives. She was a Moor, and they were surprised that she was so black and yet, among the great number of all his wives, she was his favorite.

What then did the Holy Spirit intend to say here?[15] The charming, black Moorish girl who pleases God more than all others is a God-suffering person whom God tries with constant sufferings and endows with patient detachment. Note well, daughter, it is easy to hear and talk about suffering. But to feel it oneself is a torment. Because of its intensity the person suffering is sometimes brought to the point of imagining that God has forgotten him and says to himself, "O God, have you forgotten us? Don't you know we are alive? What do you want from us? How can your hand be so heavy

340

and yet your heart is so very tender?" In response to these loving words of chiding he says, "Look at the great number of saints. Behold the beautiful, living wall of heavenly Jerusalem. How the sparkling stones of the city have been cut and polished with suffering, how brilliantly they shine in the bright light.[16] What happened to dear St. Elizabeth?[17] Paul was for this world garbage.[18] Job and Tobias followed this same path. St. Athanasius suffered as though the whole world had sworn to kill him. See how all the saints spilled the blood of their hearts, or both their physical blood and the blood of their hearts." A person in suffering should see this and be happy that through suffering God has made him equal to his very dearest friends. And so, put aside your practices of mortification and physical penances, your wasting away and fasting, since suffering can bring us such a great benefit.[19]

But if a person in suffering does not at all times have an even attitude of self-surrender, this does not mean he has lost God—it takes morning *and* evening to make a whole day—as long as he does not want to rebel against God. If a person in suffering loses his healthy color, if his mouth dries out and if his natural friendliness is lost, let him look upward and say: "Like the skin of Solomon,"[20] that is, the outer man of the King who was so ravaged on the cross that he did not resemble a man. Let the person step forward who can equal his wretched disfigurement. He says, "*Ego sum vermis*, I am a worm."[21] O dazzling worm, brighter than the sun, whoever looks upon you should not complain. He should resign himself with a cheerful heart to any suffering that befalls him. My child, you might easily imagine that because God has tried you so rigorously, your sufferings are the most severe of all. You should not think that. Every man is closest to himself. In this regard I, too, find an attitude arising at times within me that makes me consider my suffering very severe. But that one should leave in God's hands.

I should not have written you about all this except that God's love forces me to put my shoulder under your burden so that it might become lighter for you. When unfortunate and needy people gather, they sometimes invent a distraction so that they forget their hunger. I wanted to send you the doormat that I took away from the dog and kept as a reminder,[22] but I like it so much that I cannot let go of it. Let us keep our spirits up and suffer in patience, because after this there follows joy in the beautiful kingdom of heaven.

341

THE EXEMPLAR

How an Inexperienced Person Should Turn to
Himself Alone and Not Bare His Soul to Others

"Can one blind man lead another?"[23]

Among many other spiritual children whom the servant had attracted to God there was a daughter who was self-indulgent and
irresolute. She wanted and yet did not want, wanted to be utterly
blessed yet at the same time wanted to get her fill of pleasure and
comfort, talking about it all in fancy phrases. He wrote her the
following:

Dear daughter, why do you give in to yourself? Why do you so
turn your back on the well-intentioned instruction of your spiritual
father that you begin again to surrender yourself to things from
which I had just barely weaned you, things that weakened you in
soul, body and honor. Do you now think you can go and do whatever you feel like? Do you now stand so firmly that you can allow
yourself anything? Alas, why don't you think back on what God has
forgiven you, how you just barely got to where you are, and that
you are not yet anything at all? Be concerned about yourself and let
all other people be. Don't you see the devil has wrapped a silk
thread around your neck and would like to lead you off after him?
You never could give yourself good counsel. You are weaker than
Eve in paradise, and yet you expect to lead other people to God?
You want to spread straw over the fire that was just covered over a
little and has not really been extinguished.

You claim you want to act in a spiritual manner. Indeed, it may
well begin in the spirit, but it will quickly end in the flesh. Do you
still have no sense? Don't you think God has put up with enough
from you? I'm sure you won't give up until you are bound to the
devil's rope. I have often told you: You think you can deceive both
God and men by your refined manner, but in the end you are the
one deceived. You must stand firm and let go of all attachments.
Otherwise, you can never succeed. Be content if you yourself can
escape the devil!

One thing I must say to you: One day the servant had gone out to
contrive a spiritual theft from the devil and return it to God. The
theft had to do with a seemingly religious person like you. This
person had entangled her heart in an infatuation and could not

escape. She wanted to find proper what was not proper or appropriate. And when by the good advice of the servant this person received the impetus to turn away from these things and to hold fast to
God, the evil spirits began lurking about to make their losing her
and her conversion difficult, so that she thought a huge mountain
had fallen on her heart. That very night after matins it seemed to the
servant in a vision that a large swarm of giant birds was storming his
cell from outside. They were hideous each in its own way. Puzzled,
he went and leaned out the window and asked a young man who
was standing there what kind of strange company they were. The
young man said, "This changing horde is a gathering of devils.
They are angry and raging at the nun because she wanted to part
company from them, and they are flitting about here and there to
see whether they can prevent her good resolve and bring her back
again to her old way of life." When it was morning, the servant
wrote her a letter, which said:

"Be brave, etc."[24] When a respected knight first leads a squire into
the tournament ring, he says to him encouragingly, "Now, noble
hero, show what you are capable of today. Be bold and defend
yourself keenly. Don't lose heart like a coward. It is better to die
with honor than to live in dishonor. Once the first contest has been
gotten through, it gets easier." This is what holy David does in a
spiritual framework with regard to an accomplished knight of God,
when he should and must leave temporal things at the beginning.
He says, "*Viriliter*," etc. This means: Be brave and manly, all of you
who trust in God! This is what you need, my daughter, that you
stand firm and do not follow the evil counsels of the devil. You are
now in the worst situation possible. If you can pass over this narrow
stretch, you shall quickly pass over into the beautiful and spacious
meadow of a peaceful spiritual life. Would to God that I might stand
in your place and fight, taking for you the fierce blows that your
besieged heart is now receiving. But this would be a shame because
then you would not receive the green palm branch that you, along
with other special knights of God, shall wear in your eternal glory if
you conquer. For every arrow shot at you there shall be a ruby in
your crown.

And so, my child, be firm, stand firm, act boldly. What you
suffer is short. What you look forward to is eternal. Act as though
you can neither see nor hear until you have won the first contest
of your spiritual beginning. After big storms there follow bright

days. Remember that many a good-looking, young, noble and gentle person like you has prevailed in this kind of knightly contest, and they stood many an hour in the kind of fight you are engaged in and were very fiercely attacked. And that is now the joy of their hearts.

And so, my child, give me your hand and hold firmly, not to me but to our strong Lord in whose service you came to fight. Know that he will not forsake you if you surrender yourself to him completely. Two things will help you overcome in all things. One is that you do not remain standing or sitting by anyone, or listen to anyone, be it friend or foe, who wants to direct you away from the path. The second, that you not act with affectation and do not give in out of indulgence to the sucking vipers of your heart. Do what I say. If you do not want them to return tomorrow, tear their heads off. Do it quickly and thoroughly. If you only take them by the tail, they will stick to you all the more and will bite you so much the worse. Say to them that have so clearly robbed your heart of peace with their guile: "I make no peace with you!" Flee to God. Let the silly fools call after you as much as they want. Never look back! Then you will have quickly conquered all your enemies and will easily be freed from your heavy shackles.

There is one more thing I want to tell you, and do not take it amiss. I have noticed about you that you are still not completely in God with your senses, that you have not boldly stripped yourself of all things. Indeed, you must either possess things or leave them. Otherwise you will not experience happiness. Can one serve two masters?[25] Certainly not! Take a free leap and you can make it. Leave completely this person—you understand me, I know—and all the commotion that is connected with such fleeting love—meetings, messages; and don't let yourself be led astray either by threats or by blandishments. Bid an unambiguous farewell to all the companions who urged you to such actions or helped you in them or are themselves still living in that manner. These you must and shall leave because, put bluntly, they are poison for you, and you know it very well. You should abstain from all trips outside the convent and all subterfuges, trying to think up reasons why it is necessary to make such trips. God and men know well that not much good has come from this. You should constantly be occupied with how you can reform your sinful life, how you can get rid of your numerous failings, and how you might reconcile yourself to your stern judge.

Certainly it is not enough for you to bite daintily into the clover.[26] You must attack your rebellious body, curb your sharpened tongue, recollect your distracted mind, so that your heart is not like a public house, a common wine cellar, a tavern, where anyone can come in and where everyone can do as he pleases. Drive them out, drive out this low company or you can certainly never receive our gentle Lord. Remember that he has bidden you to be his bride. And so see to it that you don't become a barmaid!

LETTER 5

The Elation That the Angels and Angelic People Feel
When a Sinner Repents

"Let the angelic throng of the heavens rejoice."[27]

Our Lord says in the gospel that the angels rejoice when a sinner repents,[28] and the joy of the angels is a celestial jubilation.

Once the servant made the acquaintance of a young woman whose radiant beauty was very pleasing to everyone and whose attractive appearance seduced many a heart. The servant would have liked to put a stop to this and lead her to the God of love so that God would thereby be praised and this person's guardian angel, and along with him all angels, might rejoice, and that mankind might be improved. With this request concerning the woman he approached God very seriously and our Lady as well, who is a bright morning star. He asked her beseechingly to illumine the worldly attitude and the darkened heart of this person and to lead her away from harm to God. Our Lady granted to him that her worldly heart received the grace of God by means of which she quickly turned from the world to God with devotion. Because of this such a great heavenly joy sprang up in the servant's heart that, in the midst of this celestial elation, he sent her the letter below.

Much later, when he was putting together this small selection of all his letters and was leaving out much for the sake of brevity, he came upon this letter as well and he thought: This letter is nothing but pure jubilation. When arid souls or hard hearts read it, they will find it in poor taste. And so he, too, rejected the letter. The next morning—it was within the octave of the feast of the angels—there came to him in a spiritual vision I know not how many youths of the company of angels who chided him for destroying it, and they told him to write it again. This he did and began writing thus:

"Let the angelic throng of the heavens rejoice." When the bright star of morning, Mary, in splendor broke through the dread gloom of your darkened heart, it received a joyful greeting. I raised a joyful voice aloud at this happy moment and it resounded in the heights, "Oh, may God greet you, bright star of the sea. May God greet you, rising, delightful and gentle star of morning, from the unfathomable ground of all loving hearts!" I urged my companions on to greet the resplendent morning star with sound; I mean the sweet Queen of heaven who with the bursting forth of her brilliant radiance lit up your gloomy heart after I had secretly approached her. In exhilaration I sent spontaneous praise to the land of the skies and bade the crested larks aloft and the other delightful larks of the meadows above that they help me sing the praises of the Lord. With my heart full I raised my eyes and said:

"Let the angelic throng of the heavens rejoice." Dear God, if I ever felt suffering, it then disappeared. Golden days encompassed me. I imagined that I was floating along in the springtime valley of heavenly joy. I said, "Rejoice, O noble angel throngs of the heavenly meadows. Rejoice, leap and sing because of the glad news. Look, all of you, in astonishment. The younger son has returned. The lost son who was dead has been found. Ah, the dear, dead child lives again!29 The village common30 naturally alive with flowers, where the cattle had been kept and which had thus been made barren, now again begins to shine with supernatural beauty. The livestock have been driven off. The delicate flowers are beginning to surge forth. The gate is closed. You again have what is yours. Therefore, O heavenly strings, start up and play a new dance tune that may be heard in the court of heaven, that there be no alleyway that does not ring with it. Rejoice the more since the goddess of love, Venus, has been robbed of a heart. She has been denied her elegant summer garland. Her amusing melodies grow silent.

"Ha, false world. Deceiving, transitory love: Lower your head! Who will praise you now? Whom will you now engage in charming trivial occupations? Your beloved leader is no more. She has become a respected spiritual leader. Because of this all the heavens rejoice, and all the hearts that love God say, 'Glory to you, Lord, for these great marvels which you alone work in so many sinful, helpless, and despairing hearts.'

"O handsome and powerful Lord, how very winning and loving you are in all your deeds. And yet you are many thousands of times more loving and worthy of praise in the sight of us poor sinners whom you deign to shower with grace, undeserving though we be, and whom you draw to yourself. Lord, this most befits you above all your works. It corresponds most to your goodness. O loving, boundless Goodness, in this work[31] the forged-iron mountain of your rigorous justice shows a crack.

"Now come to me today, all you whom God has lovingly shown such mercy, and let us gaze upon, love and praise the goodness, yes the boundless goodness of our Lord and gentle Father. Beloved God, witness a miracle: Hearts that used to embrace manure now love and embrace you, O Lord, with infinite longing. Those who yesterday were seductresses are today preachers of your sweet love. Lord, it is a marvel and a pleasant thing to hear: Those who before could scarcely endure their self-pampering existence now practice strict moderation and discover new sources of great austerity and practices of love for praise of you that they might reconcile themselves to you. Those who were too concerned with their own body now treat it as a stranger. Those who adorned themselves elegantly as they pursued (worldly) love now cover themselves to please God. Those who before were as wrathful as fierce wolves are now as forgiving as quiet lambs. And those who were previously sorely burdened and were bound by the iron rings of depression and by the sadness of a punishing conscience, look! gentle Lord, they rise aloft unencumbered, above everything that the earth can offer, in exhilarating buoyant freedom. Unshackled they float into the celestial homeland. They cannot understand how they could ever have become so blind and have so little sense regarding the gloomy night of deceptive love. Lord, what I used to read about I have now experienced myself. When what is corporeal is added to what is spiritual, and what is fine by nature is added to what is eternal, then a bright flash of your beneficent love arises. Indeed, eternal Wisdom, this is a change wrought by your right hand. Gentle Lady of heaven, this is the work of your boundless kindness."

Now listen still, my child, to what you, I, and those like us should do for our dear God. We should continue so to live that no one can take God from us. We should act as though a noble king had placed his scullery maids above the ladies of his court. How gratefully would the maid embrace her lord, how intimately would she

347

love him, how warmly would she praise him! And the baser-born she were, the more intensely would she love him. We should demonstrate ourselves to be such guiltless people that we drown out all others. If they do one thing for him, we should do two. If they love him onefold, we should love him a thousandfold. Consider the matter rightly. All the different ways we used to strive in our days of foolishness to stand out as something special in our sophistication in order to attract all hearts to ourselves by how pleasing we were—now we should strive night and day to see how we might improve all hearts and be especially pleasing to God.

Remember, my child, in our senseless days how good we felt when someone would praise us as special, or think and love as we did. Now, how good we feel when our dear Love shows us special love and attention. Remember, my child, how very bitterly temporal love has to be atoned so that out of fear we often have little enjoyment from it. Hence it is only right if this (divine) love, too, sometimes becomes bitter. Look, my child, I desire one thing: that people who have not felt this[32] believe that it gives one much more enjoyment than it (transitory love) does. They think that no one is so happy as he who is lured by the red bait on the bent hook. O eternal Wisdom, dearly Loved One, if all these hearts would see you as my heart sees you, all fleeting love in them would scatter. Lord, it can never again seem strange to me, no matter how strange it seemed to me before, that any boundlessly loving heart can have anything but you as its goal, you deep pool, bottomless sea, deep abyss of everything dear. My Lord, my fair Love, why do you not show yourself to them? Look, eternal Wisdom, at what the deceiving lovers do: Whatever is displeasing, ugly and deficient about them they diligently conceal. But if they possess any beauty or pleasing manners, which they have thievishly obtained, they display it openly. And they would be sad if the eye of the beloved missed anything that they found pleasant. And as they carry on this way and that, they are really nothing but a sack full of dung. The thought comes to me (regarding them): If someone would just pull off the outer shell from you, then the truth about you would be evident. What a monster one would see in you. But you, dear Loved One, eternal Wisdom, you hide what is lovable about you and you show the suffering involved. You show what is bitter and keep what is sweet. Alas, dear gentle Love, why do you do that?

O beloved Lord, with your permission let me, a sinner, say a little something to you. Indeed, I have to say it. Dear Love, if you only loved me. O Lord, Lord, do you love me? Oh, if only I were your beloved! Does anyone on earth imagine that our dear Lord loves me? My soul talks about it and my heart pulses within me when I think you might love me. When such a thought comes into my mind, then I am so happy that anyone looking at me can tell it. Everything within me dissolves in pure joy. Lord, if I could have anything I wished for, the loftiest, most desirable and most pleasing thing that my heart and soul could imagine would be that you love me in a special way and that, dear Lord, you look upon me with especially loving eyes. Look, all you hearts, would that not be heaven? Lord, your eyes are brighter than the sun. Your divine mouth is sweet to him who knows it. Your shining countenance both as God and as man, your beautiful appearance is above all earthly power to wish. The more one can divest you of everything material, the more one can behold in joyous delight how lovable you are. The more profoundly one can perceive all delight, adornment and beauty, the more superabundant one finds it all in you, gentle Love. Is there anything lovable or pleasing about any dear person that does not exist in utter purity a thousand times more lovable in you, dear Loved One? Now look, all you hearts, look upon him. Behold: "*Talis est dilectus meus*—such is my sweet beloved,"[33] and he is the intimate friend of my heart. Let this be known to you, daughters of Jerusalem. O gentle God, how blessed is he whose beloved you are and who remains in this love forever!

LETTER 6

That a Person Should Be Unafraid When He Comes to Die

"Absalom, my son, who might grant that I die in place of you?"[34]

One of the servant's dearest spiritual children lay dying. When he heard that she would definitely die and that she was behaving badly because of it, he consoled her by writing the following letter.

My child, who will allow me, a devoted father, to die in place of my dear daughter who turned out so well? If I do not die physically, I certainly die in spirit along with the beloved child of my heart. I am physically far away from you, but my heart is present at your deathbed with bitter tears and loyal lament. Give me your failing hand and, if God should call you, remain steadfast in the Christian faith and die cheerfully. Be happy that your fair soul, which is a pure, rational, godlike spirit, is to be released from the confines of this wretched prison and can from now on enjoy unimpeded its blessedness joyfully; for God himself says: "No one can see me and live."[35]

There is one thing that reveals itself to an undiscerning person at death and makes death difficult for him: When he considers the years gone by and that his life has been consumed by insignificant things, he discovers that he stands covered with guilt before God, and in his final hour he does not know what to do about it. I want to show you a sure path from holy scripture and from truth that will let you escape this (predicament) with definite security.

If ever in all your days you have committed sins—as few people have not—you should not because of this be too greatly frightened at the hour of death. When you have received the last sacraments as best you can, if this is possible, then do this: Take the crucifix and, holding it before your eyes, look at it and press it to your heart. Incline yourself to the bleeding wounds of God's infinite mercy and ask him in his divine power to wash away all your wrongdoings with his bleeding wounds, both to his own glory and because of your need. And then be confident of what I say: According to the Christian faith, which cannot deceive, you can be absolutely certain that you will be completely purified of all obstacles and can die in good spirits.

There is one other thing that you should consider at this time so that you can better disdain death. There is a country where they have the custom that when someone is born all the relatives gather and, weeping and wailing, they carry on inconsolably. But when a person dies, they are all cheerful and happy. Their reasoning for this is that no one can know what great trials are foreordained for a person, and so they weep at his birth. When all this is over at death, they are happy. Anyone thinking it through rightly can well call the birth of a person into this wretched world "death" because of the distress and toil that awaits him. And physical death can well be called a new birth, because of the release from an onerous body and because one enters unencumbered into eternal blessedness.

If one opens one's eyes to recognize the truth of this, death becomes easier; but if one cannot see it, one's grief increases and the uncertainty of death becomes much grimmer. See what misery there is in this world, likewise what suffering, worry and want exist everywhere you turn. Even if it were only fear for body and soul and the changing uncertainty of this world, we should desire to leave. For every good thing a person experiences, he encounters ten bad things. Many a person, if asked, would say, "I have never yet had a good day on earth." The world is full of snares, deception and inconstancy. No one can count on anyone else because everyone is seeking his own advantage. If someone were to desire to live long to increase his reward (in heaven), one could ask whether his reward or his guilt would become greater. He has reward enough who shall forever behold the dear, gentle countenance of our fair Lord and dwell in the blissful company in heaven. If the hour of death is painful, if it is bitter, it must still come sometime. No one was ever excused from the hour of death. Whoever is unprepared today may be even less prepared tomorrow. The older one gets, the more evil one becomes. One finds more people who deteriorate than who improve. If the confrontation with death is bitter, it also puts an end to all bitterness.

And so, my child, direct your heart, hand and eyes upward to the celestial homeland. Greet it with the longing of your heart and surrender your will to God's will. Be free of the whole affair. Whatever he finds best for you, be it to live or to die, accept it from God as the best because it is the best, even if you do not recognize it as such at the moment. Fear not. The holy angels are with you and all around you. Our kind and merciful God wants to help you as your Father out of all your misery if only you can trust in his goodness.

When this consoling message was brought to his dying daughter, she was happy and had it read to her twice. And when she heard the soothing words, her heart was somehow greatly strengthened by them. Her previous anxieties about death disappeared, and she surrendered herself eagerly to God's will, dying in a very holy manner.

LETTER 7

How a Person in a Position of Authority
Should Conduct Himself

"Christ became obedient for us unto death."[36]

Whoever struggles against what he must do under obedience makes life difficult for himself, because doing little unwillingly is

351

worse than doing much willingly. Therefore, since this office has fallen to you through a decree of God from whom all power comes, as St. Paul says,[37] and without your wanting it, carry it out in such a way that God is not thereby dishonored and you do not visibly go astray.

It is in part necessary that you do not like to be in this office. Where you should hope to find help and advice, you find sadness and helplessness. Where you should find submission, you discover arrogant insubordination. And so, to have authority and responsibility in our times and to handle them well is not a leisurely task but rather a living martyrdom. And so take up the cross upon your back for the sake of him who took up his miserable cross for your sake. Practice resignation as long as this is what is demanded of you. Don't complain about your powerlessness and lack of ability. If you have done the best you know how, you are free (of blame), even if it is not the absolute best.

In all things you should look more to God than to material advantage and, if you can prevent it, you should not allow that any in your flock suffer harm to their souls. Be evenhanded in your outward dealings so that friend and foe carry an equal burden. This promotes peace. The young sisters you should keep under strict control because badly brought up youth is the destruction of religious life. You should display a kind seriousness, and command more by love than fear. What is beyond your strength you should turn over to your superior. And where you cannot bite, you should at least bark. If you cannot achieve religious discipline completely, so see to it that it not be relaxed or suffer serious infractions under you. If one does not mend an old torn garment, it quickly disintegrates completely. When what is spiritual is dissipated, one is quickly in a bad way in material things. He who does not care to consider small things sinks down most deeply of all.[38]

You should present your subjects with a good model, instructing with actions more than with words. Be prepared for this because it will happen for certain: If you strive to do your best in all things, people will take it as being the worst thing possible from you. And those whom you strive to treat most circumspectly will reward you most ungraciously. No one can please everyone to the same degree. If, however, you want to try it, you will be out of step with God and the truth. Base people's rebukes are the praises of good people.

Make certain that you forcefully break up inwardly reckless relationships and outwardly harmful friendships. If you do your part, you will be rid of them. Too bad for the convent where these two break in! It will become full of discord and will finally lose its reputation. You say: If I interfere, I shall have no peace. I say: Blessed is conflict because conflict produces eternal concord. Alas for those who let it all pass and thereby seek peace for their heart. Isaiah says about them, *"Pax, pax, et non est pax."*[39] This means: "They say peace, peace, but there is no peace." They seek their own comfort. They enjoy passing glory and buy it by losing all their spiritual honor. Too bad for them! They have already received their reward.[40] But you, my child, you should not act that way. Seek the praise and glory of God, just as our dear Christ sought the glory of his eternal Father.[41] This is why he let himself be executed. You complain exceedingly, but blood is not yet running down your face from wounds inflicted on you, as it did the martyrs'. One used to choose the most zealous people for such offices, not those who were looking out for themselves.

You would like to have peace for reflection and contemplation. St. Gregory says that perfect discipline should be sufficient for both,[42] if things are well-ordered. But unfortunately, since you have not yet achieved this, reflect on your insignificance and guard against arrogance. Remember who you are and how soon you will be no more. Therefore, when you want to reprimand someone, reprimand yourself first. You should strive to overcome evil with good. One devil does not drive out another. From a meek heart you should send forth harsh and mild words as the situation demands.

Before all else, I commend to you the furthering of God's service. You should also not forget yourself and should frequently during the day turn within yourself. Especially twice, in the morning and in the evening, you should seek yourself and for a time forget things, raising yourself up to God, receiving all your sorrow and suffering in him, suffering for his sake and overcoming it with him and thus making everything well again. In one short hour you can make up the whole day.

Perfection does not consist in experiencing consolation. It consists in surrendering one's will to God's will, whether this be burdensome or easy, submitting in humble obedience to a man representing God. In this context I would prefer aridity with this obedience to overflowing sweetness without it. This was shown us in the obedience of the eternal Son, which was carried out in arid bitterness. I am not saying this so that you offer yourself for this, as many of you do, but that you suffer patiently and do the best you can. If you did not have this problem, you would quite possibly fall victim to another one, and a worse one. The Lord, who is the object of your striving, has put you in this position with no help from you. He can certainly look after what is best for you in it in accordance with what praises him and brings you eternal happiness.

LETTER 8

How a Religious Person Experiencing Divine Bliss Should Act

To Elsbeth Stagel.

"Announce to my beloved that I am languishing out of love."[43]

If one person were to sit in a wine cellar and satisfy his thirst according to his heart's desire, and if another person were standing on the parched heath next to a rugged juniper tree and, thirsty himself, was picking the berries for a potion to heal asthmatics—if the person who had satisfied his thirst were to ask the one with the parched mouth how he should dance to the pleasant music in the wine cellar, the other would answer and say, "This fellow must be drunk. He thinks that everyone is in the same mood as he. I am in a completely different mood. We have nothing in common. It's easy to be happy with a full stomach."

My child, this is actually what I can say to you in response to the message you sent me, namely, that a burning torch was aflame in your heart because of your strong desire and burning love for dear eternal Wisdom and because of the new light and unusual experiences Wisdom is bringing about within you—how your heart felt a sweet pain, a tender melting and an elation that you cannot describe. And now you desire instruction on how you should act as lovingly as possible toward him (eternal Wisdom) in this state and how you should react to these unusual experiences.

Daughter, the joy in my heart is boundless upon hearing that our dear God has shown himself so loving and has let you and many others experience what I have expressed in words time and again: that he is very loving. And that all hearts might experience this directly I would be happy to remain thirsty. I am astonished that in a few short years you have come this far. This is the result of your turning utterly to God and of turning completely away from all things, and of your absolute earnestness and physical suffering, by means of which you have obliterated your former life and have trod all things underfoot.

A person who drinks wine for the first time feels its effects strongly, and I assume that this is what has happened to you from the clear, sweet love of eternal Wisdom, which has so powerfully taken hold of you. Or it could mean that God wants to attract you and take you to the inexhaustible well from which you have tasted a drop.[44] Or it could mean that he wishes to show his marvels, using you according to the abundance of his goodness. Act in this matter so that you look to his will and do not seek to indulge yourself. You do not have to be afraid. It all comes from God and is an allurement of God's love in the soul. It is what happens. It is as it should be. However, you must keep aware of your physical well-being, that you not be too much consumed by such experiences. It can also happen, as things progress, that a goodly amount of it is taken from you and that you are placed on a more perfect level.

The beautiful vision you experienced on the holy feast of Christmas, in which you saw how clearly and lovingly eternal Wisdom was united with the soul of the servant in rich joy and he was told he could rightly be a happy servant of eternal Wisdom—this caused me to sigh from my heart because I am not God's lover. It seems to me I am his cart driver and drive through puddles with my clothes tucked up, as I pull people out of the deep mire of their sinful lives and bring them to what is beautiful. And so it is enough for me if he puts a loaf of rye bread in my hands.[45] And yet I must tell you something that our Beloved has allowed to happen in me quite often.

One bright morning, when the joyful song about the paternal splendor of eternal Wisdom was about to be intoned at mass, "The light shall shine,"[46] the servant was in his chapel in a state of rest for his external senses. It seemed to him in a vision that he was being led into choir where mass was being sung. In the choir there was a great throng of the heavenly court sent there by God to sing a sweet melody of celestial music. They sang a new jubilant song that he had never heard before. It was so delightful that he thought that his soul would dissolve in pure joy. The *Sanctus* especially was sung very powerfully and he began to join in. When they came to the words, "Blessed is he who comes . . . ," they raised their voices aloft and the priest then also raised on high the body of the Lord. The servant gazed at him (in the host) in his true physical presence with humble self-surrender, and it seemed to him that somehow a lovely spiritual glow emanated from him (the Lord in the host) toward his soul, inexpressible for all tongues. And in this glow his heart and soul became so full of fresh, fervent longing and interior light that he was suddenly robbed of all his strength. It was somehow as though heart had been united to heart in a purely spiritual manner. His soul so dissolved that he was not able to find any physical equivalent for it. As he was feeling so weak and powerless, a young man of heaven who was standing there, whom he did not recognize, began to laugh. The servant said to him, "What are you laughing about? Don't you see that I am now about to collapse from sheer faintness and burning love?" And while speaking he sank to the ground like a person fainting from weakness. While singing he returned to himself and so opened his outer eyes. They were full of tears and his soul was full of resplendent grace. He went up to the altar where the body of our Lord was, and he privately intoned the song, "Blessed is he who comes . . . ," while the spiritual strains were still running through his soul.

LETTER 9

How a Person Should Achieve Peace of Heart in God

"Among all these I sought rest."[47]

Eternal Wisdom says: I have searched for rest in all things, thus teaching people gone astray how in the varied course of their life they can attain peace, as far as this is possible.

Although it is the case that truth in itself is pure and free (of representations), because of the characteristics of the nature we are born with we have to imagine it for ourselves through the analogy of images until our frail body is put aside and the purified eye of the soul's spirituality is placed immediately in the circle of the eternal sun. Until then we shuffle around like blind men, groping about us and knowing not where nor how. If we sometimes possess the truth, we do not realize we have it, and we act like someone who is looking for something that he has in his hand. There is not a person on earth who is completely free of this condition because it is an echo of original sin.

As I understand things, it would be very desirous for a soul searching for God to be able to know what God's dearest will was for it so that it could delight and please him, so that he (God) might develop a special attraction, love and intimacy for this soul. A loving person would often like to gain a clear understanding of it in every chance thing and would be willing to suffer death for this. This desire caused faithful Abraham to leave his country and his dear friends. He did not know where he was going and sought God far away, that he might find him close by. This (desire) has pursued and driven all chosen people from the beginning of the world until this very day, and this will always be the case. This dear pursuit has more attraction than any magnet has for iron, and it binds more than a thousand ropes. Fortunate is the person that he was ever born who finds it and never turns away from it.

I remember now a saying about this that I read while studying philosophy in school. I read it but did not understand it at all. The exalted teacher says this: The universal Ruler, who simply is, moves all things but himself does not move.[48] He causes motion as a desirable and lovely beloved should: He causes one's heart to beat faster and one's desires to race, and yet he is motionless, as an immovable goal that all beings strive for and desire. But the motion and the attraction vary. With the course of the heavens he causes the ant to crawl, the swift stag to run, and the wild falcon to fly. The manner of each is different and yet they have but a single goal—that they dwell with their being at the source of love flowing out from the first being.

We find this same thing in the great diversity that is noticeable among the friends of God, who are all receptive to the same good. One will race forward with great austerity; another speeds onward in pure detachment; another soars in lofty contemplation—each as he is attracted. What is most important among all these is clear from scripture; but what is special for each person and the most important for each one's particular self no one can say for sure. Trying all kinds of things, says Paul,[49] to find what is fitting, as St. Gregory says,[50] divine illumination, as Dionysius says,[51] help a person achieve rest. Corporeal penances help some if there are not too many of them, but true detachment in all things, in what we know and do not know, in submission to the Will above, which knows all things—this helps a person escape all the waves and puts him at peace with all things if they can be seen in proper perspective.

There was a man who had undertaken something that he wanted to complete to God's glory. He was asked whether he knew if it were God's will. He said, "No, and I prefer not to know. If I knew it for certain, my self would derive too much spiritual satisfaction from it; but now it is for me a question of submission."

A prudent person does not throw aside his interior life for external things, nor does he reject external things because of his interior life. He should diligently perform external works with holy zeal in order to return to what is within. And within himself he should be so detached that he can do justice to external things when it is timely and proper. Thus does he within and without find peace in all things according to the teachings of Wisdom,[52] which nourishes the soul, as Christ said.[53]

I write this to you because you have followed God into a distant and strange land in order to find him near and far, for he dwells in all things. I know a person who in his wretched suffering once came beneath the cross to poor Christ. Christ responded to him inwardly and said, "You shall be without love so that you can become my love, and be despised so that you can reflect praise on me, and you shall be of no value so that you shall serve to honor me."

LETTER 10

Some Things That Are Part of Perfection

"Be perfect."[54]

This is what eternal Wisdom says to his chosen disciples who were striving for a sublime way of life: "You should be perfect!"

Brilliant Dionysius in his book *On the Celestial Hierarchies* says that the lower angles are purified, illumined and brought to perfection by the higher angels. This all happens by means of the brightness of the sun, which is above all beings as it bursts forth. In flowing forth it shares (with them) unrecognized truth by shining within them.[55]

We discover something similar to this taking place in many people on earth. Purification consists in driving out everything that is creature or smacks of creature and that one wrongly desires, worries about or is attached to; anything that is in some way an obstacle for man. Even if this were the highest spirit of the Seraphim, St. John himself, or anything whatever that is a creature, one must abandon it. Good people can become confused by things in this matter even if they act with a good intention. A good intention in all things is not enough. In earlier times the Lord commanded through gentle Moses and said, "What is just and good you must justly and properly carry out."[56] Otherwise, justice becomes injustice.

After purification come light and truth because truth is light that drives out the dark gloom of ignorance. This light that renews the soul in joy and fills it with divine forms is sometimes received indirectly and sometimes directly. The more a person can partake of it on earth, the more all worldliness falls away from him; and the immortal garment of the future everlasting light becomes increasingly his as he finds earthly things tiresome.

Out of this arises true perfection, which consists in the union of the highest powers of the soul with the origin of being in sublime contemplation, in fervent love and sweet enjoyment of the highest Good to the extent this is possible for our frail bodies. But because the soul, given the weakness of our burdensome bodies, cannot continually cling to pure Good in a completely spiritual manner, it must have some concrete model to lead it back to this union. And the best thing for this that I know is the dear image of Jesus Christ. In him one has God and man. He is the one who made all the saints holy. In him one finds life. This is the supreme reward and highest benefit. And as a person becomes formed according to this image, he is transformed as by God's Spirit into the divine glory of the Lord of heaven, growing brighter and brighter, from the brightness of his (Christ's) humanity to the brightness of his divinity.[57] For the more often we gaze upon him lovingly with desirous eyes and form our whole life according to him, the more nobly shall we enjoy the beatitude of his Being in eternity.

LETTER 11

How One Should Be Devoted to the Divine Name of Jesus

"Set me like a seal on your heart."[58]

Our eternal God makes a request of the pure soul and says, "Place me as a sign of love on your heart."

THE EXEMPLAR

A seasoned friend of God should always have some good model or saying in the mouth of his soul to chew on that will inflame his heart for God, because therein lies the most sublime thing we can attain on earth—that we often reflect on our divine Beloved, that we often send out our hearts to him, often speak of him, take in his words of love, for his sake abandon or perform all things, and have no one but him alone as the focus of our attention. Our eye should look upon him with love. Our ear should open to his bidding. Our heart, mind and spirit should lovingly embrace him. If we make him angry, we should beg his pardon. If he tries us, we should endure him. When he hides, we should seek our dear Love and never give up until we find him again and again. When we find him, we should hold him tenderly and reverently. Whether we are at rest or going somewhere, whether we are eating or drinking, the golden clasp IHS should be inscribed on our heart.[59] When we can do nothing else, we should press him with our eyes into our soul. We should turn over his tender name in our mouth. We should be so intent on this while awake that we dream about it at night. Let us say with the prophet, "O dear God, eternal Wisdom, how good you are to the soul that seeks you, that longs for you alone."[60]

Realize that this is the best habit you can have, for constant prayer is the crown of all activity. Everything else should be directed to it as to its goal. What other activity is there in heaven but gazing at and loving the object of all love, loving it and praising it? Therefore, the more dearly we press the divine object of our love into our hearts, and the more often we look upon him and intimately embrace him with the arms of our hearts, the more lovingly shall we be embraced by him here and in our eternal happiness.

Take as a model that lover of God, Paul, how he grasped the dear name of God, Jesus, in the deep ground of his heart. When his head had been severed from his holy body, it nonetheless said three times, "Jesus, Jesus, Jesus." And St. Ignatius (of Antioch), who in his intense suffering kept calling out the name Jesus and was asked why he was doing this, responded by saying that *Jesus* was engraved on his heart. When they had killed him and out of curiosity had cut open his heart, they found written in it everywhere in gold letters: Jesus, Jesus, Jesus. May this name be praised by us all forever. All people who love God wish this together with me from the depths of their hearts and say with joy: Amen, Amen.

Sermons

SERMON 1

"Lectulus noster floridus"[1]

These words are written in the Book of Love and are spoken in praise of a pure conscience. In German they mean: "Our bed is covered with blossoms."[2]

A lovely bed covered with roses, lilies and many other flowers, and on which one rests and sweetly sleeps is as unlike an uncultivated field filled with sticks and weeds as is the soul of a blessed person to the conscience of a disordered person. For it is God's fondest desire to take his rest in a place covered with flowers. This is why the loving soul rejoiced when she yearned for the loving embrace of her bridegroom, and she spoke thus to her beloved: "*Lectulus noster floridus*—our bed is covered with blossoms," just as though she were to say: Our cozy little secluded abode is bolted. The bed of our love is covered with blossoms. Come, dearest beloved! All that is lacking is for you to let me fall blissfully asleep in the arms of your unfathomable love."

Now there are some people whose consciences are not decorated with flowers; rather, their hearts are strewn with dung. There are some people whose failings turn outward, while there are other people all of whose failings go inward, and these are difficult to help beyond all measure, just as is the case with people whose physical wounds have spread internally. There are very many of these internal failings, but there are three of them especially that are so very serious that one can hardly compare them to any other failings because they

363

are so completely crippling. The first is indiscriminate sadness; the second, inordinate dejection; the third, turbulent despair.[3]

First of all, you should know that indiscriminate sadness occurs when a person is so utterly sad that he can do nothing good and yet does not know what is wrong with him. Even if he asked himself about it, he would not know in the least what was wrong with him. This is the sadness dear David felt when he said: "*Quare tristis es, anima mea*—my soul, why are you so very sad and why do you make me sad?"[4] This is as though he were saying: Something is wrong with you, but you do not know what. Trust in God and things will get better. You will yet often enjoy his praise. This sadness is such that it has driven a thousand men away from their good beginnings, for among all people who live on earth no one has such need of a good disposition as does the person who, like a knight, is to pierce through the onslaught of his own failings.[5] How can bodily austerities on earth be difficult for one who inwardly possesses high spirits?[6] Or what can afford someone pleasure outwardly who is continually beset with a somber disposition? Therefore, a person should resist this weakness with all his might as far as he can. But one can find out, among other things, how to get rid of this failing by what happened to the preacher who had this unbearable defect for a very long time.[7] He often prayed to God about it and once, as he was sitting in his cell defeated, it was said to him: "Why are you sitting here? Stand up and immerse yourself in my suffering. Then you will lose all your suffering!" And it happened just that way, and he was then rid of it.

The second internal failing is inordinate dejection and is different from the first defect because whoever has this defect has enough insight to realize what is wrong with him, but he has not ordered it according to God's will. This is why it is called *inordinate* dejection. It comes about either when a person causes himself suffering by taking seriously what he should not, or from sufferings God gives a person, especially those that affect one internally.

Now one finds four distinct kinds of suffering, which are the most severe that a human heart on earth can bear. They are so great that no one could really believe these disconsolate hearts but him who has felt it himself or to whom it has been given by God. For their suffering never leaves them and when they turn to God, which should relieve their suffering, they have the most painful suffering of all. And the harshness of this suffering is to be judged solely by the continuous pain that it causes, and not from any harm it does to the soul. And these are the four sufferings: doubts concerning faith, doubts about God's mercy, thoughts against God and his saints, and temptations to take one's own life.

First of all, I shall take up the second suffering separately, and then treat them all together. This suffering—that a person begins to doubt God's mercy and to doubt whether there will ever be any help for him[8]—this arises especially from three causes. These are that such people are not able to grasp what God is, what sin is, and what sorrow is.

Look! God is such an inexhaustible wellspring of boundless mercy and natural goodness that never was there a devoted mother who as willingly stretched out her hand to her own child that she had carried under her heart, seeing it in a raging fire, as God does to the penitent, even if it were possible that he had the sins of all men himself and committed them a thousand times every day. Alas, dear Lord, why are you so very dear to many a heart, why does many a soul yearn for you, why is many a person happy because of you? Is it only because of their innocent way of life? Certainly not! It happens when they consider who they are, how very sinful, weak, and unworthy of you they are, and that you, benevolent Heart, you sovereign Lord, you give yourself to them so freely. Lord, this is what makes you so great in our hearts, that you have absolutely no need of any human goods. For you, canceling a debt of a thousand marks is the same as canceling one of a penny; and forgiving a thousand serious sins is like forgiving one. Lord, this is dignity beyond all dignity. Lord, such people can never thank you enough without their hearts overflowing in praise of you. According to scripture this gives you more praise than if they had never fallen into sin at all and, living spiritually lukewarm lives, did not love you as much.[9] For according to the teaching of St. Bernard, you do not consider what a person has been, but what he desires in his heart to become.[10] Therefore, whoever denies that you constantly forgive serious sins robs you of great honor. Sin, after all, brought you down from heaven to earth. Fortunate is the sin, says St. Gregory, that brought us such a loved and gentle Redeemer who is willing to receive us so lovingly at any moment.[11] And so David says: If a person can grasp what God is, he cannot but trust him.[12]

The second cause is that such people cannot grasp what sin is. Properly speaking, sin consists of this alone: that a person with a conscious and deliberate act of the will knowingly and freely, not objecting despite what he knows, turns away from God and toward what is sinful. For if it were to happen that a person suffered many frequent temptations and these were so terrible and evil that no human heart can imagine them and no tongue can describe them, neither God's nor man's, and even if a person were to remain in this condition a whole year or two or however long it lasted—if his good sense struggles at all against them and does not find the pleasure in them that is natural in such matters, so that his good sense does not with full knowledge and will succumb to them, then no serious sin is committed. And this is just as certainly true according to holy scripture and sacred doctrine, out of which the Holy Spirit speaks, as it is true that God is in heaven.

Now there is a hidden perturbation contained in this, the most subtle and chafing fetter in the whole matter, and it is this: When the detestable attack occurs and one suddenly succumbs with perhaps some pleasure and acts wrongly by not quickly turning away, then one thinks that one has willingly and knowingly succumbed, transgressed and committed a serious sin. But this is not the case. According to holy teaching, such attacks and pleasures often precede reason and continue for a good while and a long time before reason really becomes aware of them. When, then, reason becomes aware of them and considers them fully, it can accept or reject them, sin or not sin. This is why people should not have any perturbations in the question of serious sin if they want to believe Christian doctrine. St. Augustine says that sin must happen with the will completely free. If it does not happen willfully, it is not a sin.[13] Theologians think that if Eve alone had eaten the fruit in paradise and Adam had not, it would have caused no harm.[14] Similarly, whatever effect sensuality has apart from the full participation of reason does not cause a serious sin.

The third thing that causes harm is that such people cannot grasp what sorrow is. Sorrow is a virtue that, when practiced with full awareness, takes away a person's sin. St. Bernard says that irrational sorrow displeases God.[15] Evil Cain also felt sorrow, but it was immoderate since he said: "My evilness is greater than God's mercy."[16] Judas, too, felt sorrow, but his regret was too extreme. Such people sometimes fall into such a state of inordinate sorrow that they say to themselves: "It is an evil thing that I am even alive. Lord, why was I ever born? O Lord, if only I would die!" Saying these and similar things they anger God more than by sinning, if sin was really involved in what they did. But according to holy scripture there was no sin involved. Thus, whoever wants to have real sorrow must possess humility about himself, detest sin, and have complete trust in God. Eternal and beloved Wisdom says: "My child, in your suffering you should not despise yourself. Turn to God who will help you overcome it."[17] A person is a real fool if, because he cannot see out of one eye, he wants to pluck out the other eye.

Concerning all these failings one should know the following six things: The first is that such people are incorrigible and do not want to believe someone in these matters whom they should believe, especially someone telling them something the least bit consoling far less than someone telling them depressing things. This is the result of the restless, heartfelt pain that they all constantly suffer. They freely bemoan their fault aloud in order to see if someone might come to their aid. They should not do this with such clamor because there are few who can help in this situation. And the more they talk about it, the worse their fault becomes. They should choose a teacher who is well-versed in holy scripture, and they should believe him without any hesitation. For on the day of judgment God will demand this of them and hold nothing against them if they have done their part.

The second thing is that they have many illegitimate fears. It always seems to them that they have not confessed properly, no matter how careful and learned their confessor is, or that they have done the best they could. And they never achieve peace of heart in all this. This is the result of their not knowing exactly what they are required and not required to confess. According to pertinent literature, one is only required to confess serious sins exactly, if one can do this. The everyday sins may be mentioned in a more general way. Because these people are generally not guilty of any mortal sins, they need not and should not enumerate exactly all their slight offenses, but rather should confess them in a general way according to the advice of a knowledgeable and pious confessor. It is the devil who is thus disturbing their peace of heart and one should therefore resist him, because the more one gives in to him, the more confused one's conscience becomes.

The third thing is that they are seeking a kind of knowledge in these matters that one can never have. They are striving to know for certain that they are not in the state of serious sin. No human being on earth, no matter how good or blessed or well-instructed in holy doctrine, can know for certain whether or not he is in the state of grace, except by a special revelation from God. In this matter it is enough if, after carefully examining one's conscience, one is not conscious of any serious offenses. Wanting such certitude arises from mistaken notions, as when a child expects to know what lies hidden in the heart of an emperor. Therefore, just as one who is bodily ill must believe his physician, who knows the nature of his disease better than he does himself, so must a person believe a prudent physician of the spirit.

The fourth thing is that they are too impetuous with regard to God. This is the result of the constant bitter suffering they unremittingly experience. They are generally not well-versed in other kinds of suffering and they behave like a young colt hitched up to a wagon. He can thrash about with all his might until he is skin and bone. When he finally sees that it cannot be otherwise, he gives in and begins acting like a tame animal. This is what happens to these people. As long as they are struggling and have not conformed completely to God's will, not yet wishing to suffer it for his sake, they are in great torment. And they have to suffer until God mercifully recognizes their sorry state and their patience. He knows when it is profitable to release them from it. Thus there is nothing else for one to do but humbly give oneself over to this affliction, as long as God wills it, and patiently beg help from him and prayers from good people.

The fifth thing is that nothing on earth confounds these people so completely as their wanting to listen to the foul whisperings (of the devil), wanting to respond to him, to argue convincingly and to dispute with him. They should be on their guard against this as they are against death, because in resisting they sink down helplessly. As soon as these whisperings approach their spiritual ears, without offering resistance they should immediately turn their attention away and toward the closest thing they see, hear or know, as though they were saying to him (the devil): "Keep your whisperings to yourself. They have nothing to do with me. You are just too contemptible for me to want to respond to you." See what then actually happens: The less they pay attention to him, the more quickly they escape. They should use this maneuver again and again until they

are in a position to turn away normally. No one can really understand what I have said except these people themselves.

Sixth, the more sacred the liturgical feast day is and the more a
person wants to turn to God, the worse these tribulations are, so
that he cannot utter an Our Father or a Hail Mary in peace without
hearing these insidious whisperings. Thus such people fall into a
depression, cast aside prayer, and say to themselves: "How can you
imagine that such befouled prayers are a help to you?" They are
mistaken in this, because in so doing they conform completely to the
devil's will, for he seeks nothing else than to keep a person from
spiritual activity. They do not realize that their prayer, with all
these incursions they deplore, is very pleasing and delightful in
God's eyes. St. Gregory says that the human spirit often falls into
such darkness that it cannot help itself except through the experience of pain and suffering. It is this repugnant existence itself that
calls them to God's caring attention. In his eyes the bitterness of
their sufferings[18] turns into a pleasing prayer that approaches him
more closely than otherwise, more quickly making him favorably
disposed to them.[19] Therefore, no one should ever omit a good deed,
prayer or a visit to church—which are all especially repugnant to
this same evil spirit. Whatever purity in prayer one loses because of
the inroads of suffering becomes pleasing in God's eyes for this very
reason, just as one is often more ready to listen to a sick and weakly
person who can hardly talk than to a strong and healthy person.
And so the more one abstains from prayer, the more one pleases this
same evil spirit.

Now since it is confirmed by holy scripture that such things do
not involve sin, one might ask why a merciful God might afflict
these persons with sufferings as severe as these, which they would
all rather exchange for some bodily affliction. These people, as well
as some simple folk, untaught and inexperienced, mistakenly believe that they are simply at fault. This is not the case. Many a holy
person has obviously been tried in this way. We see this all the time
and find it in holy scripture. And many low and unsavory persons
are free of it. Some experience it in childhood while they are still
without any serious guilt. But if this kind of affliction and severe
punishment were to befall someone because of his real or imagined
guilt, this person should praise God fervently because of it, for
according to scripture this is more than anything else a very clear

sign of God's love, enabling one to atone quickly for sins here on earth by means of such dire visitations. But why God tries these people through suffering more than others is hidden among God's mysteries. They should accept it from God because God knows the heart, mind and nature of man, both inwardly and outwardly, better than anyone. Like an experienced physician and devoted father, he dispenses to each what he alone knows to be best for them.

Now a person might well ask what good there could possibly be in this for anyone. I answer according to the scripture and say: A person can derive a great inexpressible good from it. One thing is this. Some people are proud by nature, and they could never be brought low in humility to such a degree or so covertly. And humility is the true beginning of all virtue. Such people think that the hideousness of the affliction is the measure of the hideousness of the sin. This is not the case. A self-complacent person can become more sinfully deformed in God's sight than if he had suffered a thousand of the most degrading afflictions. This is clear in the case of the highest angel, who fell without having such afflictions. So, too, does it happen on earth that a man who in his arrogance does not want to see his true self comes to see himself through suffering. And he who used to look down on others now seems to himself worthy of everyone's contempt. What can be more useful to someone or make him more dear to God than this? It is impossible for a humble person to be lost.

Certainly, therefore, according to the scripture and in truth, such people should fall on their knees and should increase the worth of their dreadful suffering by thanking God fervently for this suffering through which they can attain such a virtue. This same suffering rescues them from hell and places them in heaven. It helps protect people from the snares of the body and from many sins. Such people are thereby so busy that they nearly forget all vanity, and this is a valuable advantage. These sufferings promote all virtues because such people are so very much in pain because of them that they continually seek and do all things possible solely to be released from them. And even if they are serious about this, God often lets them remain in this condition until they have accomplished many good works and have become vessels full of all virtues and grace.

Notice, dear children, how lovingly eternal Wisdom knows how to order all things so that people imagine that they have suffered a great loss, but God has turned it to their great advantage. It also diminishes their purgatory and garners them a great reward. They think they are evil, and are good. They think they are great sinners, and are martyrs in God's eyes because it is a thousand times worse to be constantly thus martyred than to lose one's head with one blow. Stated briefly, according to holy scripture and according to the truth, it is a true sign of love, of boundless grace, and of the great intimacy that they shall hereafter enjoy. And therefore they should suffer it cheerfully and willingly because after this adversity eternal happiness is theirs for certain. This happened once to a woman in a convent who experienced this kind of suffering.[20] When she died, she returned (in an apparition) and said that her purgatory had been on earth and that she had been received by God immediately into eternity. May our dear Lord Jesus Christ help us to achieve this. Amen.

SERMON 4

"Iterum relinquo mundum et vado ad patrem."[1]

All of our dear Lord Jesus Christ's striving, his teaching and his example had as their goal that he teach his beloved friends and lead them inward into the pure ground, into the service of truth. And he saw that they were so occupied with his outward humanity that they were incapable of pursuing what is truly good. Hence he had to leave them.

Children, away with all cloaks that conceal! Since the Son of the heavenly Father, eternal Truth, could not help being an obstacle for them, there is no creature that does not obstruct, no matter what it is called or how it appears. They have to be thoroughly eliminated if we are to receive the inward goodness that is God.

One can distinguish three kinds of people. The first are those leaving behind; the second are those approaching; the third are those entering in. Or one can call them beginners, those progressing, and the perfect.[2] When a person is a beginner, he should go through and thoroughly examine all the corners of his soul to see whether he can find anything that he has fastened onto with pleasure, whether he suspects some creature (hiding) in some corner. Drive it out now! Before all else this must be the first thing, just as one teaches children first of all their ABCs. If you do not achieve all of this right

371

away, do not be intimidated and give up. With children one repeats a word until they know it well—again and again: *iterum*. If this is what is asked, then I leave the world behind. But in leaving the world I abandon all things. In the morning, when you open your eyes, you should say, "Ah, dear pure Goodness, look! Now I shall begin again to abandon myself and all things." And this should happen a thousand times a day. As often as you find yourself, you should leave yourself. Everything depends on this. One can look at it as one will, without this no progress is possible.

One discovers people who have served God for forty years, practicing and accomplishing many good works, and they are as far from him in their last work as they were in their first. This is what happened to the children of Israel when they wandered through the desert for forty years with much toil and deprivation. When they thought they had reached their goal, they found themselves at the very point from which they had started.³ Alas, what amounts of toil, energy and time do many people lose who in their own mind and in the mind of others are faring very well. They think that everything has been achieved, yet they are really still at the starting point. This abandoning is the most difficult thing in the beginning and remains so to the very end. No matter how much one abandons oneself, one repeatedly finds more of oneself to abandon. Then some become weak, imagining they do not need to do this any longer. The more purified one becomes, the more refined are the things to be left behind.⁴

Now one finds people who, having abandoned themselves, take themselves back again. Some do this deceitfully, others brutishly, and still others diabolically. Here is how the deceitful ones act: Their nature is so clever and seeks what belongs to it with such deftness that, God help me, it gets it and knows how to excuse itself very ably, using all sorts of pretexts and considering itself wiser than God. Consider this. If someone put a disc made of gold or a black one out of iron in front of his eyes, he would see as little through the gold as through the iron. Precious metal blocks one's sight just as much as base metal does. You see as much through the one as through the other. And so, no matter how precious creatures are or you think they are, let them go and help yourself as best you can. Some people are so attached that in an assembly in the convent, because of some household object or something else as trivial, they behave like mad dogs, barking and scolding. A spiritual person should be so detached that if someone were to strike him on one cheek, he would offer the other.[5] Whatever one would do to him, he should remain at peace. Regarding our dear model, our Lord Jesus Christ, people called him a seducer, a false prophet, a glutton and one possessed by the devil. But he kept silent, taking it and bearing it without malice.[6]

One reads in the *Lives of the Fathers* that a disciple asked his teacher how to become perfect. He told him to go to where the dead were lying and to praise them lavishly for a while and then criticize them bitterly. It was all the same to them. "So should you be," said the master.[7] Our dear master Christ says, "In the world you shall suffer deprivation and adversity, but in me you shall have peace."[8]

Second are the people who take themselves back brutishly. By this I do not mean brutish people. I mean those seeking dearest Goodness, which is called and is God, but who desire this in a natural manner. Man should not perform his deeds irrationally or out of natural inclination or desire, as an animal does that nature controls, but rather with free will and the rational intention of serving and living for God. Whether one eats, sleeps, talks or keeps silent—whatever in the world it is or one does—eliminate this brutish inclination and perform your actions according to reason in praying, thinking and living: "Dear Lord, it is for you and not for me that I eat, sleep, talk, live, suffer and abandon all things."

A spiritual man seriously desired to live perfectly.[9] And it seemed to him that he was conducted before a group of students who were very diligent, studying intently. Then this friar asked one of them, "Dear friend, I have heard marvelous things about this place of advanced learning. Tell me, what school of thought do you represent?" And the other said, "Nothing else but a thorough abandoning of self in all things." "Ah, here I wish to remain even if I had to die a thousand deaths to do so. Here I am going to build my cell!"[10] "No," said the other person. "Continue your life calmly and without frenzy. The less you accomplish, the more you have accomplished."

People are terribly blind and want to do great feats, undertake something as though they wanted to take God by storm, doing everything themselves according to their own will and self-confident in their own nature. No, not by fighting but by abandoning, by dying, by decreasing and abandoning! As long as there is a drop of blood in you that is unmortified and unconquered, you are imperfect. Dear St. Paul said this: "*Vivo ego, iam non ego:* I live, not I, rather Christ lives in me."[11] Know that as long as anything—whatever it is—lives in you that you can see is not God, then God does not live in you and never will.

The third kind of person takes himself back in a diabolical manner. Listen to how this happens. God created Lucifer with appealing qualities and endowed him nobly. And what did he do? He turned his attention toward himself, took pleasure in himself, and wanted to be something. Exactly because he wanted to be something he became nothing and he fell. Without question we find this same thing in our first parents whom God adorned in a marvelously noble way. The devil spoke offering Eve the apple. No, of course she did not want it, lest she die and become nothing. "On the contrary," he said. "You shall become, you shall be something: *eritis!*" She found the word so pleasant and it echoed so in her heart's ear, her nature found this so attractive and rooted within it, that she quickly and without thinking took the apple and ate of it.[12] And we were all ruined, and for all generations to the last man we were changed for the worse. He who would become something must necessarily become less.[13]

This is the ground and foundation of our happiness—a becoming less and an annihilation of oneself. Whoever wants to become something he is not, must of necessity become less of that which he is. Pure desirable Goodness, which is called and is God, exists in itself and dwells in its own substantial being, one substantial, immutable being existing and being for itself. All things should exist for him, not for themselves, but for him and through him. He is being, activity, life and all things; we are nothing except in him.

Your detachment must be bottomless. How bottomless? If a stone were to fall into a bottomless pool, it would have to sink forever because it would never reach bottom. So should a person sink and fall endlessly into the unfathomable God and have his ground in him, however serious a thing might befall him, be it internal or external suffering or his own failings, all of which God often allows to happen for one's own great benefit. All this should draw a person still deeper into God without his ever sensing, touching or becoming distressed in his own ground. Nor should one seek anything or intend anything for oneself, but should have God as the object of one's thoughts, into whom one has plunged. Whoever seeks anything, he does not seek God. All man's desire, ground and intention shall be to him—to him glory, to him the will, devotion; never our own advantage, pleasure, exaltation or reward. Seek him alone. Say with the beloved Son, "I do not seek my glory, but the Father's."[14] Know that if you are seeking anything else, things are not right with you and you are going astray. Glass, no matter how beautiful it is, if it has a small hole the size of a pinpoint, is not intact. However small the flaw is, it is not intact and perfect.

Do not become troubled about this, dear children. You will certainly make it. One finds great and small people in heaven, just as one finds here also big men and giants as well as men so weak one can knock them over with a finger. And yet they are all human beings. So is the case here. Among a thousand people one will find not one or hardly one person who is perfect. Some have abandoned themselves and discover themselves once a year failing in detachment. "Alas," they then say. "I find you still here. I thought I had buried you but unfortunately you are still alive!" Others find themselves failing once a month, others once a week, others once a day, and still others several times a day. With hearts weeping they should say, "Alas, dear God. In what a sad state I am! What is going to happen to me since I am continually finding myself? Certainly I shall abandon myself again and again—*iterum relinquo mundum*—I shall begin again." You shall die, overcome and become less again and again until it is accomplished. The flight of one swallow is not a sure sign of summer. But if they come often and there are many of them, then one knows that summer has arrived. Just because a person abandons himself once, twice or twenty times does not mean he is perfect. But if, in fact, he does it repeatedly, again and again, then he may accomplish it. One studies a lesson as long and as often as it takes to know it very well. In like manner, if a person abandons himself again and again, he learns to do it and everything is solved. Now nothing else is needed but hard work and watchfulness. Some people come and talk on and on about lofty perfection and have never taken the first step. They do not know how to abandon themselves the least little bit, and they have abandoned neither creature, nor the world, nor themselves.

May God help us achieve that detachment which he wants from us. Amen.

Notes

INTRODUCTION

1. See David Knowles, "A Characteristic of the Mental Climate of the Fourteenth Century," in *Mélanges offerts à Etienne Gilson de l'Académie Française* (Toronto and Paris: Vrin, 1959), pp. 315–25; and Richard Kieckhefer, *Unquiet Souls: Fourteenth Century Saints and Their Milieu* (Chicago and London: University of Chicago Press, 1984), p. 3. For more on the calamities of the times, see Robert Lerner, *The Age of Adversity. The Fourteenth Century* (Ithaca: Cornell University Press, 1968), chap. 1, "Catastrophe," pp. 7–34.

2. See below, pp. 16–18.

3. The last section of chapter 41 in Suso's *Life* (pp. 165–166) is probably an example of his work with beguines.

4. On this whole subject, see Robert Lerner, *The Heresy of the Free Spirit in the Later Middle Ages* (Berkeley, Los Angeles, London: University of California Press, 1972). See also Malcolm Lambert, *Medieval Heresy. Popular Movements from Bogomil to Hus* (New York: Holmes and Meier, 1976), pp. 173–81.

5. Lerner, *Free Spirit*, pp. 185–86.

6. See below, Introduction, pp. 31–32; *LBT*, chap. 6 (pp. 326–329). Also, in the *Life* (chaps. 46, 47, 48 and 51) several of the spiritual daughter's misconceptions, which her spiritual advisor felt compelled to address, reflect views ascribed to the brethren of the Free Spirit.

7. From the papal bull *In agro dominico, Essential Eckhart*, p. 77.

8. The most reliable studies on biographical details are Bihlmeyer, pp. 63*–140*; Künzle, pp. 1–6; and for details concerning the years of study, I. M. Frank, "Zur Studienorganisation der Dominkanerprovinz Teutonia in der ersten Hälfte des 14. Jh. und zum Studiengang des seligen Heinrich Seuse OP,"in *Seuse-Studien*, pp. 39–69. I have accepted Künzle's corrections of the material found in Bihlmeyer. (Concerning page references to the

NOTES

Bihlmeyer edition: pages with asterisks refer to Bihlmeyer's introduction; normal page numbers refer to pages of text in Suso's work themselves.)

9. Unfortunately, a prime source of information, the archives of the Dominican house in Constance, was lost during the Reformation. See Bihlmeyer, p. 65*.

10. See *Life*, chap. 16 (p. 91).

11. This information about Suso's parents is from early sixteenth century sources. Despite their lateness, most Suso scholars accept this information as accurate.

12. For comments about Suso's parents, see *Life*, chap. 6 (p. 75) and chap. 42 (p. 167). Concerning the nature of the *Life* and how it should be read, see below, pp. 38–50.

13. See *Life*, chap. 24 (pp. 110–113).

14. See *Life*, chap. 20 (p. 100).

15. See *Life*, chap. 21 (p. 104) for Suso's description of this.

16. *Life*, (pp. 63–64).

17. *Life*, (p. 64).

18. The syntax, extensive vocabulary and literary style of the *Horologium sapientiae* demonstrate that Suso's command of Latin went far beyond that of the average medieval intellectual.

19. See Introduction, pp. 19–20 (simony) and below, pp. 27–32 (re: *LBT*).

20. *Life*, chap. 6 (pp. 74–75). Colledge (*Essential Eckhart*, pp. 18–19), following Thomas Kaeppeli, *Scriptores ordinis praedicatorum medii aevi* (Rome, 1970), I, 358–60, accepts the view that the Eckhart Suso referred to here is not his former teacher in Cologne but rather Eckhart the Younger, a doctor of theology of the province of Saxony known for his holiness and learning, who died returning from a general chapter of the order held in Valenciennes in 1337. There are two reasons for this view. First, to recount that someone condemned for heresy had appeared to one would be an act of open contempt for the papal decree of condemnation. Second, the Tuscan Dominican Leander Alberti (1479–1552) in his *Of the Illustrious Men of the Order of Preachers* seems to be referring to this Eckhart the Younger as the one who appeared to Suso after his death. These are certainly serious considerations, but they are hardly overwhelming. The *Life* was published more than thirty years after Eckhart's condemnation by the pope. Mentioning the incident so much later could hardly be considered an act of raw defiance. Besides, it was not Eckhart whom the pope had condemned but rather his teachings. To imply that Meister Eckhart was among the blessed can hardly be considered terribly rash. As we shall note, in the *Little Book of Truth* Suso distances himself from aspects of Eckhart's thought. As for the man himself, Suso clearly had nothing but admiration. As for the report of the Tuscan Dominican, one can think of several reasons for his maintaining that this other Eckhart was the one who appeared to Suso. For example,

NOTES

concerns for ecclesiastical propriety may have pushed him, two hundred years later, to interpret Suso's words thus or may have allowed such a tradition to arise. And men of the same name are frequently confused in history. Though the matter is far from certain, when one considers the total context there are good reasons for assuming, as most critics have done, that it was indeed this better-known Meister Eckhart, Suso's revered teacher, who after the sad events of his last years reassures his former student about his final triumph and warns him about "wolfish men."

21. Frank, in *Seuse-Studien*, p. 69, thinks that Suso spent part of the time of the *studium generale*, either at Cologne or elsewhere, as a sublector or assistant to a professor in either biblical theology or in the teaching of the *Sentences*. If this is the case, he would have had some solid teaching experience before his return to Constance.

22. See below, Introduction, p. 33.

23. *Hor.* pp. 480,26-481,3; and see Bihlmeyer, pp. 100*-101*.

24. For further details, see Bihlmeyer, pp. 96*-100*.

25. See below, pp. 363-375.

26. See above, p. 16.

27. It is very probable, for example, that Meister Eckhart was heavily engaged in the *cura monialium* during his years in Strasbourg and Cologne.

28. That this father-daughter relationship could sometimes be resented is evident in the pseudo-Eckhartian tract "Sister Catherine," *Teacher and Preacher*, pp. 347-87, where the "father" confessor-advisor is put in his place by the mystical experiences and wisdom of his "daughter."

29. Some older studies claim this happened at a chapter in Magdeburg in 1363. No one has brought this up again since Bihlmeyer's (p. 131*) refutation.

30. *Prologue*, p. 58.

31. *Prologue*, p. 58.

32. Works not included in the present volume are the *Large Book of Letters* (*Das große Briefbuch*), from which Suso took the material for the *Little Book of Letters*, the *Little Book of Love* (*Das Minnebüchlein*), whose authenticity is doubtful, and his Latin *Horologium Sapientiae*, which will be discussed in connection with the *Little Book of Eternal Wisdom*. James M. Clark has translated the *Little Book of Eternal Wisdom* and the *Little Book of Truth* (London: James Clarke, 1953) and *The Life of the Servant* (London: James Clarke, 1952). The *Life*, however, is abridged, with about thirty percent of the original omitted, including all of chapters 46-53. (Having attempted to translate them, I can sympathize with Clark's decision to omit them.) The entire *Exemplar* has been translated by Sister M. Ann Edward (Dubuque, Iowa: Priory Press, 1962); however, the translation was made from the modern German version of N. Heller.

NOTES

33. Clark, *Little Book of Eternal Wisdom and Little Book of Truth*, Introduction, p. 18.

34. For more on the influence of Eckhart, besides the comments here, see Herma Piesch, "Seuses 'Büchlein der Wahrheit' und Meister Eckhart," *Seuse-Studien*, pp. 91–134.

35. See Josef Koch, "Kritische Studien zum Leben Meister Eckharts," in Koch, *Kleine Schriften* (Rome: Edizione di storia e letteraturae, 1973), I, p. 345.

36. *LBT*, (p. 308).

37. *LBT*, chap. 3 (p. 311).

38. *Essential Eckhart*, pp. 199–203.

39. German Sermon 6, *Essential Eckhart*, p. 188. See also the bull of condemnation *In agro dominico*, article 10, *Essential Eckhart*, p. 78.

40. See, for example, German Sermon 4, *Teacher and Preacher*, p. 250; and the papal bull *In agro dominico*, article 26, *Essential Eckhart*, p. 80.

41. See Lerner, *Free Spirit*, especially p. 82.

42. *LBT*, chap. 5 (p. 319).

43. German Sermon 9, *Teacher and Preacher*, p. 257; see also Article 28 in the bull *In agro dominico*, *Essential Eckhart*, p. 80.

44. See Lerner, *Free Spirit*, especially pp. 78–84.

45. *Life*, chap. 23 (p. 109).

46. See above, p. 23; and Künzle, p. 30.

47. *Hor.* II, 1 (pp. 518–26) and II, 4 (p. 548).

48. *LBEW*, prologue (p. 209). For clarification on what Suso meant by this and how it was misinterpreted by early critics, see Maria Bindschedler, "Seuses Auffassung von der deutschen Sprache," *Seuse-Studien*, pp. 71–76.

49. See Künzle, p. vii.

50. *Hor.*, Prologue, pp. 364,13—365,5.

51. Bihlmeyer, p. 105*.

52. Künzle, pp. 50–51.

53. Bihlmeyer, p. 47*.

54. Bihlmeyer, pp. 104*–5*.

55. *LBL*, (p. 335).

56. For a more detailed discussion of the relationship of the *Great Book of Letters* to the *LBL*, see Walter Blank, "Zum Stilwandel in Seuses Briefbüchern," *Seuse-Studien*, pp. 171–190.

57. *LBL*, Letter 4 (p. 345).

58. *LBL*, Prologue, (p. 335).

59. Bihlmeyer, p. 135*. Others would make this claim for Ulrich von Lichtenstein, who wrote his *Frauendienst* in 1255. However, many question how justly the term can be applied to this work.

60. *Life*, p. 63.

61. The most eloquent defenders of this *sententia communior*, which has not

380

been seriously questioned recently, have been Karl Bihlmeyer in his introduction to Suso's German works, especially pp. 132–36; Bihlmeyer, "Die Selbstbiographie in der deutschen Mystik des Mittelalters," *Theologische Quartalschrift* 114 (1933), 504–44; Julius Schwietering, "Zur Autorschaft von Seuses Vita," most readily available in *Altdeutsche und altniederländische Mystik*, ed. Kurt Ruh (Darmstadt: Wissenschaftliche Buchgesellschaft, 1964), pp. 309–23; and Georg Misch, *Geschichte der Autobiographie*, IV,1 (Frankfurt am Main: Schulte-Bulmke, 1967), especially pp. 136–56.

62. *Life*, p. 63.

63. *Exemplar*, Prologue, p. 59.

64. Bihlmeyer, p. 133*, and note 2 on this page. Misch, *Geschichte der Selbstbiographie*, IV,1, p. 141, downplays Stagel's role even more and proportionately emphasizes the imprint of Suso on the final version. For even more insistence on the *Life*'s being Suso's creation, see Christine Pleuser, "Tradition and Ursprünglichkeit in der Vita Seuses," *Seuse-Studien*, pp. 137–39.

65. K. Gröber, *Der Mystiker Heinrich Seuse* (Freiburg: Herder, 1941), pp. 177–83.

66. Uta Joeressen, *Die Terminologie der Innerlichkeit in den deutschen Werken Heinrich Seuses* (Frankfurt am Main: Lang, 1983), p. 11.

67. The remark of Georg Misch, *Geschichte der Autobiographie*, p. 144, that Suso was playing a bit of "hide and seek" regarding the question of authorship is persuasive, especially in light of his continuing concern about being called upon to answer questions about his orthodoxy.

68. Concerning the question of reality vs. *topos*, see Pleuser, "Tradition und Ursprünglichkeit in der Vita Seuses," *Seuse-Studien*, pp. 135–60.

69. Richard Kieckhefer, *Unquiet Souls. Fourteenth-Century Saints and Their Religious Milieu* (Chicago: University of Chicago Press, 1984).

70. Kieckhefer, *Unquiet Souls*, p. 6.

71. *Life*, chap. 37 (p. 146).

72. *Life*, chap. 41 (pp. 165–166).

73. See his remarks at the beginning both of the *LBT* (p. 308) and of the *LBEW* (p. 208), and his more expanded comments in the *Hor.* (p. 366,20-22).

74. *Exemplar*, prologue, pp. 57–59.

75. Schwietering, "Zur Autorschaft von Seuses Vita," (pp. 313–23) gives a brief history of Suso as seen against the background of chivalry and corrects what he considers a defect in previous studies by asserting that Suso should not be seen as a singer of spiritual courtly love (*Minnesänger*) but rather as a knight of spiritual love (*Minneritter*). He also claims that the courtly romance strongly influenced the structure of the *Life*.

76. However, for a thoughtful comparison of the *Life* with courtly romance, see Bindschedler, "Seuses Begriff von Ritterschaft," *Seuse-Studien*, pp. 233–40. See also, Künzle, pp. 84–104.

77. Chaps. 24, 25 and 26 respectively.

78. *Life*, chap. 43 (p. 169).

79. For Suso's humor in a broader perspective, see Ignaz Weilner, "Heinrich Seuse und die Aszese des Humors," *Seuse-Studien*, 241–54.

80. Cf. Mk 9:30–32 and Lk 9:43–45.

81. See Dn 13.

82. Those of us who spend much of our lives formulating perfect rejoinders for critical situations in the past where our verbal acuity failed us may well admire (or consider improbable) the servant's presence of mind in speaking here to the woman as well as in many other of his moments of crisis.

83. Like the angel who consoles Christ in the garden (Lk 22:43).

84. The largest concentration is in chapters 51 and 52 of the *Life*.

85. *Ez duhte in*, or *im waz vor*.

86. Three of the numerous visions following this pattern are found in chapter 19 (p. 97), chapter 36 (p. 142) and chapter 38 (p. 148).

87. Matins, the first hour of the Divine Office, was finished before daybreak.

88. See p. 208 and p. 302.

89. *Life*, chap. 51 (pp. 195–196).

90. See Augustine, *Literal Commentary on Genesis*, 12, 4 ff.

91. *Life*, chap. 51 (p. 195).

92. *Life*, chap. 2 (pp. 66–67).

93. 2 Cor 12:2–4.

94. *Hor.* p. 366,20-22. Although the statement is made only concerning the visions mentioned in the *Horologium*, one can easily agree with Bihlmeyer (p. 84*) that it is legitimate to apply it to many of the visions of the *Life* as well.

95. *Life*, chap. 18 (p. 97).

96. *Life*, chap. 15 (p. 88).

97. *Life*, chap. 46 (p. 174).

98. See *Life*, chap. 33.

99. *LBL*, Letter 11 (pp. 359–360).

100. See *Life*, chap. 13 (pp. 83–86) and the *LBEW*, especially the "Hundred Meditations" (p. 294–304).

PROLOGUE

(translated from Bihlmeyer, pp. 3–6)

1. This prologue is considered by Bihlmeyer to have been added later by Suso after completion of the four books included in the *Exemplar*. For the time of its composition, see the Introduction, p. 26. Most scholars

accept the Prologue as authentic, although in the past some have disputed its authorship.

2. "By concrete example" translates *mit bildgebender wise*, a phrase that is both rich and ambiguous. It might also be rendered "to provide a model" or "in a figurative manner."

3. Suso frequently refers to himself as "the servant of eternal Wisdom," or simply "the servant."

4. This explains the title given to the collection of four books that follows. However, *exemplar* also refers to the content of the books. The author's life and teachings are to serve as an exemplar for those seriously pursuing the goals of the interior life.

5. Elsbeth Stagel, Dominican nun in the convent at Töss. See Introduction, p. 25 and pp. 38–40.

6. These pictures, gouaches, were probably originally done by Suso himself and appear in some of the manuscripts as well as in the first printings of the *Exemplar* (1482, 1512).

7. The thought that humankind is not progressing but is rather in decline occurs frequently in various ages, but in Suso's time the feeling that humanity was regressing, morally and otherwise, was particularly strong, perhaps because of the calamitous experience of the Black Death (1348–50).

8. Part of Suso's concern is probably connected to the misuse to which he felt the thought of Meister Eckhart had been put and to his own experiences with the *Little Book of Truth*. See *LBT*, chap. 6 (pp. 327–329), and Introduction, pp. 31–32.

9. Bartholomew of Bolsenheim had a brilliant career in his order both as a theologian and as an administrator. He was provincial of the German province Teutonia from 1354 until his death in 1362.

LIFE

(translated from Bihlmeyer, pp. 7–195)

1. This sentence, as well as its equivalents at the beginning of the other books in the *Exemplar*, is probably a later addition. I have used the version appearing in manuscript N because it makes better sense than the version found in most of the better manuscripts.

2. The duchy of Swabia included at that time the city of Constance where Suso was born. In language and ethnic origin Suso was Alemannic.

3. That is, may he be in heaven.

4. This person is the Dominican nun Elsbeth Stagel. See Introduction, p. 25 and pp. 38–40.

NOTES

5. These final chapters (46–53) are in the form of a dialogue between the good sister and her spiritual father.

6. This change (*abker*) implies a turning *from* former ways.

7. January 21.

8. This is no doubt an allusion to Paul's experience in 2 Cor 12:2–4.

9. See previous note.

10. The Latin version bears the title *Horologium sapientiae*. See Introduction, pp. 34–35.

11. According to various versions of the *Physiologus* (or bestiary), a widely read medieval account of animals and their behavior, which existed in many versions, the panther exuded a sweet smell which its prey found attractive. The animals in the *Physiologus* were looked upon as having archetypal qualities that were viewed as being symbolic of Christ, the devil or man.

12. The following books of the Old Testament: Proverbs, Ecclesiastes, The Song of Songs, The Book of Wisdom and Sirach.

13. This section in quotation marks includes, in the order of their occurrence, thoughts from Prv 4:1–2, 3:19–20 and 3:24.

14. Cf. Prv 6:10 and 21:17.

15. Cf. Sir 24:18–21 and Eccl 7:27.

16. Cf. Boethius, *The Consolation of Philosophy*, Bk. 1, Prose 1.

17. Cf. Wis 8:1.

18. Cf. Prv 23:26.

19. Cf. Wis 7:10–11.

20. A scapular is a broad strip of cloth worn over the religious habit of some orders. It goes over the shoulders (Latin: *scapulae*), descending to the ankles in front and back. It is a symbol of spiritual protection.

21. IHS are the Greek letters for the abbreviated name *Jesus*.

22. See *Life*, chap. 42 (pp. 167–168).

23. For more on this book, see below chap. 35, and note 126 below.

24. This is from the response from matins for the feast of the Nativity of Mary (September 8) according to the Dominican *Divine Office*.

25. A *venia* was a complete prostration on the right side recommended on certain occasions by the constitution of the Dominican order.

26. "My soul has longed for."

27. This is the beginning of the fourth response from Matins for the feast of the Epiphany in the Dominican *Divine Office*. Cf. Is 60:1.

28. September 29.

29. A traditional Christmas hymn.

30. Concerning who this Eckhart was, see Introduction, note 20.

31. John der Fuoterer was a member of a Strasbourg merchant family who became a Dominican attached to the Dominican house in Basel. A few of his sermons are extant.

NOTES

32. This is an Eckhartian idea according to which one leaves one's limited and comfortable conception of God to seek him as he really is.

33. This behavior is reminiscent of that of St. John at the Last Supper. Cf. Jn 13:23.

34. Cf. 2 Cor 1:17–18.

35. "Lift up your hearts."

36. The author repeats the Latin word *sursum* here probably because he then chooses a similar sounding word to translate it into the vernacular: *susent*.

37. The last two sentences with their references to "arising" and "being lifted" continue the play with the word *sursum*.

38. February 2. Also called Candlemas Day.

39. "Inviolate one."

40. "O gentle one." These are the beginnings of two hymns from vespers in the Dominican *Divine Office* for this feast.

41. "Decorate." Sung during the procession on this feast.

42. In medieval Europe the period preceding lent was given over to unrestrained celebrations, which had various names in various regions. Since the expression *Shrovetide* is not well-understood in this country and since *mardi gras* is so regional, I have resorted to the more general expression *Carnival* to refer to this pre-lenten celebration.

43. The *alleluia* is dropped from the liturgy from Septuagesima Sunday (third Sunday before lent) until Easter.

44. This is Psalm 51, which is often recited as a penitential act.

45. Compline is an hour of the Divine Office sung in the evening.

46. See note 25 above. A *venia* accompanies each of the six decorations offered below.

47. "Hail, Holy Cross."

48. Matins is an hour of the Divine Office sung very early in the morning, even before daybreak.

49. The chapter room, where members of the religious community gathered daily to hear part of the rule read, to discuss important matters affecting the community, or to vote for a new superior, would not be in use after matins.

50. "My God, my God, why have you deserted me" (Ps 22).

51. The cloisters are in the form of a square or a rectangle and thus make up four paths or ways.

52. Cf. Ps 22:6.

53. Cf. Ps 22:15–16.

54. "Hail, our King, Son of David." Antiphon sung during the procession on Palm Sunday (Second Passion Sunday) in the Dominican liturgy.

55. "Hail, O cross, only hope." From a Good Friday hymn (*Vexilla regis*: Banner of the King).

NOTES

56. Cf. 2 Sm 15:15.

57. "Lord, who believed what we heard." Cf. Is 53:1.

58. This is a reference to the *LBEW*. See therein, Prologue (pp. 207–208).

59. A whip made of cord for penitential practices.

60. See note 25 above.

61. "Therefore, our advocate."

62. "O clement, O pious, O sweet Mary."

63. A chapter is an assembly of the order. A general chapter is a meeting of the provincials with the general of the order. A provincial chapter is a meeting of the priors with their provincial. Both kinds were held annually.

64. St. Dominic (1170–1221): the founder of the Order of Preachers of which Suso was a member. St. Arsenius (+449): a hermit in Egypt whom Suso revered. St. Bernard of Clairvaux (1090–1153): the famous Cistercian preacher and church leader.

65. "Lord, tell me to bless." This is a request for a blessing which is part of the Divine Office as well as grace before meals.

66. That is, the door separating the cloister from the outside world.

67. The iron chain was worn next to the body like a belt. The inside surface ended in points that would press against the body.

68. Bloodletting was considered of medicinal value at the time and was prescribed four times a year in the constitution of the Order of Preachers.

69. These five signs of love would be the four wounds in the hands and feet caused by the nails at the crucifixion and the wound in Christ's side caused by the lance.

70. See note 59 above. Here, obviously, his fist and not a whip was used.

71. November 23.

72. Called Quinquagesima Sunday.

73. March 21.

74. A mealtime during a period of fasting at which only beverages were consumed.

75. Second Sunday after Epiphany.

76. The reference is to Vincent of Beauvais, *"Speculum hist."* 8. 84. This story is told of many other saints as well.

77. The servant is described here as leaving one type of spirituality for another that is definitely higher. The level described in the last several chapters and now being transcended is usually called the purgative way. The highest way on earth is the illuminative way. The third level, one that transcends the conditions of life on earth, such as life in space and time, is the unitive way.

78. Jb 7:1. The author translates the Latin *militia* (military service, warfare) with the Middle High German *riterschaft*, which means "knighthood," "knightly service," or "knightly activity."

79. Perhaps the author had the first strophe of the *Nibelungenlied* in mind here. He is almost paraphrasing it.

80. Probably September 29.

81. See below, chap. 35 (pp. 137–139).

82. "While the meat was yet in their mouths" (Ps 78:30).

83. Suso entered the Dominican order at the age of thirteen (cf. *Life*, pp. 63–64), two years earlier than usually permitted. For admission at this early age, the special permission of the provincial was required. Apparently some gift to the order was involved in his early admission. This would not necessarily mean that the sin of simony had occurred or that, if it had, Suso himself was guilty of it. This seems to be his own final judgment in the matter since he calls his fear "inordinate" or "excessive."

84. The word *liden* (suffering), which occurs in the previous sentence four times, is what one is supposed to connect to the four red roses mentioned here.

85. These wax figures, votive offerings for favors granted, are still found at shrines in parts of Europe.

86. Dominicans never traveled alone. A fellow Dominican always went along as a companion. Also, they traveled only on foot.

87. That is, to a meeting of his order.

88. A reference to *LBW* and possibly *LBEW*. See Introduction, p. 33.

89. Gethsemane, the Mount of Olives.

90. January 21.

91. Such formality toward a priest, even though he was a member of one's own family, was usual. The sister also uses formal pronouns (*ir, uch*) rather than the familiar *du* in addressing her brother.

92. In times of plague Jews were often accused of poisoning wells. In 1348–49, from the area around Cologne through southern Germany and into Austria, large numbers of Jews were burned at the stake as a result of such accusations. In Constance alone 350 Jews were thus killed on March 3, 1349.

93. That is, the kind of breakfast allowed on one of the order's days of fasting.

94. Apparently Suso had to pay a stiff fine.

95. Note the parallels with Psalm 22 and the synoptic accounts of the passion of Christ.

96. This little book is probably the *LBEW*, which was completed most likely in 1330 and certainly by 1334. See Introduction, p. 34.

97. That is, Suso conversed with the nuns through a grille that separated the cloistered nuns from those visiting them.

98. The nobleman seems inclined to consider suspect or worse all at-

NOTES

tempts to lead a spiritual life that depart from tradition. For more on the spiritual movements of the times, see Introduction, pp. 16–18.

99. Cf. Rom 12:15.

100. Cf. 2 Cor 11:26 and Gal 2:4.

101. Lk 10:3.

102. Ps 22.

103. St. Nicholas was the patron saint of the Dominican house in Constance and was much venerated around the Lake of Constance area besides being generally a patron of those in need.

104. Ps 31:6 and Lk 23:46.

105. Cf. Lk 23:34.

106. Cf. Jn 17:9–26.

107. Cf. Jn 17:21–23.

108. "Breakthrough," a term occasionally used by Meister Eckhart (cf. *Essential Eckhart*, Sermon 52, p. 203), here seems to signify the attainment of union with God. However, because it appears so abruptly here, it is difficult to know exactly what all its implications have been for Suso.

109. One attains the power of having all one's wishes fulfilled by uniting completely with God and going out of oneself completely, leaving all things behind. In such a state of union, whatever happens fulfills one's wishes because it is God's will.

110. Cf. Rom 8:28.

111. According to Bihlmeyer (p. 133*, note 2), this whole chapter is a later addition. Perhaps Suso added it along with the final chapters of Part Two.

112. "Courage, daughter." Cf. Mt 9:22 and Lk 8:48.

113. Töss is near Winterthur in Switzerland. The convent was founded in 1233, and at the time of the Reformation (1525) was abolished by the city council of Zurich.

114. Cf. Introduction, pp. 24–25 and *Life*, prologue. The daughter of a respected family in Zurich, Elsbeth Stagel became acquainted with Suso in the mid-1330s and died between 1350 and 1360.

115. The teachings that follow have an Eckhartian ring, but it is doubtful that they are the result of direct contact between Stagel and Eckhart.

116. Literally the "imagelessness of all images" (*bildlosigkeit aller bilden*), but this phrase probably refers to the Eckhartian notion that God cannot be grasped in any real sense through images or even through rational concepts.

117. "Sir" translates *herr* which is the word used to address both a lord and a priest.

118. This "fact" about pelicans appeared in the bestiaries. The pelican is usually a symbol for Christ, who nourishess his followers with his own blood.

NOTES

119. Cf. Lk 7:38–50.

120. Cf. Mt 15:22–28.

121. Mt 9:22.

122. Suso seems to be referring to philosophical problems about the nature of angels as such problems might have come up in the schools; e.g., since angels are completely spiritual beings, they are not differentiated from each other within a species by their forms being received into different matter. What then does make them different from each other?

123. That is, through the instrumentality of the heart of the servant.

124. See chap. 20, p. 103.

125. That is, the gate separating the cloistered friary from the world outside.

126. This is the *Vitae Patrum* in Migne, *Patrologia Latina*, Vols. 73–74.

127. Cf. 2 Cor 12:7–10.

128. Cf. Mt 16:24, and *Teacher and Preacher*, Sermon XLIX, p. 231.

129. Cf. Phil 4:13.

130. Cf. Ps 18:29.

131. Cf. Ps 68:35.

132. See note 68 above.

133. This incident is filled with the conventions and vocabulary of the poetry of courtly love.

134. "There the Queen of virgins rising above the (heavenly) ranks, etc."

135. The rebec was a three-stringed, violin-like instrument played with a bow. It derived from the two-stringed Arabian rebab.

136. Benedictines and Augustinians had some monasteries of this kind.

137. The nine choirs or ranked orders of angels are traditionally considered to be (from highest to lowest): Seraphim, Cherubim, Thrones, Dominions, Virtues, Powers, Principalities, Archangels and Angels. Cf. *LBEW*, chap. 12, p. 242.

138. "Many tribulations of the just."

139. Note the parallel to Christ's remarks about his future sufferings and the lack of understanding on the part of his disciples. Cf. Mk 9:30–32, and Lk 9:43–45.

140. Each house of mendicants was given exclusive rights to preach and beg for alms within a certain area (*terminus*). Those engaged in this begging were called *terminarii*.

141. There are many parallels to and even verbal borrowings here from the story of Susannah. See Daniel 13.

142. Here a line is omitted that appears in only one manuscript. It reads: "And because I love him (God), so you must be my darling child."

143. The wheel of fortune, a popular image in medieval times, was usually depicted with Lady Fortune, a female figure standing next to a wheel with four crowned figures on it. Next to each was a saying. Next to the

figure sitting on top of the wheel was written, "I rule." Next to the figure half way down the right side of the wheel, who is falling off, was written, "I was ruling." Next to the figure under the wheel, "I ruled." Next to the figure half way up the left side, "I shall rule." Lady Fortune at her caprice turns the wheel, thus changing the figures' fortunes.

144. An hour of the Divine Office recited at about 3 P.M.

145. Cf. Is 62:4.

146. Cf. Mt 26:50.

147. Cf. Mt 26:42.

148. These last two paragraphs are missing in one manuscript (M), which has the following lines instead: "The superior over Teutonia also exonerated him from fault and said that he and the head of the order had held a formal visitation, as is required, and found nothing against him except that this one evil woman, who should not be believed, had spoken maliciously about the honest man, and that this could happen again if someone wanted to heed evil tongues."

149. Cf. Mt 12:31.

150. From the Dominican Divine Office for a feast of Mary.

151. This is Sermon 1, pp. 363–371.

152. That is, by committing suicide, which is a mortally sinful act, his soul would die a spiritual death and be consigned to hell.

153. Cf. Jn 9:3.

154. Cf. Lk 23:43.

155. About the middle of July.

156. This description of the effect of celestial music on the heart is reminiscent of Suso's contemporary, Richard Rolle.

157. This vision is similar to one attributed to St. Francis of Assisi. Concerning the wings of the seraph, see Is 6:2.

158. Künzle's explanation (Hor., p. 6) that this is not a reference to the general famine of 1343–44, as Bihlmeyer (p. 145, note to line 14) suggests, but rather to a financial crisis of the Dominican house in Constance seems the more plausible explanation.

159. A canon is a secular priest (with no vow of poverty) attached to a cathedral.

160. That is, after his conversion and resolve to lead a serious religious life, as narrated in the Prologue, pp. 63–64.

161. Aachen (also called Aix-la-Chapelle) was a popular destination for pilgrimages.

162. This final sentence seems to function as a conclusion not just for this chapter but perhaps for the whole *Life* up to this point. In any case, this chapter concludes the narrative part of the *Life*. The final eight chapters are made up of theoretical discussions and instruction about mysticism.

163. Cf. Dt 32:11.

NOTES

164. Cf. Jn 16:7. Cf. also, Sermon 4, p. 371.

165. This is tantamount to saying: "Sin does not injure a truly good person." Such unorthodox sayings were attributed to several quietistic sects, especially to the brethren of the Free Spirit. The import of such statements seems to be that, for one who is truly united with God, ordinary concepts of good and evil do not apply. Such people are "beyond good and evil." See Introduction, pp. 31–32.

166. This line of thought is based on the conception (developed by Meister Eckhart, among others) that creatures have a twofold existence: They exist in the material world distinct from God; however, they exist in God as well. God did not create them irrationally. Just as a chest exists in the mind of a cabinetmaker before it exists as a material object separate from its maker, so creatures also have existed from eternity in the mind of God, utterly one with him. Suso's point is that it is all fine and good to recall man's eternal existence as one with God in the divine mind, but that this existence has very little to do with determining how corporeal man, existing as a creature and distinct from God, should determine what he is to do or avoid doing.

167. That is, the actions I perform as a creature distinct from God.

168. That is, he is to submit to this one person as his spiritual guide, but this person is no more mature or circumspect in spiritual matters than he is himself.

169. Here the following words are found in only one manuscript (M): "they even look with contempt upon the suffering humanity of Christ." Holding this belief was a common accusation made against heretical groups of beghards and against the brethren of the Free Spirit. The Council of Vienne (1311–12) had condemned it.

170. "This or that" is a term borrowed from Eckhart's vocabulary. It signifies finite being which, as *finite*, can be *defined* as being this or that being. Infinite being or "all in all" is simply being without qualification, without this or that.

171. This is taken up in chapter 52 below.

172. "Withdrawing" is a translation of *vergangenheit*.

173. That is, when a person dies.

174. Cf. 2 Cor 12:2 ff.

175. This is possibly a reference to the body.

176. The One, or oneness, is a favorite name neoplatonists and mystics have for God.

177. That is, one loves that about a thing which is not of the essence or substance, but rather that which is passing.

178. Lk 23:46.

179. Jn 19:30.

180. This is probably a reference to the Dominican position that man's

beatitude consists primarily in knowing God. The Franciscan position was that beatitude consisted foremost in loving God.

181. Cf. Rom 1:20.

182. The Latin word for mirror is *speculum*. Hence to "speculate" is to know something through its reflection. This etymology is common to many medieval thinkers.

183. The seven planets of the Middle Ages are sun, moon, Mars, Mercury, Jupiter, Venus and Saturn.

184. The last several lines describing nature in the summertime owe much to the vernacular and Latin lyric poetry of earlier generations.

185. This jubilation or *jubilus*, an ecstatic bursting forth in voice, is frequently mentioned in the lives of nuns of the period.

186. No doubt Suso is speaking of himself.

187. A vigil here means a part of the Divine Office for the Departed, which Dominicans recited twice daily in Suso's time.

188. "Bare" here translates *bildlos*, which more literally means "imageless" or "formless." Suso means he wishes to embrace the divinity in its pure state and not just as it is revealed to our limited capacities of understanding through the medium of images or forms.

189. "Genuine" translates *weslich*, which could be rendered more literally as "essential," "substantial" or "in being." But such translations would give Suso's words here a heretical coloring. That this is not the case becomes clear from his attempts to define *weslich*, which immediately follow.

190. This could refer to a number of Christian thinkers.

191. God simply *is* being without qualification. Creatures have a different relationship to being. They share in being that is not simply divine being. Their being is limited to being this or that.

192. That being is a negation of nonbeing or, in other words, that the only negation to be found in perfect being (God) is the negation of negation is a favorite thought of Meister Eckhart. See *Teacher and Preacher, Comm. Wis.* n. 148, pp. 167–68, and Sermon 21, p. 281.

193. According to Thomas Aquinas, created being is composed of act and potency. For example, in order to sing one must have the capability of singing. Actual singing is act. The mere ability to sing is potency. But potency is, in a sense, nonbeing because it is non-act. Creatures are a mixture of act and potency. Only God is pure act.

194. A saying appearing frequently in the works of medieval authors. It may have begun with the *Book of 24 Philosophers*, second definition of God.

195. *Trinity* 4. 20. 29.

196. *Divine Names* 2. 5. 7.

197. *Summa Against the Gentiles* 4. 11.

198. Jn 1:1. The eagle is a frequent symbol for John. According to medi-

eval animal lore, the eagle is the only creature that can look directly into the sun (God) and not go blind.

199. Here, as throughout this chapter, Suso is attempting to express central thoughts of scholastic theology while avoiding the formidable technical vocabulary of scholasticism. A scholastic thinker would express the thought of this last sentence by saying that the formal object of the will is "the good" as such.

200. This image is, of course, the Son.

201. This teaching was attributed to the brethren of the Free Spirit. Cf. also *Essential Eckhart*, Sermon 52, p. 200 and pp.201–2.

202. Cf. Jb 31:23.

203. Cf. Rom 8:15.

204. Cf. Gal 2:20. The complete idea is: It is no longer I who live, but Christ lives in me.

205. Mt 5:3, ". . . theirs is the kingdom of heaven."

206. Suso is here following the teaching of Augustine. Cf. *Literal Commentary on Genesis*, Bk. 12.

207. Gn 41.

208. *Confessions* 4. 13.

209. Jn 12:26.

210. Bihlmeyer (p. 184, note to line 20 ff.), following Heinrich Denifle, *Die deutschen Schriften des sel. Heinrich Seuse* (Munich: Literarisches institut von dr. M. Huttler, 1880), pp. 280–92, assumed that much of this chapter from here on had been taken from the Eckhartian poem *Von dem überschalle* and its gloss (pp. 517–20) and the tract *Liber positionum* (pp. 668–71) in Franz Pfeiffer, *Deutsche Mystiker des 14. Jahrhunderts*, Vol. 2: *Meister Eckhart* (Göttingen: Literarisches institut von dr. M. Huttler, 1857). Neither of these works is still considered to be a genuine work of Eckhart. Kurt Ruh, "Seuse, Vita c. 52 und das Gedicht und die Glosse 'Vom Uberschall,' " *Seuse-Studien*, pp. 191–212 argues convincingly that the poem and its gloss derive from the *Life*, chap. 52, but that Suso did take some formulations from the already existing so-called *Liber positionum*.

211. *On the Trinity* 7, 4–6.

212. That is, creatures imitate the characteristics of the Trinity and thus both remain within God and flow out from him. This thought occurs frequently in Eckhart's works.

213. Cf. Jn 1:1–3.

214. The author is here playing with the word *wise*, which means "manner" or "mode." Being in creatures is always limited to a certain manner or mode of being. Since God is limitless, his being is without manner or mode.

215. According to the apophatic tradition of pseudo-Dionysius and oth-

ers, what we can most properly say about God is that he cannot be named and is the nothing that is above being.

216. *On Loving God* 10. 27–28.

217. I Cor 13:12.

218. That is, the spirit is blind to the fact that in its state of withdrawal into God it still remains separate in being from God.

219. See *LBT*, chap. 5 (p. 320).

220. Cf. Pseudo-Dionysius, *Mystical Theology* 1. 1. and 1. 3.

221. See chap. 51 (p. 192) and note 194 above.

222. That is, it gazes upon the form of the first man.

223. It is precisely the intellect, spiritual in nature and thus immortal, that allows one to say that man is the image of God.

224. The "shining image" is the intellect reflecting the divinity.

225. 2 Cor 12:2 ff.

226. *Grades of Humility* 8.

LITTLE BOOK OF ETERNAL WISDOM

(translated from Bihlmeyer, pp. 196–325)

1. Suso is referring to himself.

2. See *Life*, note 25.

3. Cf. *Life*, chaps. 13 and 14.

4. At the beginning of the *Horologium* the author goes into more detail: "The visions contained in the following are not all to be taken literally, although many of them literally happened. It is rather a figurative way of speaking." *Hor.*, p. 336, 20–22.

5. See below, chaps. 17, 19 and 20.

6. See chap. 5 below.

7. An allusion to the three parts of the *LBEW*.

8. Cf. Sg 5:10.

9. Wis 8:2.

10. Much of the rest of this chapter draws on Augustine's *Confessions*, especially 10. 6.

11. Wis 5:7.

12. Cf. Augustine, *Confessions* 1. 1.

13. The garden on the Mount of Olives, Gethsemane.

14. Cf. Rom 11:33.

15. In the poetry of courtly love the lover is constantly pleading with his mistress to give him some token of her love (*minnezeichen*). The wounds of Christ's passion are to be understood as such tokens of love.

16. Gn 9:13.

17. The courtly lover blushed red and blanched white at the sight of his beloved. Christ's passion caused Christ also to take on various colors.

18. Mt 11:30.

19. Ps 42:1.

20. Mt 22:14.

21. Cf. Mt 18:6.

22. Cf. Jb 6:16.

23. Cf. Jn 16:7, and Sermon 4, p. 371.

24. That is, houses of religious orders.

25. Again, a metaphor for a religious house.

26. Sir 24:26–28 and 40:20. Ecclesiasticus was considered and called one of the Books of Wisdom.

27. Sg 2:3 and 5:2.

28. Ps 45:10.

29. Phil 3:8.

30. That is, these words do not begin to describe what I really am.

31. 1 Cor 2:9.

32. Sg 2:1.

33. That is, it cannot share the object it loves with anyone.

34. Sg 5:6.

35. From the Divine Office (antiphon at matins) for the feast of St. Agnes.

36. *Nisi* is a Latin conjunction that introduces a negative condition: "if . . . not" or "unless."

37. Rom 1:20 and 11:36.

38. Sg 6:12.

39. Cf. Sir 11:27.

40. Cf. Prv 13:12.

41. Cf. Lk 17:21.

42. Rom 14:17.

43. Jer 12.

44. Jn 15:9.

45. Cf. Wis 2:6.

46. Cf. Wis 5:4.

47. Cf. Jb 38:7.

48. Many of the images of the last few sentences are staples from courtly poetry: the meadows alive with springtime flowers, lovers' glances, music and dancing. However, the courtly world is here surpassed because "perfect joy" was described in courtly poetry as an unattainable goal, and joy was never without sorrow (Cf. *Nibelungenlied*). Nor was joy secure from time and change.

49. Sg 8:5.

50. Sg 2:1.

NOTES

51. The Thrones are, after the Seraphim and Cherubim, the third-highest order of the angels.

52. The lowest three ranks of angels are Principalities, Archangels and Angels.

53. This bridal gift (*morgengabe*) was presented by the husband to the bride on the morning following the wedding night.

54. These are the chief characteristics of creatures' bodies in heaven after the resurrection of the body.

55. Cf. Thomas Aquinas, *S. Th.* I, q. 95, a. 4.

56. Mt 27:46.

57. Mt 25:34.

58. Rom 11:33.

59. Rv 7:12.

60. Mt 17:4.

61. Prv 3:12.

62. That is, the vision of hell and the vision of heaven.

63. Mt 20:16.

64. Wis 11:21.

65. Cf. Mt 26:42.

66. This is an attempt to reproduce Suso's word play. The idea is that suffering turns out not to be suffering when the whole truth is known.

67. That is, knowledge, learning and sacred eloquence can be the property of both good and bad people. They have nothing directly to do with sanctity.

68. That is, there is no one . . . .

69. Sir 34:9.

70. Purple is the color of royalty.

71. Red roses signify suffering. Green palm branches signify victory.

72. See the beginning of *LBEW* above, pp. 208–209.

73. The psaltery is a kind of stringed instrument plucked with or without a plectrum.

74. 2 Cor 12:4.

75. The former: contemplating Christ in his glory. The latter: contemplating him in his suffering.

76. This is loosely translated by Suso from St. Bernard's Sermon 43 on the Song of Songs.

77. Cf. Mt 27:39–43.

78. Cf. Lk 23:39–42.

79. Lk 23:49.

80. Jer 11:19.

81. Jn 19:26–27.

82. Cf. Mt 27:51.

83. Cf. Mt 16:24.

NOTES

84. Rom 11:33.

85. That is, Mary is above all the angels.

86. Jer 29:11.

87. That is, Christ.

88. Cf. Mk 13:31 and Lk 21:33.

89. Cf. Est 2:9.

90. The unicorn, according to the bestiaries, could only be captured by a pure maiden. The unicorn was often equated with Christ and the maiden with Mary.

91. Cf. Sg 2:16.

92. Cf. 2 Sm 19:1.

93. Lam 1:12.

94. Mt 27:46.

95. Jn 19:30.

96. Cf. Phil 2:8.

97. Lk 23:46.

98. These signs are the wounds and death Christ suffered.

99. A favorite subject of late medieval sculpture was the pietá: the dead Christ in the lap of his Mother. The thought was usually present that he had played on this same lap as a child. This thought, as here, added poignancy to the scene.

100. That is, make my soul again that fresh and bright image of you that it should be.

101. Suso's word play here cannot be duplicated in English. He calls Mary the *mittel*, which has been translated "mediatrix." Literally it can mean either "means" or "middle." Thus Mary is the beginning, middle, and end as well.

102. These four points make up the content of Part Two (through chapter 24).

103. Literal translation of the Vulgate version of Ps 17:5–6.

104. Cf. Wis 5:12.

105. Cf. Wis 5:11.

106. Jb 23:2; and immediately following, 23:6 and 3.

107. Mt 25:9.

108. That is, before it actually happens.

109. Heb 13:14.

110. Cf. Sir 1:16 and 7:40.

111. This entire chapter borrows heavily from Cassian's *First Conference*, especially chaps. 4, 7, 8, 12 and 13.

112. Prv 1:8.

113. Ps 76:2.

114. Cf. Ps 137:3.

115. Cf. Is 45:15.

NOTES

116. 2 Sm 6:14.
117. Cf. Augustine, *Confessions* 7. 10.
118. That is, he makes use of the sacrament of penance.
119. Sg 1:14.
120. Ps 145:1.
121. God is good without his goodness being restricted to a certain mode or manner of being good. He is infinitely good, or good beyond all modes or manner.
122. Ps 33:1.
123. By "the praise in eternal glory" Suso might mean the praise the triune God gives itself. This is the only truly adequate praise God receives. Or he might mean the praise given God by the angels and saints in eternity: the most perfect praise creatures can give.
124. Is 29:13.
125. Lk 23:41–42.
126. Suso, of course, is the cuckoo; the heavenly spirits the nightingales.
127. That is, the fallen angels.
128. Rom 8:28.
129. See *Life*, note 25.
130. Probably a reference to chap. 16, above.
131. A medieval woodwind instrument.
132. That is, a piece of music.
133. This concluding paragraph appears only in manuscripts that contain the *LBEW* separately (and not as part of the *Exemplar*). It may not be authentic, but it coincides well with Suso's thoughts on the matter, as expressed in the Prologue to the *Exemplar*. See p. 58.

LITTLE BOOK OF TRUTH

(translated from Bihlmeyer, pp. 326–59)

1. The *LBT* follows the *Life* and the *LBEW* in the manuscripts of the *Exemplar*. For its chronological relationship to the other works, see Intro., pp. 26–27.
2. Ps 51:6.
3. Cf. *Life*, chap. 6 (pp. 74–75), where in his vision of Eckhart the relationship of detachment to truth is touched upon.
4. This is most probably a reference to the teachings of the brethren of the Free Spirit. See Introduction, pp. 17–18.
5. Cf. Ex 7:8–12.
6. Cf. Mt 24:5 and 11.
7. Cf. Jer 15:19.

NOTES

8. See note 4 above.

9. "Explained allegory" is an attempt to translate *usgeleite bischaft*. The verb *ûzlegen* means to "explain" or "interpret." *Bischaft* generally refers to a didactic piece, such as a fable. Actually, Suso casts his thoughts here in the form of a dialogue. Notice also that in saying "as though the disciple were asking and Truth answering," the author is clearly informing his audience that such a dialogue never really took place. It is a literary invention.

10. This last clause could also be interpreted "and in comparison with which nothing else is."

11. Cf. Dionysius, *On the Divine Names* 1. 4–6; Thomas Aquinas, *Summa of Theology* Ia. 13. 1.

12. "Without mode of being" translates *wiselos*. All creatures have a certain limited manner or mode of existence. In being *this* they cannot also be *that*. God's being is infinite and hence without a limited mode of being. The term *wiselos* and the ensuing train of thought is very reminiscent of Eckhart. See, for example, Sermon 9, *Teacher and Preacher*, pp. 255–261.

13. The point of this last sentence is that in God being is the same as knowing, and that the highest activity within God is his knowing himself.

14. "Giving birth" is perhaps the most famous and pervasive concept in Eckhart's works.

15. "Godhead" is the divinity in its purity and immutability. "God" is this divinity conceived as capable of acting and giving birth.

16. That is, our minds distinguish between God and the Godhead, but there are not two things in the divinity that correspond to this distinction.

17. These qualities are the so-called general perfections, which imply no limitations; such as, *one, true, good, just*, and so on. *Green*, on the contrary, is a perfection or quality limited to a material object.

18. This is standard Aristotelian and Thomistic thought. Form gives actual existence. Matter without form has only the potential to exist.

19. For a similar way of expressing this, see Eckhart's Sermon 52, *Essential Eckhart*, p. 200.

20. John Damascene, *On the Orthodox Faith* 3. 11. What is meant is that Christ took on an individual human nature.

21. I have translated *blutli* as "blossom." It might also mean "blood."

22. That is, his body.

23. In saying Christ assumed human nature in all purity and was untouched by original sin, the author may be making an allusion to the theory of Augustine and others that the pleasure in the sex act is what transferred original sin to the soul of the newly conceived human being.

24. "Means" (*mittel*), a term used frequently by Eckhart, denotes anything that functions as a hindrance or obstruction between God and the soul.

25. Cf. Eph 1:22–23.

26. Cf. Rom 8:29.

NOTES

27. The author does not mean that the fact that all men share a common human nature takes anything essential away from their individuality. He means, rather, that all men have a human nature in exactly the same way and to the same extent.

28. "Nobility" and "accident" have been rendered literally. "Nobility" is all that we share with God. "Accident" is what is ours exclusively, our individuality in itself.

29. That is, one focuses on becoming more and more an individual human being with one's own wishes and goals and turns away from uniting oneself to that which is not accidental: God's will and being.

30. The sense of this sentence seems to be: Complete detachment from self does not bring about any change in one's being or nature. One still remains the limited human creature one always was. No metaphysical change in one's nature occurs.

31. Multiplicity is the root of being an individual creature because multiplicity is the result of acting for oneself and one's own goals separate from the divine will. Acting in union with God is the root of unity.

32. Gal 2:20.

33. The following two paragraphs draw heavily upon Bernard's *On Loving God* 10 and 15.

34. Cf. Mt 25:23.

35. Cf. 1 Cor 6:17.

36. Cf. 1 Cor 15:28.

37. Cf. Bernard, *On Loving God* 15. 39 and *Letters* 11. 8.

38. Cf. 1 Tm 6:16.

39. Cf. Thomas Aquinas, *Summa of Theology* Ia. IIae. 61.5

40. This would seem to mean the condition of blessedness in heaven.

41. "Figurative example" is an attempt to translate *glichnusse*, which can mean "likeness," "comparison," "allegory," "parable" or anything denoting figurative language. Exactly what Suso means by it here becomes clearer as one reads on.

42. That is, Christ as man is unique because he exists and subsists as one with the divine Person. Other men are just formed according to his image.

43. Cf. Jn 1:12–13.

44. That is, man as existing in God and as perfectly one with him is eternal nothing. Through his distinct existence as a creature who came to be in time he is not eternal nothing. These are contraries human logic cannot reconcile, but they are both true.

45. This line of thought may be an endorsement of the negative or apophatic way of naming God. The apophatic way maintains that one can better describe God by saying what he is *not*, for example, that he is *not* material, *not* temporal, *in*finite, etc., than by saying what he is, for example, that he is good, just, etc.

400

46. That is, God's knowing is not some accidental activity of the intellect that can be turned on and off or that has steps to its completion. It is part of his being, is always going on, and is always in full possession of its object. Hence he knows without a separate activity of knowing.

47. Dionysius, *On the Divine Names* 1. 4–6, and 7. 3.

48. This is a very obscure passage. Any attempt to clarify in translating would involve unwarranted interpretation.

49. This is most likely a reference to Boethius' classic definition of eternity as the "complete and perfect possession of endless life all at once." See Boethius, *The Consolations of Philosophy* 5. 6.

50. The sense seems to be: Before man existed as a creature, he was the same as God, not *just* united with him. This interpretation fits what follows.

51. Cf. Jn 1:3–4.

52. This example of the eye appears in Aristotle's *Soul*, 2 (425 b 26).

53. Probable meaning: This fact, that the soul always remains a creature, is true whether one is aware of it or not.

54. Cf. Augustine, *On Genesis According to the Letter* 4. 22. 39 ff.

55. The chief powers of the soul are intellect and will, which are distinct from the essence or being of the soul.

56. 1 Jn 1:8.

57. 1 Jn 3:9.

58. Implied here is the question: Even if several persons act in perfect union with Christ, will this unified act not have individual and distinct empirical effects?

59. In the state of union one's faculties act, but one has no consciousness of any separate act or its effect.

60. The following discussion of rebirth in man and the eternal birth is very obscure. Commentators are not able to throw much light on exactly what Suso means or what the sources for his use of these terms might be.

61. That is, pagan philosophers, unaided by faith or grace.

62. Augustine, *Trinity* 8. 3. 4.

63. Jn 8:34.

64. Jn 8:36.

65. The learned teacher is Meister Eckhart, though he is not mentioned by name here or in the subsequent allusions to his teachings. The "wild one's" claim that the teacher denied all distinctions could refer to his denying all distinctions in God, which would seem to be at odds with the dogma of the Trinity, or to his denying all distinctions between God and man. In the response that follows, the disciple gives an orthodox interpretation to both cases. In the papal bull "*In agro dominico*," in which several statements taken from Eckhart's works are condemned, two articles (23 and 24) reject the idea of distinctions in God, and article 10 denies any distinction be-

tween man and God. For a translation of the bull, see *Essential Eckhart*, pp. 77–81.

66. The passage Suso has in mind is possibly the following: "*Nihil tam distinctum a . . . creato . . . sicut deus, et nihil tam indistinctum.*" (Translation: Nothing is as distinct from a creature as God is, and nothing is as indistinct.) See *Teacher and Preacher*, p. 169.

67. This line of thought, with the exception of our birth being a rebirth, is frequent in Eckhart's Latin works. See, for example, his Commentary on John, n. 106, *Essential Eckhart*, p. 162.

68. This is close to article 13, "*In agro dominico.*" See note 65 above.

69. Jn 3:6.

70. An approximation of article 11, "*In agro dominico.*" See note 65 above.

71. Jn 13:3. Cf. also Mt 11:27 and 28:18.

72. Here Suso recapitulates two major points: 1. The detached person is both one with God and distinct from God. 2. This *both-and* balance that describes the actual metaphysical state of the detached person is then expressed by the statement that he is united with God. This is then contrasted with the detached person's perception of this state in which he is unaware of being distinct from God.

73. Implied here, it seems, is a rejection of heterodox activities that damage the order and oneness of the church.

74. Cf. 1 Tm 1:9.

75. This phrase can also mean "to the extent that he is a creature."

76. Suso is engaging in word play here that the translation cannot reproduce. *Tun und laszen* usually means "actions and omissions," logical contraries. *Laszen* is also the activity of becoming detached. Hence a detached person's activity is non-activity/becoming detached. And his achievement is not to achieve or not to be attached to his achievement.

77. "Without their making a deep impression on him" translates *ane inbildunge*. This seems to mean that the detached person's relationships with others should not become so intense that they disturb his being formed by or his conforming to the divine image.

78. The term "highest power" (*oberste kraft*) occurs frequently in Eckhart's works and means the highest capacity or part of the human intellect.

LITTLE BOOK OF LETTERS

(translated from Bihlmeyer, pp. 360–93)

1. This is Elsbeth Stagel. Letters 3 and 8 are addressed to her.

2. This text is part of the ceremony of blessing and consecrating new women religious.

NOTES

3. Much of the paragraph to this point is reminiscent of the first stanza of Walther von der Vogelweide's famous "elegy." Also, the figure of Lady World occurs frequently both in poetry and in religious sculpture as sensually attractive on the outside but filled with vermin and rot within.

4. Lady World was often depicted holding out an apple (of temptation) to her admirers.

5. Cf. Mt 11:30.

6. Cf. 1 Cor 4:9 and *LBEW*, chap. 13 (p. 248).

7. Cf. Is 52:1 and Rom 13:11.

8. Is 11:6.

9. Cf. *Life*, chap. 31 (p. 128).

10. Cf. *Life*, chap. 20 (pp. 101–102).

11. On the wheel of fortune, see *Life*, chap. 38 (p. 152 and note 143).

12. St. Bernard, *Grace and Free Will*.

13. This saying, found frequently in medieval spiritual literature and variously attributed, probably has its origin in Seneca, *Moral Epistles* 7: "I return more greedy, more ambitious . . . and less human because I was among men."

14. Sg 1:5.

15. The erotic Song of Songs, traditionally attributed to King Solomon, was often an embarrassment to medieval exegetes. Hence especially with this book of the Bible they felt a need to find a spiritual meaning in the text.

16. Cf. Rv 21:10–14.

17. St. Elizabeth of Hungary (sometimes called St. Elizabeth of Thuringia).

18. Cf. 1 Cor 4:13.

19. By suffering is meant here those trials sent by God in contrast to fasting and other penances that one chooses to undertake of one's own free will.

20. Sg 1:4.

21. Cf. Ps 22:6.

22. Cf. *Life*, chap. 20 (pp. 101–102).

23. Lk 6:39.

24. "*Viriliter agite*." Ps 31:24.

25. Cf. Lk 16:13.

26. That is, you must not pamper yourself.

27. This is the beginning of a hymn sung on Holy Saturday during the consecration of the Easter candle and is attributed to St. Augustine.

28. Cf. Lk 15:10.

29. Cf. Lk 15:11–32.

30. That is, the area the people of the village hold in common.

31. That is, the work of showing forgiveness, mercy and grace to sinners.

32. That is, God as their loved one.

NOTES

33. Sg 5:16.
34. 2 Sm 18:33—19:1.
35. Ex 33:20.
36. Phil 2:8.
37. Rom 13:1.
38. Cf. Sir 19:1.
39. This is rather from Jeremiah. Cf. Jer 6:14 and 8:11.
40. Cf. Mt 6:2.
41. Cf. Jn 8:49.
42. Gregory the Great, *Pastoral Rule* 2. 5.
43. Sg 5:8.
44. Cf. *LBEW*, chap. 12 (p. 242).
45. The author is saying that he deserves nothing special. Rye bread was a food of the lower classes.
46. This is the beginning of the introit from the second Christmas mass, celebrated at dawn.
47. Sir 24:11.
48. Cf. Aristotle, *Metaphysics* 12. 7.
49. Cf. 1 Thes 5:21.
50. Cf. Gregory the Great, *Morals*, 6. 57.
51. Pseudo-Dionysius, *Mystical Theology* 1.
52. Cf. Sir 24:11.
53. Cf. Jn 10:9.
54. Mt 5:48.
55. Pseudo-Dionysius, *On the Celestial Hierarchies* 8. 1; 7. 2 and 3; 4. 3. See also, Thomas, *Summa of Theology* 1. q. 106 ff. The sun symbolizes God.
56. Cf. Dt 16:20.
57. Cf. 2 Cor 3:18.
58. Sg 8:6.
59. IHS are Greek letters used as a monogram for the word *Jesus*.
60. Cf. Lam 3:25.

SERMON 1

(translated from Bihlmeyer, pp. 495–508)

1. Sg 1:16.
2. Suso uses the diminutive for *bed* (*bettelin*), which translates the Latin *lectulus*, but which would also call to the minds of the listeners the world of medieval love poetry. The "Book of Love" is a reference to the Song of Songs.

NOTES

3. Cf. *Life*, chap. 21 for such experiences in Suso's own life.
4. Ps 42:5.
5. The image here is that of a knight in a battle.
6. *Hoher muot*, translated here as "high spirits" (or exhilaration), is a term from the courtly world indicating that state of positive feeling that should characterize the ideal knight. Cf. also, *Life*, chap. 44 (pp. 171–173).
7. Suso is referring to a personal experience. The story is repeated in *LBEW*, chap. 14 (p. 251).
8. Cf. *Life*, chap. 21 (p. 105).
9. Cf. Lk 15:7.
10. Bernard of Clairvaux, Sermon 83 on the Song of Songs 4.
11. This is a reference to a passage from the Easter liturgy (*O felix culpa, quae talem ac tantum meruit habere redemptorem*), which is usually attributed to St. Augustine.
12. Cf. Ps 9:10.
13. Augustine, *On True Religion* 14. 27.
14. Adam, or man, occurs often in medieval religious thought as a symbol for man's rational powers. Eve, or woman, represents man's sensual appetites. Hence Suso is just stressing again the need for one's reason to be involved before one can commit a sin.
15. Cf. Bernard, Sermon 38 on the Song of Songs 1.
16. Cf. Gn 4:13.
17. Cf. Sir 38:9.
18. The sufferings referred to are the doubts mentioned above.
19. Gregory the Great, *Morals on Job* 8 22. 38; 26. 45. 82; 27. 14. 26.
20. Cf. *Life*, chap. 42 (pp. 166–167).

SERMON 4

(translated from Bihlmeyer, pp. 529–36)

1. "Now I leave the world again and go to the Father." Jn 16:28.
2. Cf. *Life*, chap. 36 (p. 144).
3. Cf. Nm 33.
4. This sentence seems to rest on the image of purifying precious metals. The purer the molten gold becomes, the smaller the bits of dross that must be separated from it.
5. Cf. Mt 5:39.
6. Cf. Mt 11:19; Jn 7:12 and 8:48.
7. *Vitae Patrum* (*The Lives of the Fathers*), ed. Rosweyde, 8. 83. (This work exists also as Vols. 73 and 74 of the *Patrologia Latina*.)

NOTES

8. Cf. Jn 16:33.

9. This story, with some variations, is narrated of Suso himself in *Life*, chap. 19.

10. Cf. Mt 17:4.

11. Gal 2:20.

12. Cf. Gn 3:4 ff.

13. The play here and immediately below is on the words *gewerden* (to become) and *entwerden* (to un-become). This follows *verwerden* (to become or be changed for the worse).

14. Cf Jn. 8:49–50.

Select Bibliography

I.   EDITIONS

All serious work on Suso relies on the following exemplary critical editions. For Suso's vernacular works:

Bihlmeyer, Karl. *Heinrich Seuse. Deutsche Schriften.* Stuttgart: Kohlhammer, 1907.
For the *Horologium sapientiae:* Künzle, O.P., Pius. *Heinrich Seuses Horologium sapientiae.* Freiburg, Switzerland: Universitätsverlag, 1977. Spicilegium Friburgense, Vol. 23. Father Künzle finished the work begun by Dominikus Planzer, O.P.

Besides offering the critical edition of the texts, Bihlmeyer and Künzle have provided in the introductions to their respective volumes the most important and reliable data about the texts and their author.

II.   ENGLISH TRANSLATIONS

Clark, James M. *The Life of the Servant.* London: James Clarke, 1952. Contains about seventy percent of the original text of Suso's autobiography in a generally reliable translation.
_____. *Little Book of Eternal Wisdom* and *Little Book of Truth.* London: Faber and Faber, 1953. Complete in reliable translations.
Edward, Sister M. Ann. *The Exemplar.* Dubuque, Iowa: Priory Press, 1962. Complete, but translated from the modern Ger-

man version of Nikolas Heller rather than from the Middle High German original.

III.   SECONDARY LITERATURE

Bindschedler, Maria. "Seuses Auffassung von der deutschen Sprache." *Heinrich Seuse. Studien zum 600. Todestag, 1366–1966.* Ed. E. M. Filthaut, O.P. Cologne: Albertus Magnus Verlag, 1966, pp. 71–76.

————. "Seuses Begriff von Ritterschaft." *Seuse-Studien*, pp. 233–40.

Blank, Walter. "Zum Stilwandel in Seuses Briefbüchern." *Seuse-Studien*, pp. 171–90.

Champollion, C. "Zum intellektuellen Wortschatz Heinrich Seuses." *Seuse-Studien*, pp. 77–89.

Clark, James M. *The Great German Mystics. Eckhart, Tauler and Suso.* Oxford: Blackwell, 1949.

Frank, I. M. "Zur Studienorganization der Dominikanerprovinz Teutonia in der ersten Hälfte des 14. Jh. und zum Studiengang des seligen Heinrich Seuse OP." *Seuse-Studien*, pp. 39–69.

Haas, Alois. *Nim din selbes war. Studien zur Lehre von der Selbsterkenntnis bei Meister Eckhart, Johannes Tauler und Heinrich Seuse.* Freiburg, Switzerland, 1971.

————. *Sermo mysticus. Studien zu Theologie und Sprache der deutschen Mystik.* Freiburg, Switzerland: Universitätsverlag, 1979.

Kieckhefer, Richard. *Unquiet Souls. Fourteenth-Century Saints and Their Religious Milieu.* Chicago: University of Chicago Press, 1984.

Michel, Paul. "Heinrich Seuse als Diener des göttlichen Wortes. Persuasive Strategien bei der Verwendung von Bibelzitaten im Dienste seiner pastoralen Aufgaben." *Das "einig ein." Studien zu Theorie und Sprache der deutschen Mystik.* Ed. Alois M. Haas and Heinrich Stirnimann. Freiburg, Switzerland: Universitätsverlag, 1980, pp. 281–367.

Misch, Georg. *Geschichte der Autobiographie*, IV,1. Frankfurt am Main: Schulte-Bulmke, 1967.

Piesch, Herma. "Seuses 'Büchlein der Wahrheit' und Meister Eckhart." *Seuse-Studien*, pp. 91–134.

Pleuser, Christine. "Tradition und Ursprünglichkeit in der Vita Seuses." *Seuse-Studien*, pp. 135–60.

BIBLIOGRAPHY

Ruh, Kurt. "Seuse, Vita c. 52 und das Gedicht und die Glosse 'Vom Uberschall.' " *Seuse-Studien*, pp. 191–212.

Schwietering, Julius. "Zur Autorschaft von Seuses Vita." *Altdeutsche und altniederländische Mystik*. Ed. Kurt Ruh. Darmstadt: Wissenschaftliche Buchgesellschaft, 1964, pp. 309–23.

Weilner, Ignaz. "Heinrich Seuse und die Aszese des Humors." *Seuse-Studien*, pp. 241–54.

Index to Introduction

INDEX

411

INDEX

Rhine river, 15
Rhineland, the, 16
Romanticists, German, 14

Scholasticism, 36, 50
Schottenkloster, 25
Seneca, 37
Sentences (Lombard), 21
Spirituals, the Franciscan, 14
Stagel, Elsbeth, 3, 25, 37–39
Strasbourg, 22
Susanna, 45, 46
Suso, Henry: accusations against, 33; advanced studies of, 21–22; adversaries of, 22; conversion of, 20; dishonor of, 23; early Dominican years of, 20; frailness of, 19–20; intellectual abilities of, 33; life of, 19–26; literary talents of, 51; mysticism of, 4; as a narrator, 44–45; pastoral activity of, 17; preaching of, 24; real name of, 19; talents of, 33; writings of, 4, 26–51
Switzerland, 15

Tauler, John, 4
Teutonia, 16
Tobin, Frank, 6–7
Töss, 25
Truth, 29–31, 35–36

Überlingen, 19
Ulm, 25

Visions, 47–48

"Wild One," the, 31
William of Ockham, 14
Wisdom, 35–36
Women, role of, 3–4
World, the, 37

Zurich, 25

Index to Texts

INDEX

INDEX

Other Volumes in this Series